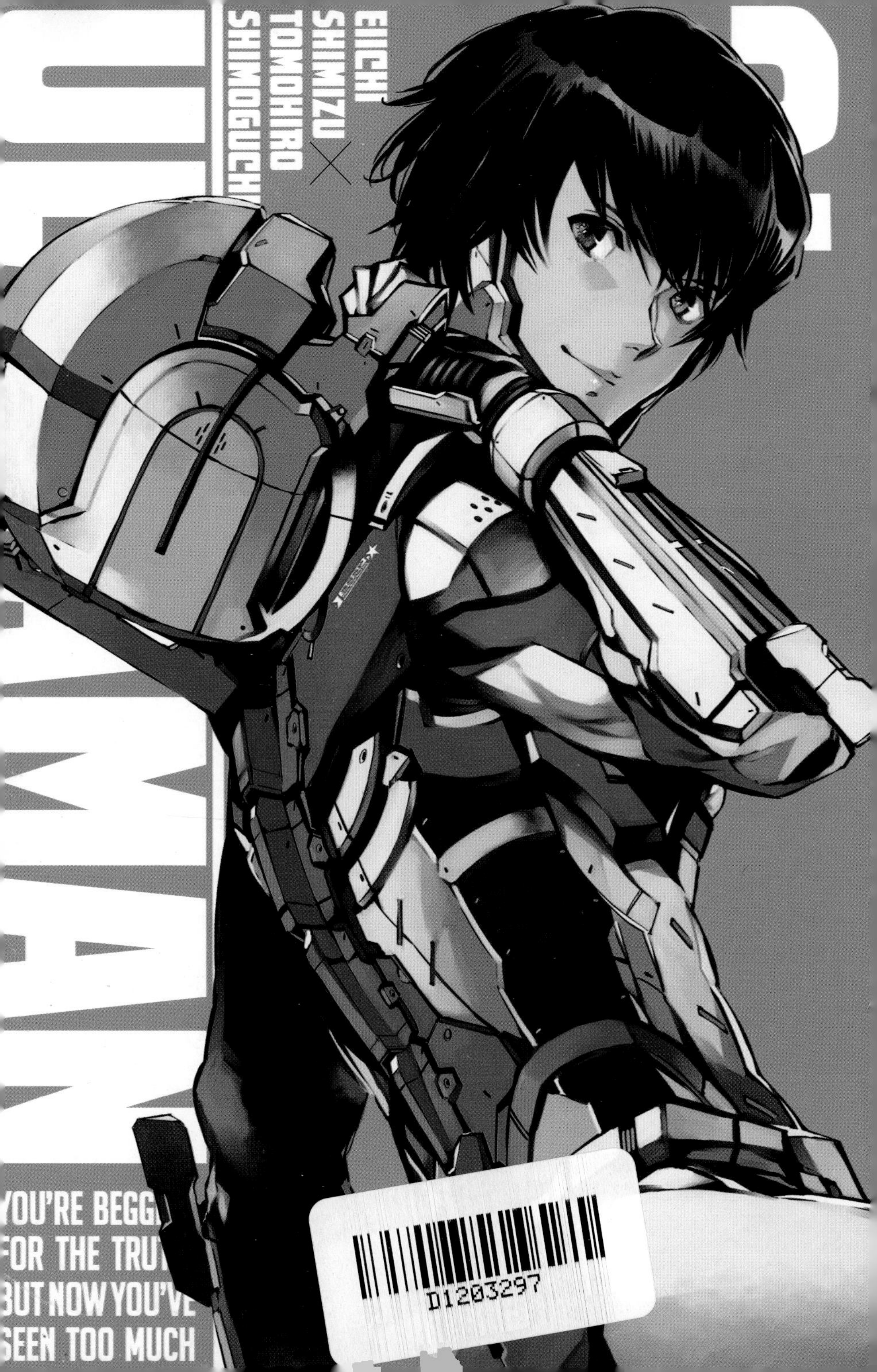
EIICHI SHIMIZU × TOMOHIRO SHIMOGUCHI
YOU'RE BEGG
FOR THE TRUT
BUT NOW YOU'VE
SEEN TOO MUCH

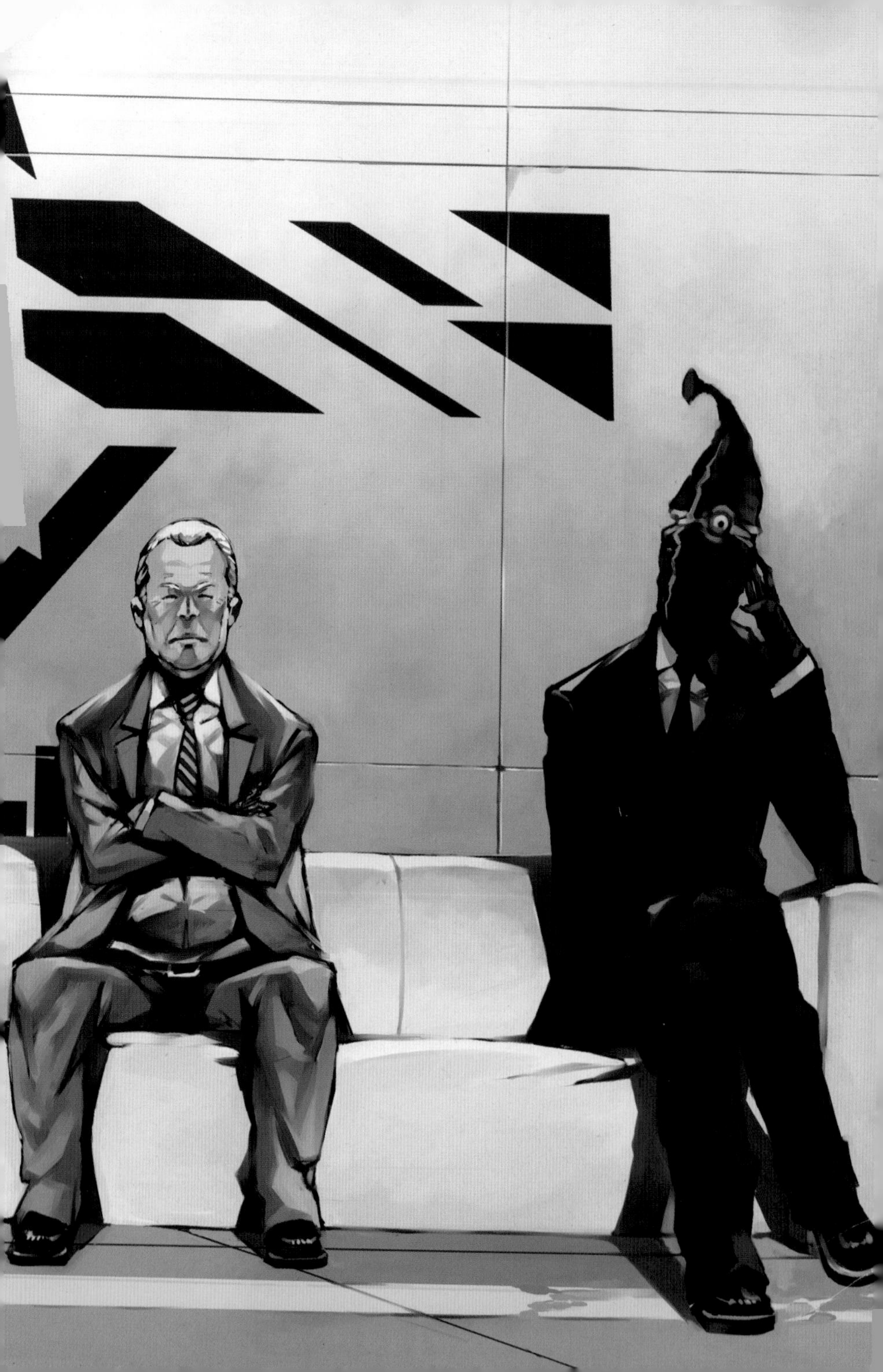

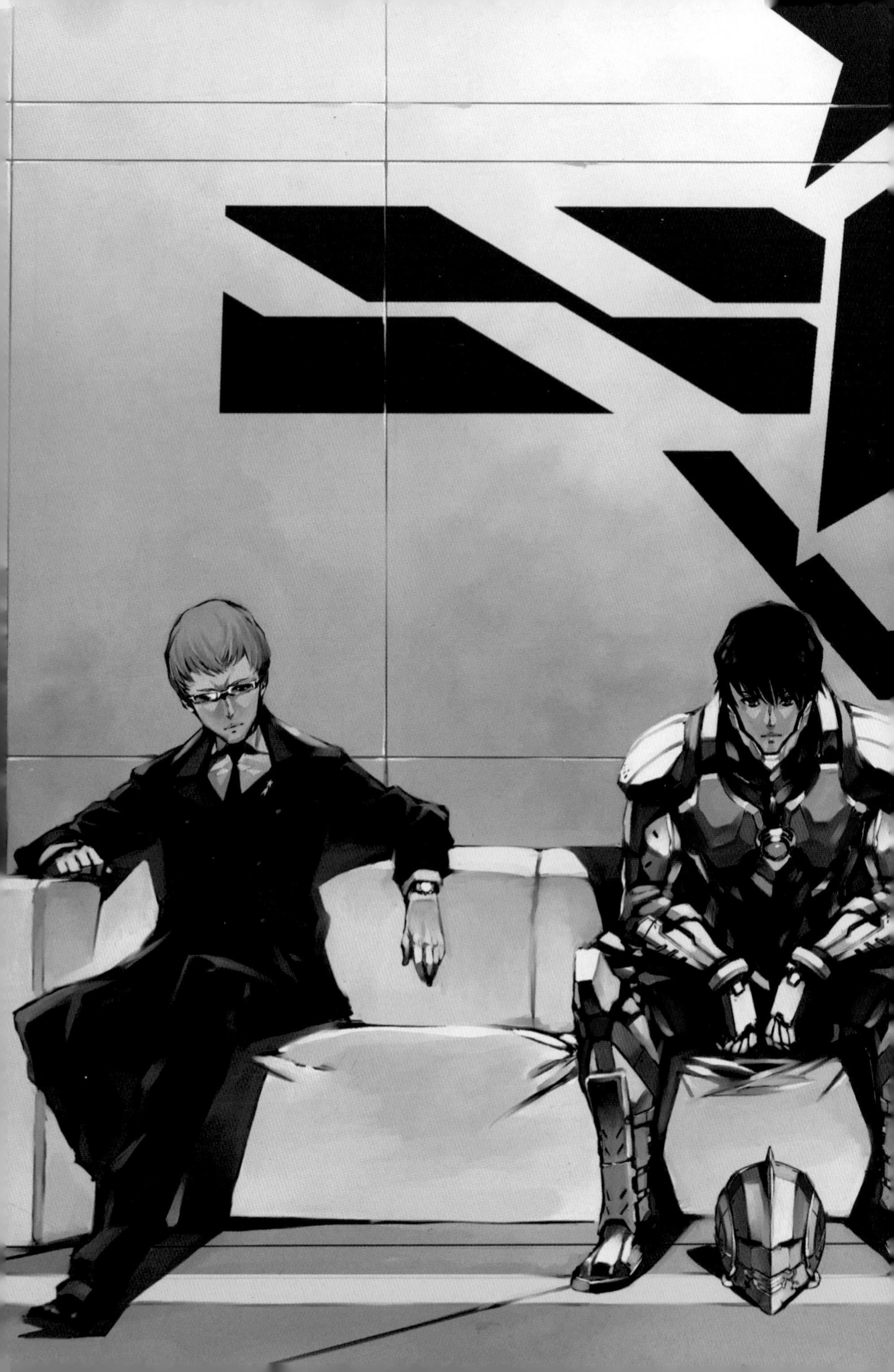

CONTENTS

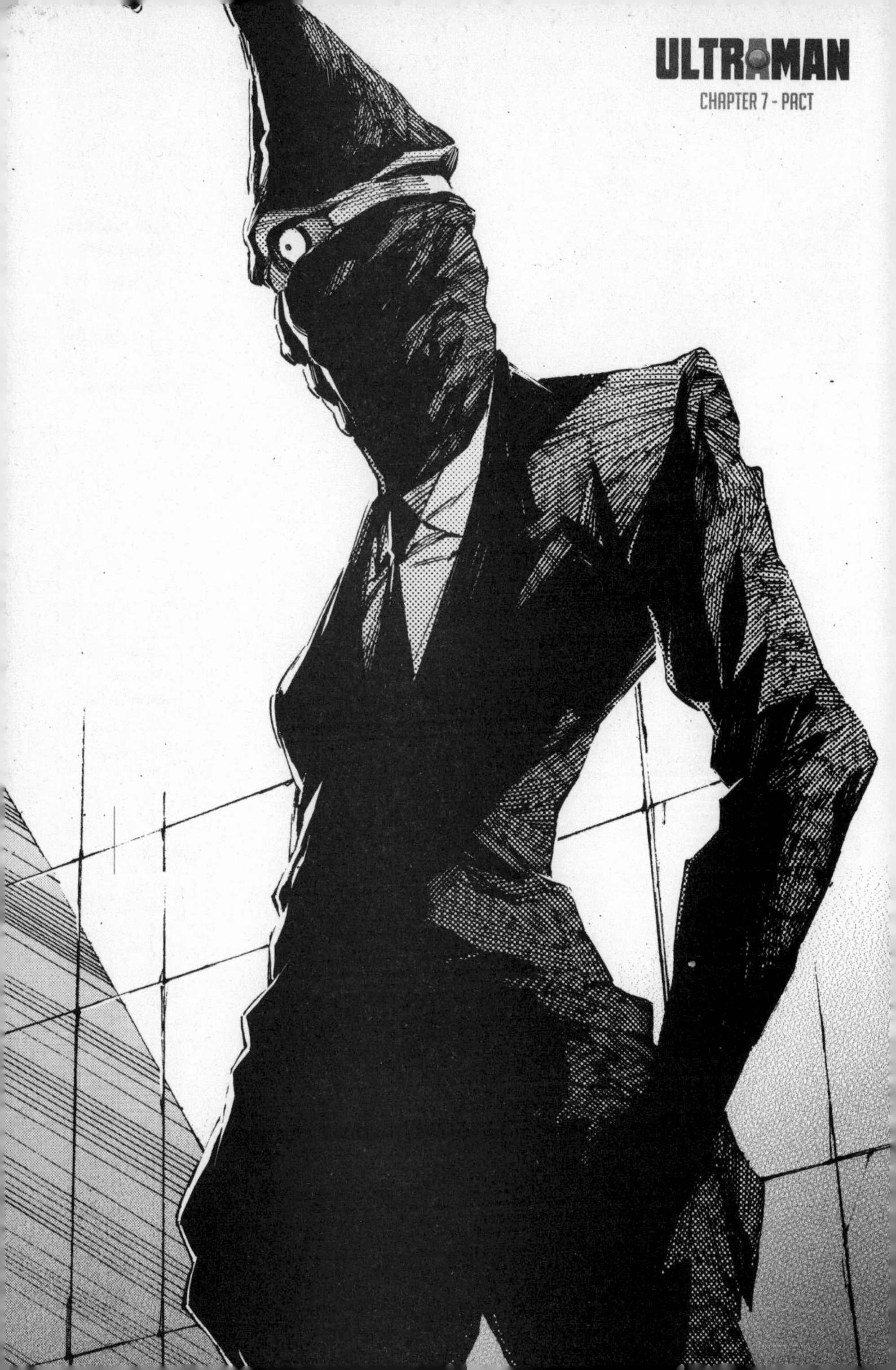
ULTRAMAN
CHAPTER 7 - PACT

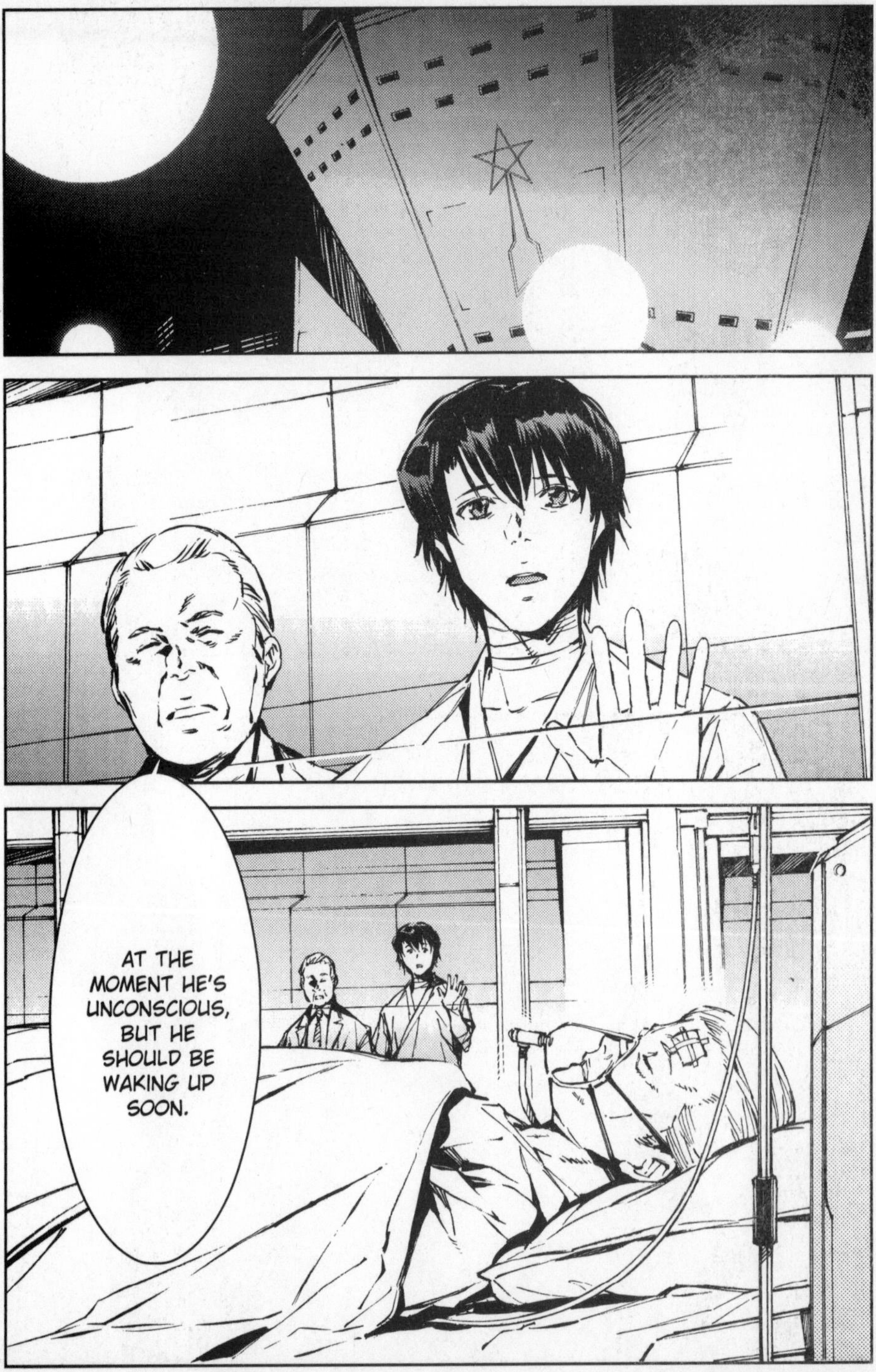
AT THE MOMENT HE'S UNCONSCIOUS, BUT HE SHOULD BE WAKING UP SOON.

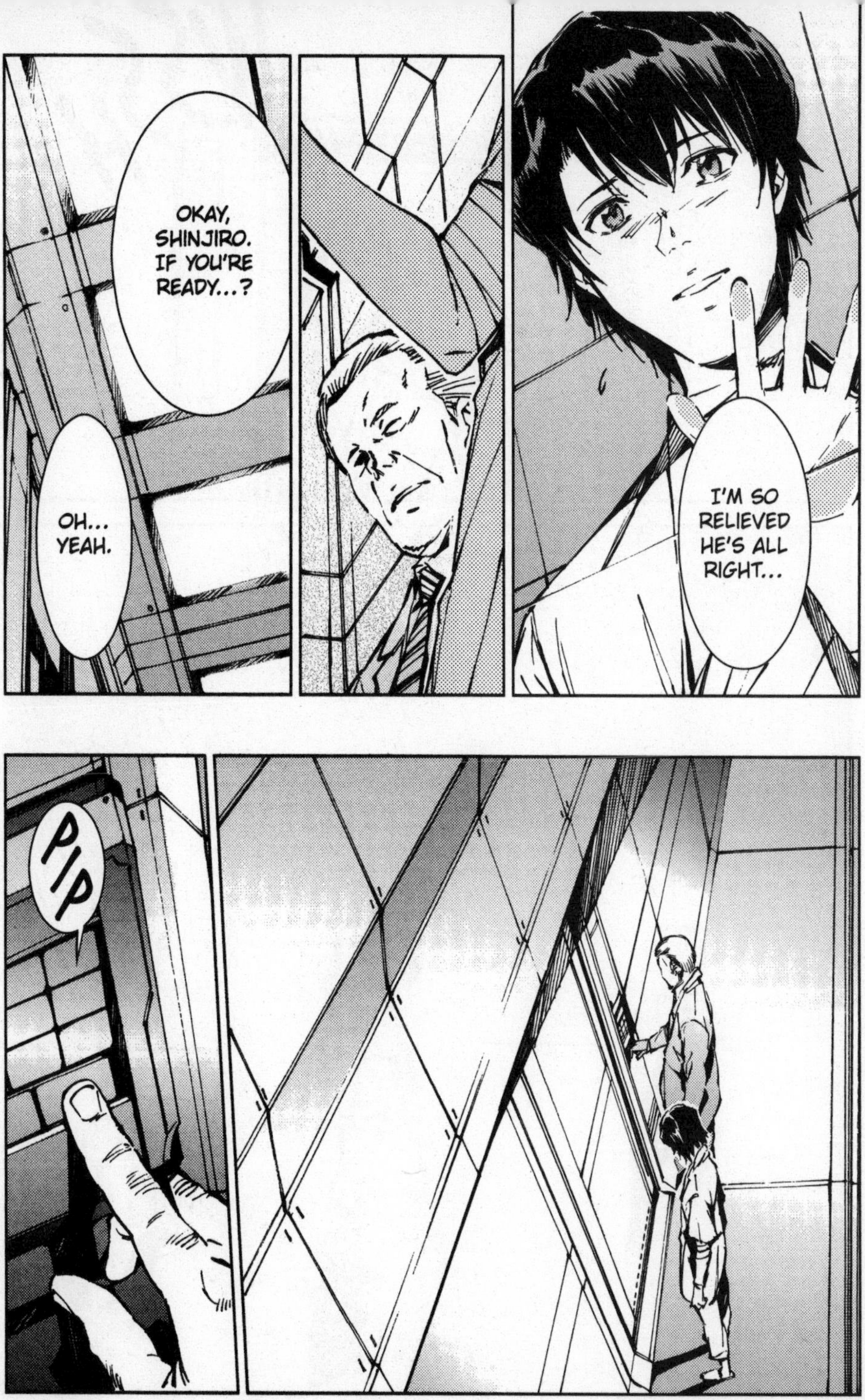
I'M SO RELIEVED HE'S ALL RIGHT...
OKAY, SHINJIRO. IF YOU'RE READY...?
OH... YEAH.
PIP

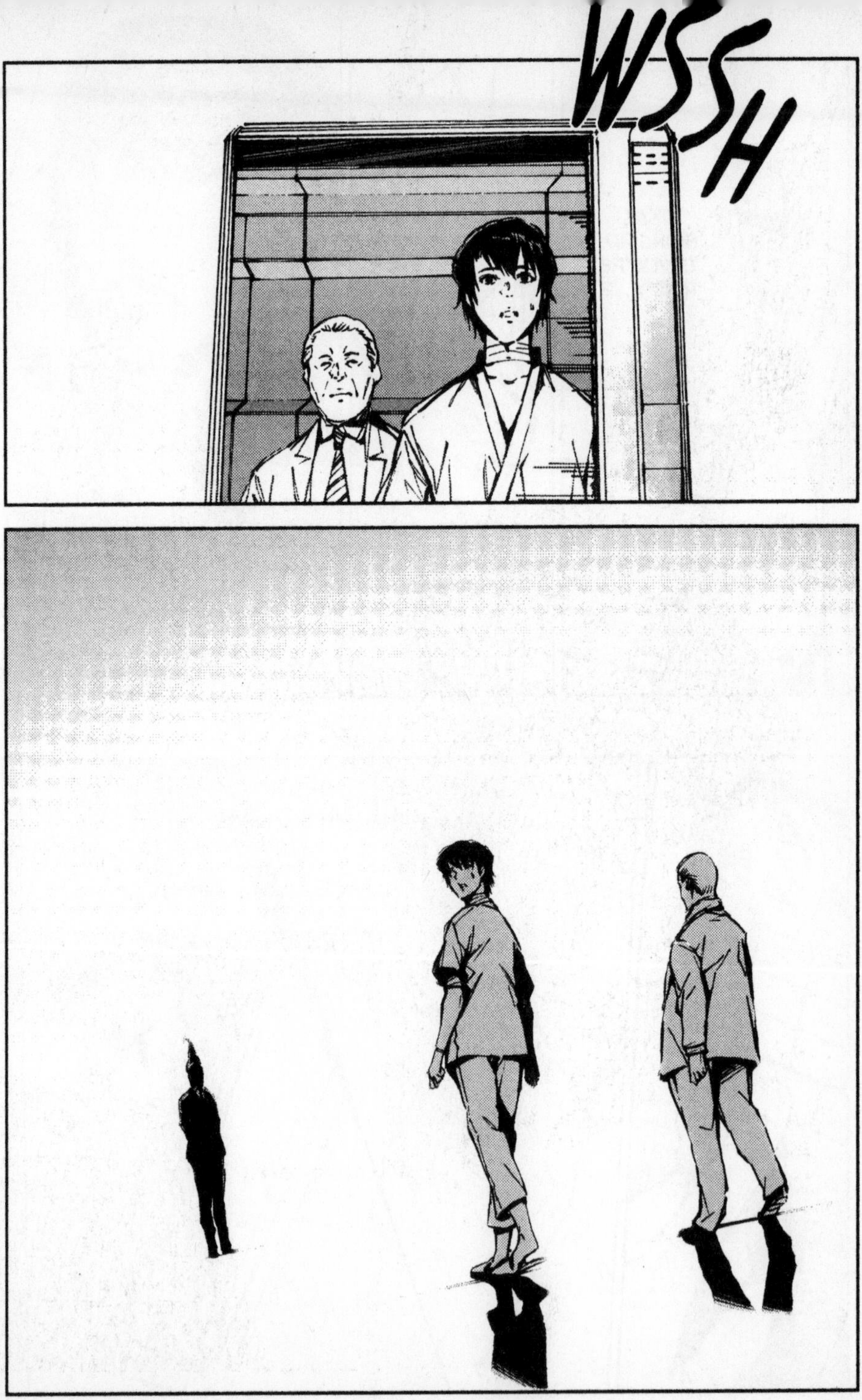
WSSH

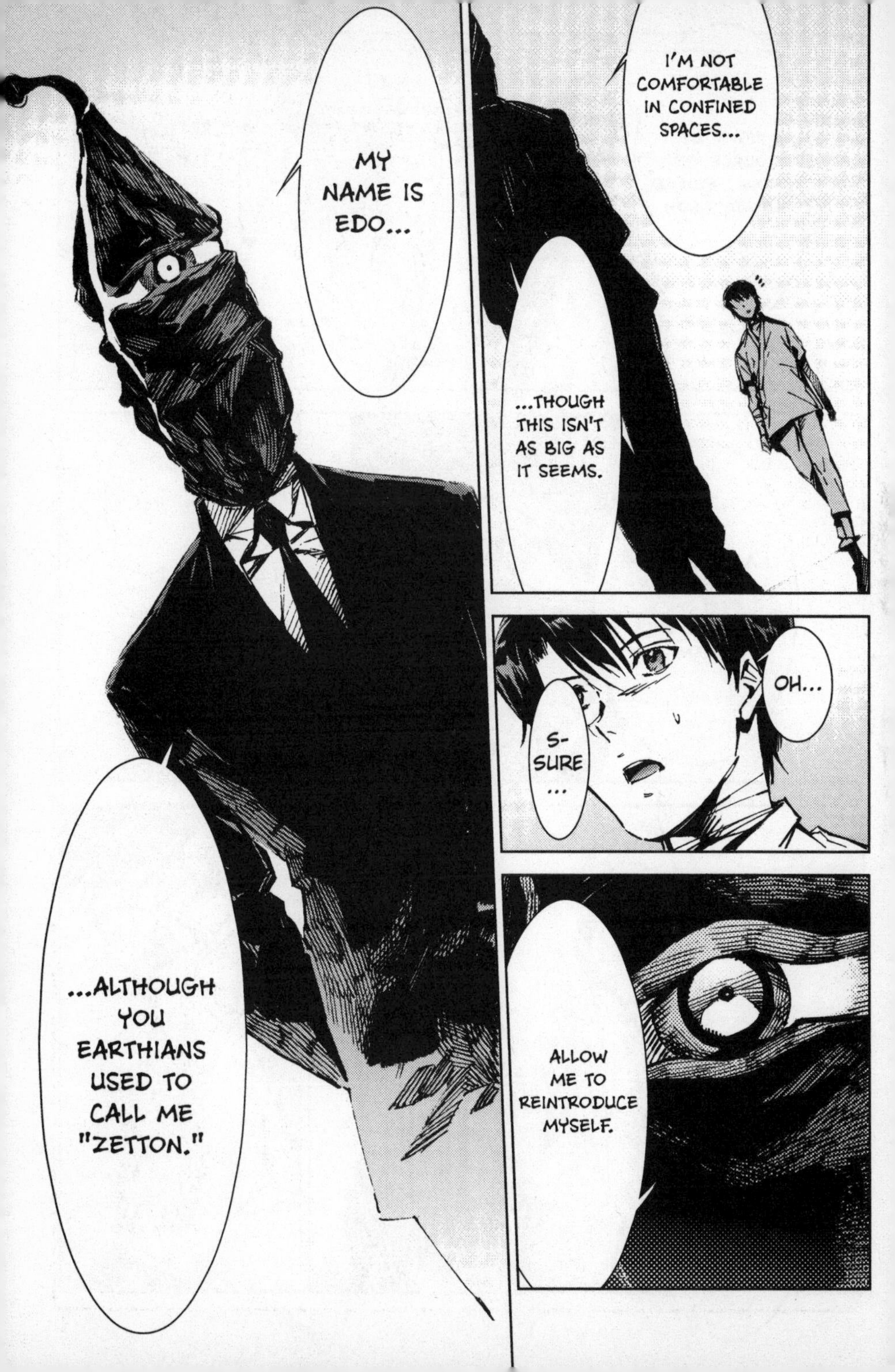
I'M NOT COMFORTABLE IN CONFINED SPACES...
...THOUGH THIS ISN'T AS BIG AS IT SEEMS.
OH...
S-SURE...
ALLOW ME TO REINTRODUCE MYSELF.
MY NAME IS EDO...
...ALTHOUGH YOU EARTHIANS USED TO CALL ME "ZETTON."

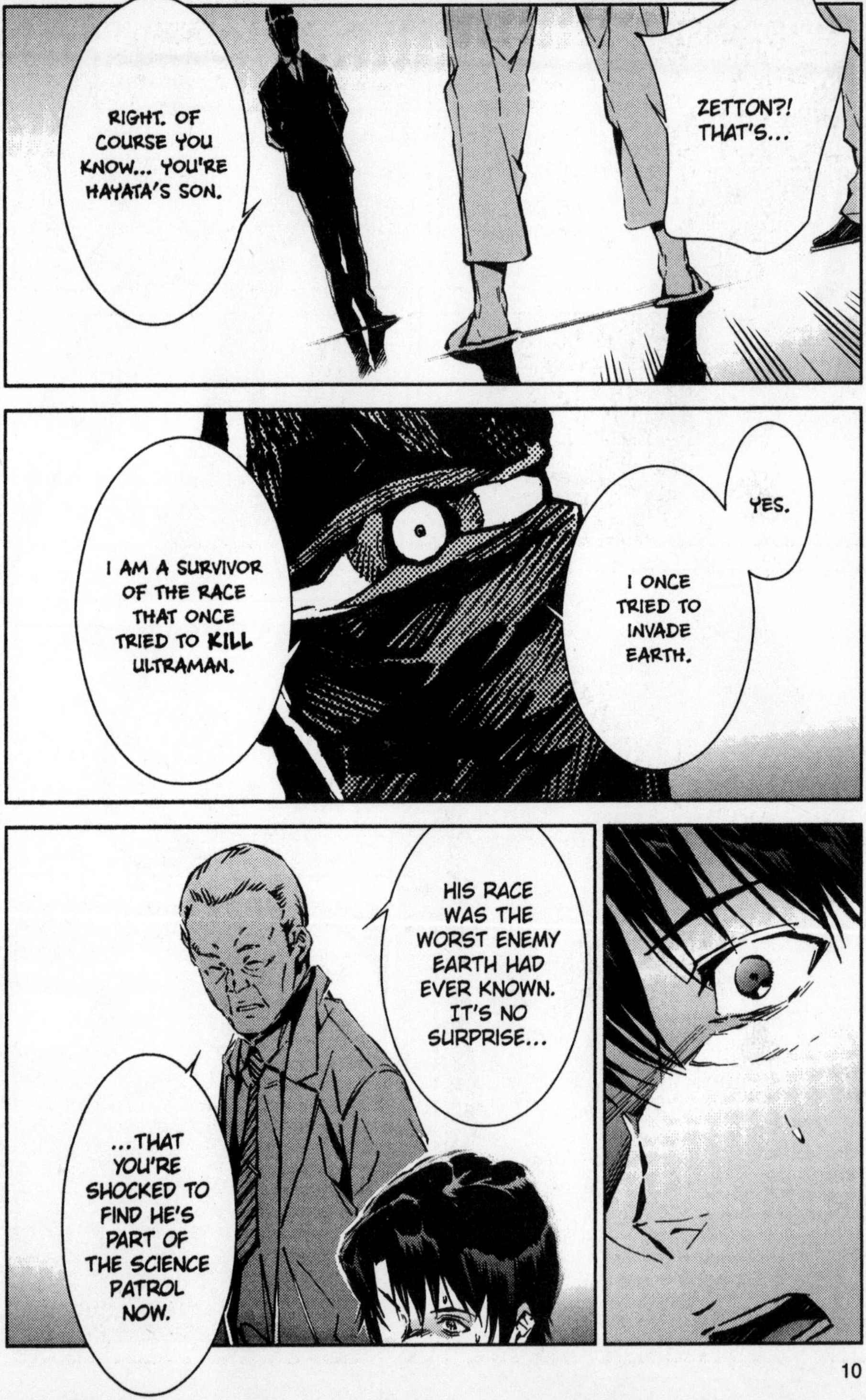
ZETTON?! THAT'S...
RIGHT. OF COURSE YOU KNOW... YOU'RE HAYATA'S SON.
YES.
I ONCE TRIED TO INVADE EARTH.
I AM A SURVIVOR OF THE RACE THAT ONCE TRIED TO KILL ULTRAMAN.
HIS RACE WAS THE WORST ENEMY EARTH HAD EVER KNOWN. IT'S NO SURPRISE...
...THAT YOU'RE SHOCKED TO FIND HE'S PART OF THE SCIENCE PATROL NOW.

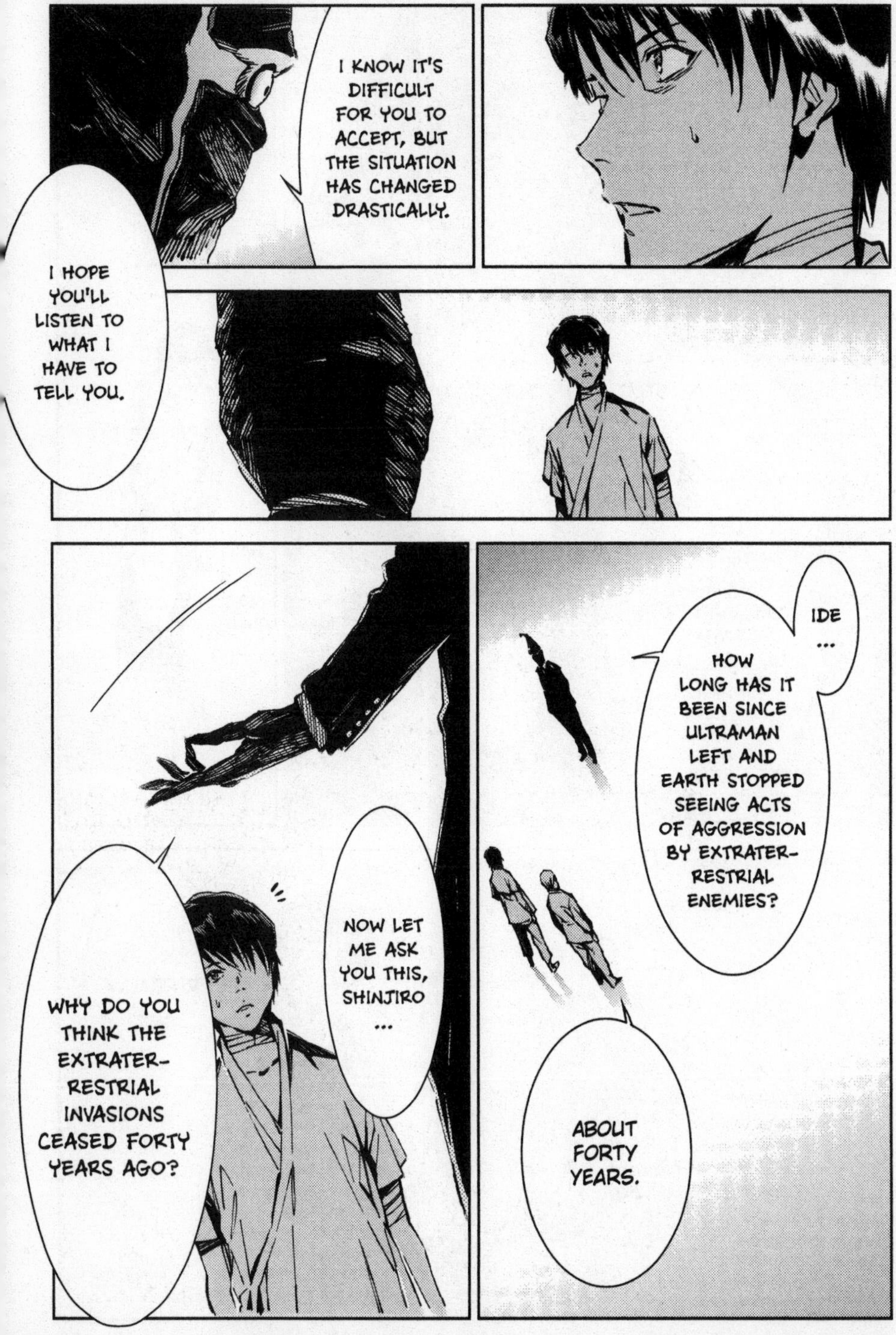
I KNOW IT'S DIFFICULT FOR YOU TO ACCEPT, BUT THE SITUATION HAS CHANGED DRASTICALLY.
I HOPE YOU'LL LISTEN TO WHAT I HAVE TO TELL YOU.
IDE ...
HOW LONG HAS IT BEEN SINCE ULTRAMAN LEFT AND EARTH STOPPED SEEING ACTS OF AGGRESSION BY EXTRATER-RESTRIAL ENEMIES?
ABOUT FORTY YEARS.
NOW LET ME ASK YOU THIS, SHINJIRO ...
WHY DO YOU THINK THE EXTRATER-RESTRIAL INVASIONS CEASED FORTY YEARS AGO?

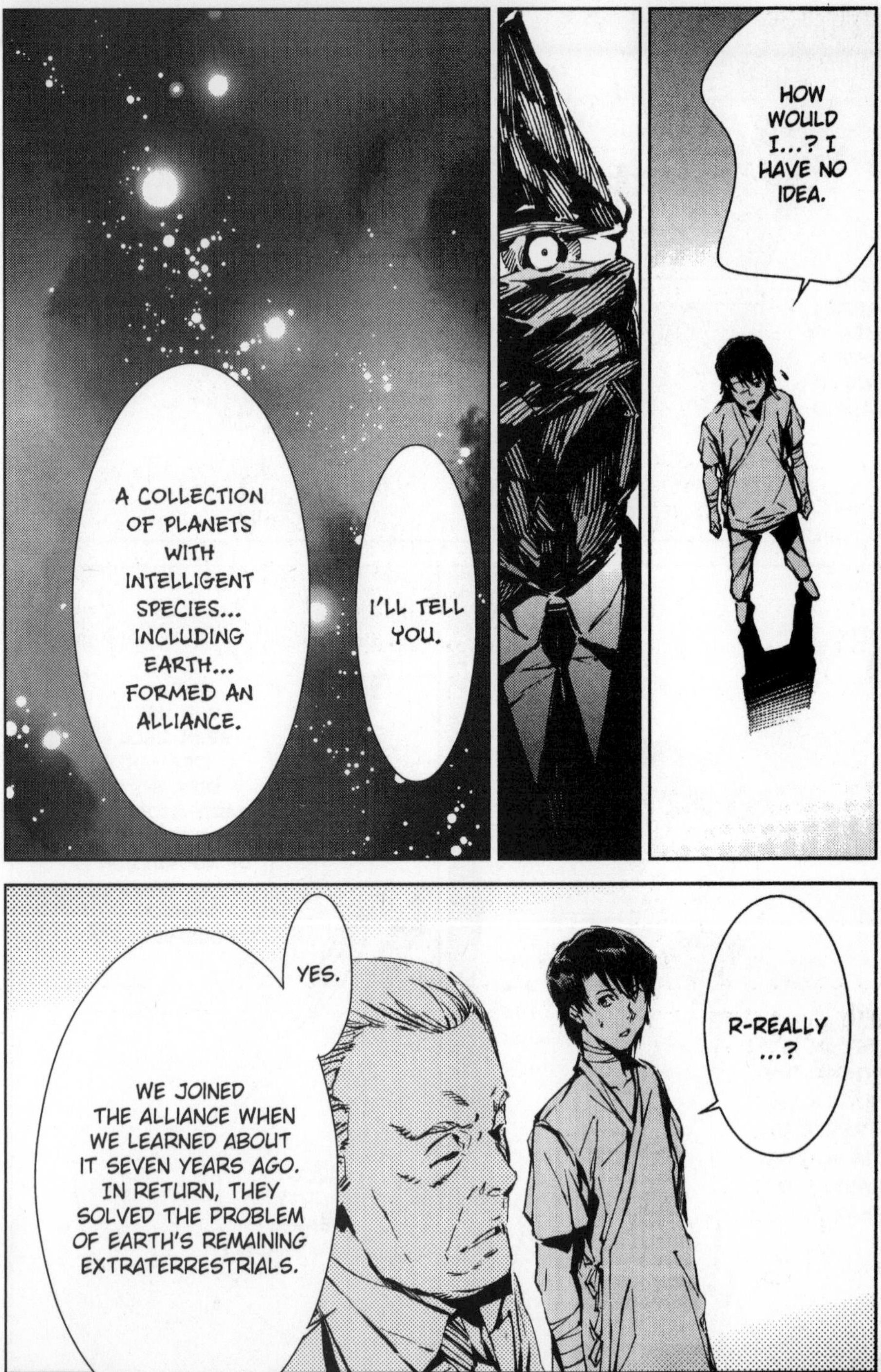
HOW WOULD I...? I HAVE NO IDEA.
I'LL TELL YOU.
A COLLECTION OF PLANETS WITH INTELLIGENT SPECIES... INCLUDING EARTH... FORMED AN ALLIANCE.
R-REALLY ...?
YES.
WE JOINED THE ALLIANCE WHEN WE LEARNED ABOUT IT SEVEN YEARS AGO. IN RETURN, THEY SOLVED THE PROBLEM OF EARTH'S REMAINING EXTRATERRESTRIALS.

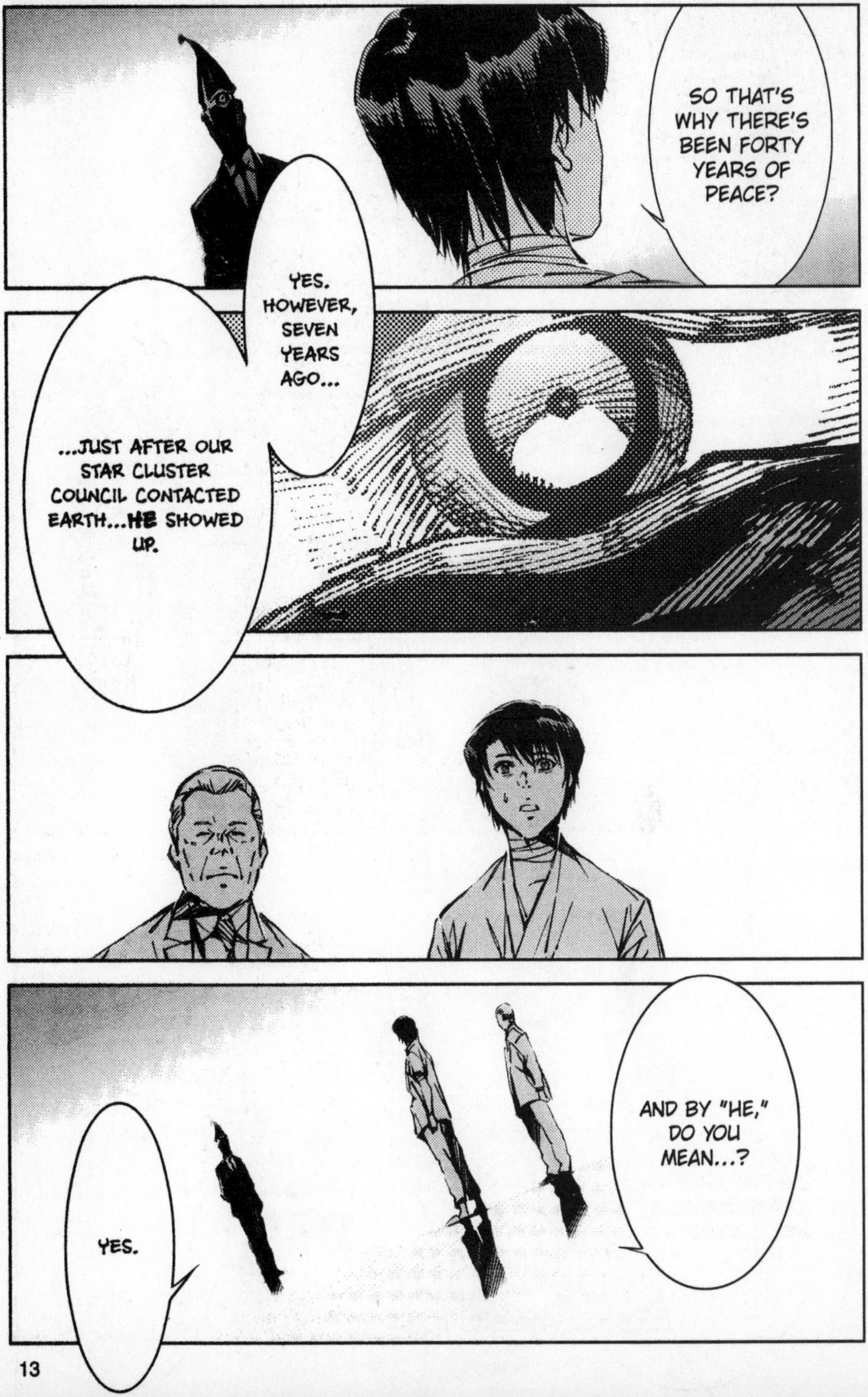
SO THAT'S WHY THERE'S BEEN FORTY YEARS OF PEACE?
YES. HOWEVER, SEVEN YEARS AGO...
...JUST AFTER OUR STAR CLUSTER COUNCIL CONTACTED EARTH...HE SHOWED UP.
AND BY "HE," DO YOU MEAN...?
YES.

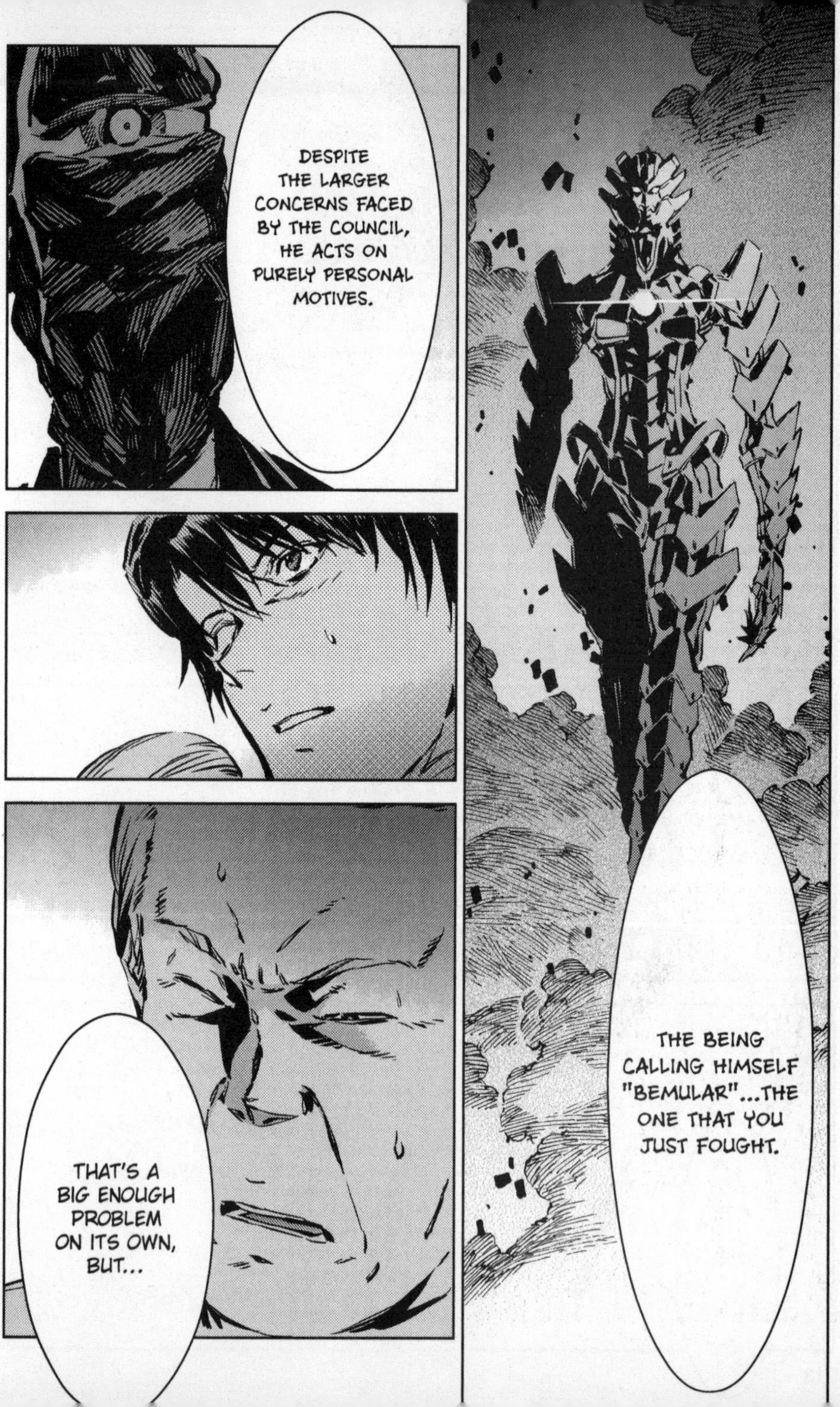
THE BEING CALLING HIMSELF "BEMULAR"...THE ONE THAT YOU JUST FOUGHT.
DESPITE THE LARGER CONCERNS FACED BY THE COUNCIL, HE ACTS ON PURELY PERSONAL MOTIVES.
THAT'S A BIG ENOUGH PROBLEM ON ITS OWN, BUT...

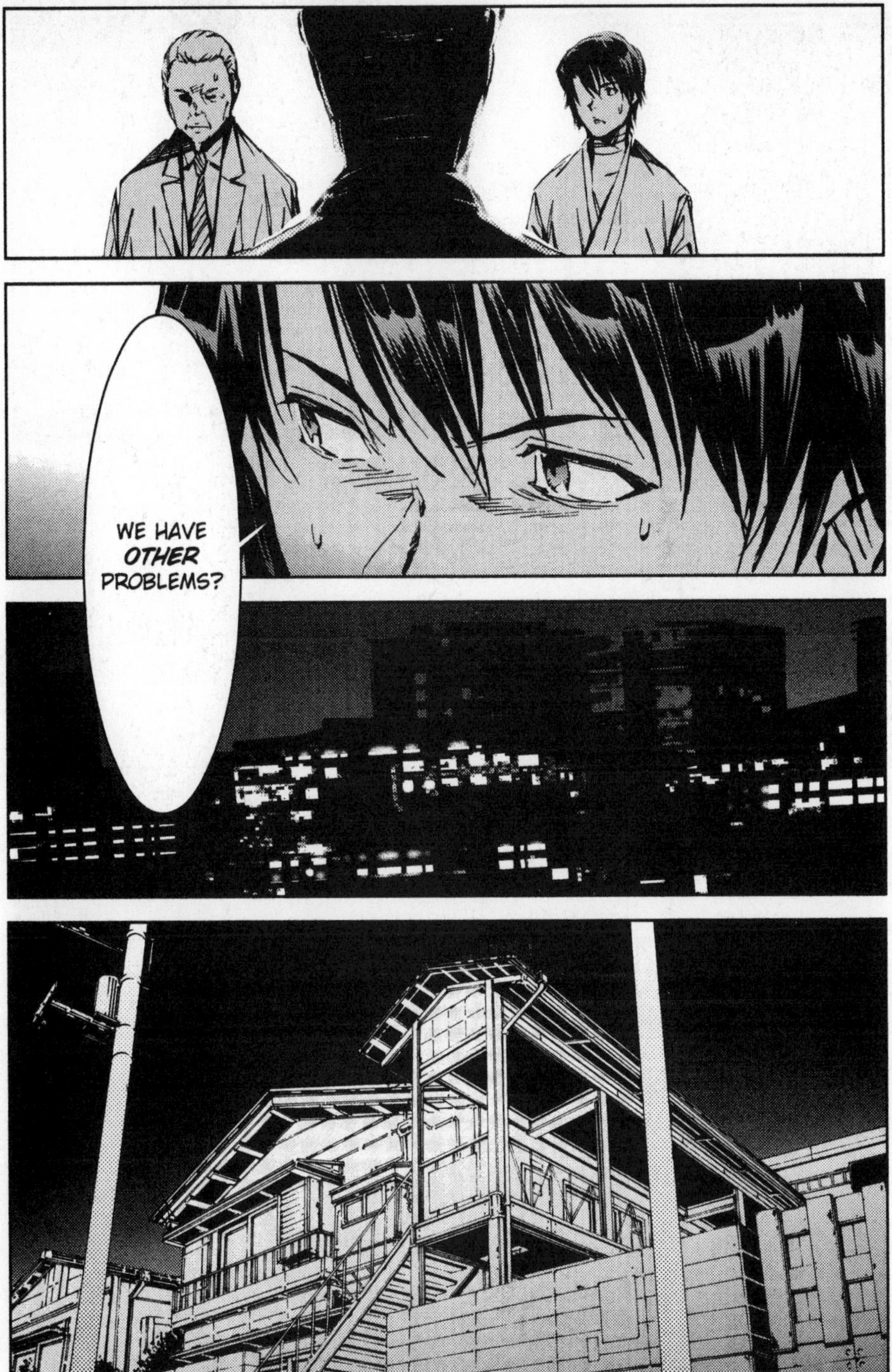
WE HAVE OTHER PROBLEMS?

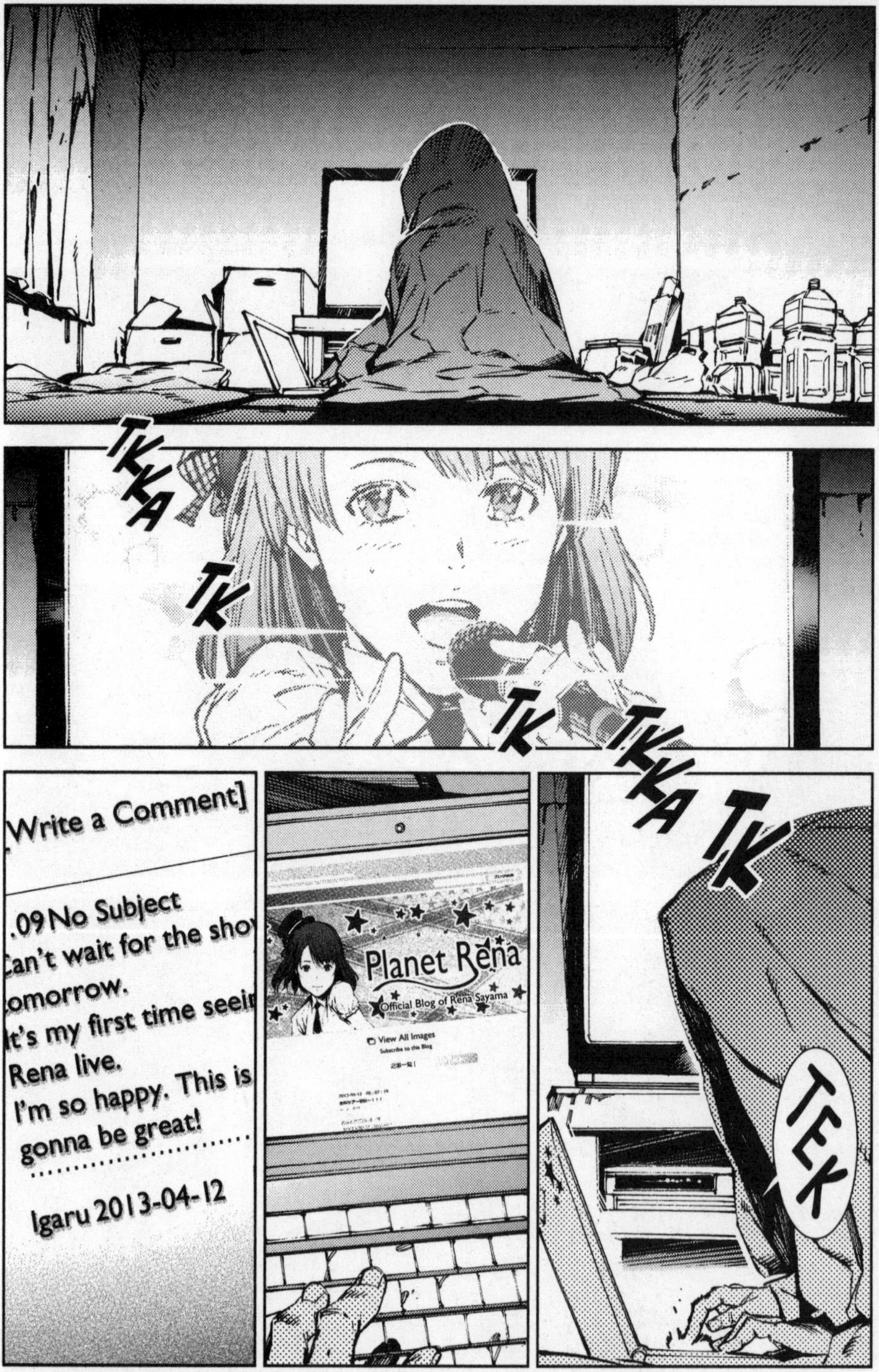
TKKA
TK
TK
TKKA
TK
TEK
Planet Rena
Official Blog of Rena Sayama
View All Images
Subscribe to this Blog
[Write a Comment]
.09 No Subject
Can't wait for the sho
tomorrow.
It's my first time seei
Rena live.
I'm so happy. This is
gonna be great!
Igaru 2013-04-12

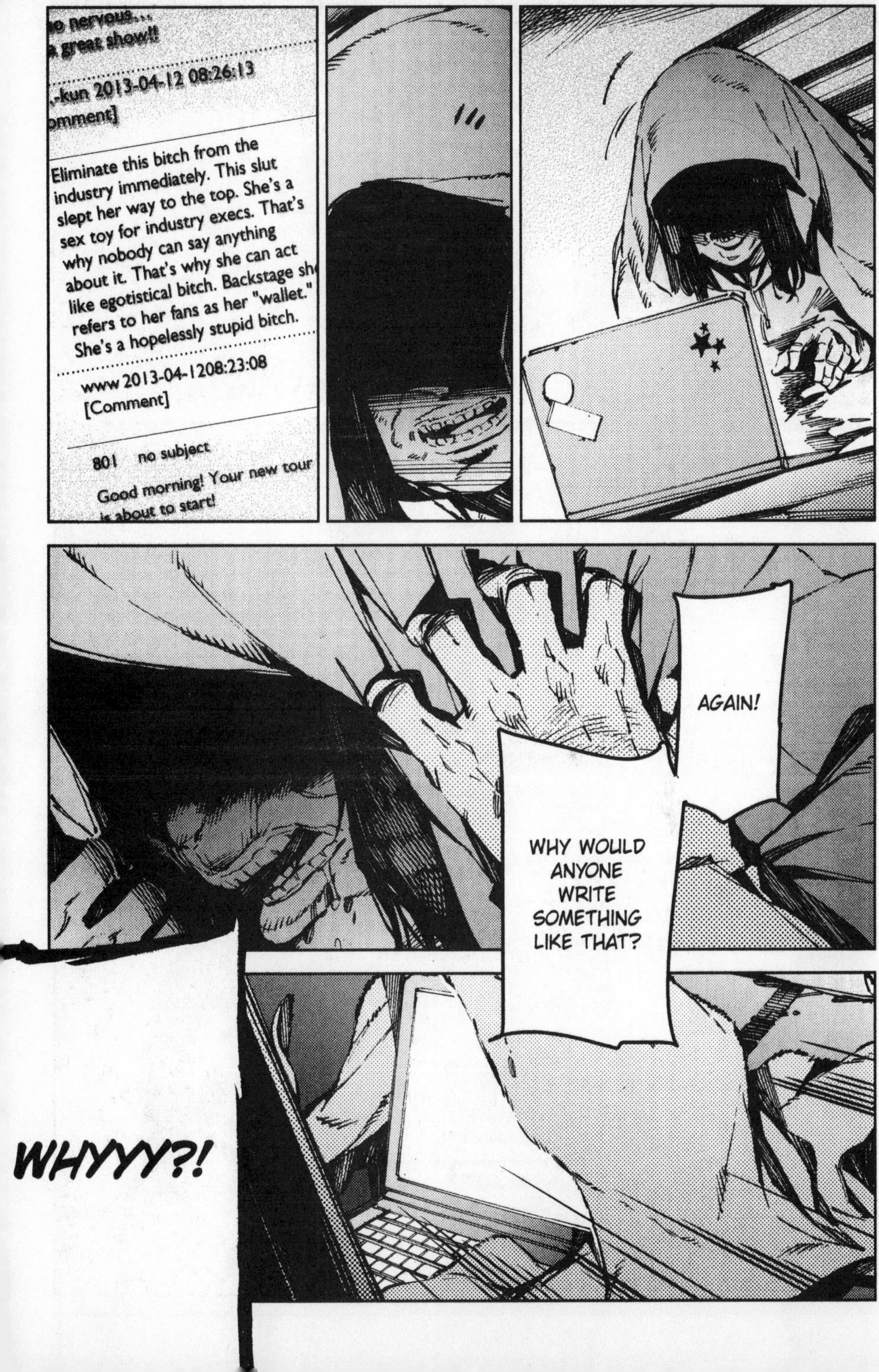

so nervous...
a great show!!
-kun 2013-04-12 08:26:13
omment]
Eliminate this bitch from the industry immediately. This slut slept her way to the top. She's a sex toy for industry execs. That's why nobody can say anything about it. That's why she can act like egotistical bitch. Backstage sh refers to her fans as her "wallet." She's a hopelessly stupid bitch.
www 2013-04-1208:23:08
[Comment]
801 no subject
Good morning! Your new tour is about to start!
AGAIN!
WHY WOULD ANYONE WRITE SOMETHING LIKE THAT?
WHYYY?!

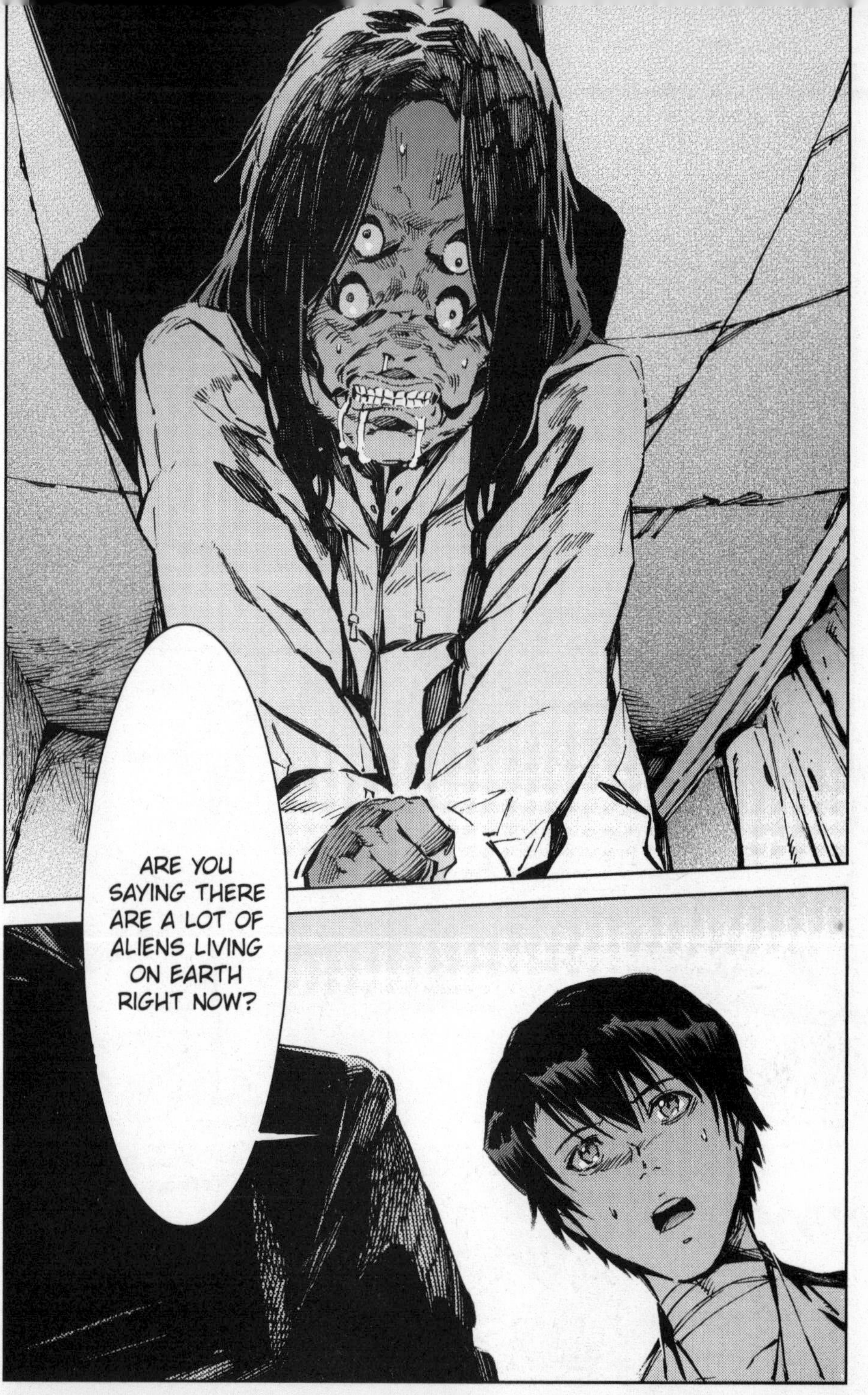
ARE YOU SAYING THERE ARE A LOT OF ALIENS LIVING ON EARTH RIGHT NOW?

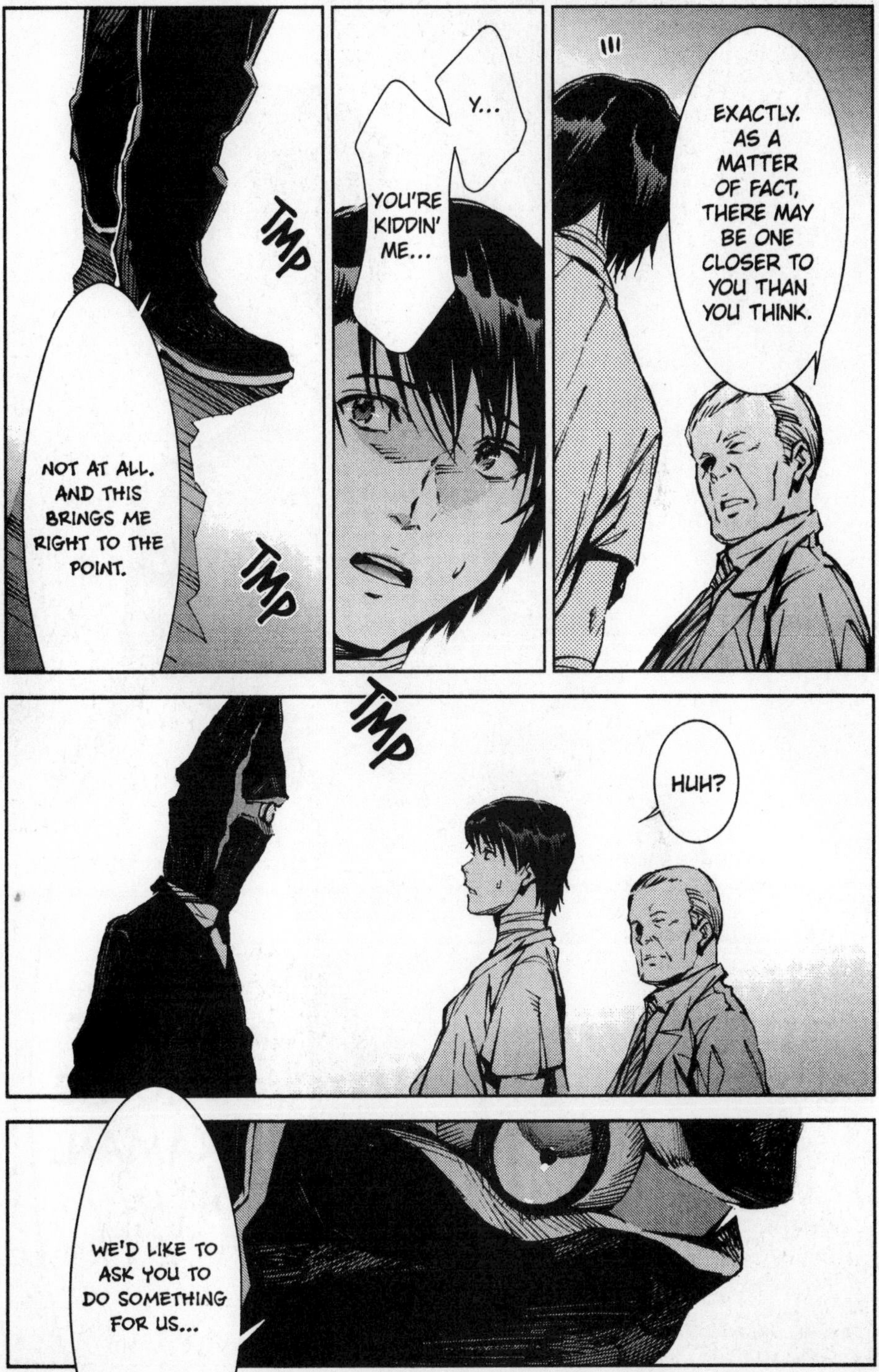
EXACTLY. AS A MATTER OF FACT, THERE MAY BE ONE CLOSER TO YOU THAN YOU THINK.
Y...
YOU'RE KIDDIN' ME...
TMP
NOT AT ALL. AND THIS BRINGS ME RIGHT TO THE POINT.
TMP
TMP
HUH?
WE'D LIKE TO ASK YOU TO DO SOMETHING FOR US...

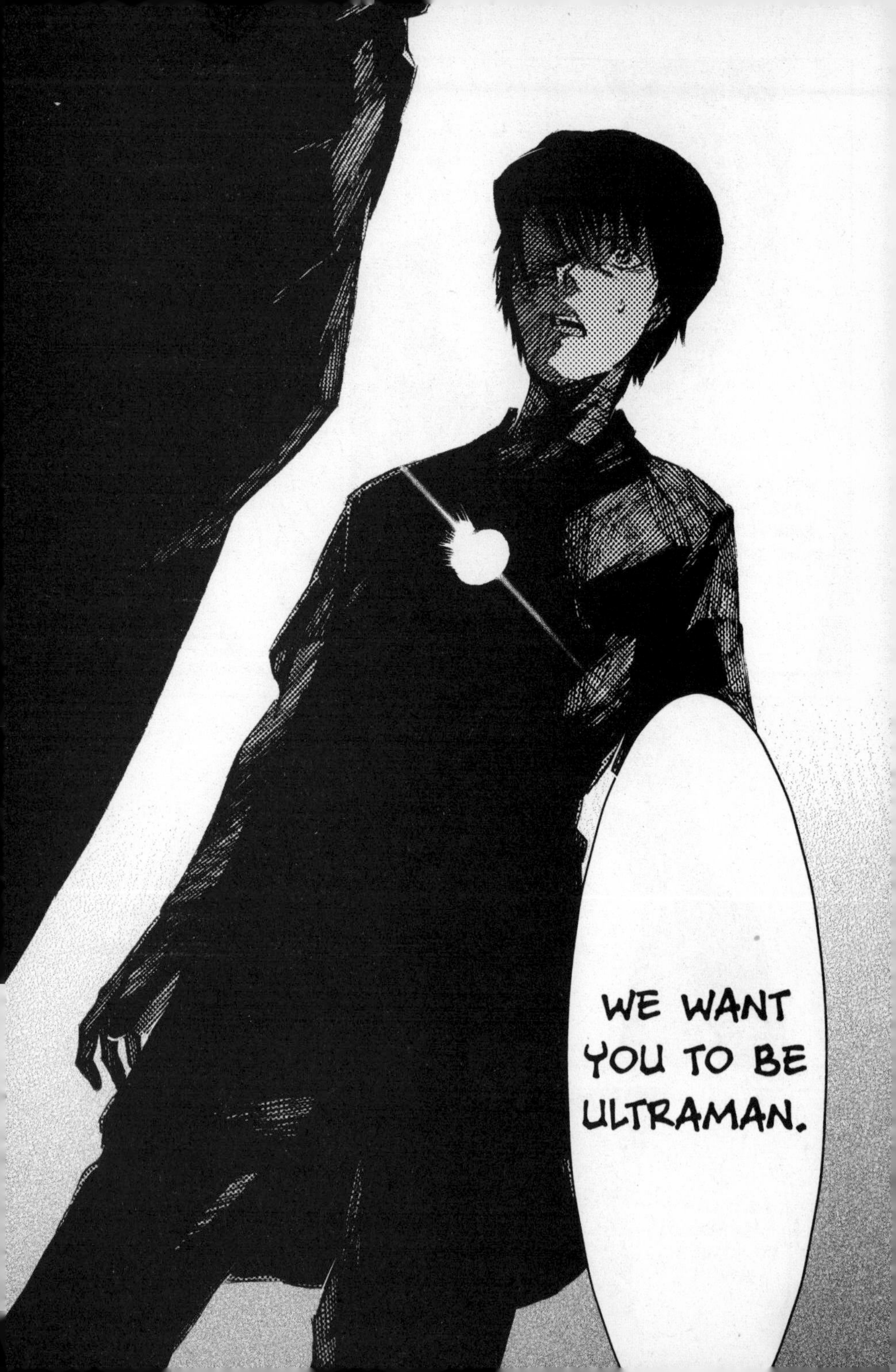
WE WANT YOU TO BE ULTRAMAN.

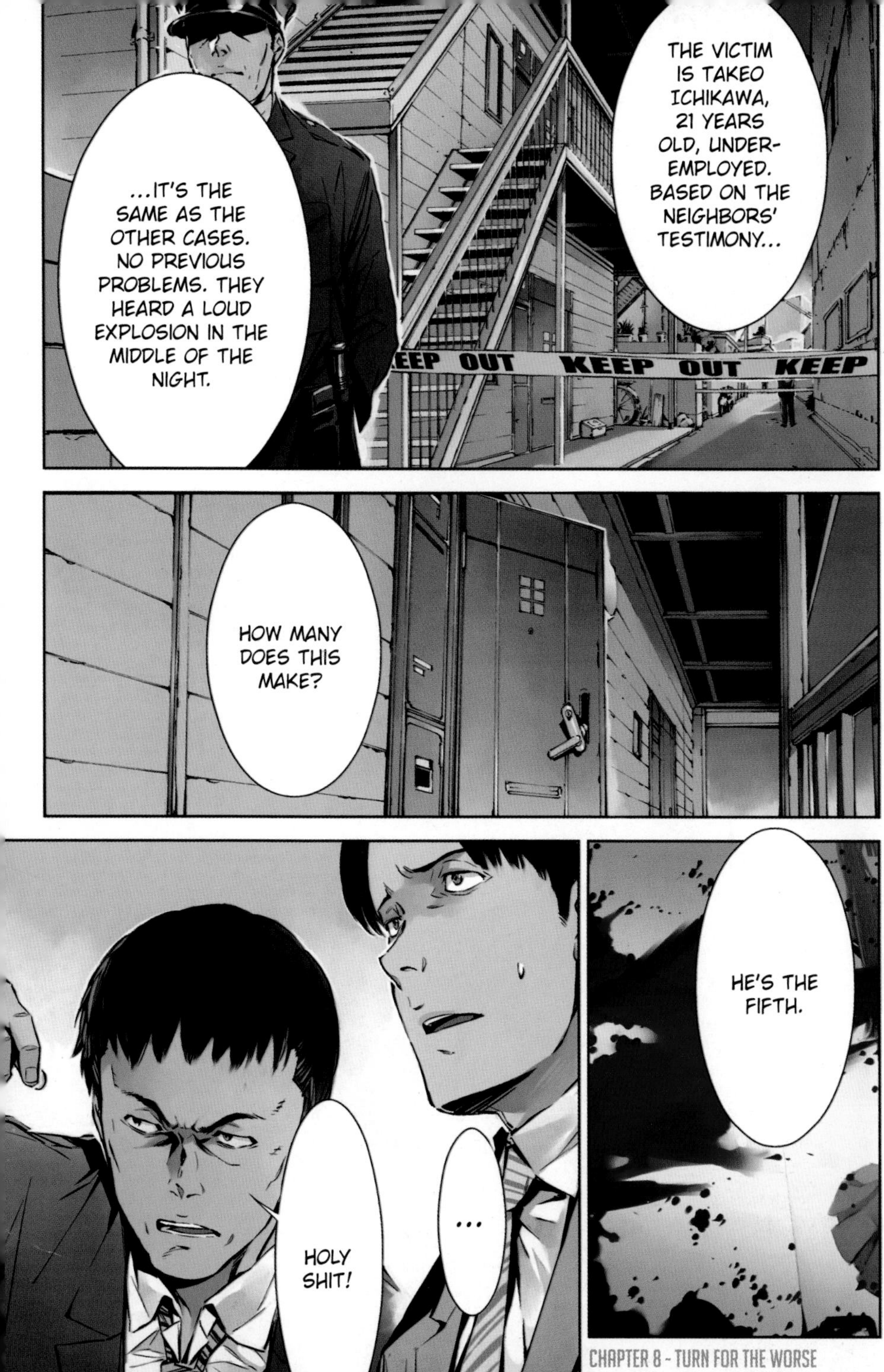
THE VICTIM IS TAKEO ICHIKAWA, 21 YEARS OLD, UNDER-EMPLOYED. BASED ON THE NEIGHBORS' TESTIMONY...
...IT'S THE SAME AS THE OTHER CASES. NO PREVIOUS PROBLEMS. THEY HEARD A LOUD EXPLOSION IN THE MIDDLE OF THE NIGHT.
KEEP OUT KEEP OUT KEEP
HOW MANY DOES THIS MAKE?
HE'S THE FIFTH.
...
HOLY SHIT!

CHAPTER 8 - TURN FOR THE WORSE

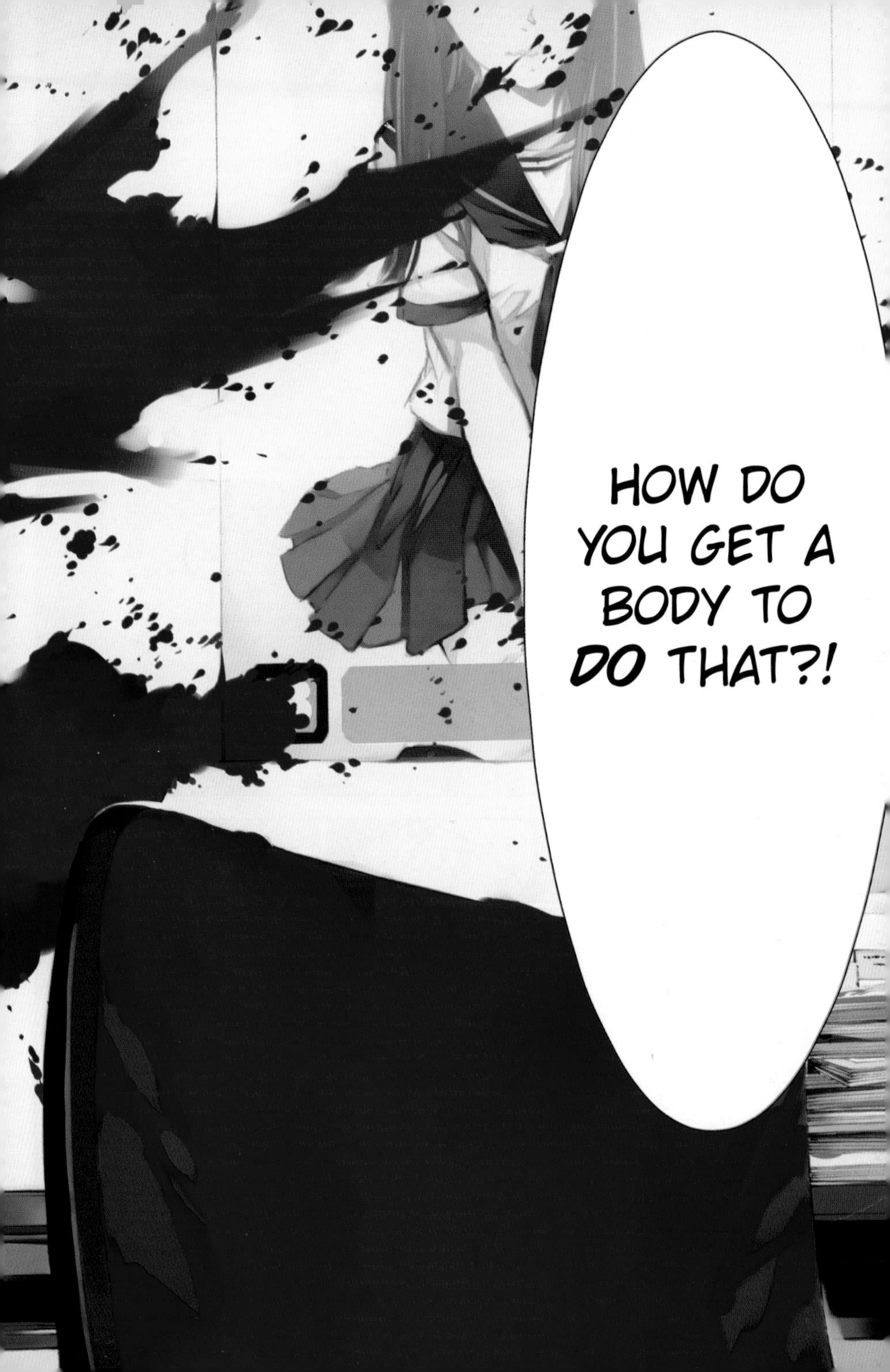
HOW DO YOU GET A BODY TO DO THAT?!

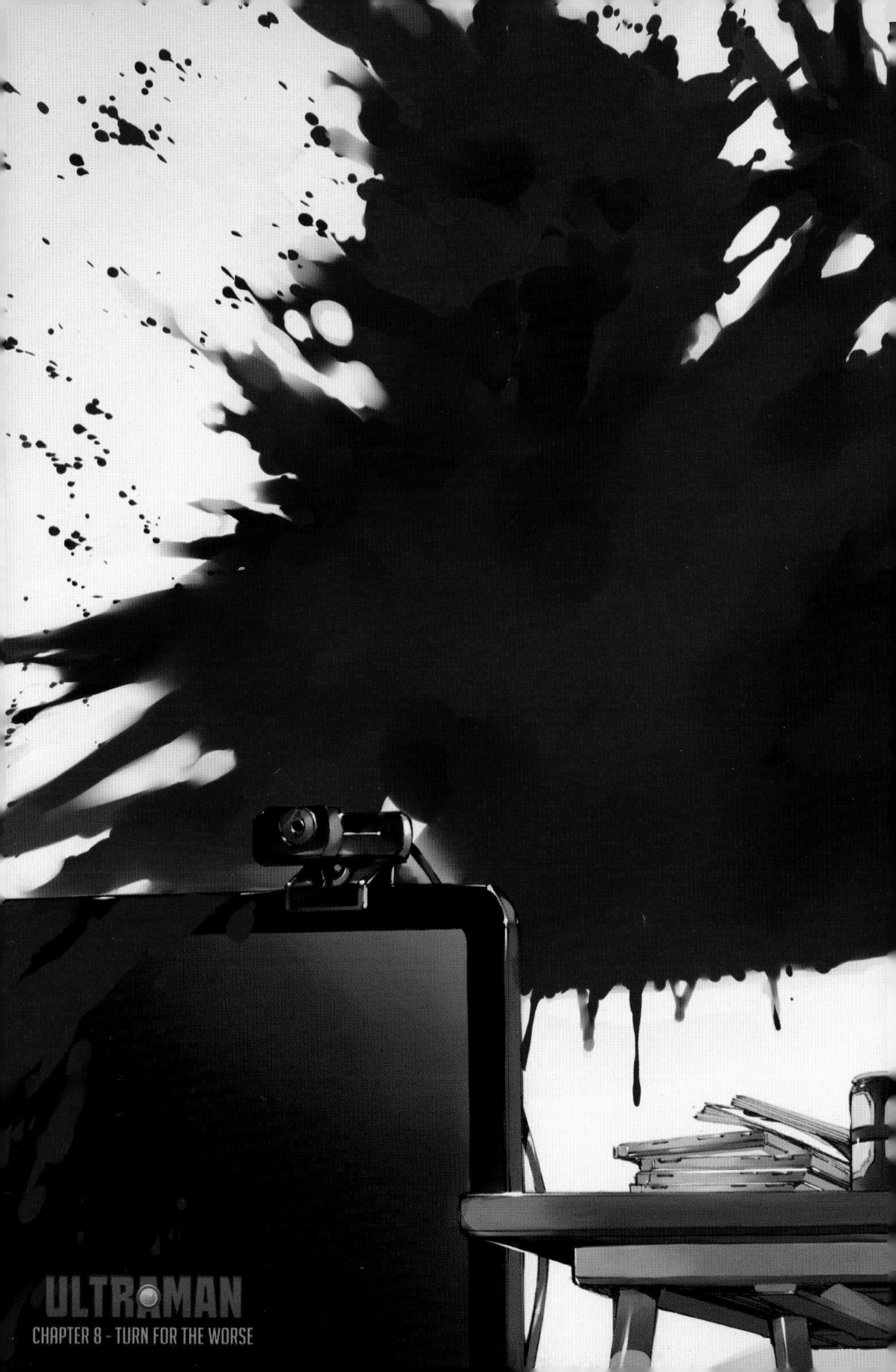
ULTRAMAN
CHAPTER 8 - TURN FOR THE WORSE

ULTRAMAN

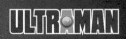

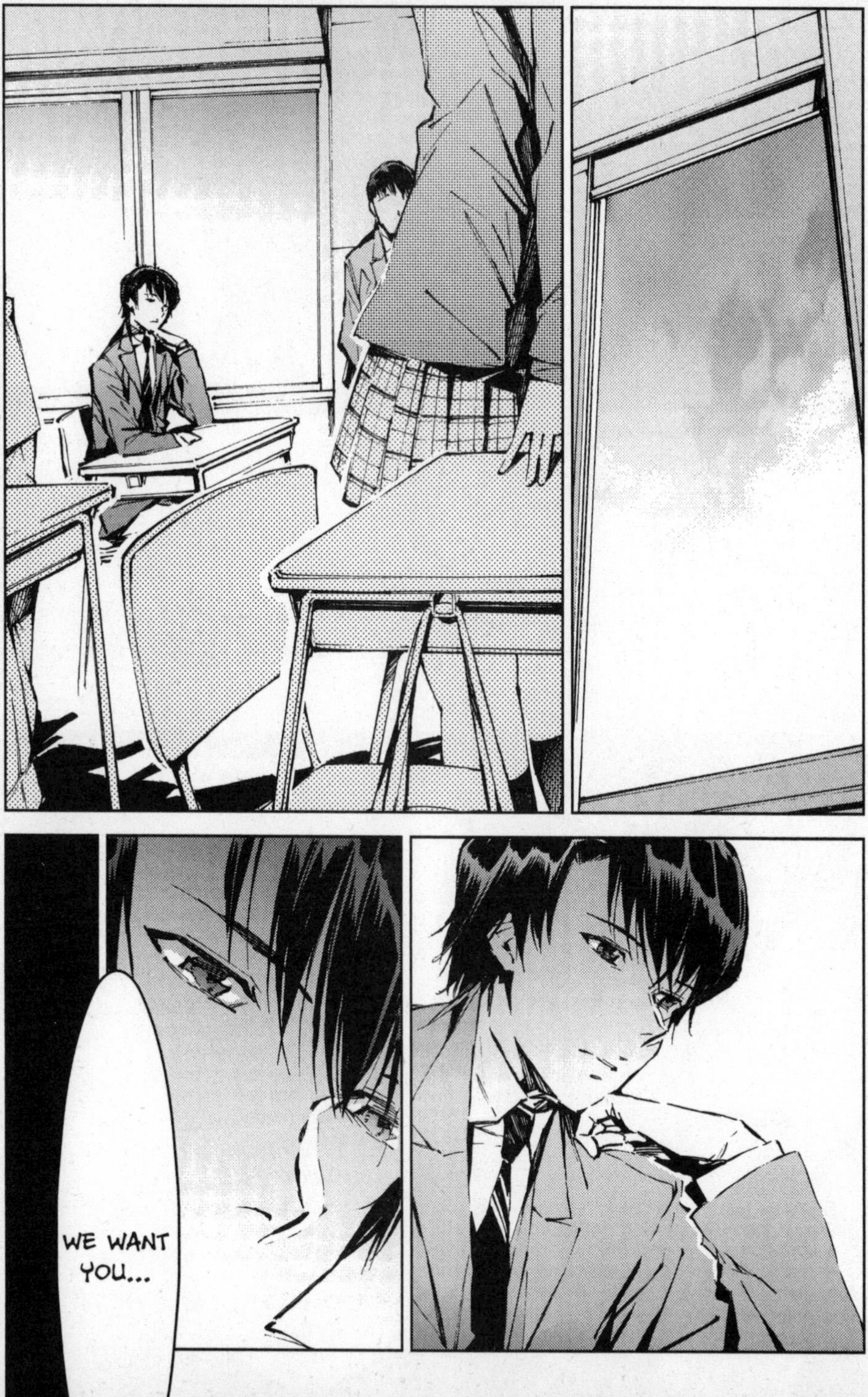
WE WANT YOU...

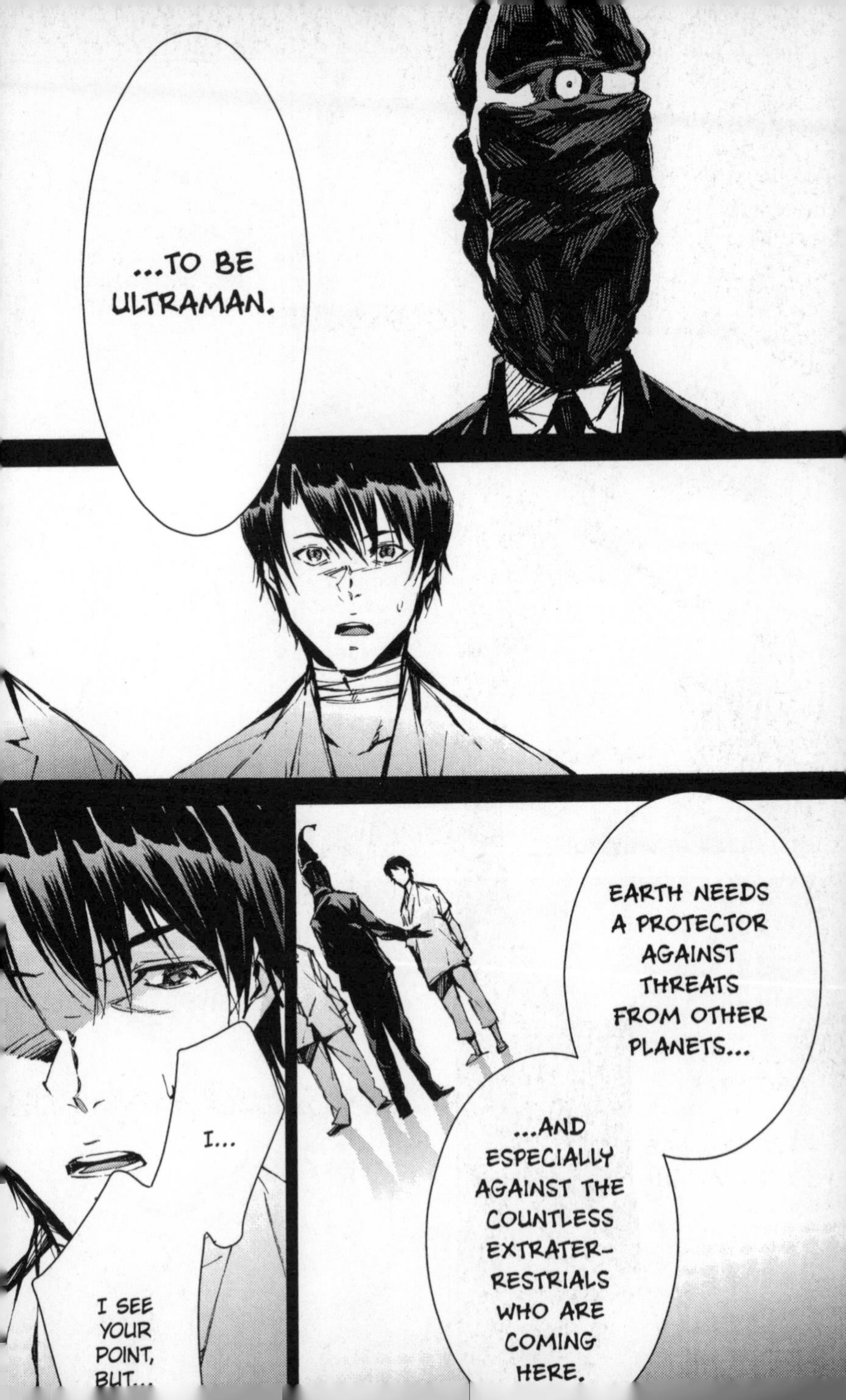
...TO BE ULTRAMAN.
EARTH NEEDS A PROTECTOR AGAINST THREATS FROM OTHER PLANETS...
...AND ESPECIALLY AGAINST THE COUNTLESS EXTRATER-RESTRIALS WHO ARE COMING HERE.
I...
I SEE YOUR POINT, BUT...

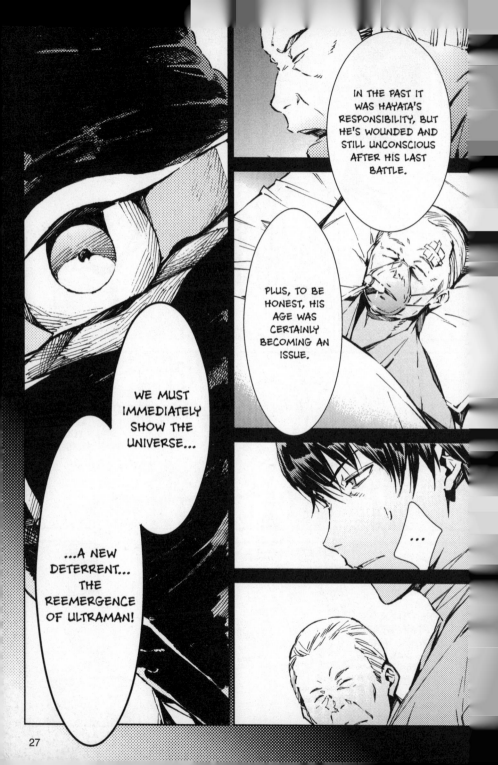

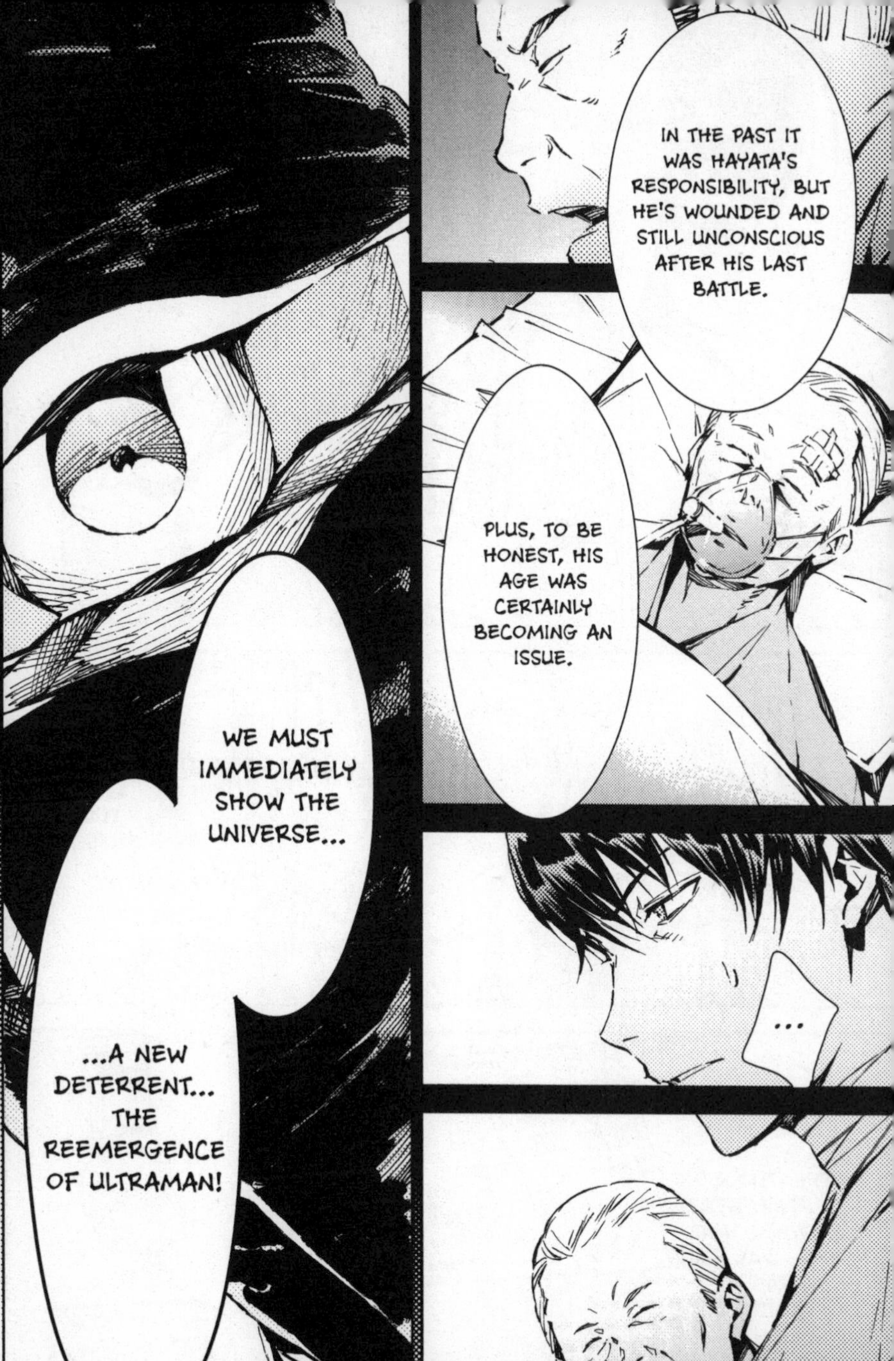
IN THE PAST IT WAS HAYATA'S RESPONSIBILITY, BUT HE'S WOUNDED AND STILL UNCONSCIOUS AFTER HIS LAST BATTLE.
PLUS, TO BE HONEST, HIS AGE WAS CERTAINLY BECOMING AN ISSUE.
...
WE MUST IMMEDIATELY SHOW THE UNIVERSE...
...A NEW DETERRENT... THE REEMERGENCE OF ULTRAMAN!

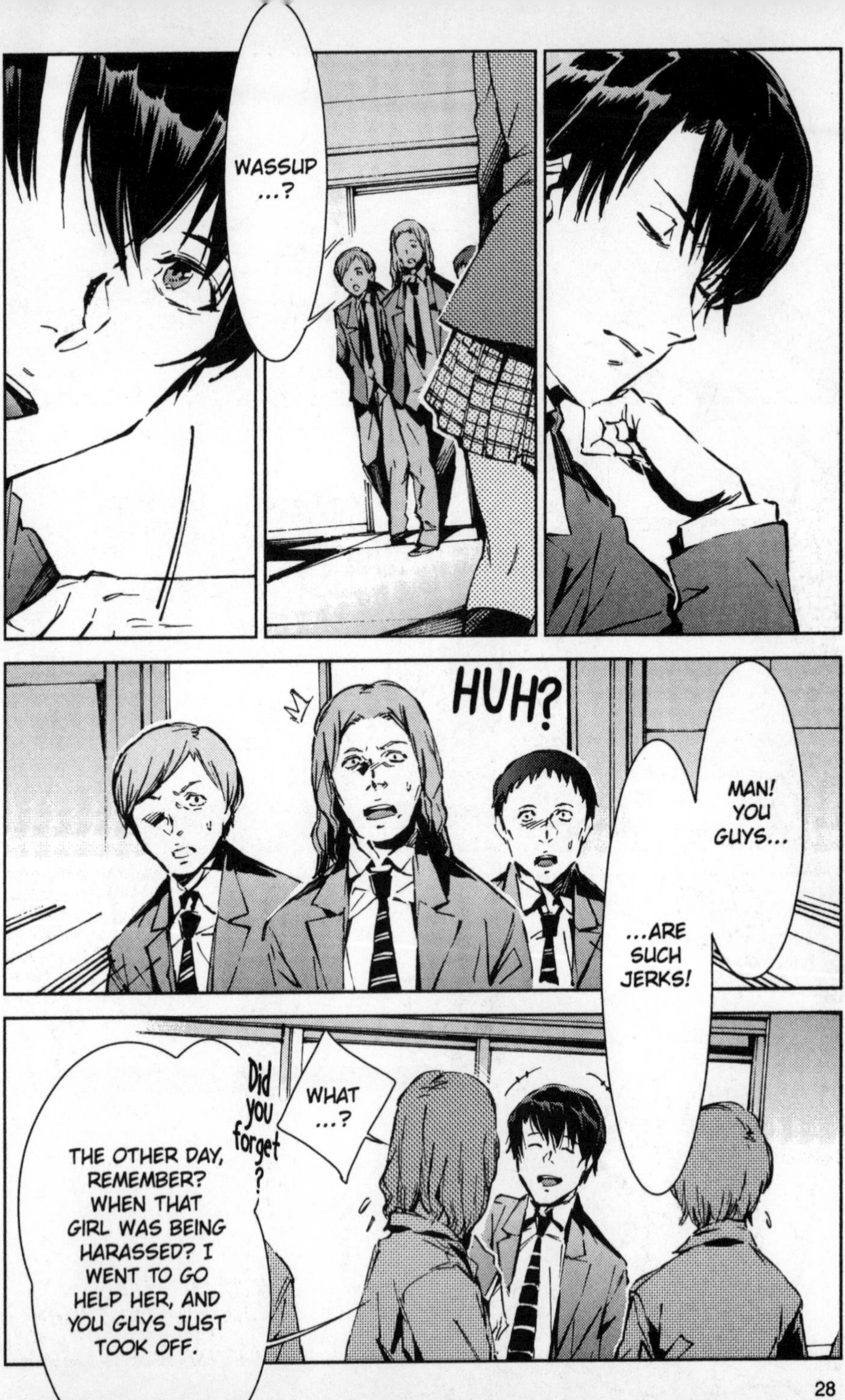
WASSUP ...?
HUH?
MAN! YOU GUYS...
...ARE SUCH JERKS!
WHAT ...?
Did you forget ?
THE OTHER DAY, REMEMBER? WHEN THAT GIRL WAS BEING HARASSED? I WENT TO GO HELP HER, AND YOU GUYS JUST TOOK OFF.

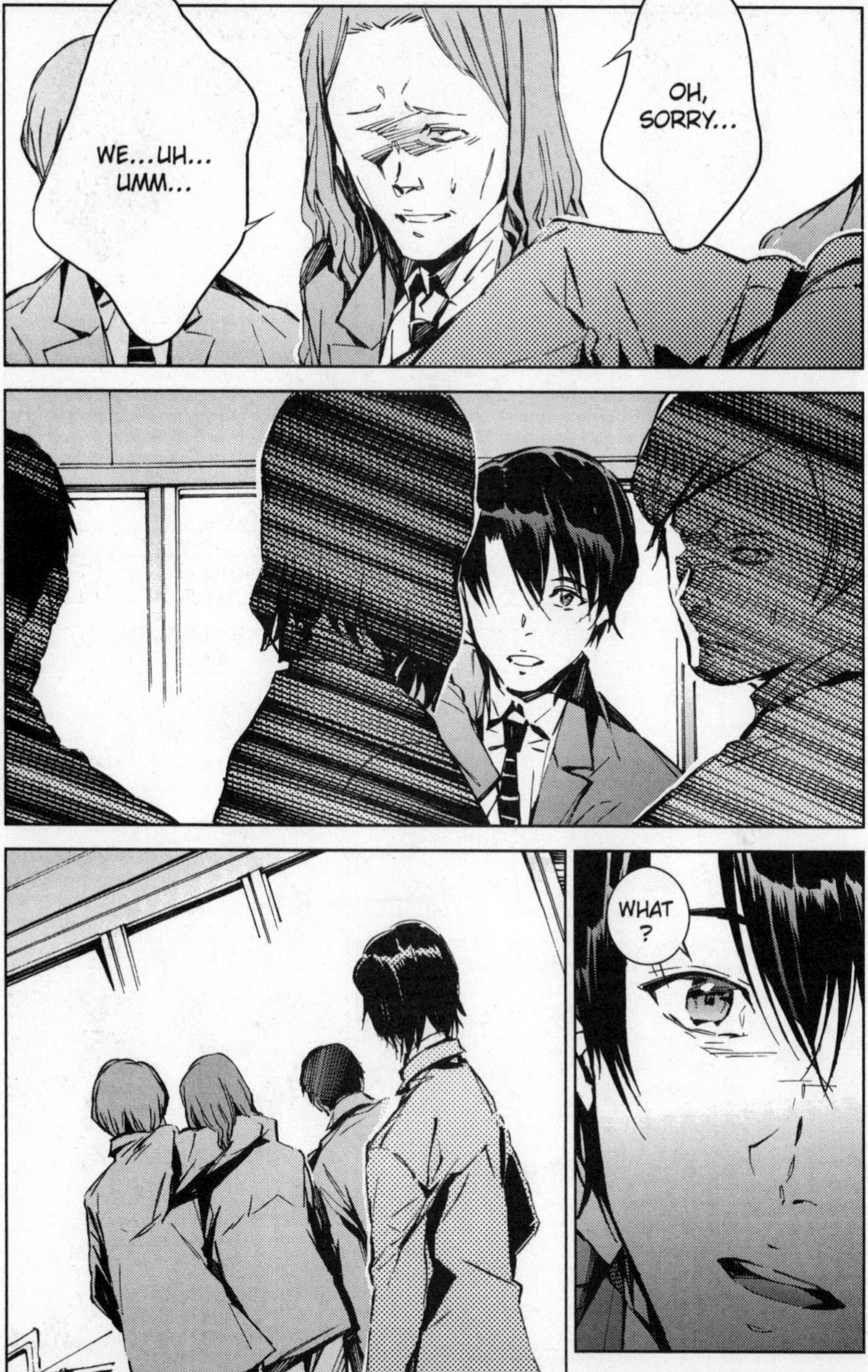
OH, SORRY...
WE...UH... UMM...
WHAT ?

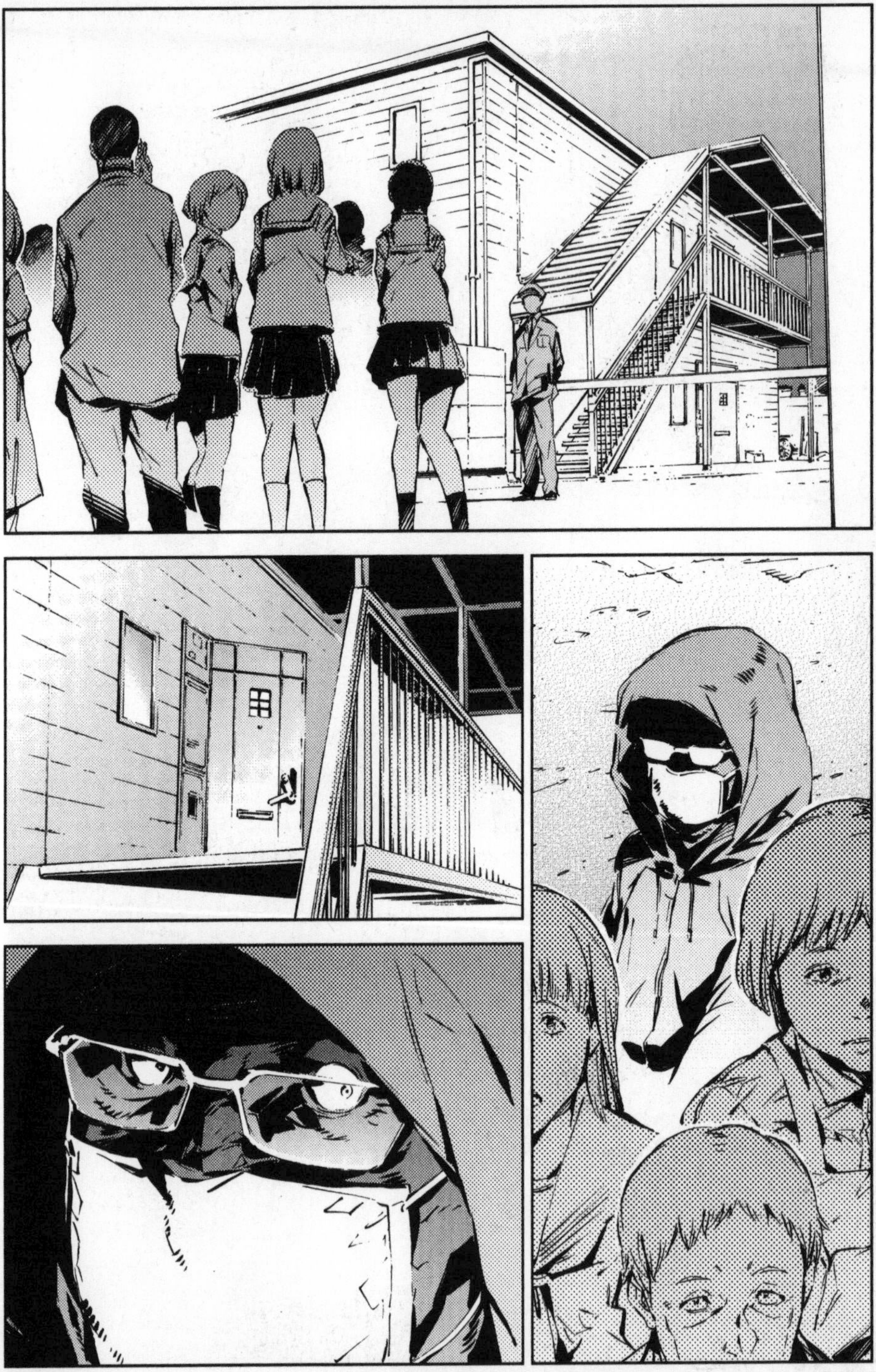

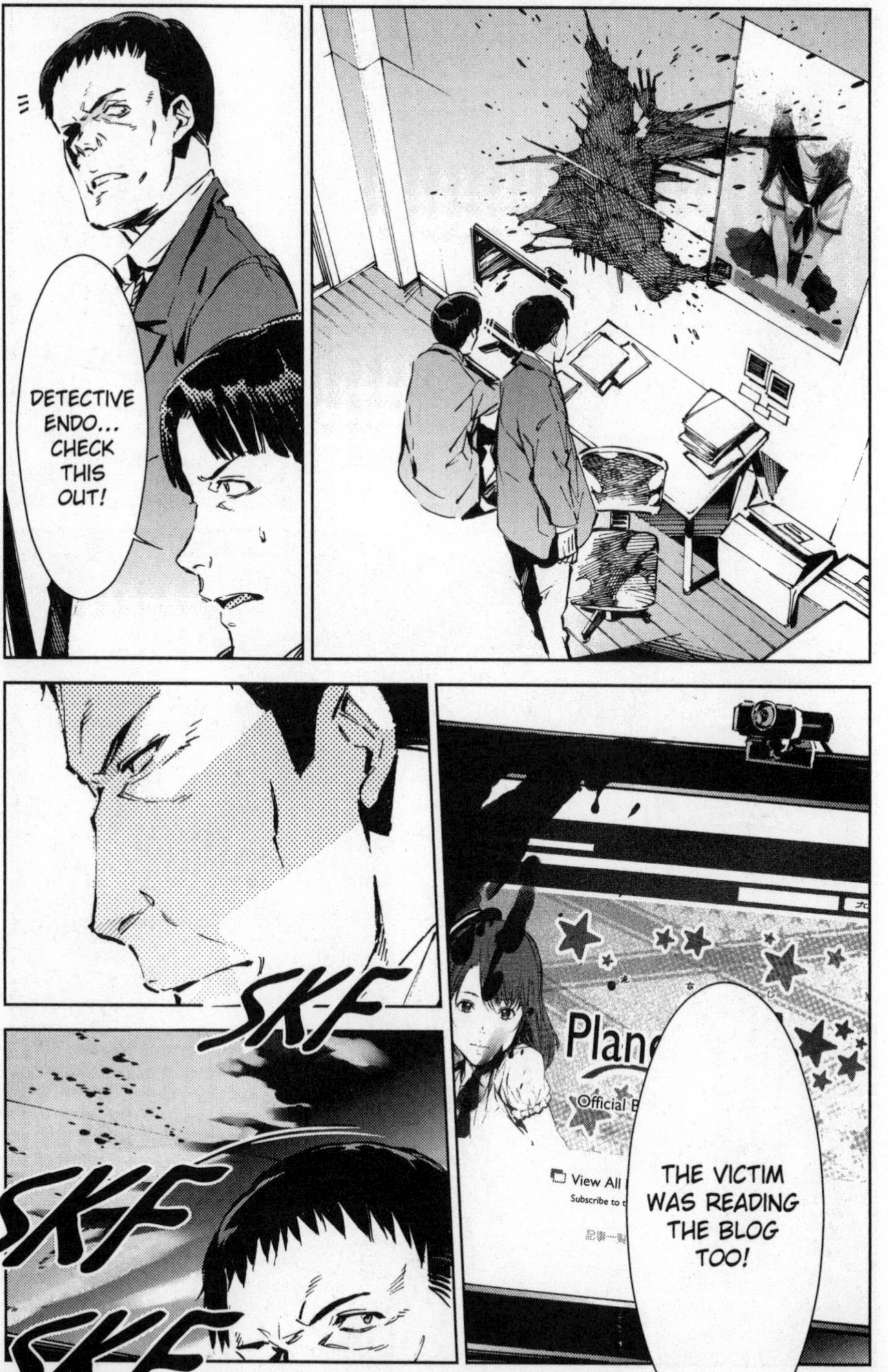
DETECTIVE ENDO... CHECK THIS OUT!
SKF
SKF
SKF
Official B
View All
THE VICTIM WAS READING THE BLOG TOO!

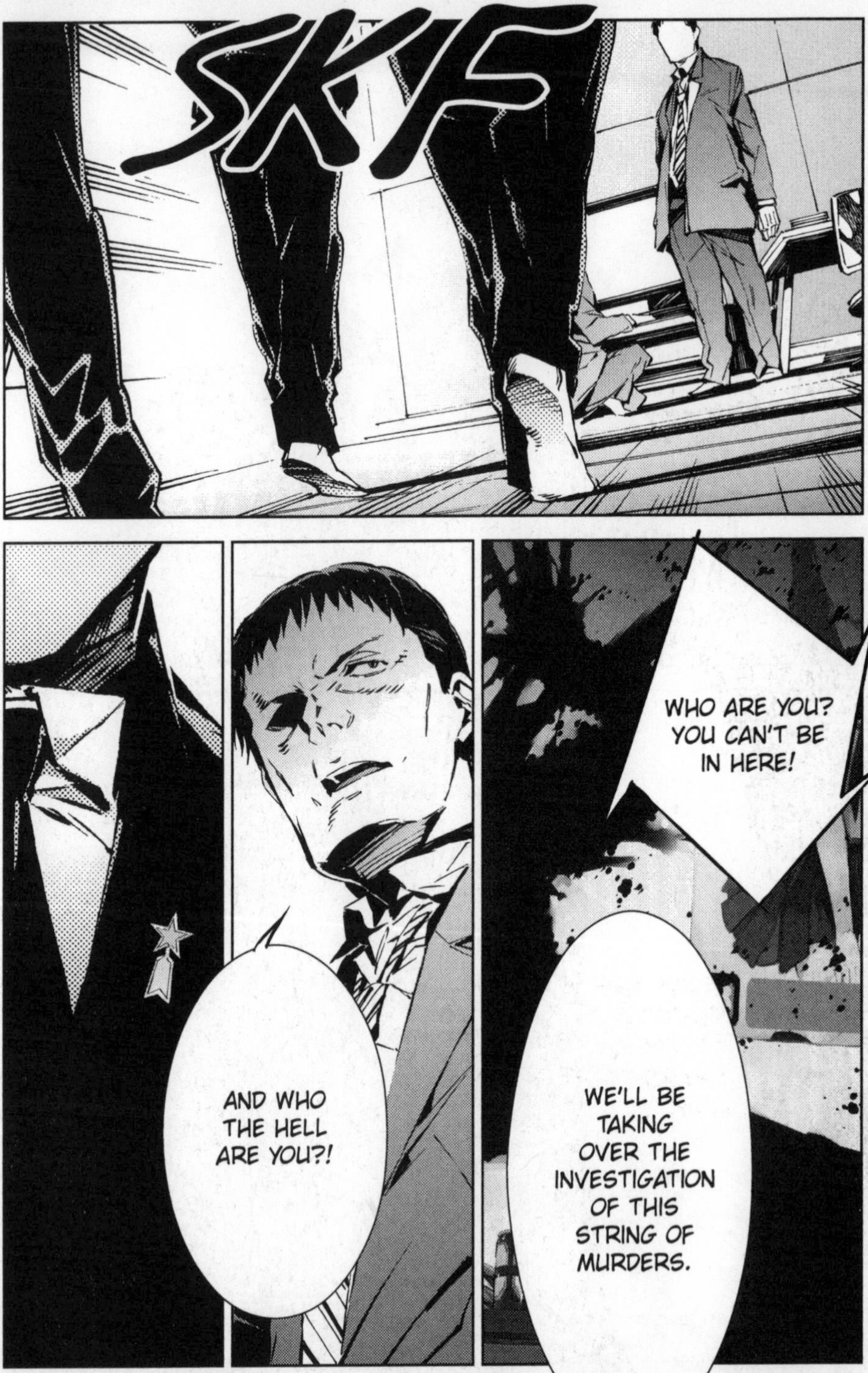
SKF
WHO ARE YOU? YOU CAN'T BE IN HERE!
WE'LL BE TAKING OVER THE INVESTIGATION OF THIS STRING OF MURDERS.
AND WHO THE HELL ARE YOU?!

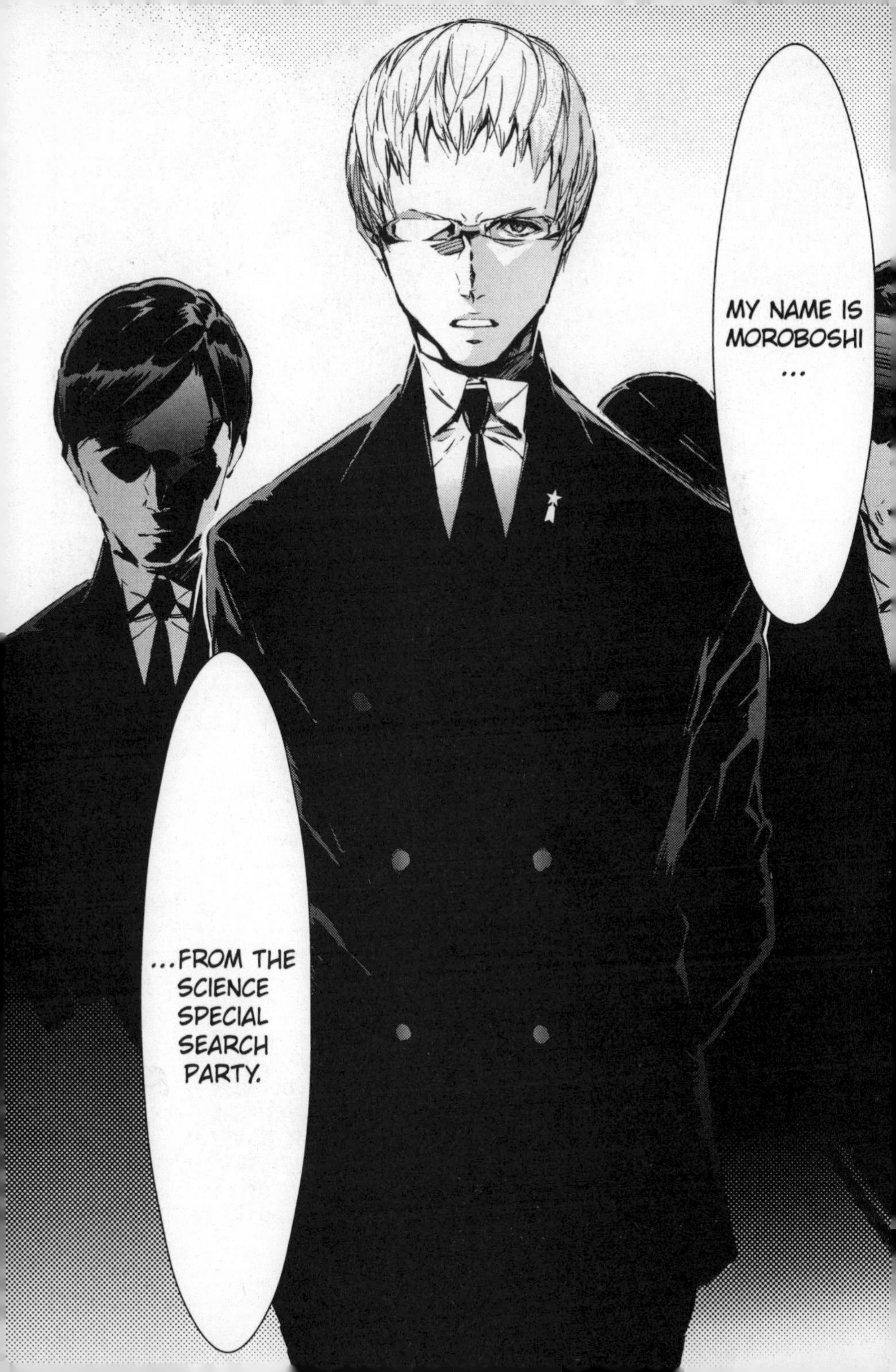
MY NAME IS MOROBOSHI ...
...FROM THE SCIENCE SPECIAL SEARCH PARTY.

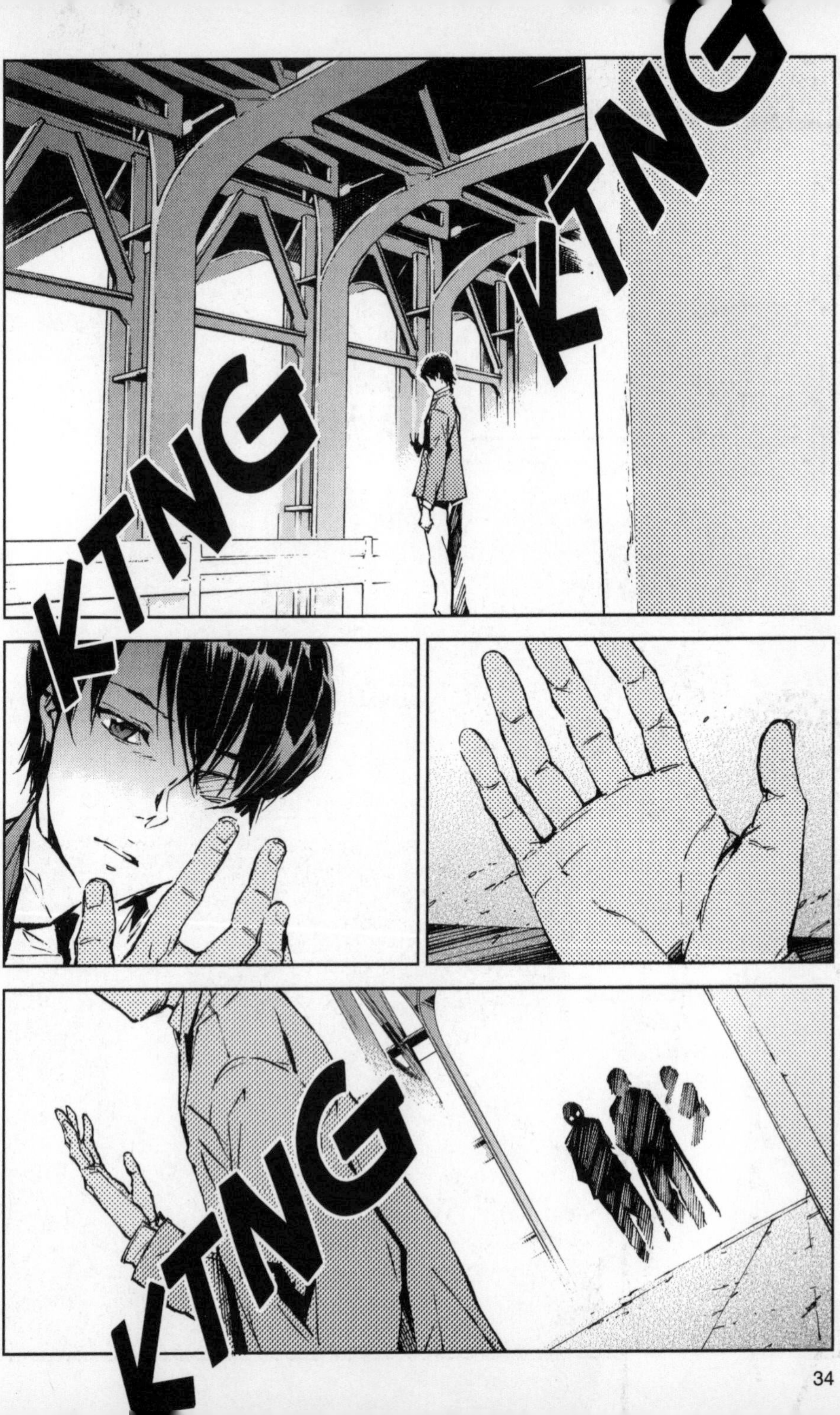
KTNG
KTNG
KTNG

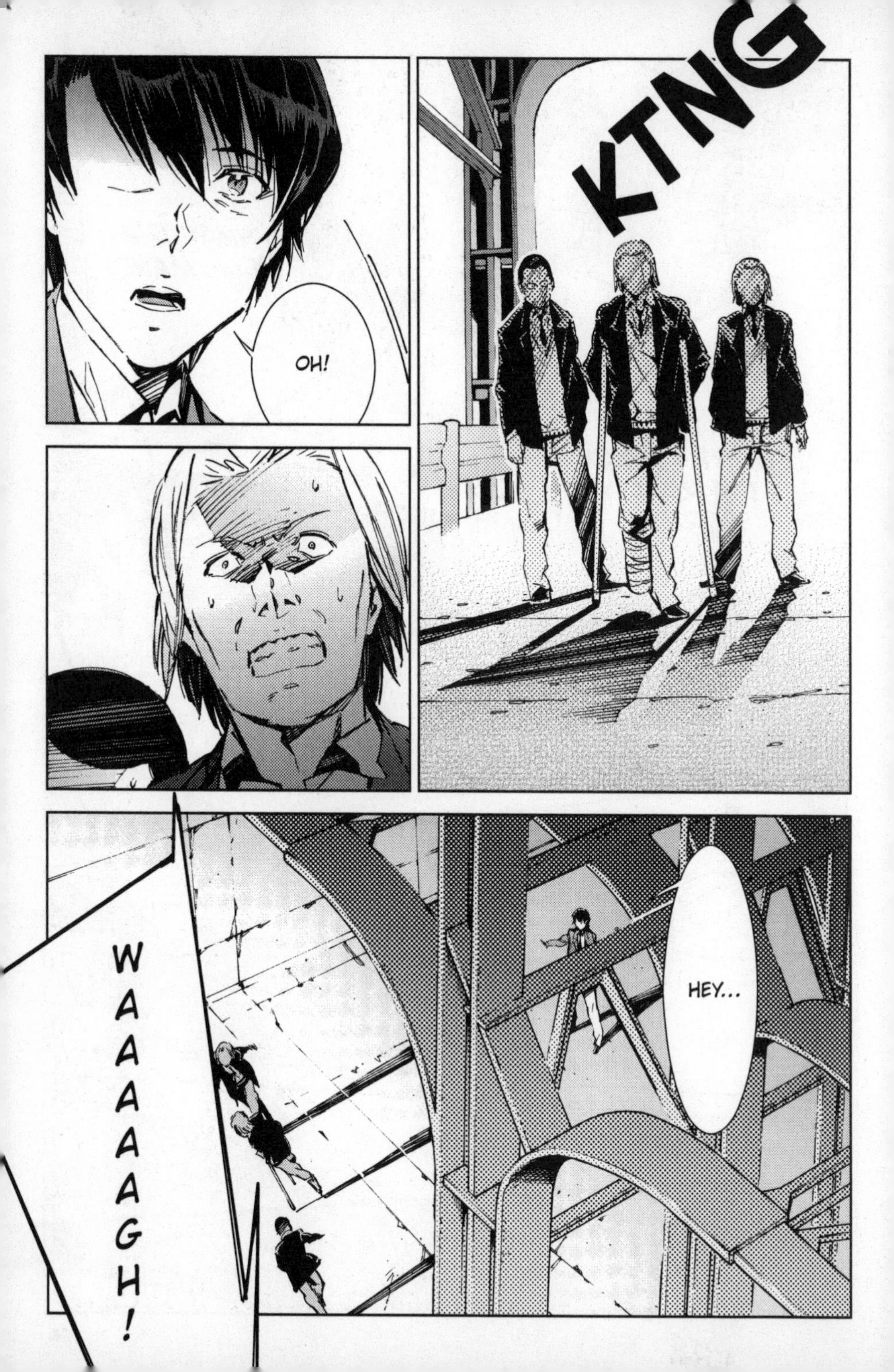
KTNG
OH!
HEY...
WAAAAAAAGH!

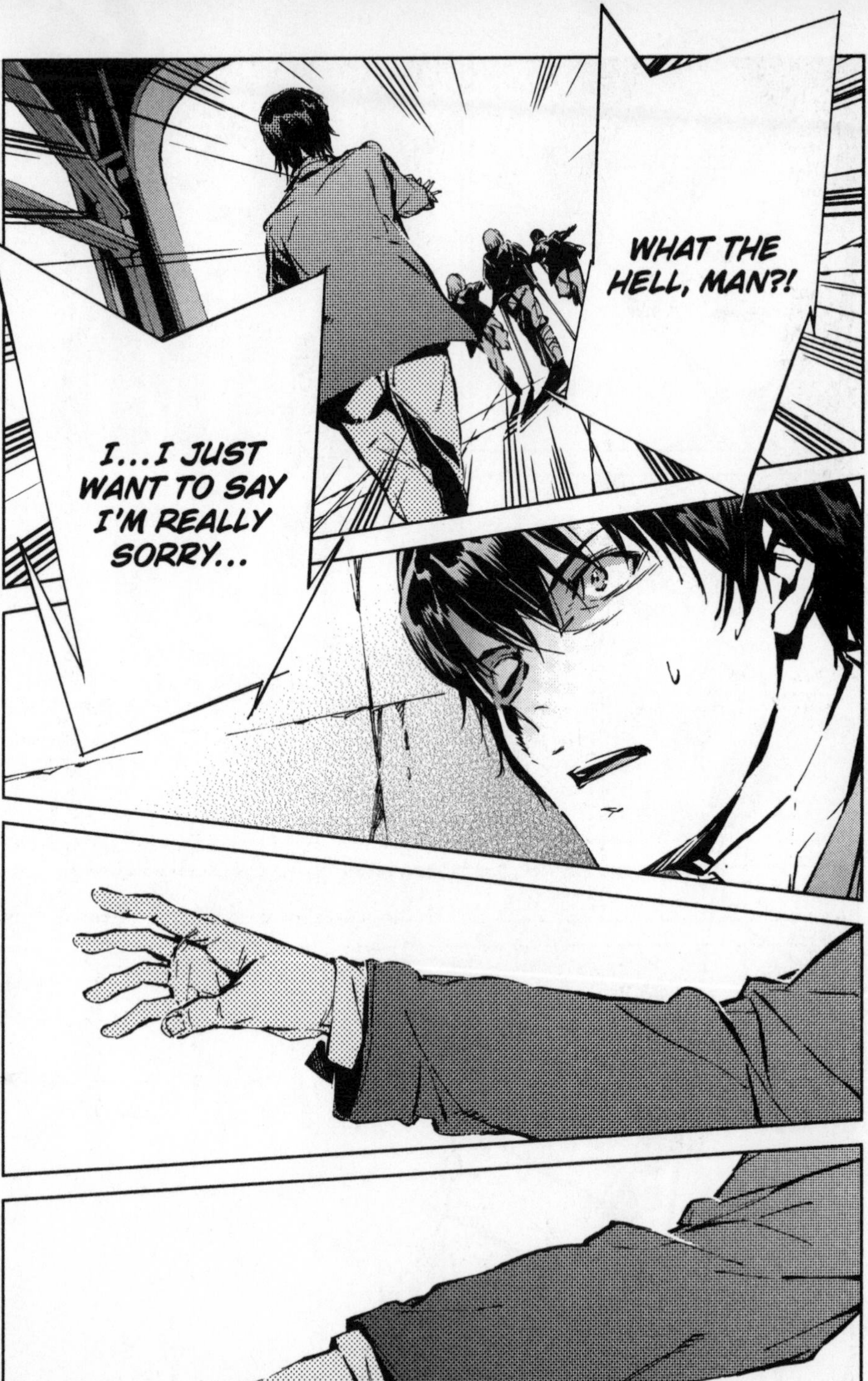
WHAT THE HELL, MAN?!
I...I JUST WANT TO SAY I'M REALLY SORRY...

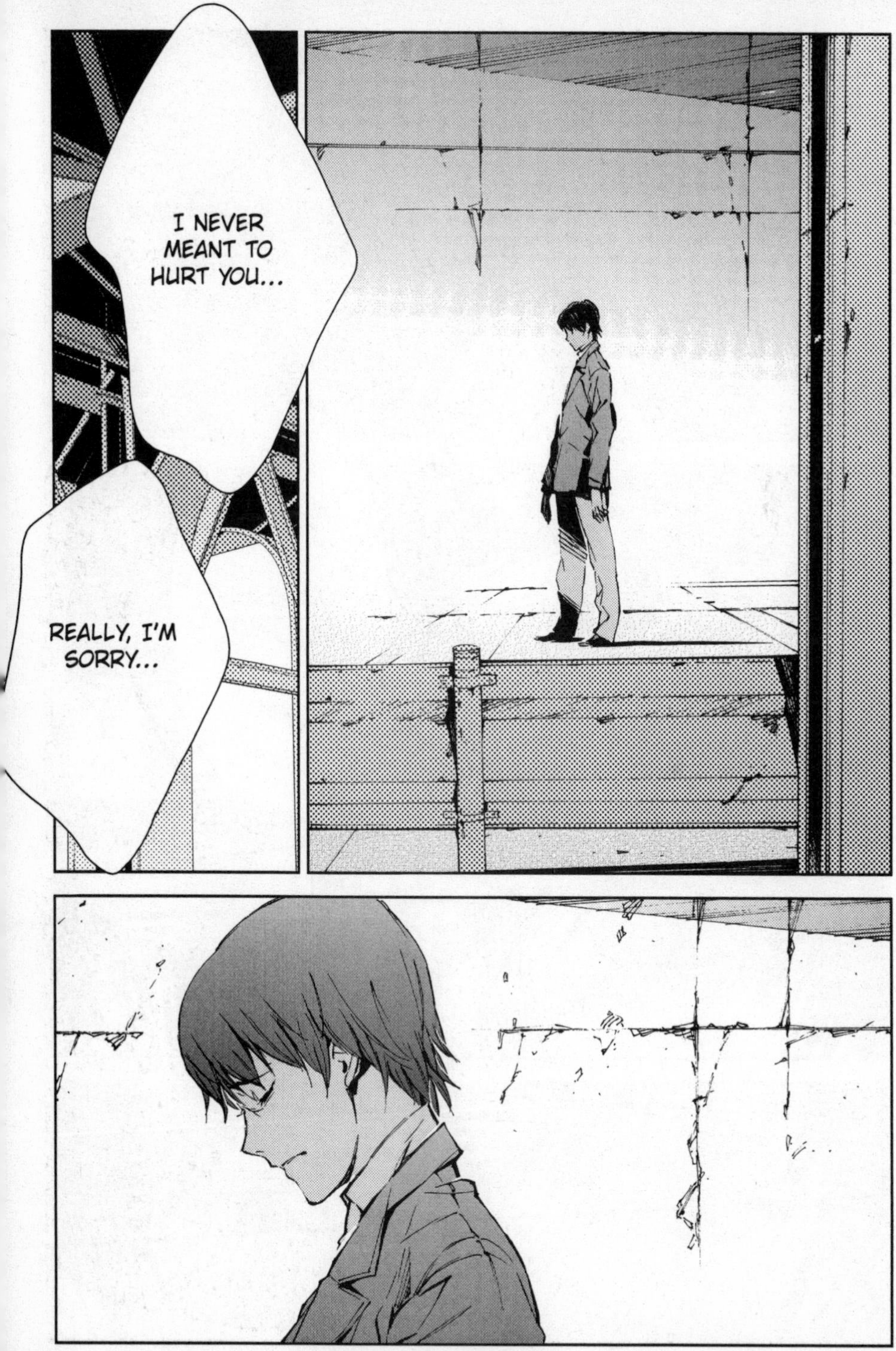
I NEVER MEANT TO HURT YOU...
REALLY, I'M SORRY...

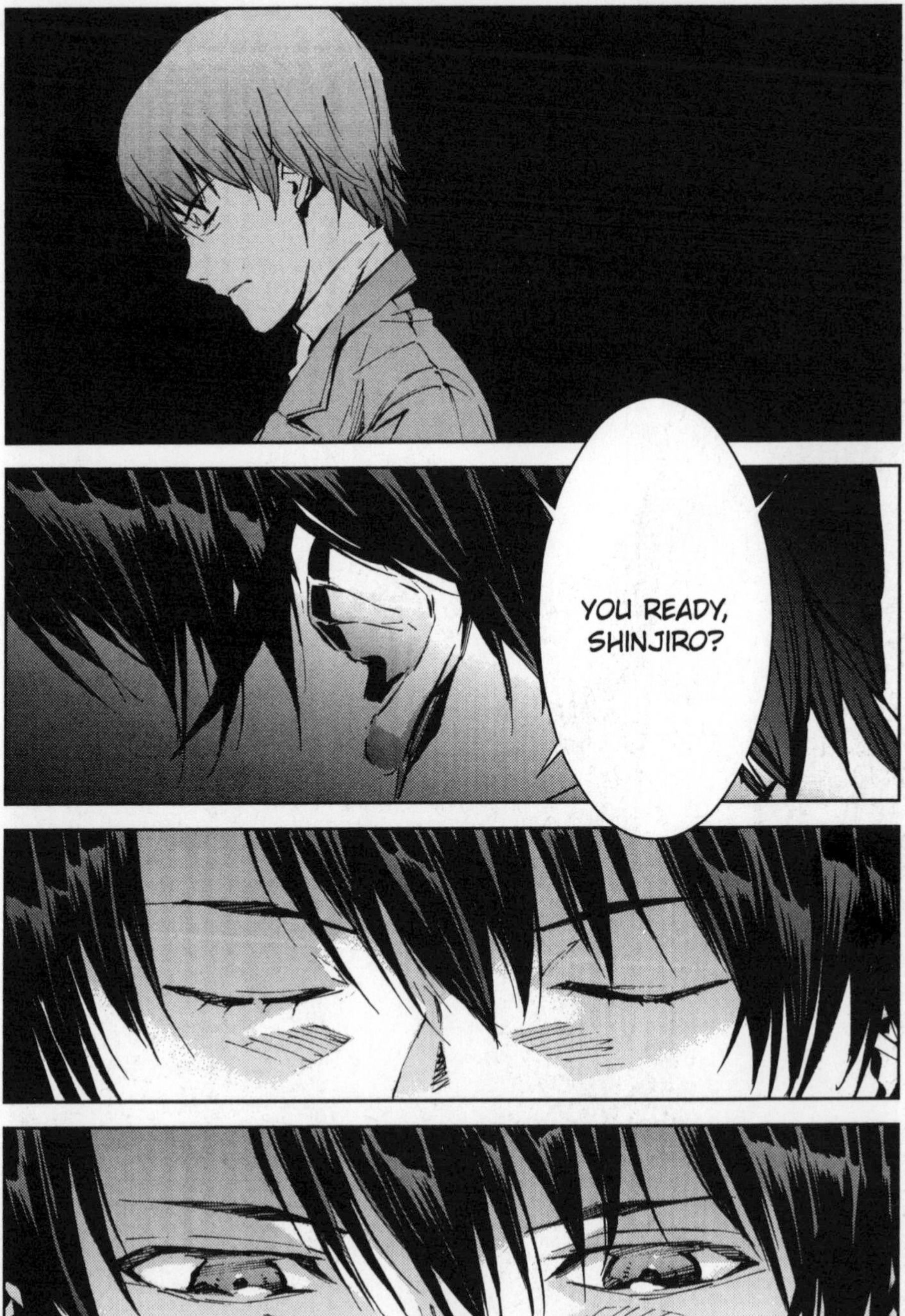
YOU READY, SHINJIRO?

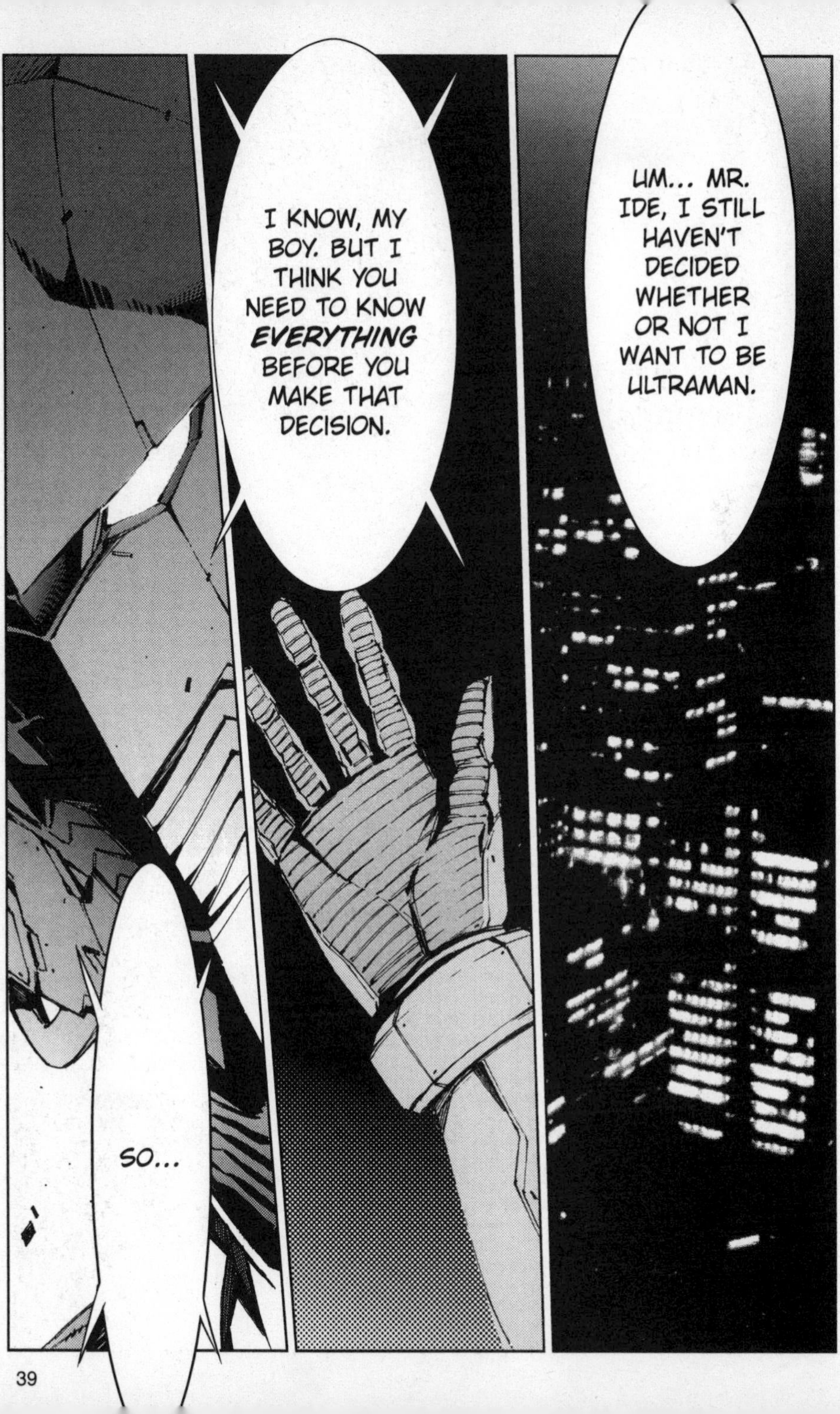
UM... MR. IDE, I STILL HAVEN'T DECIDED WHETHER OR NOT I WANT TO BE ULTRAMAN.
I KNOW, MY BOY. BUT I THINK YOU NEED TO KNOW *EVERYTHING* BEFORE YOU MAKE THAT DECISION.
SO...

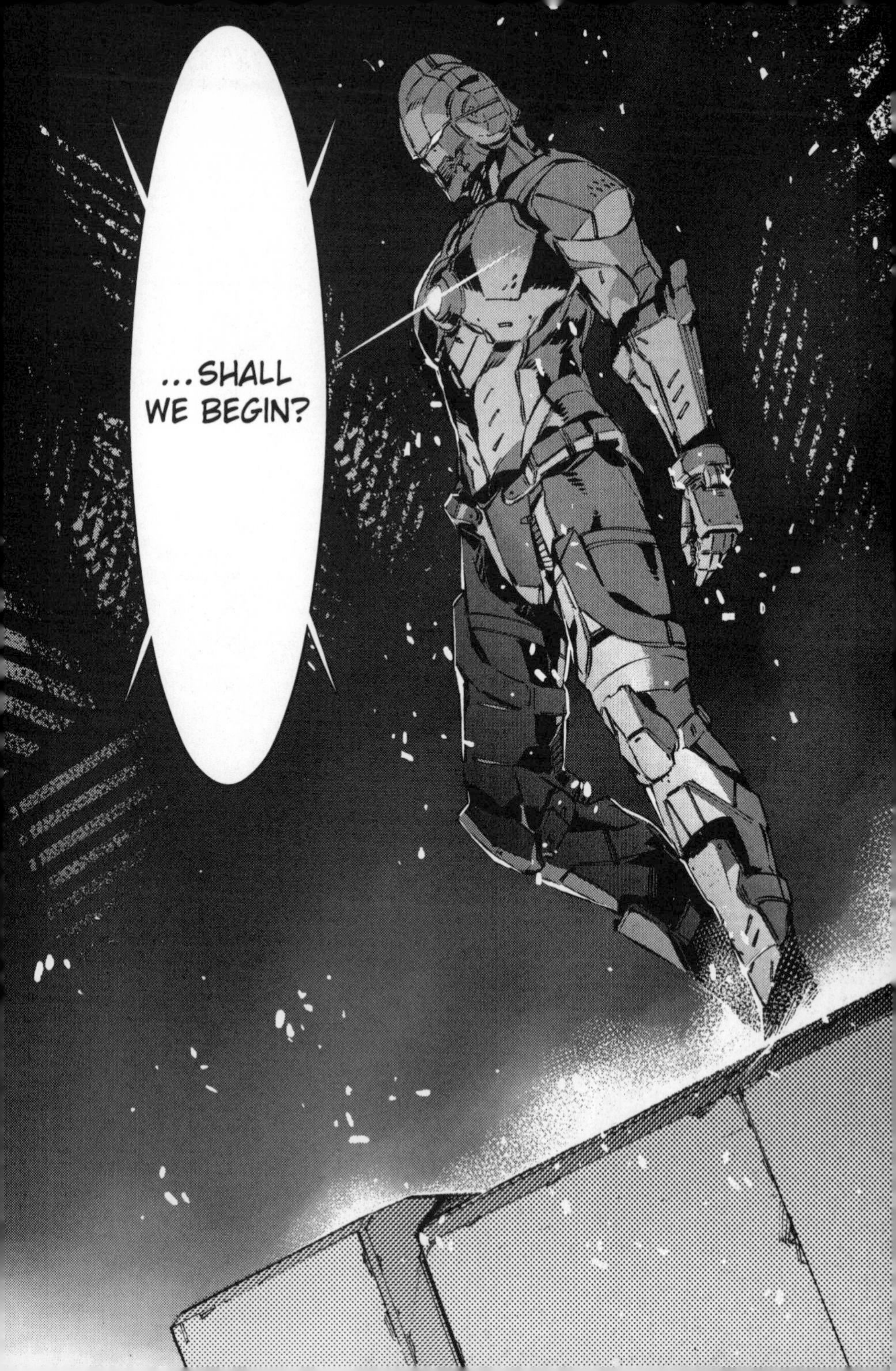
...SHALL WE BEGIN?

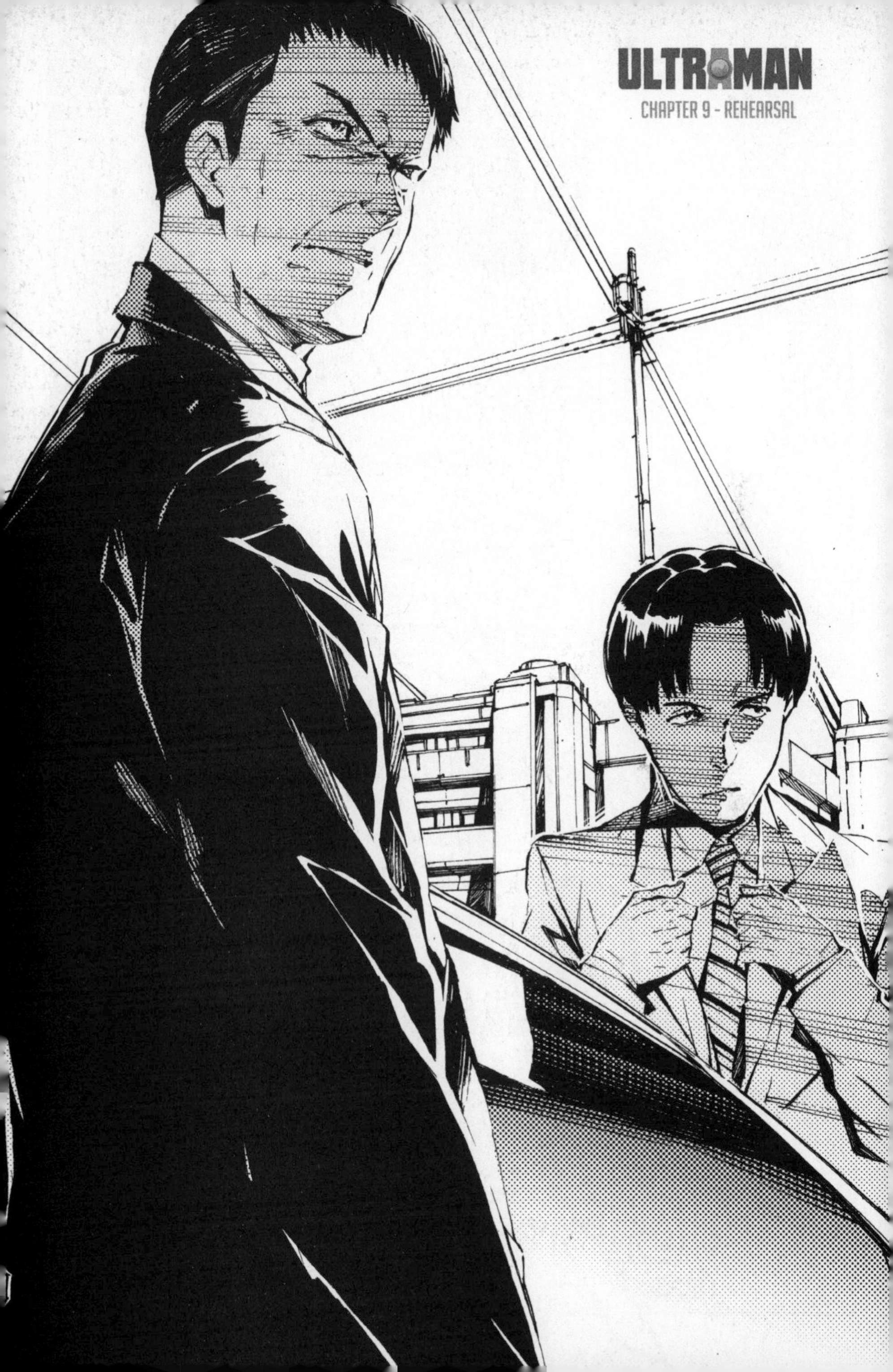
ULTRAMAN
CHAPTER 9 - REHEARSAL

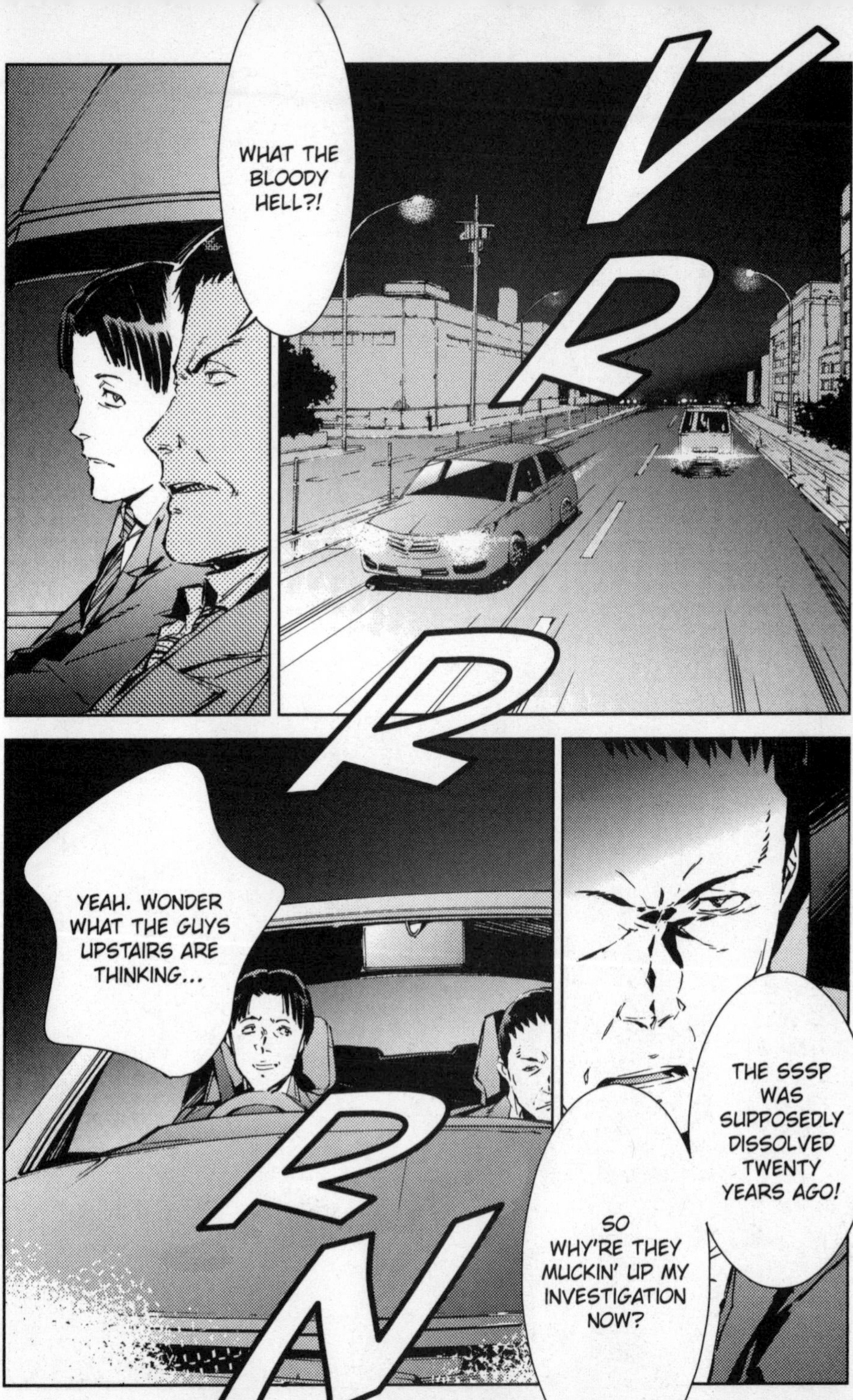
WHAT THE BLOODY HELL?!
VRRRN
THE SSSP WAS SUPPOSEDLY DISSOLVED TWENTY YEARS AGO!
SO WHY'RE THEY MUCKIN' UP MY INVESTIGATION NOW?
YEAH. WONDER WHAT THE GUYS UPSTAIRS ARE THINKING...

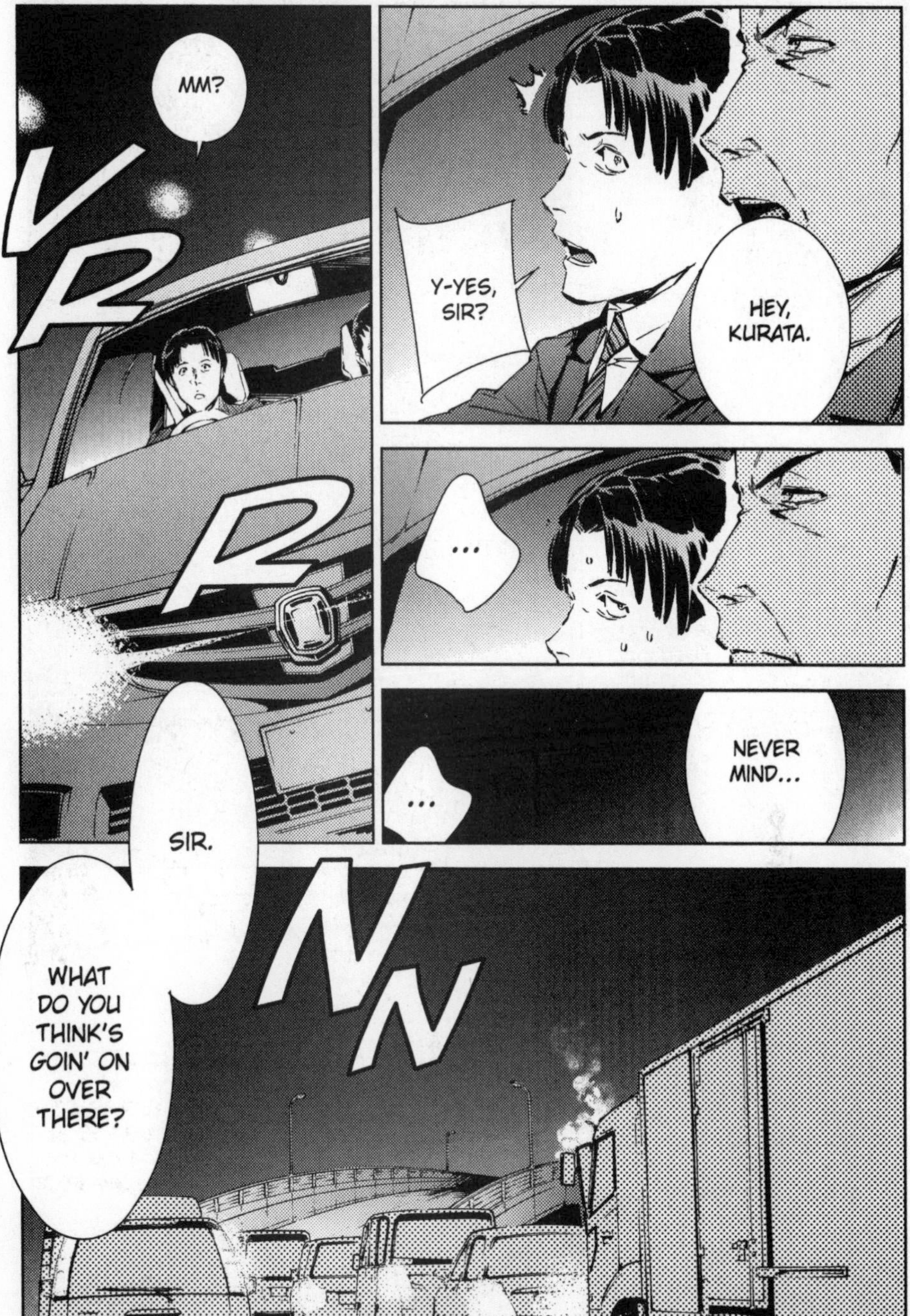
HEY, KURATA.
Y-YES, SIR?
...
NEVER MIND...
...
MM?
VRR
R
SIR.
WHAT DO YOU THINK'S GOIN' ON OVER THERE?
NN

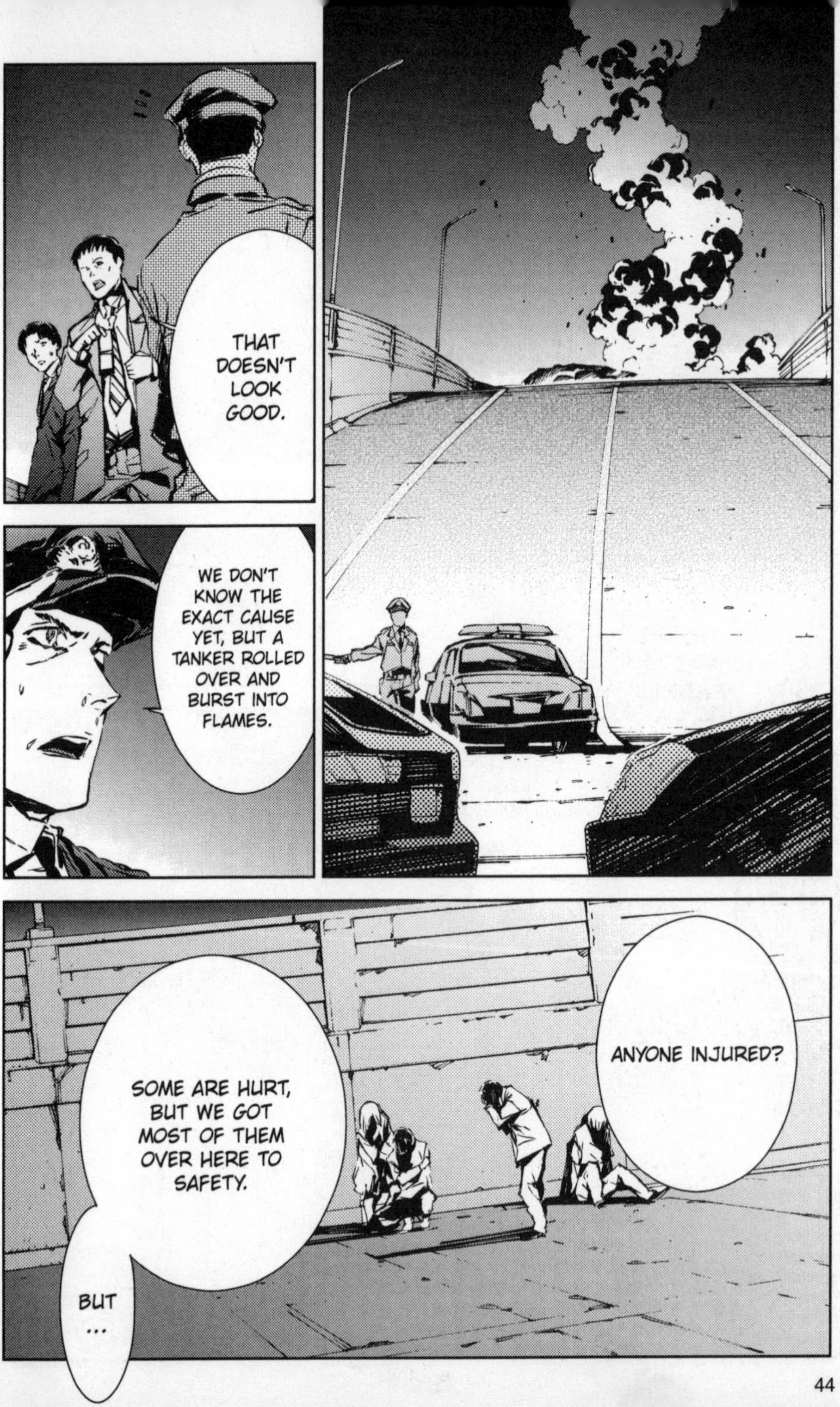
THAT DOESN'T LOOK GOOD.
WE DON'T KNOW THE EXACT CAUSE YET, BUT A TANKER ROLLED OVER AND BURST INTO FLAMES.
ANYONE INJURED?
SOME ARE HURT, BUT WE GOT MOST OF THEM OVER HERE TO SAFETY.
BUT ...

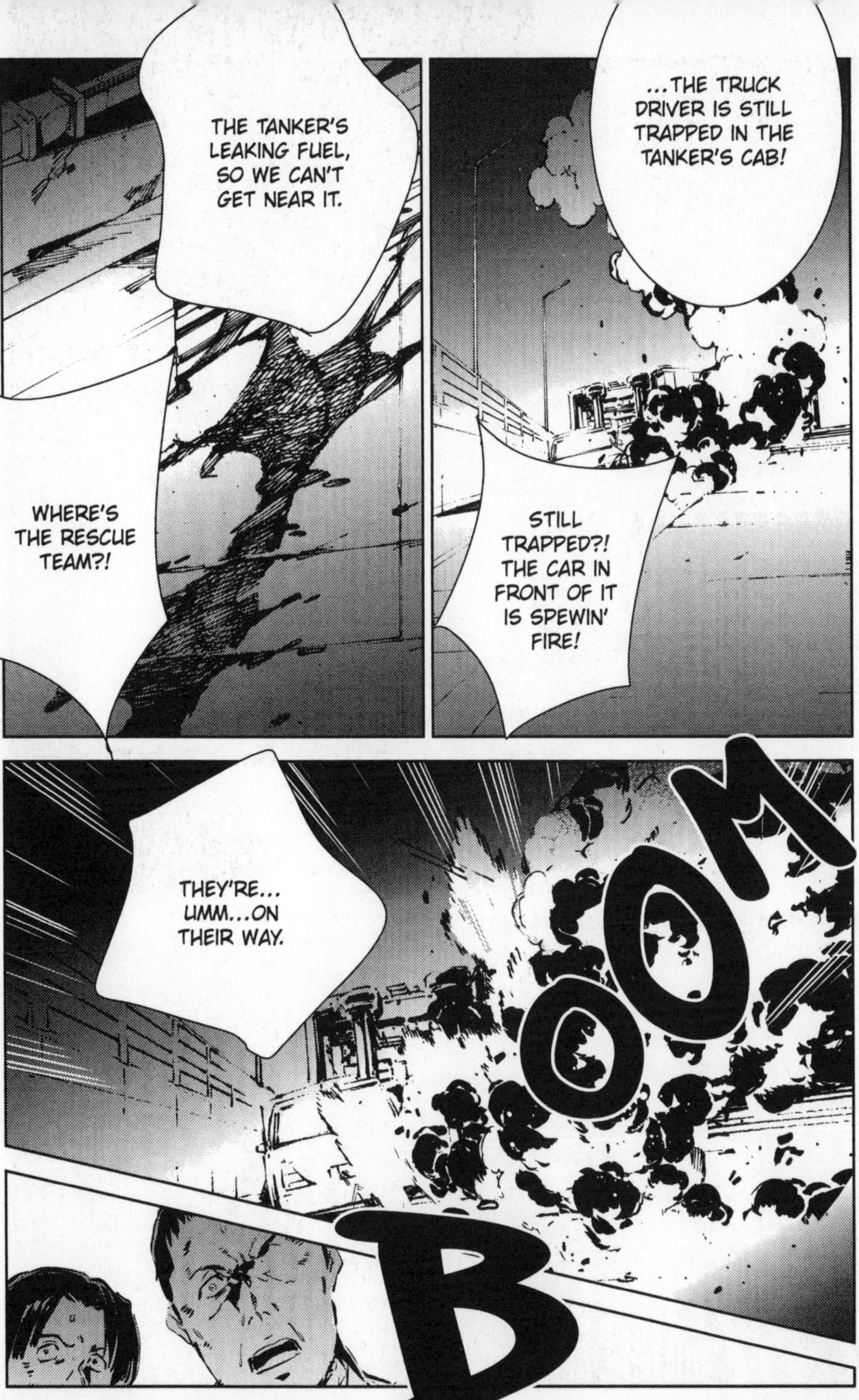
...THE TRUCK DRIVER IS STILL TRAPPED IN THE TANKER'S CAB!
STILL TRAPPED?! THE CAR IN FRONT OF IT IS SPEWIN' FIRE!
THE TANKER'S LEAKING FUEL, SO WE CAN'T GET NEAR IT.
WHERE'S THE RESCUE TEAM?!
THEY'RE... UMM...ON THEIR WAY.
BOOM

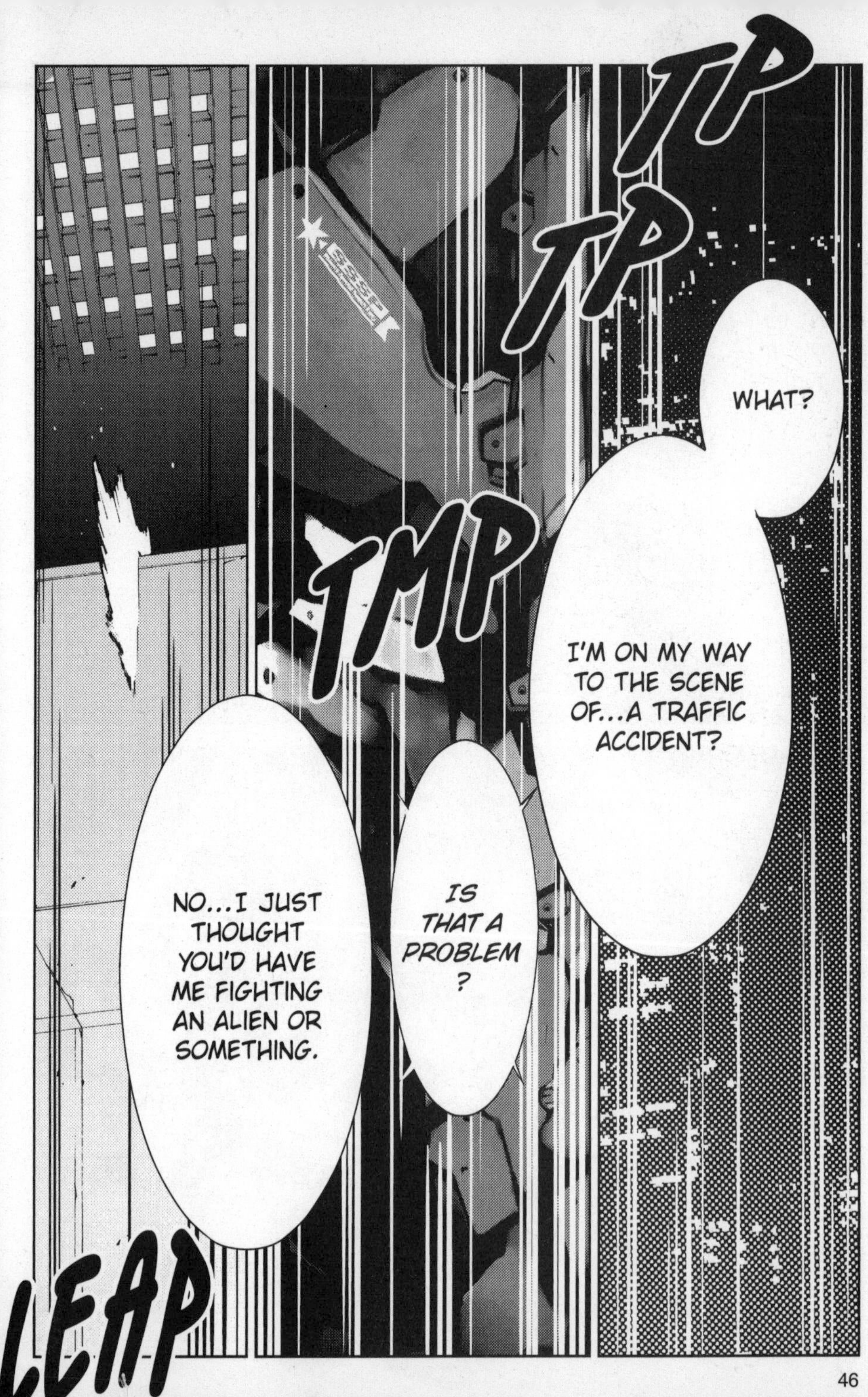
TP
TP
WHAT?
I'M ON MY WAY TO THE SCENE OF...A TRAFFIC ACCIDENT?
TMP
IS THAT A PROBLEM?
NO...I JUST THOUGHT YOU'D HAVE ME FIGHTING AN ALIEN OR SOMETHING.
LEAP

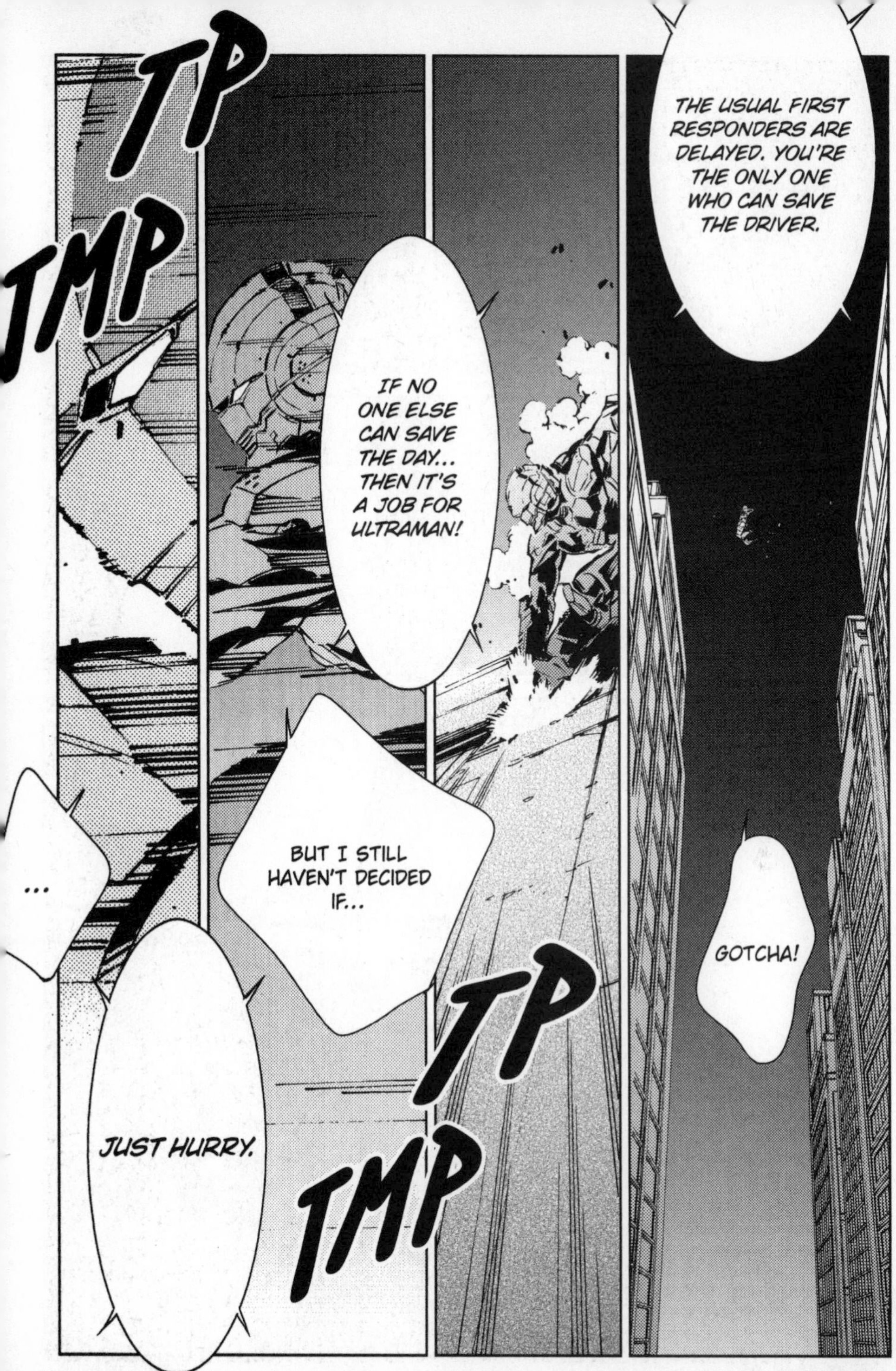
THE USUAL FIRST RESPONDERS ARE DELAYED. YOU'RE THE ONLY ONE WHO CAN SAVE THE DRIVER.
GOTCHA!
IF NO ONE ELSE CAN SAVE THE DAY... THEN IT'S A JOB FOR ULTRAMAN!
BUT I STILL HAVEN'T DECIDED IF...
TP TMP
...
JUST HURRY.
TP TMP

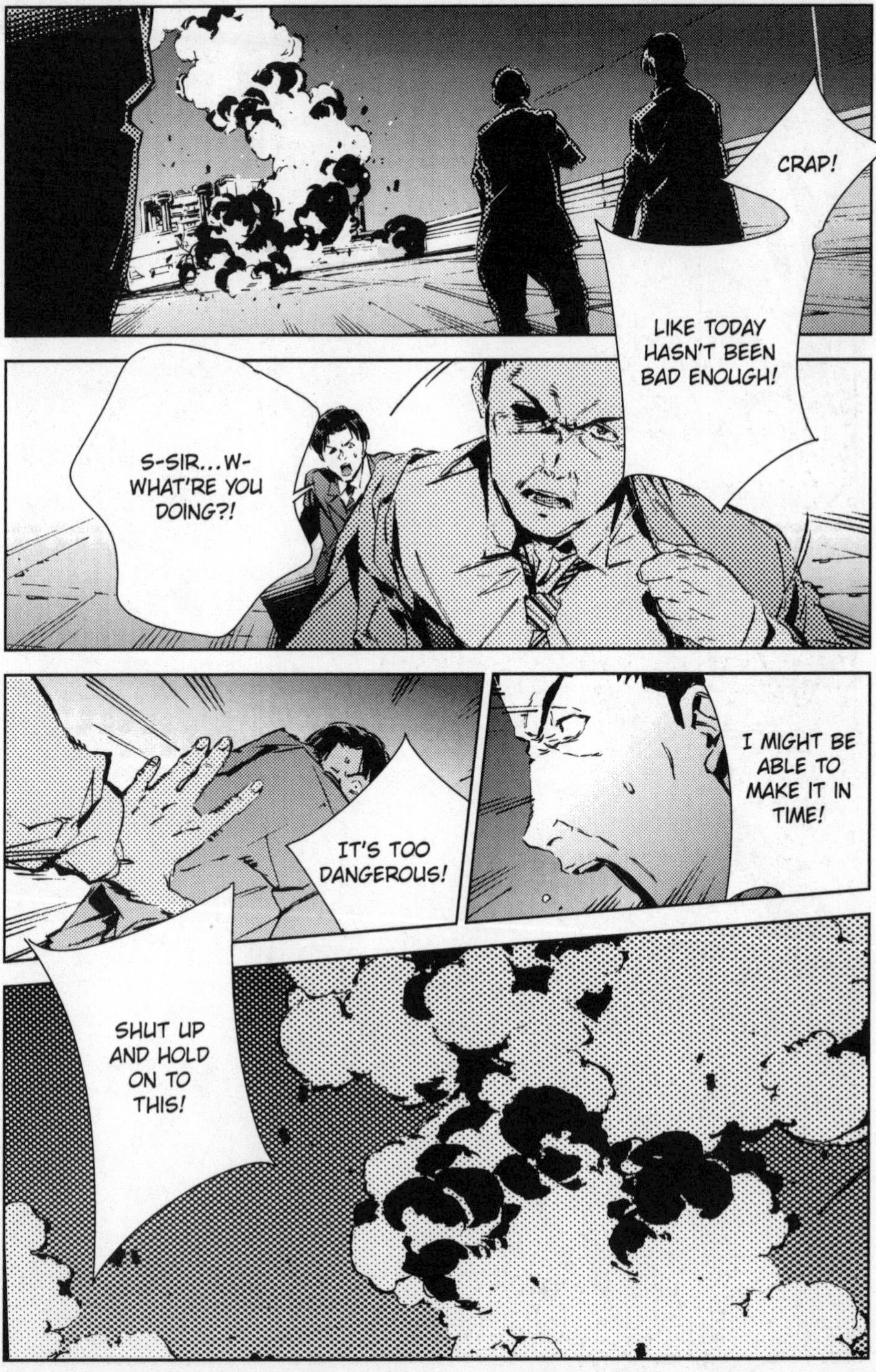
CRAP!
LIKE TODAY HASN'T BEEN BAD ENOUGH!
S-SIR...W-WHAT'RE YOU DOING?!
I MIGHT BE ABLE TO MAKE IT IN TIME!
IT'S TOO DANGEROUS!
SHUT UP AND HOLD ON TO THIS!

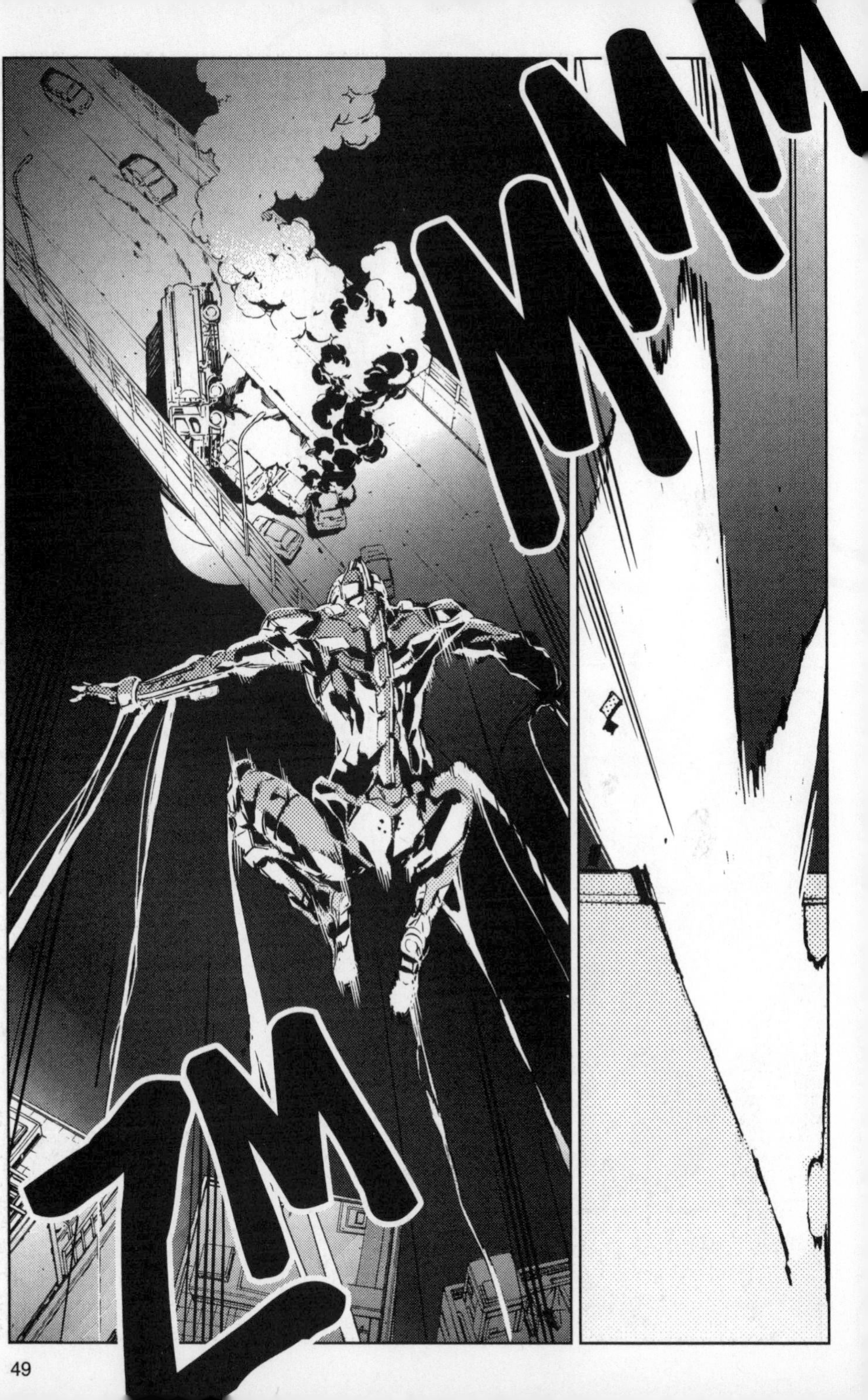
ZMMMMM

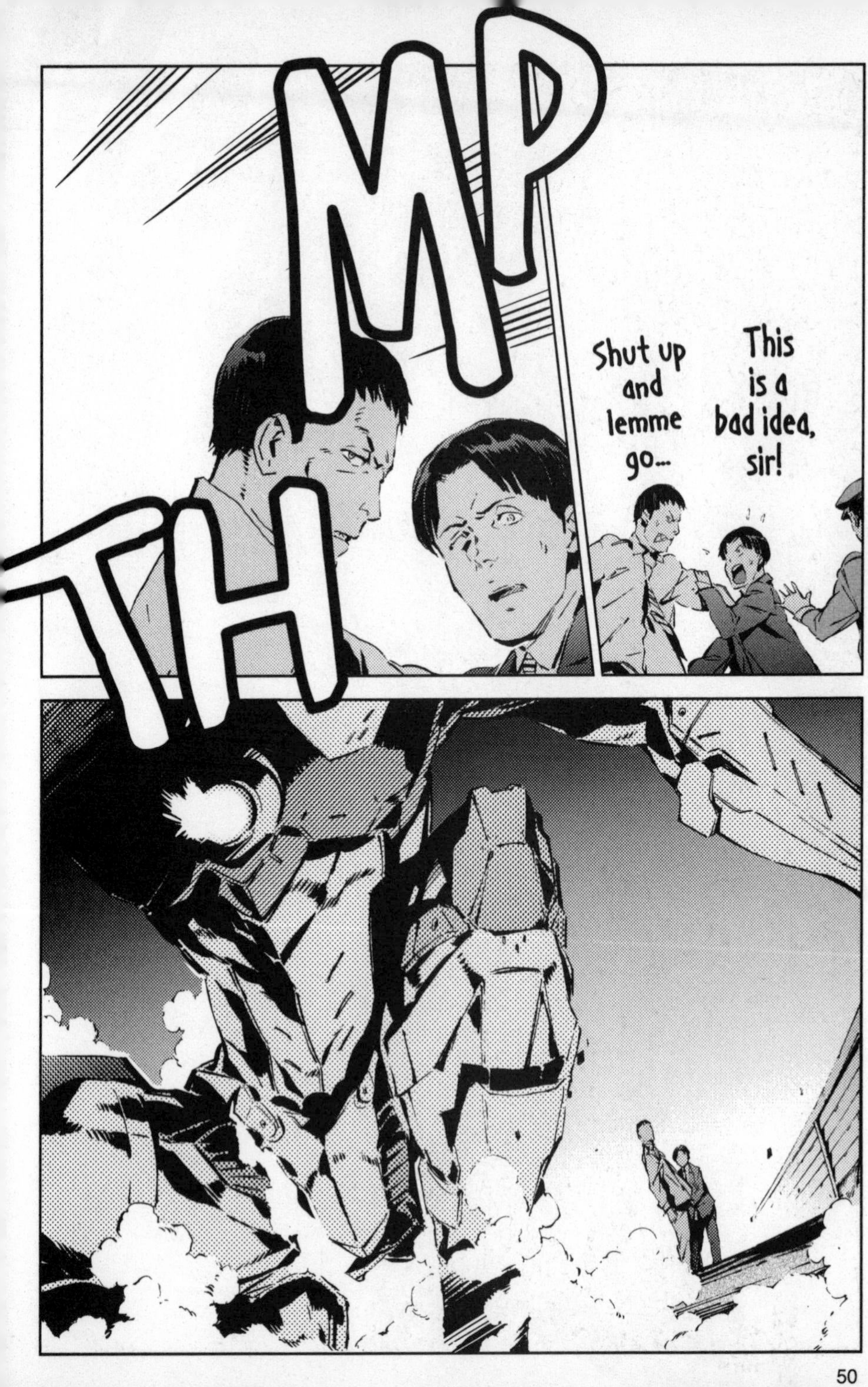
This is a bad idea, sir!
Shut up and lemme go...
THMP

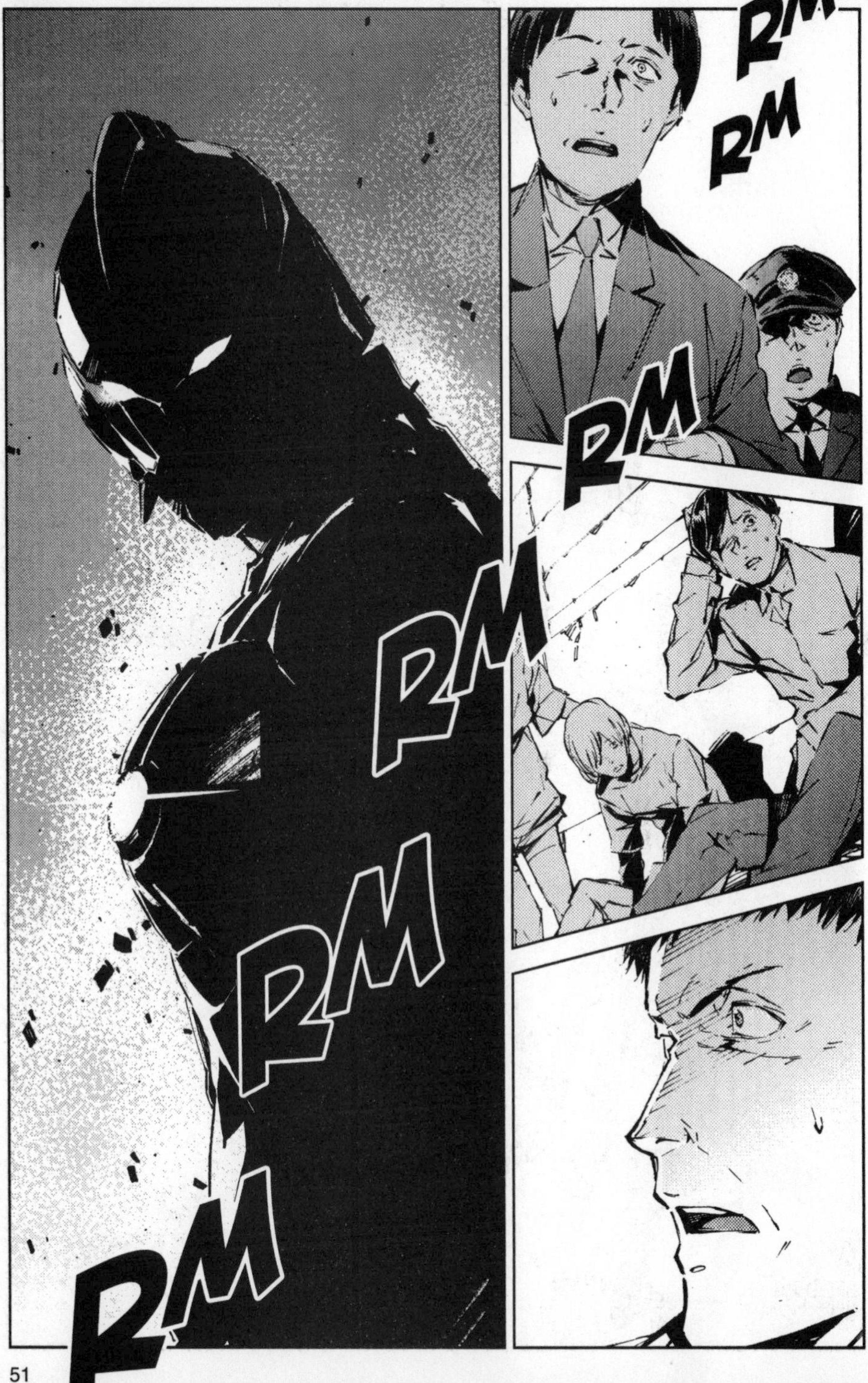
RM
RM
RM
RM
RM
RM

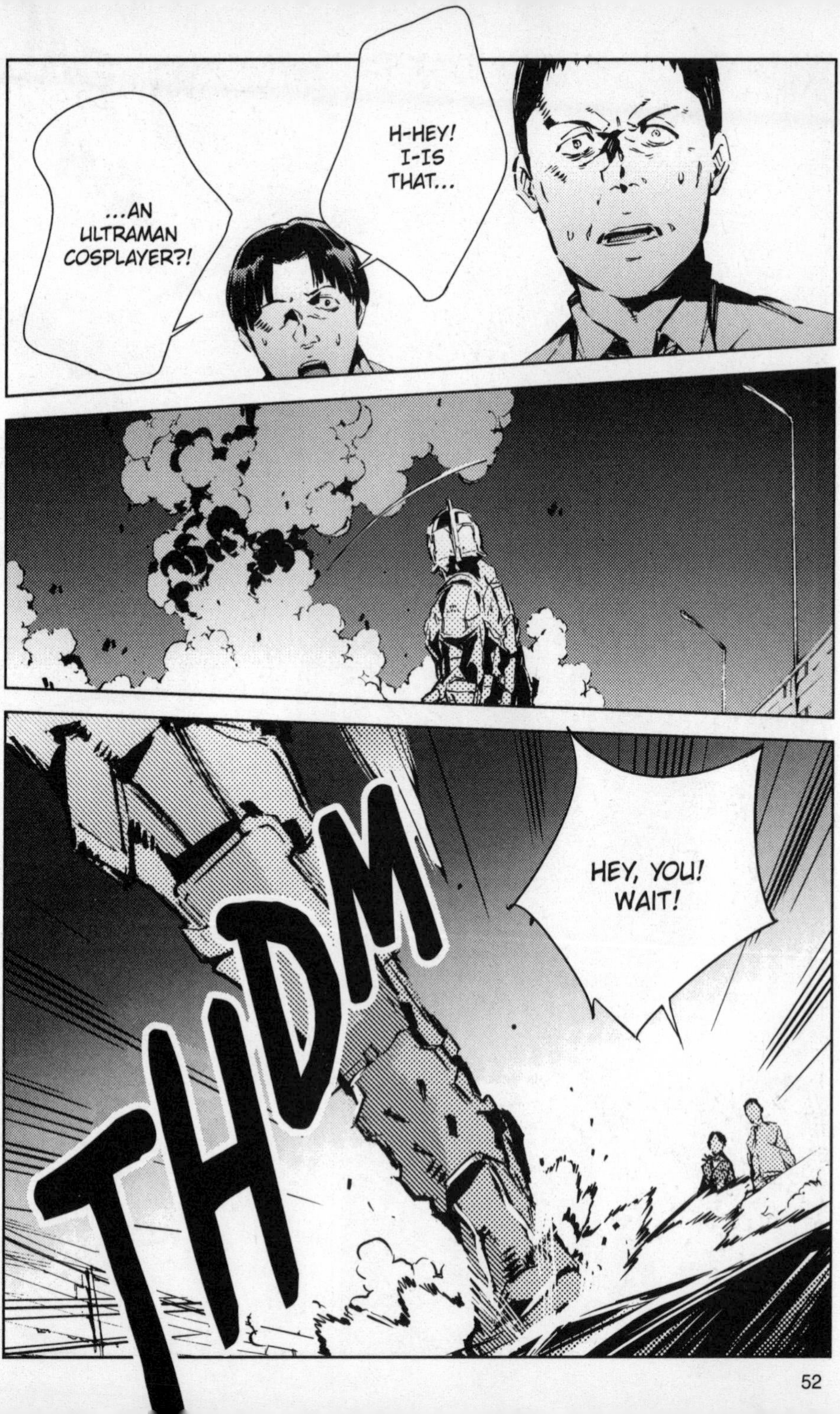
H-HEY! I-IS THAT...
...AN ULTRAMAN COSPLAYER?!
HEY, YOU! WAIT!
THDM

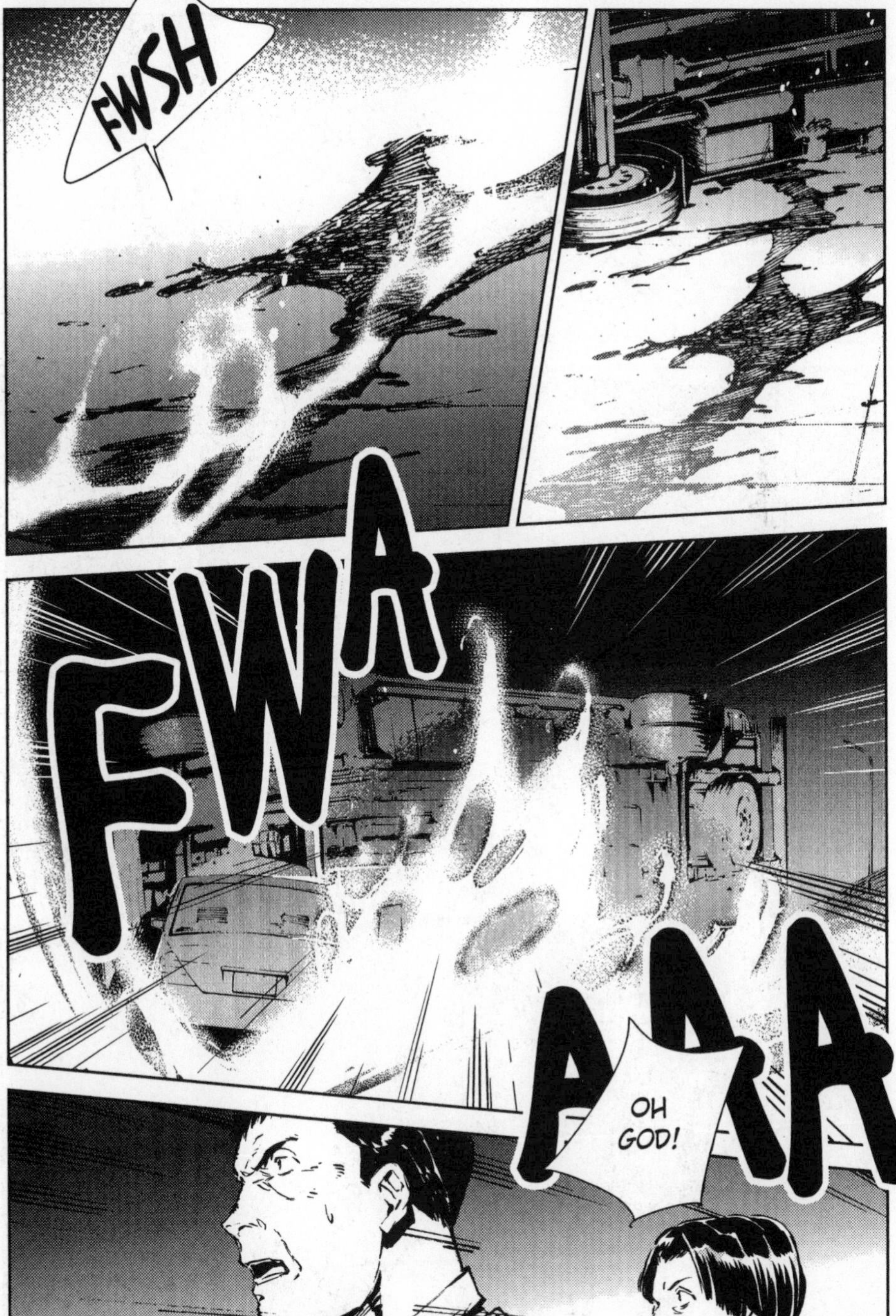
FWSH
FWA
AAA
OH GOD!

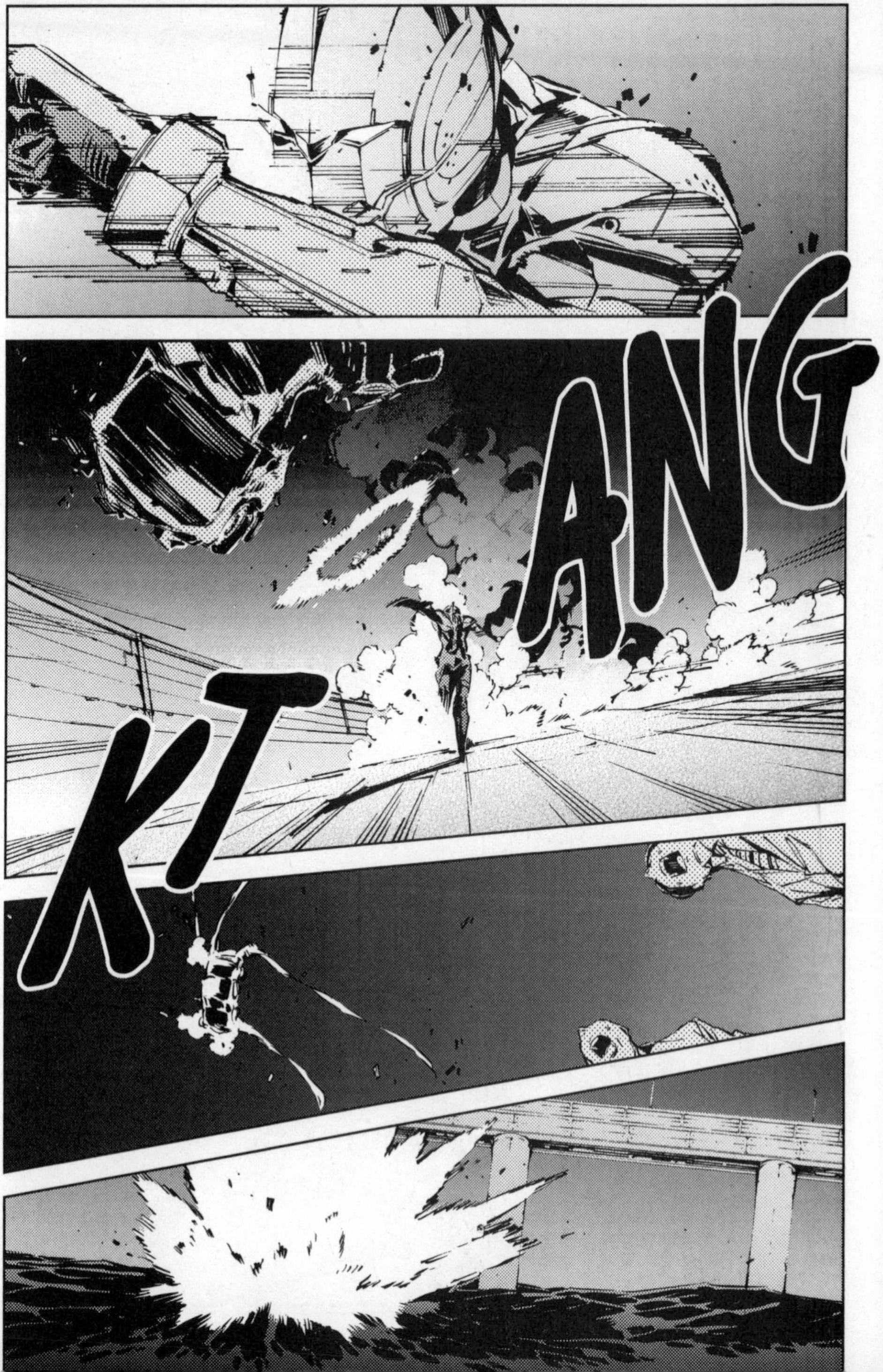
KT
ANG

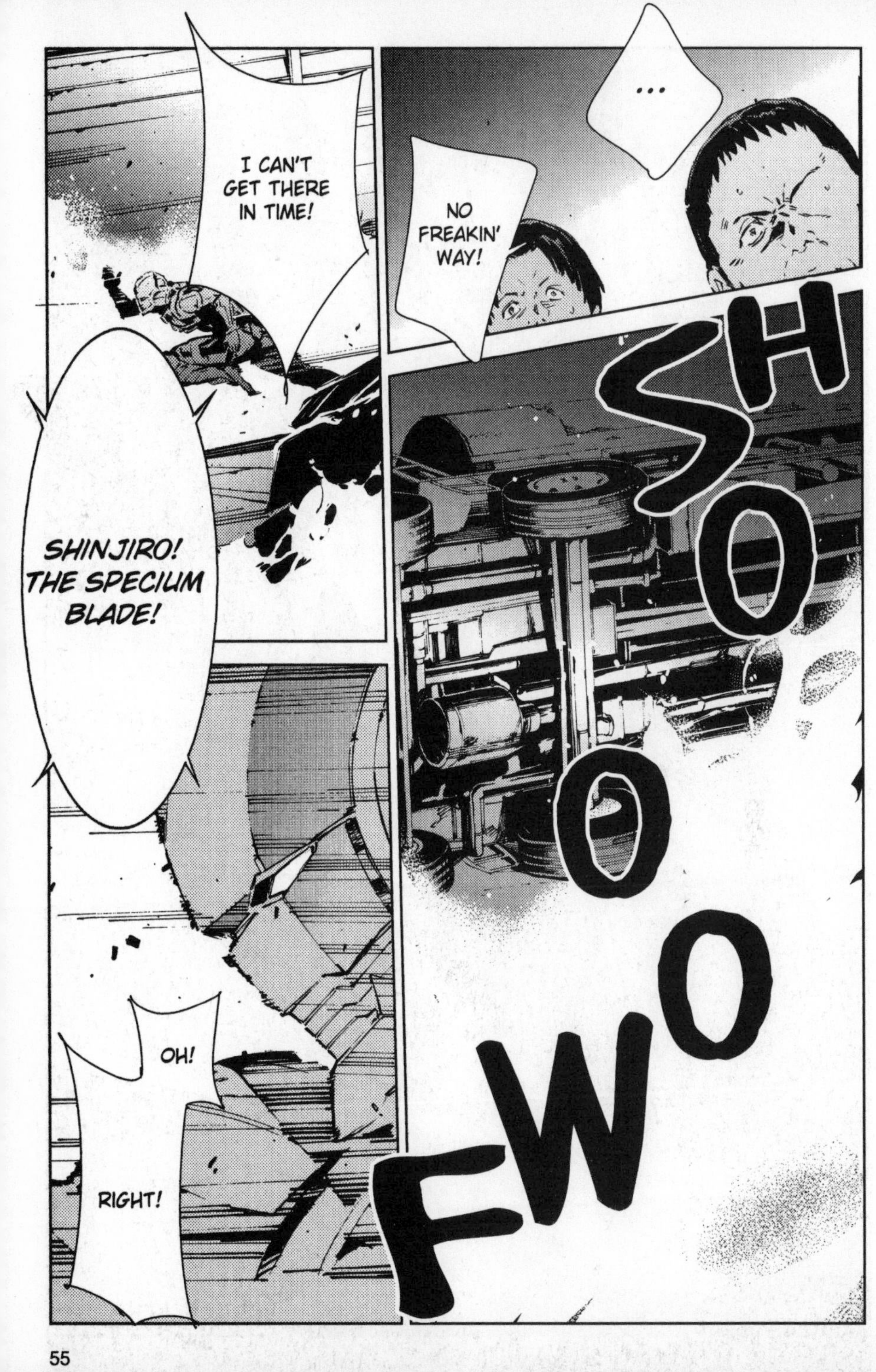
...
NO FREAKIN' WAY!
SHOOO
FWOO
I CAN'T GET THERE IN TIME!
SHINJIRO! THE SPECIUM BLADE!
OH!
RIGHT!

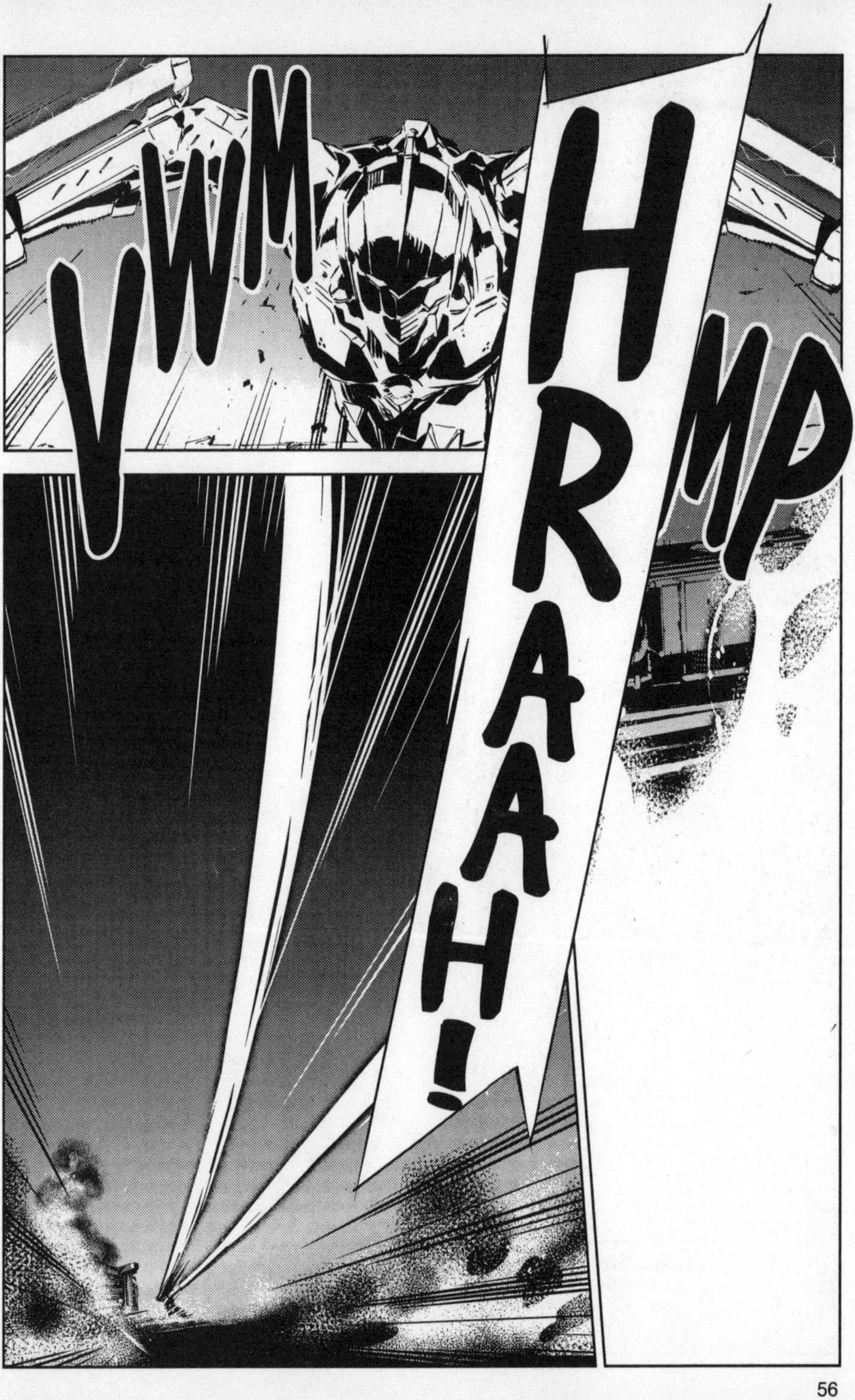
VWM
HMP
RAAAH!

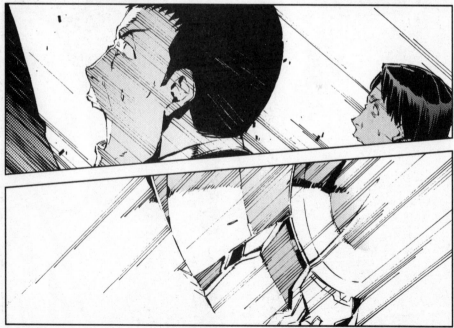

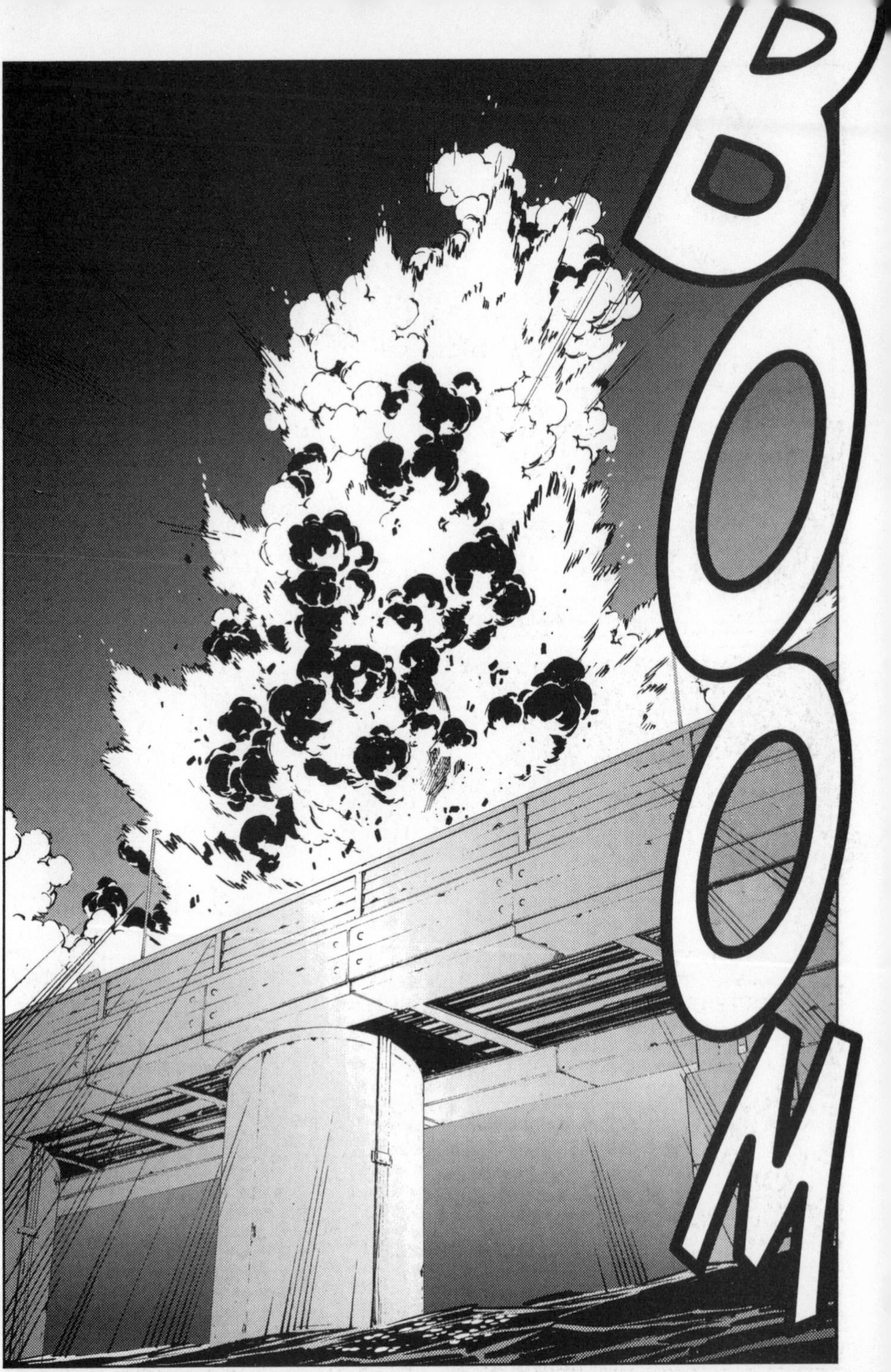
BOOM

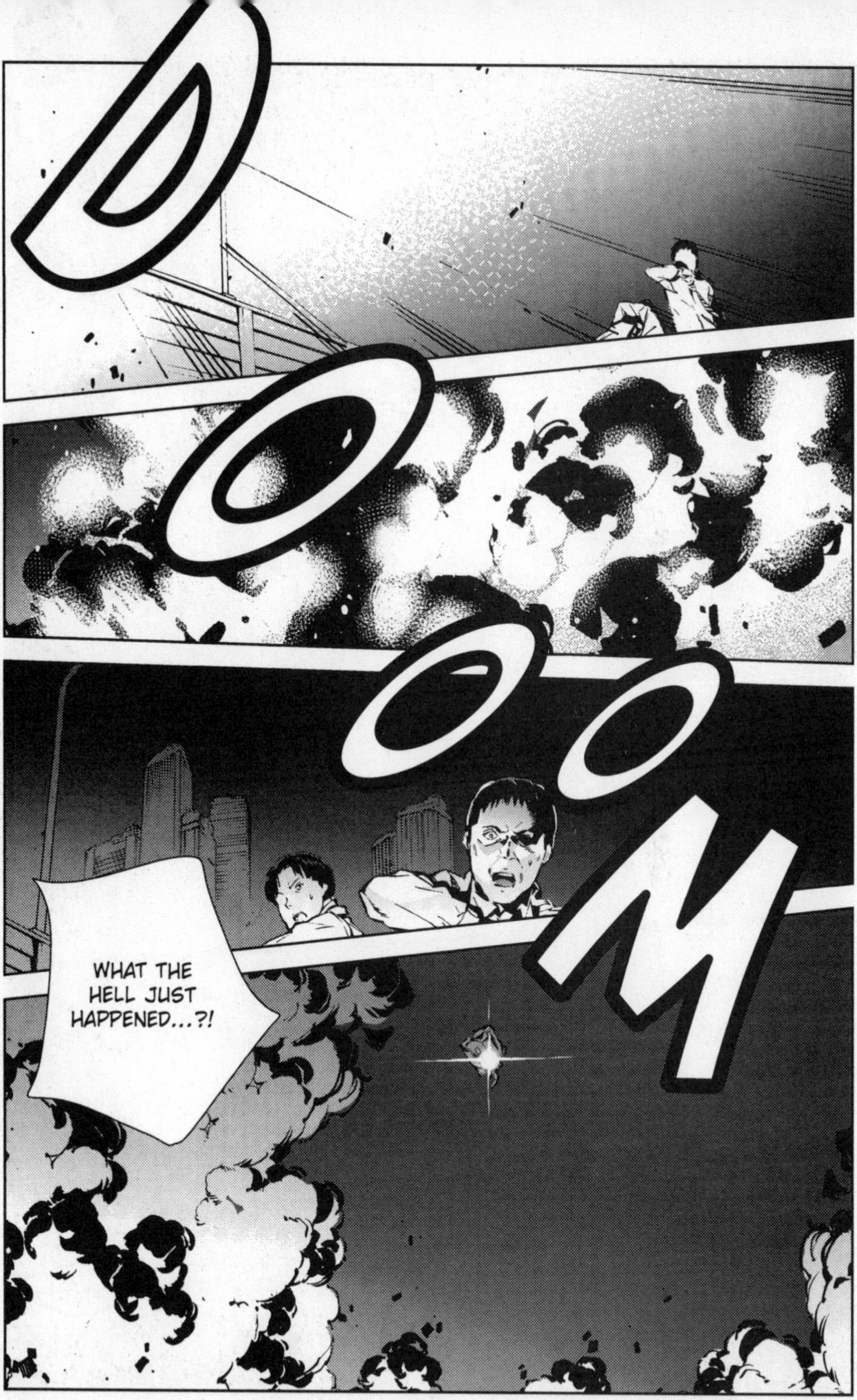
DOOOM
WHAT THE HELL JUST HAPPENED...?!

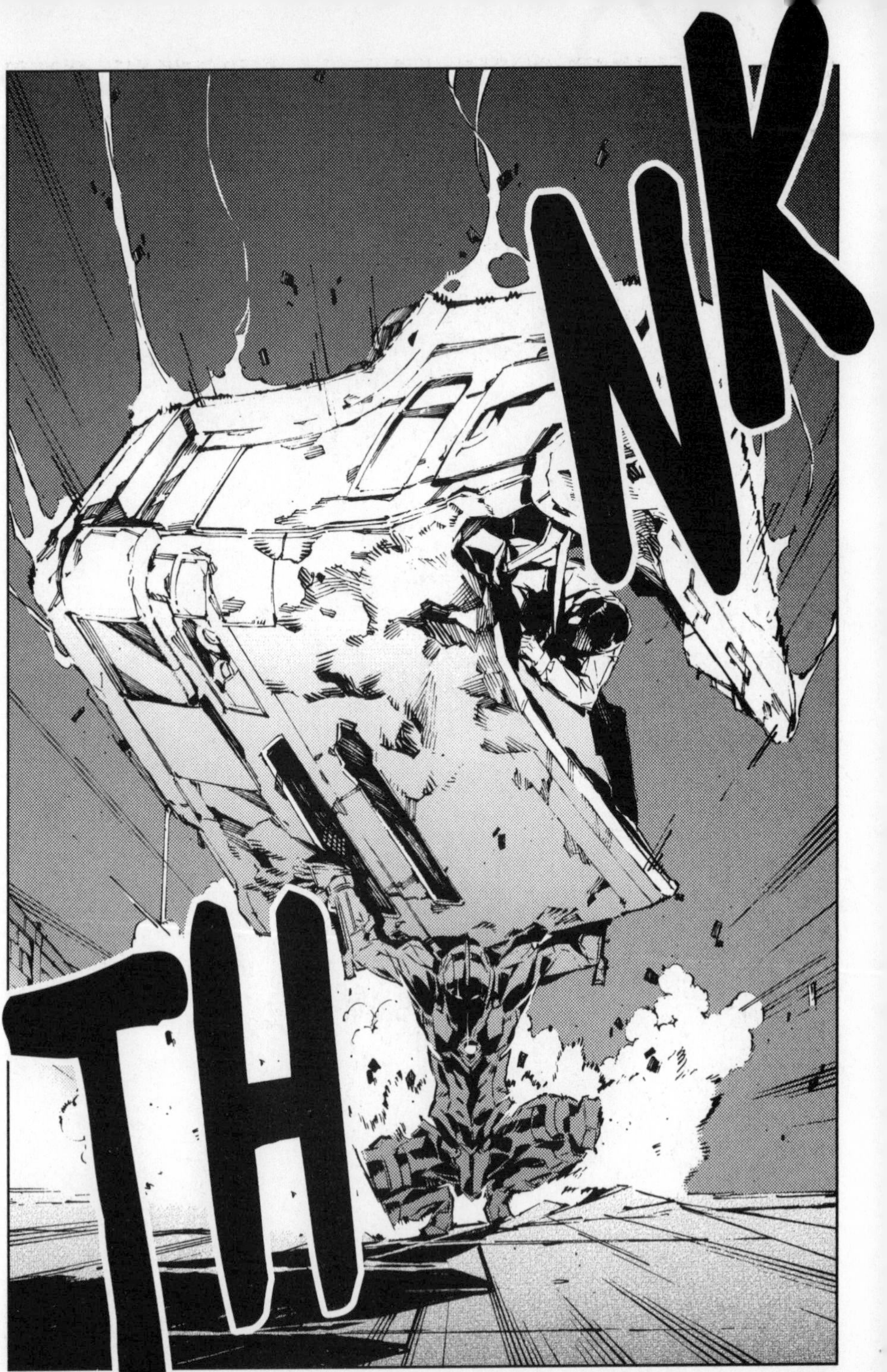
THNK

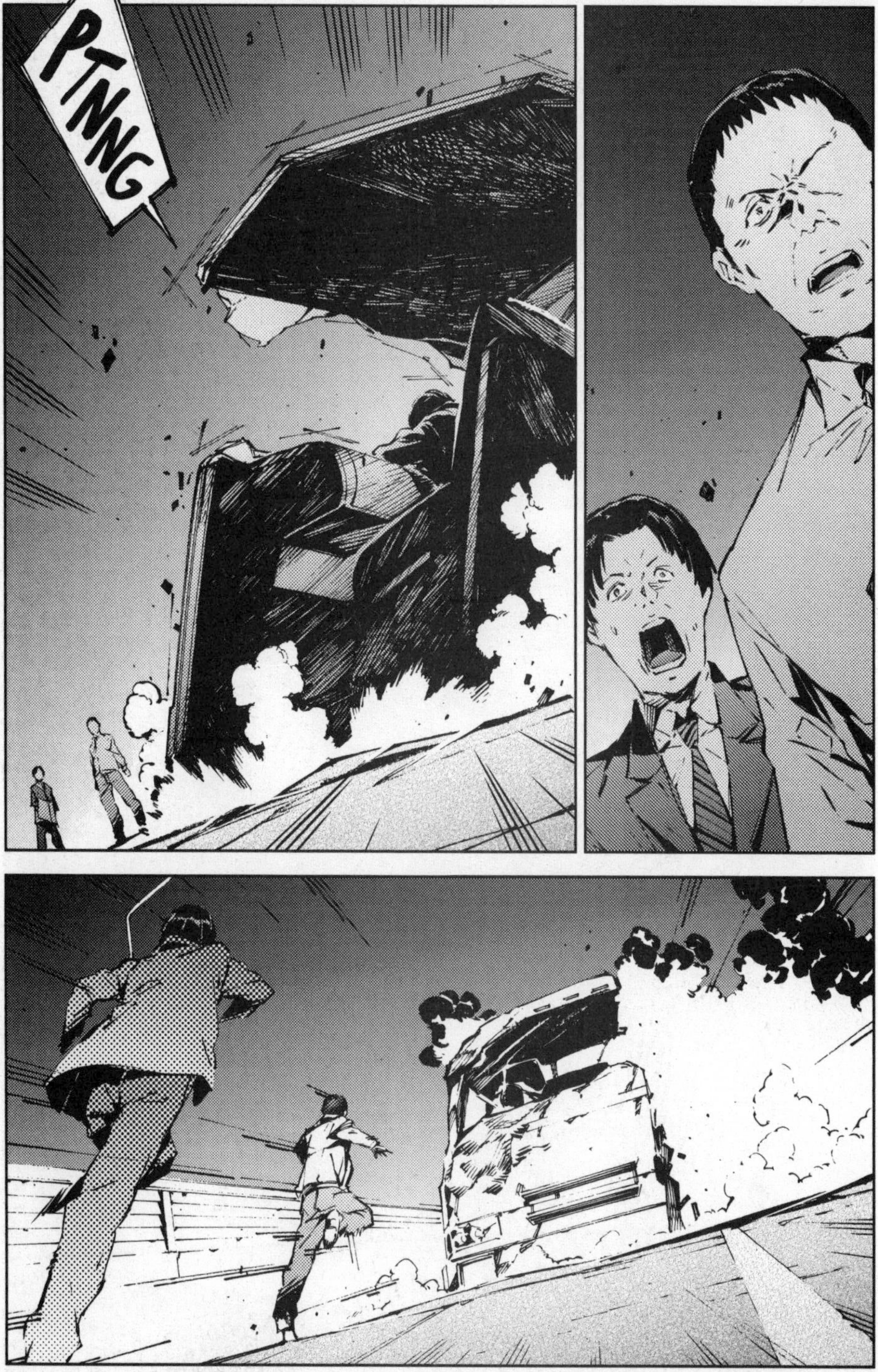
PTNNG

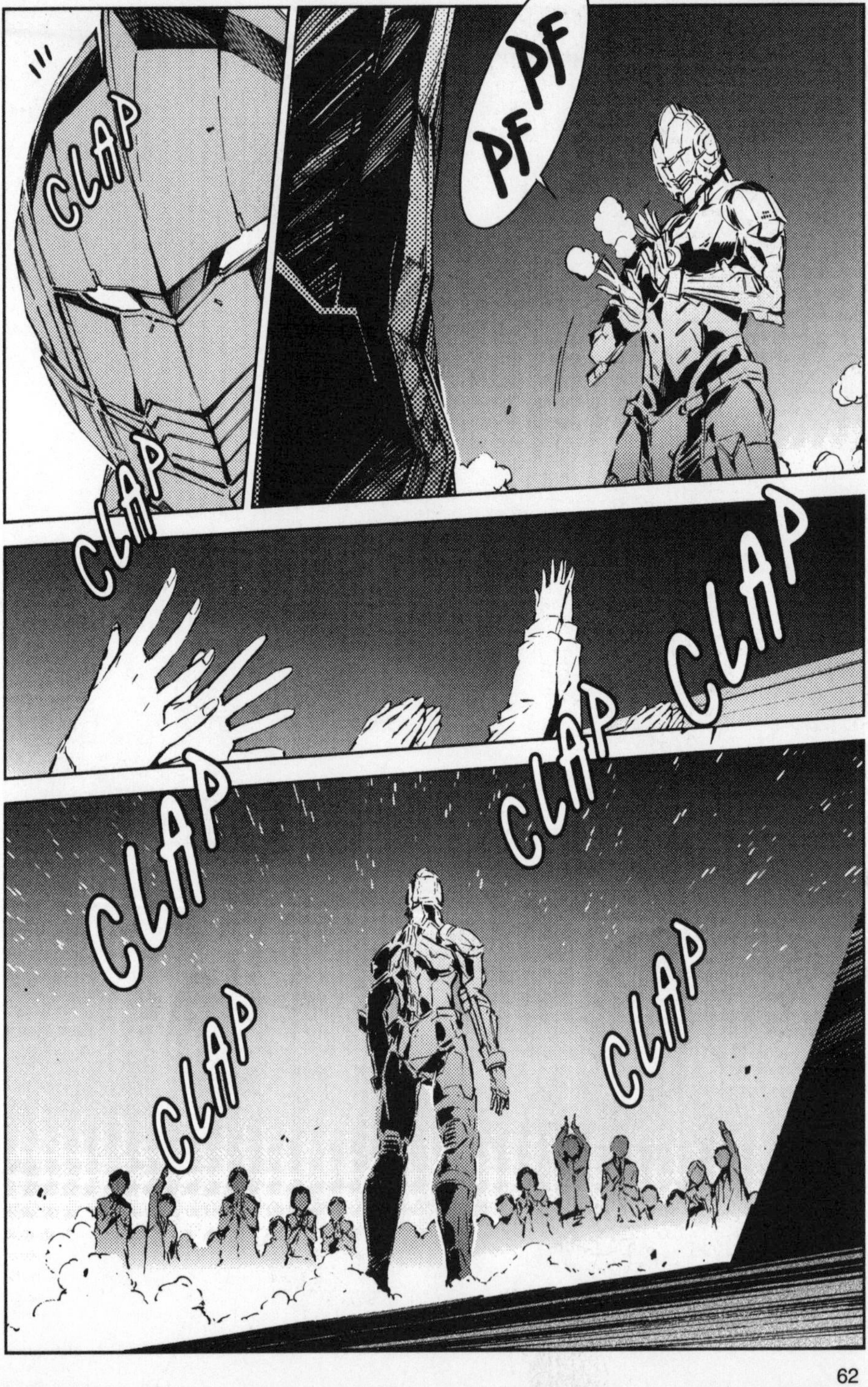
PF PF
CLAP
CLAP
CLAP
CLAP CLAP
CLAP
CLAP
CLAP
CLAP

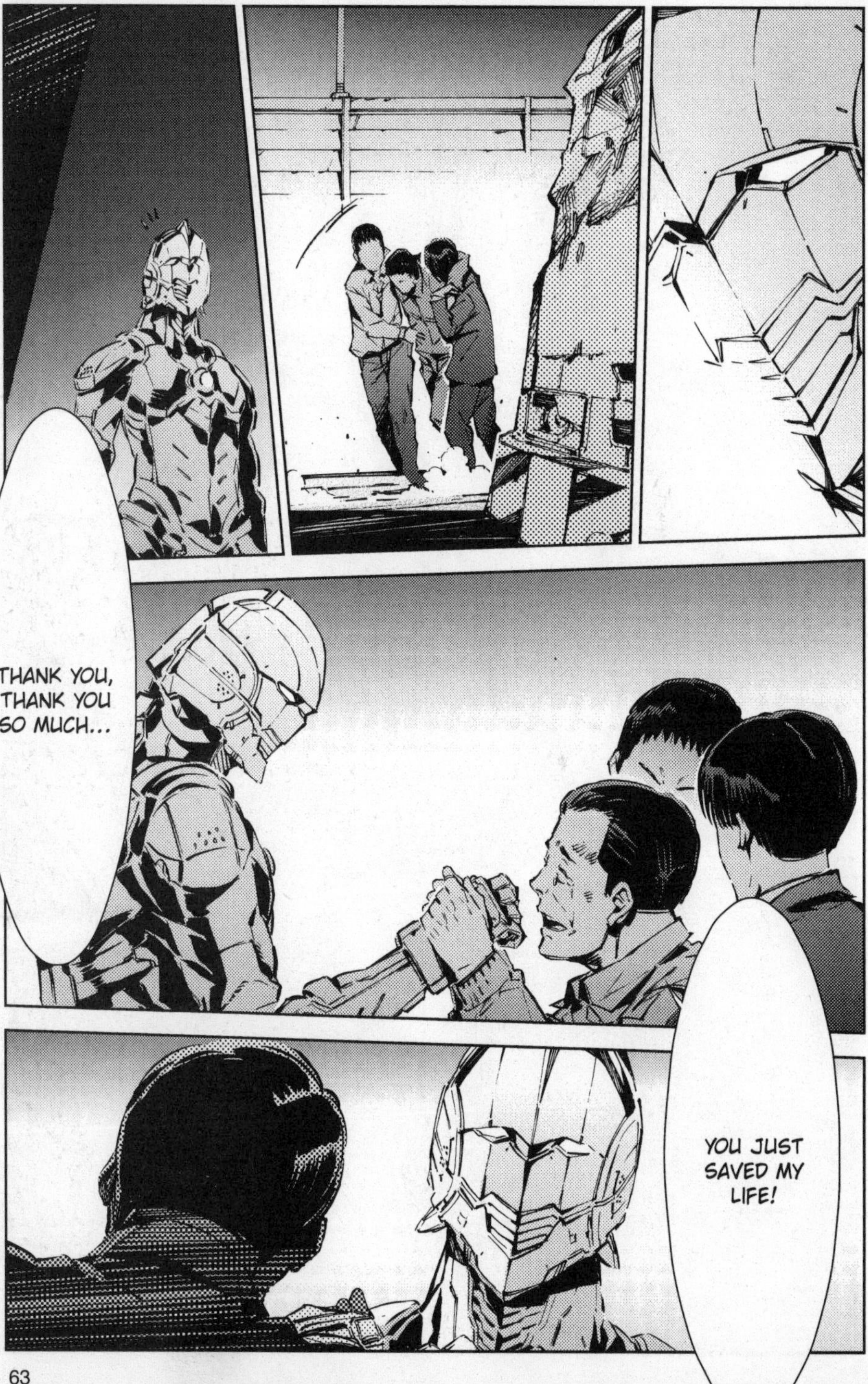
THANK YOU, THANK YOU SO MUCH...
YOU JUST SAVED MY LIFE!

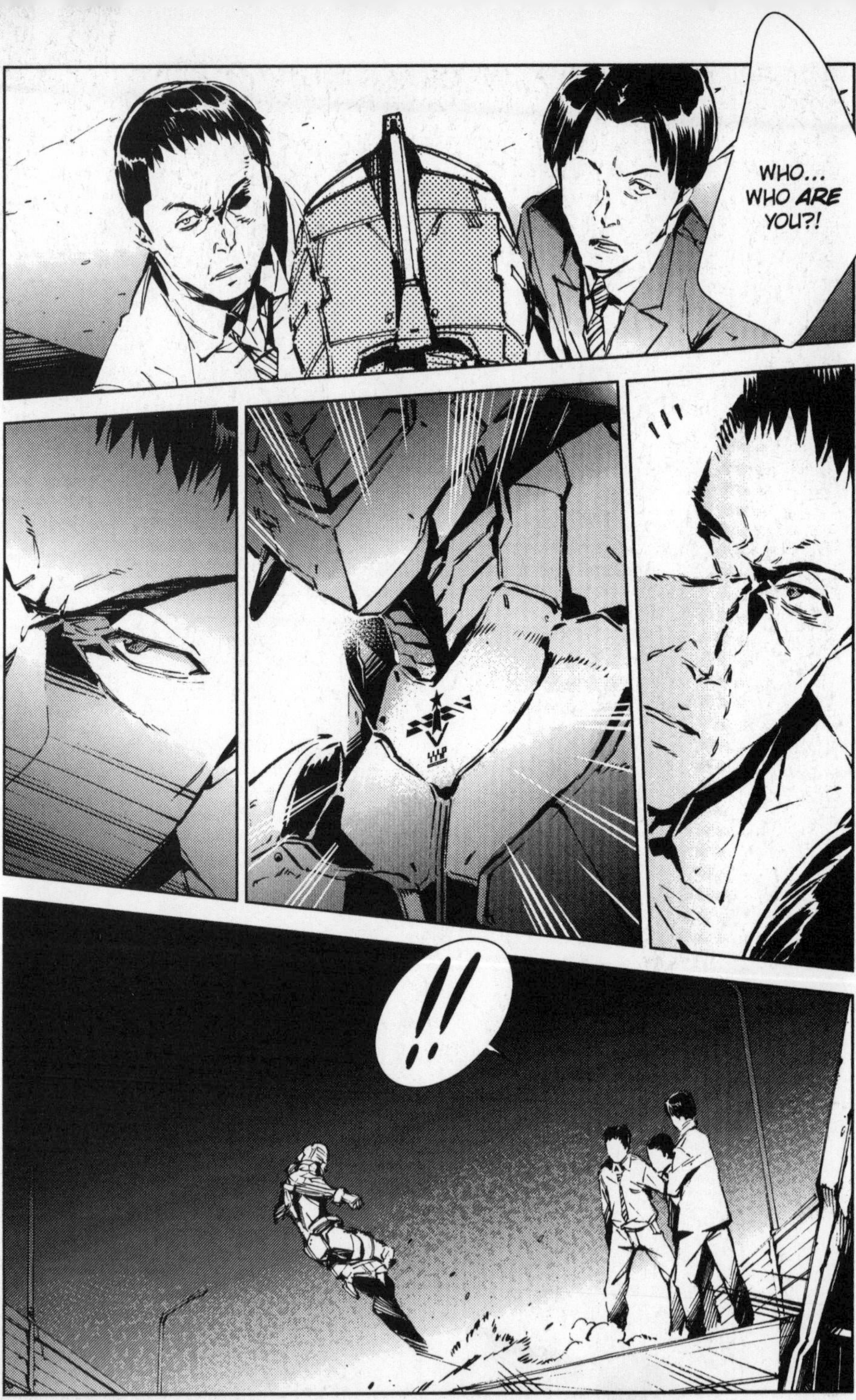
WHO... WHO *ARE* YOU?!
!!

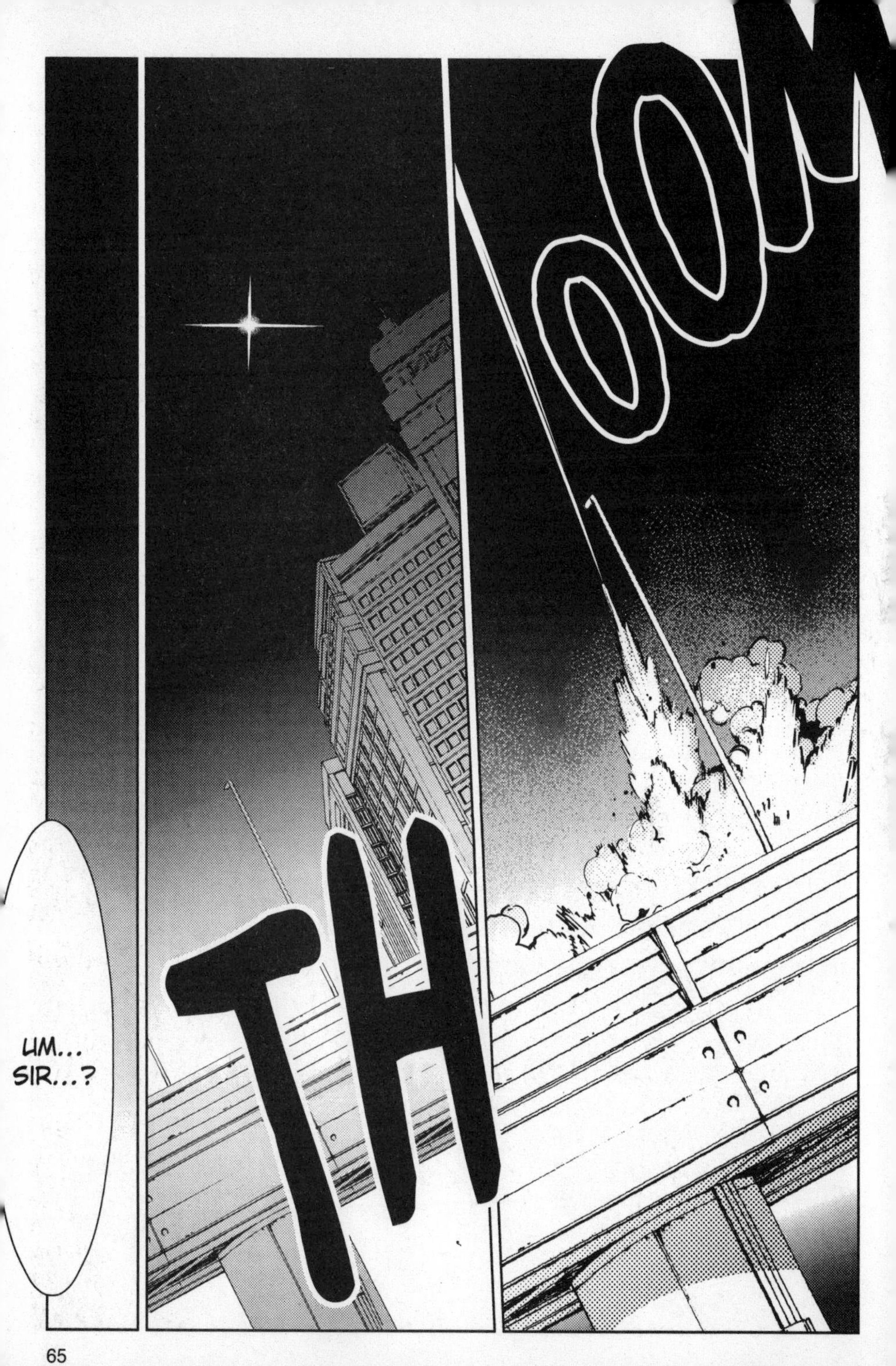
THOOOM
UM... SIR...?

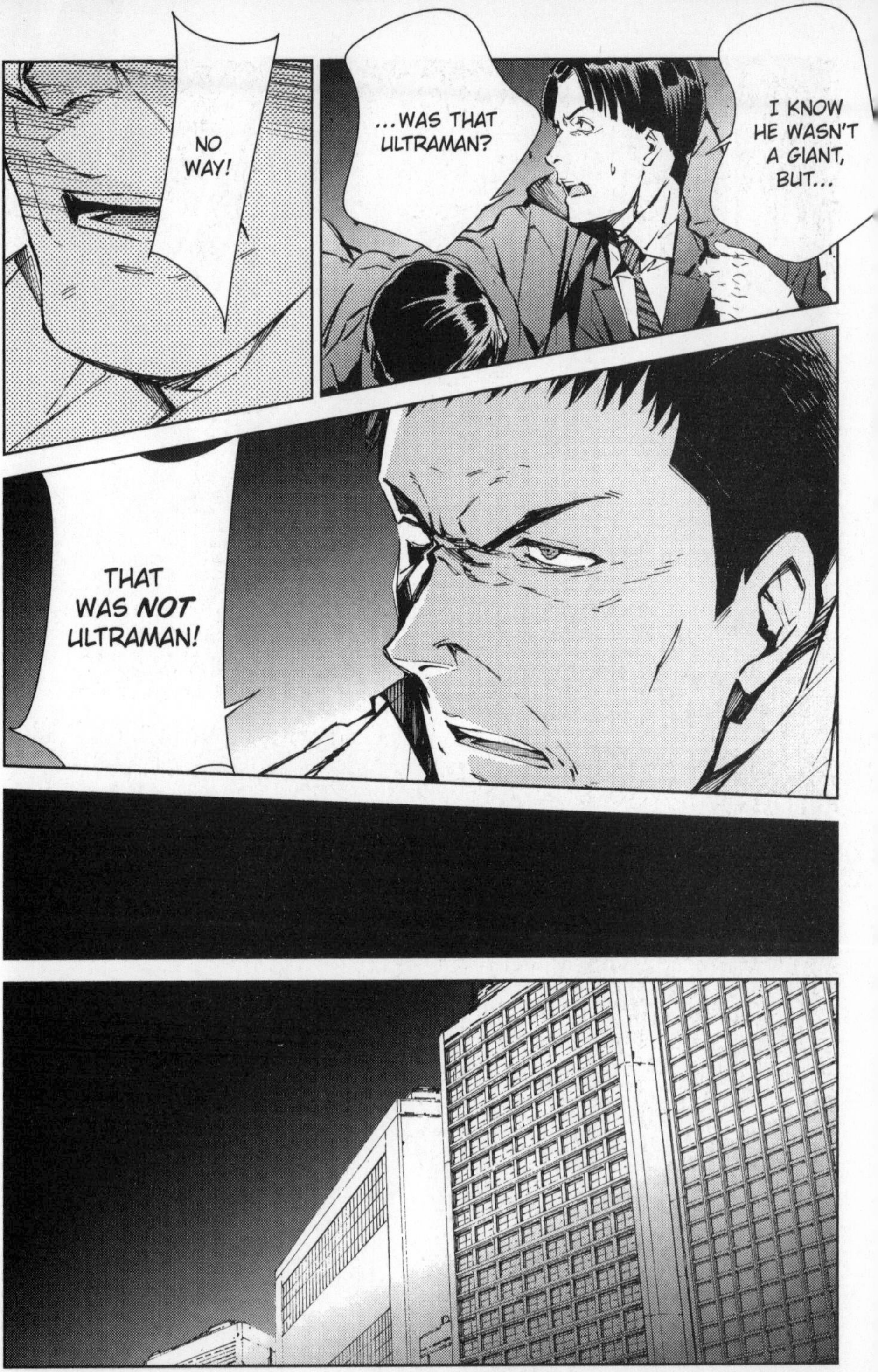
NO WAY!
...WAS THAT ULTRAMAN?
I KNOW HE WASN'T A GIANT, BUT...
THAT WAS NOT ULTRAMAN!

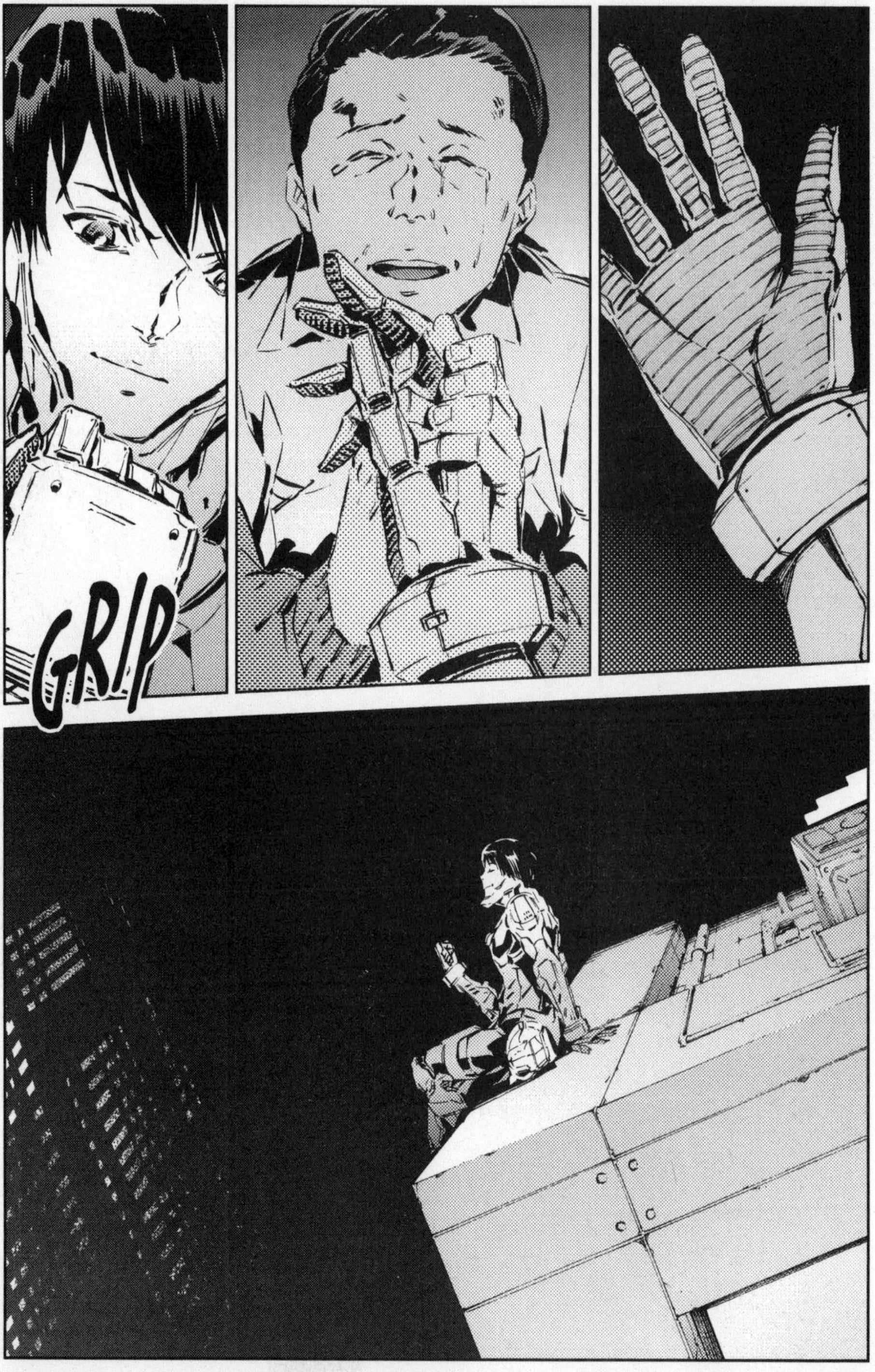
GRIP

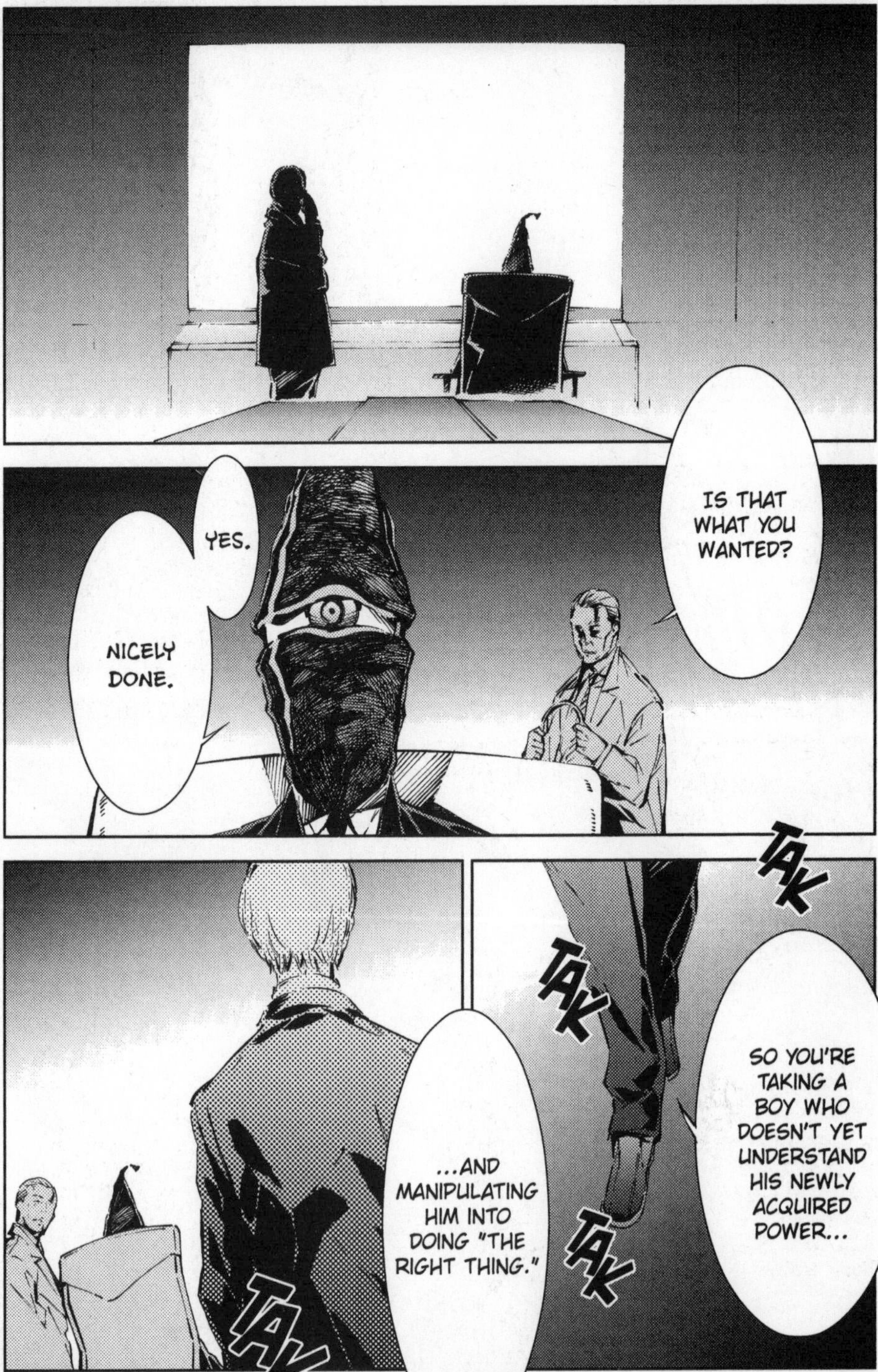
IS THAT WHAT YOU WANTED?
YES.
NICELY DONE.
TAK
TAK
SO YOU'RE TAKING A BOY WHO DOESN'T YET UNDERSTAND HIS NEWLY ACQUIRED POWER...
TAK
...AND MANIPULATING HIM INTO DOING "THE RIGHT THING."
TAK

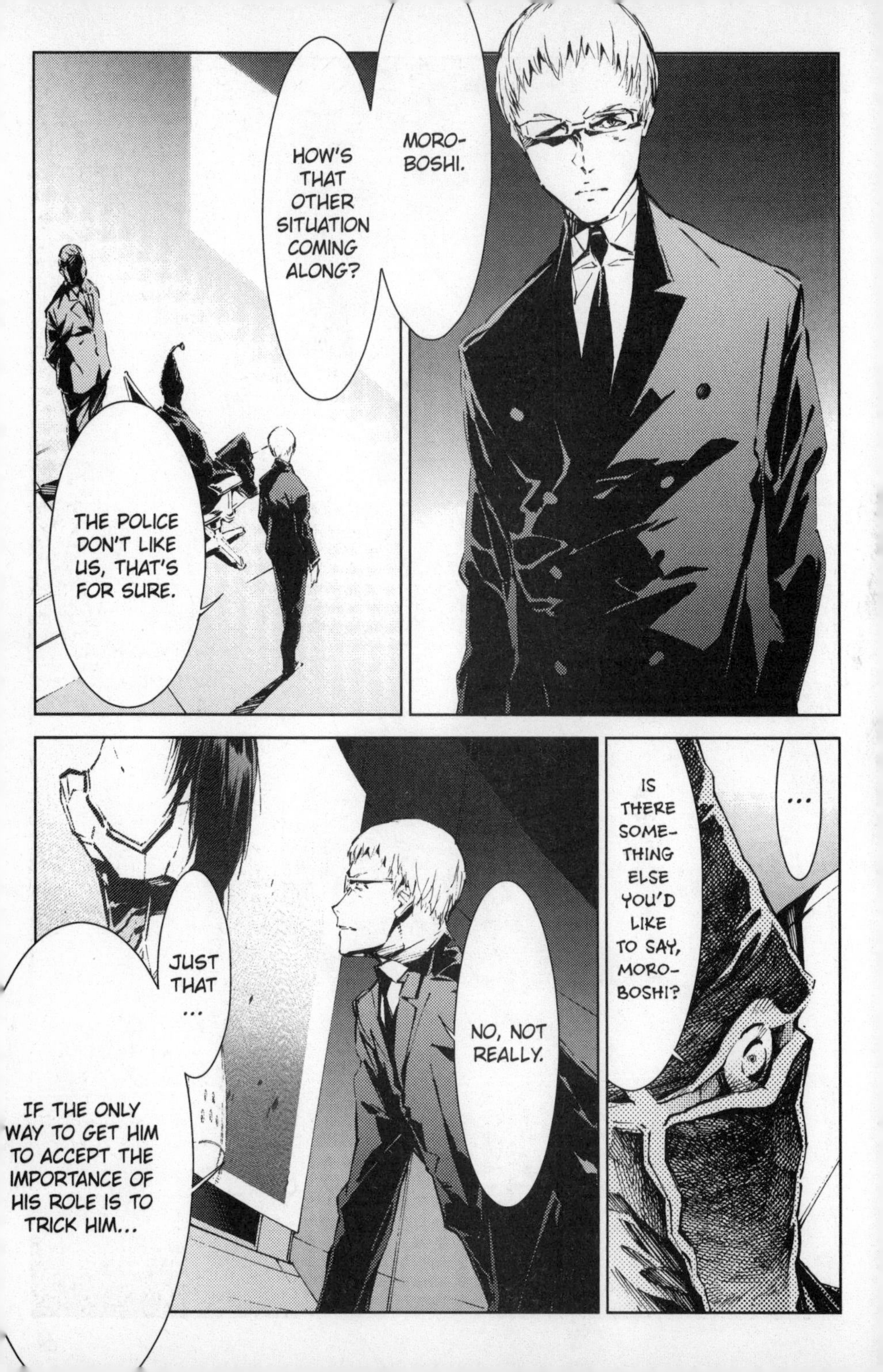
MORO-BOSHI.
HOW'S THAT OTHER SITUATION COMING ALONG?
THE POLICE DON'T LIKE US, THAT'S FOR SURE.
...
IS THERE SOME-THING ELSE YOU'D LIKE TO SAY, MORO-BOSHI?
NO, NOT REALLY.
JUST THAT ...
IF THE ONLY WAY TO GET HIM TO ACCEPT THE IMPORTANCE OF HIS ROLE IS TO TRICK HIM...

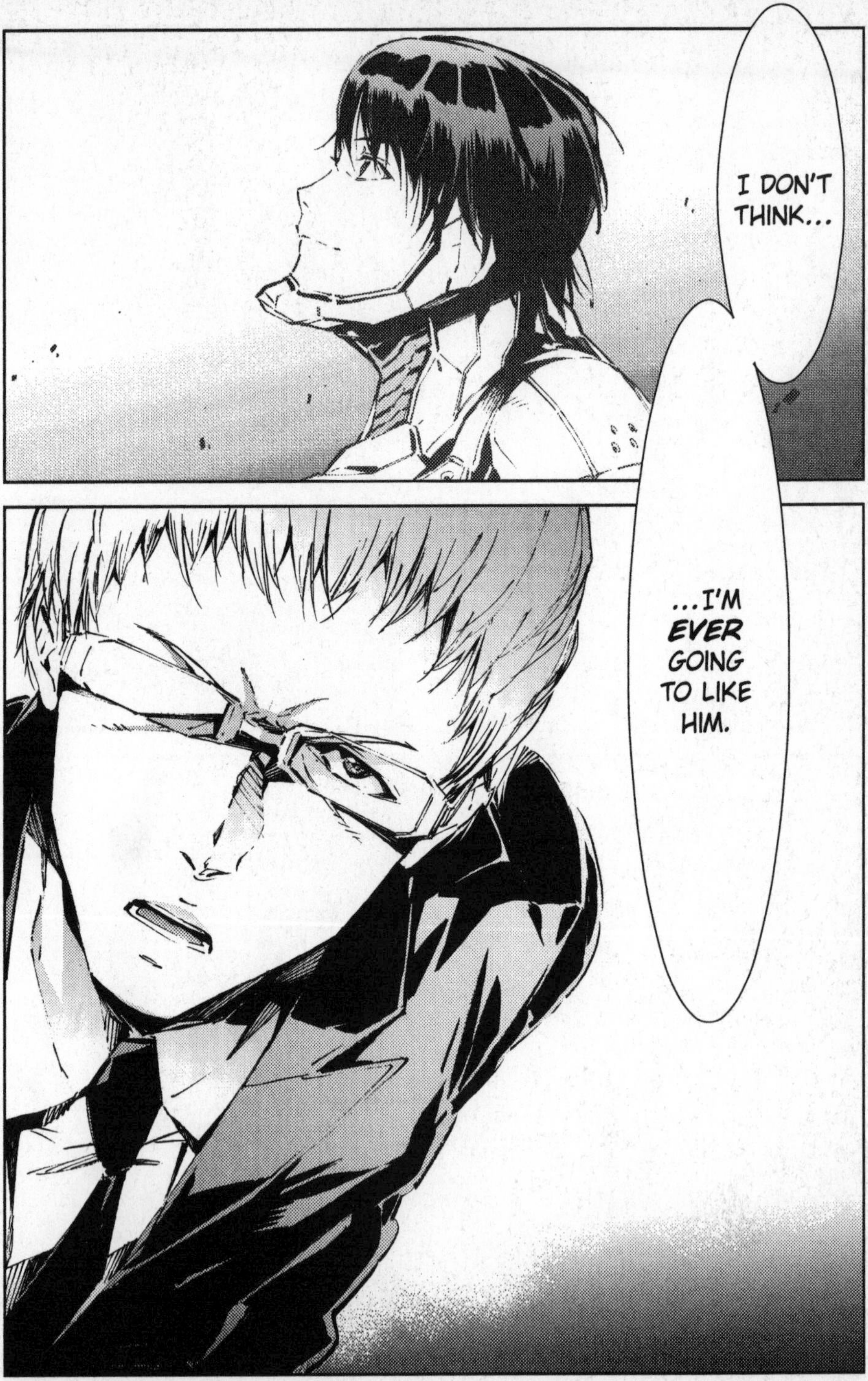
I DON'T THINK...
...I'M EVER GOING TO LIKE HIM.

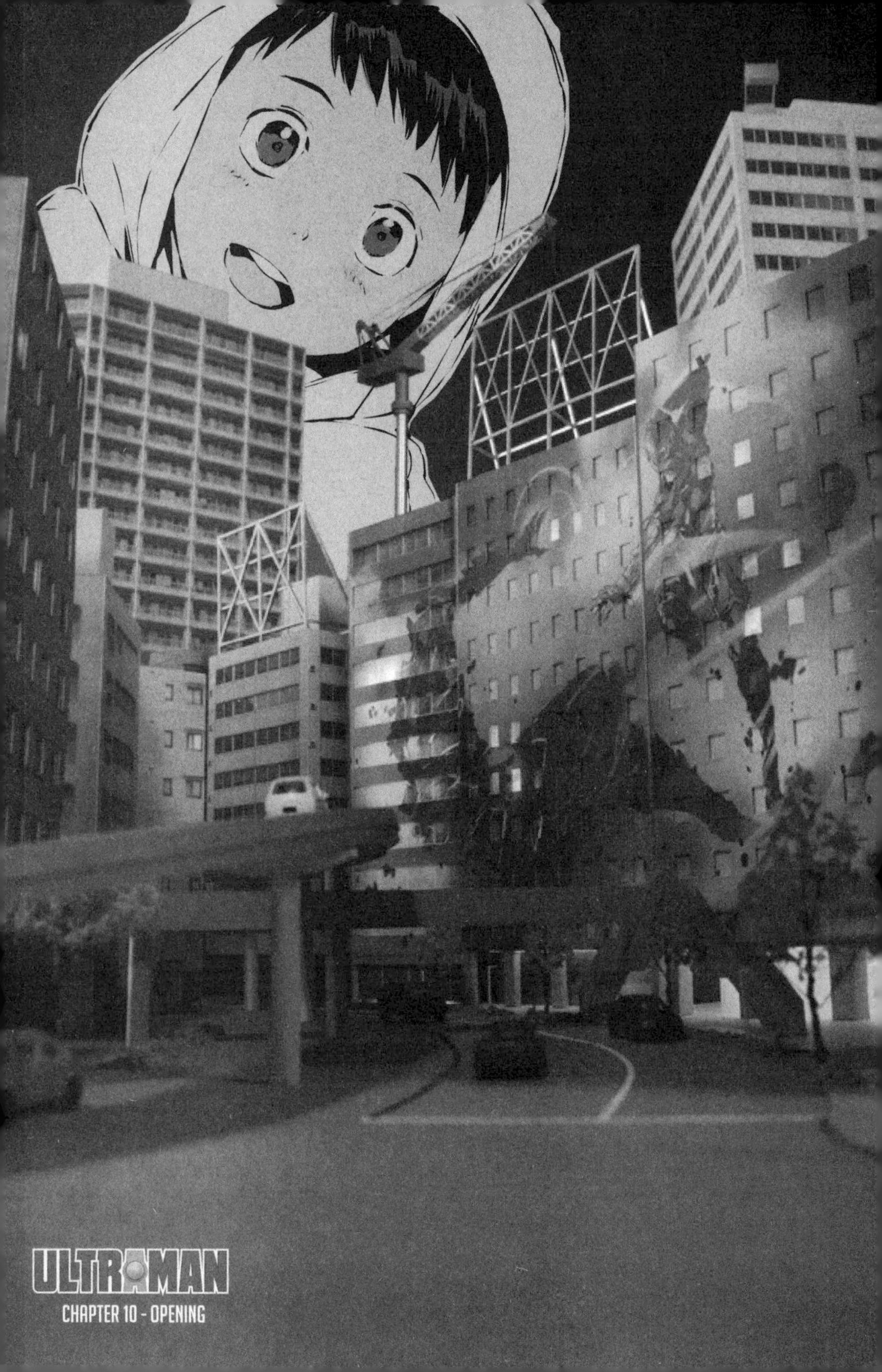
ULTRAMAN
CHAPTER 10 - OPENING

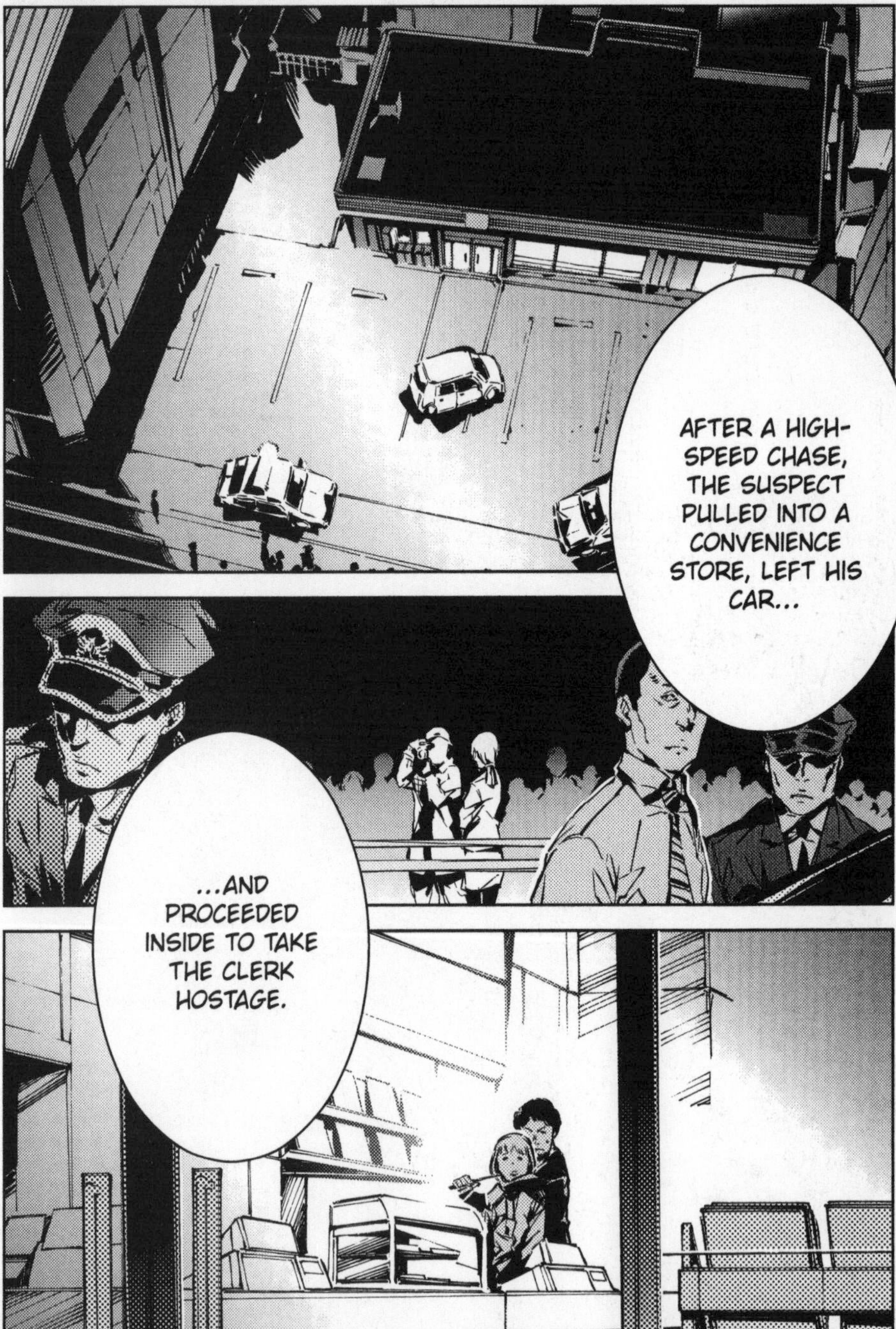
AFTER A HIGH-SPEED CHASE, THE SUSPECT PULLED INTO A CONVENIENCE STORE, LEFT HIS CAR...
...AND PROCEEDED INSIDE TO TAKE THE CLERK HOSTAGE.

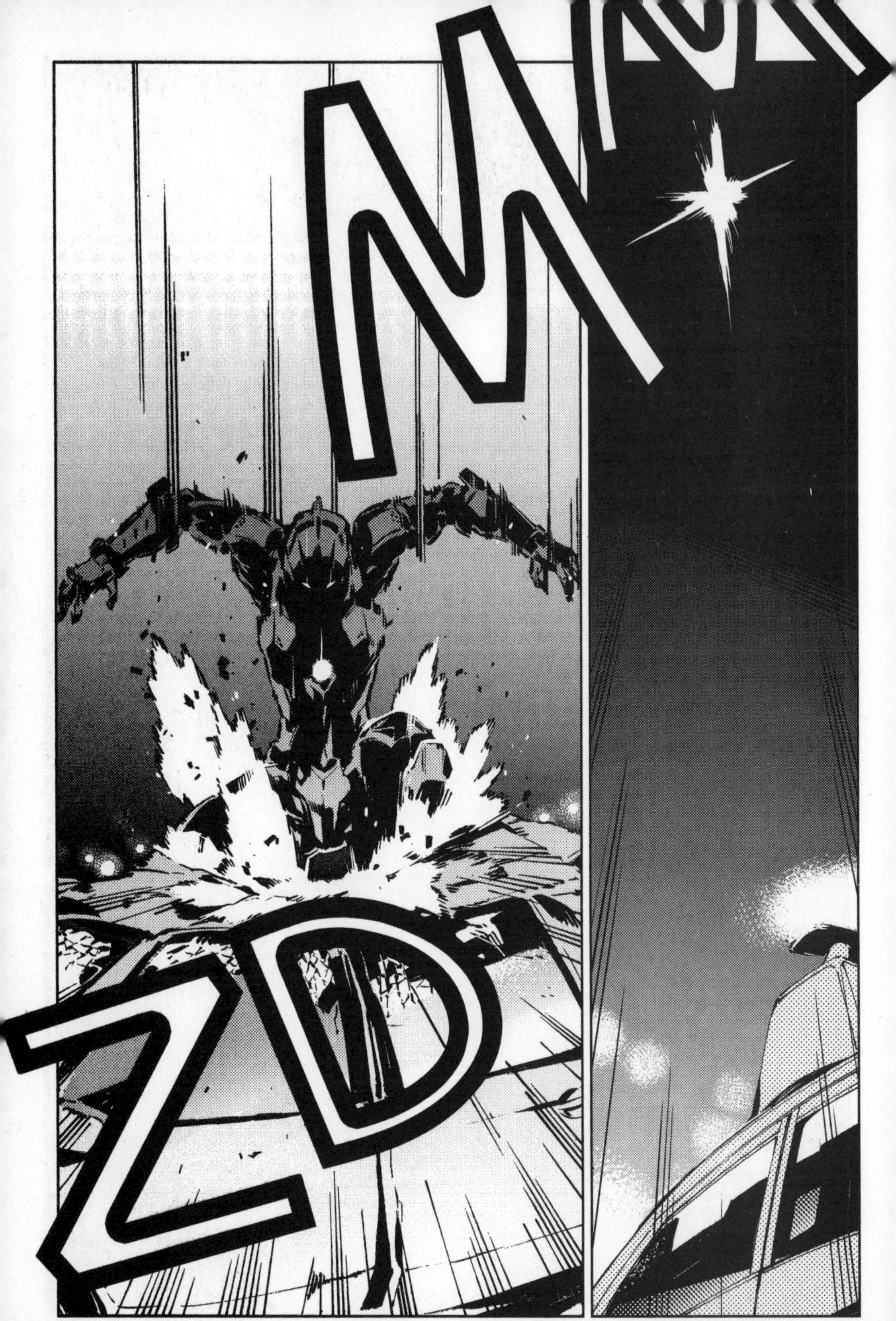
ZDM

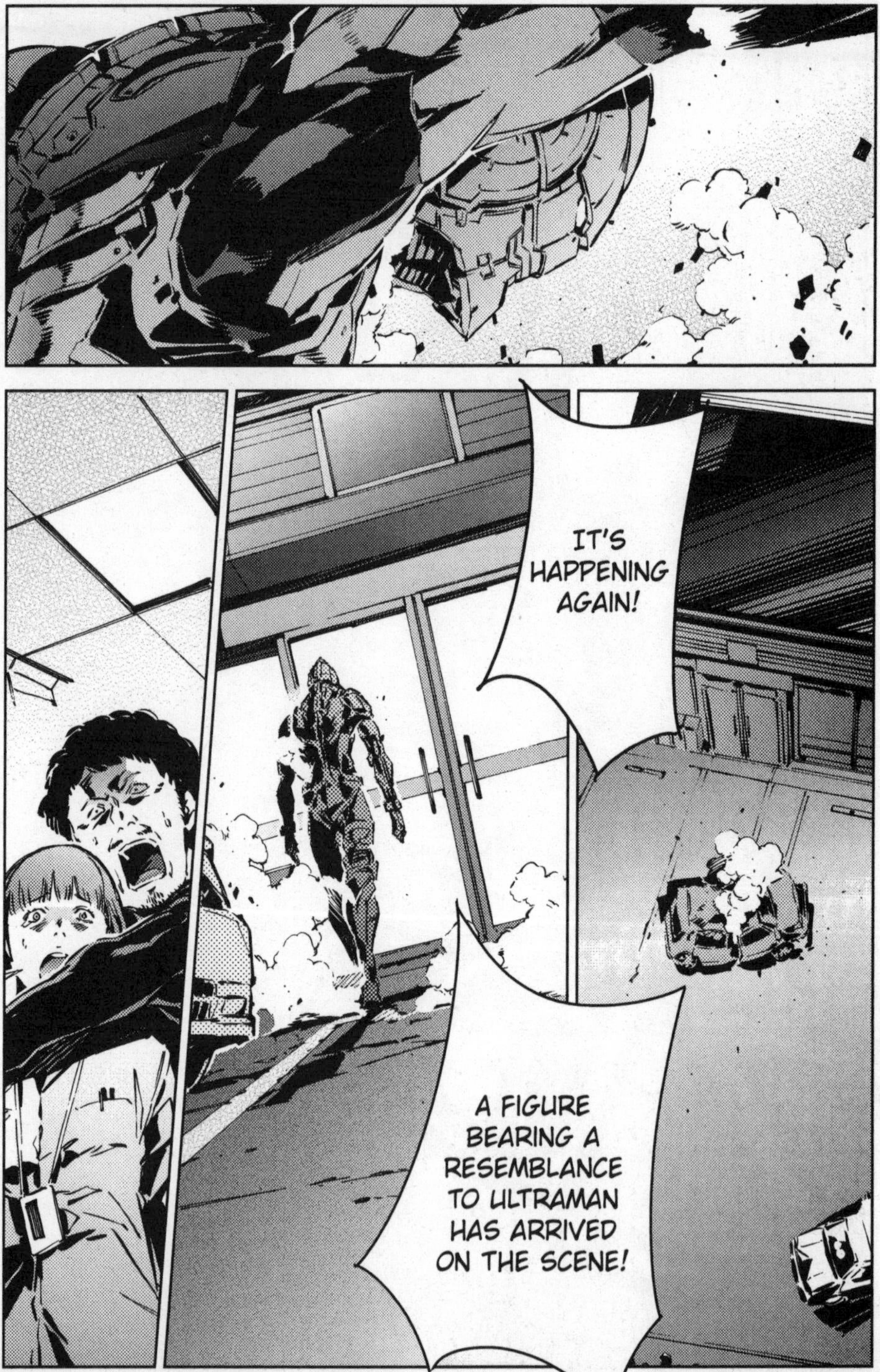

IT'S HAPPENING AGAIN!
A FIGURE BEARING A RESEMBLANCE TO ULTRAMAN HAS ARRIVED ON THE SCENE!

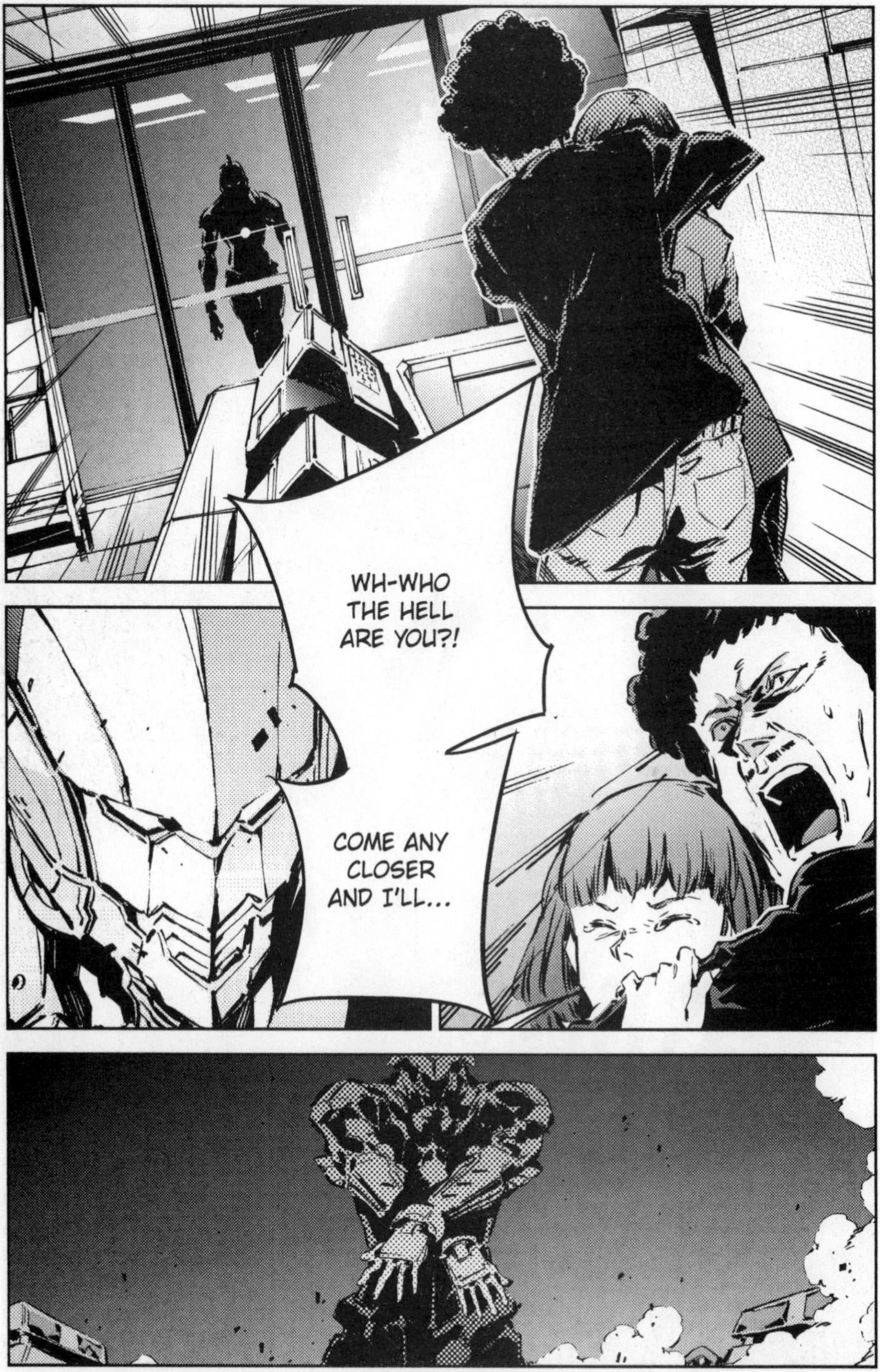
WH-WHO THE HELL ARE YOU?!
COME ANY CLOSER AND I'LL...

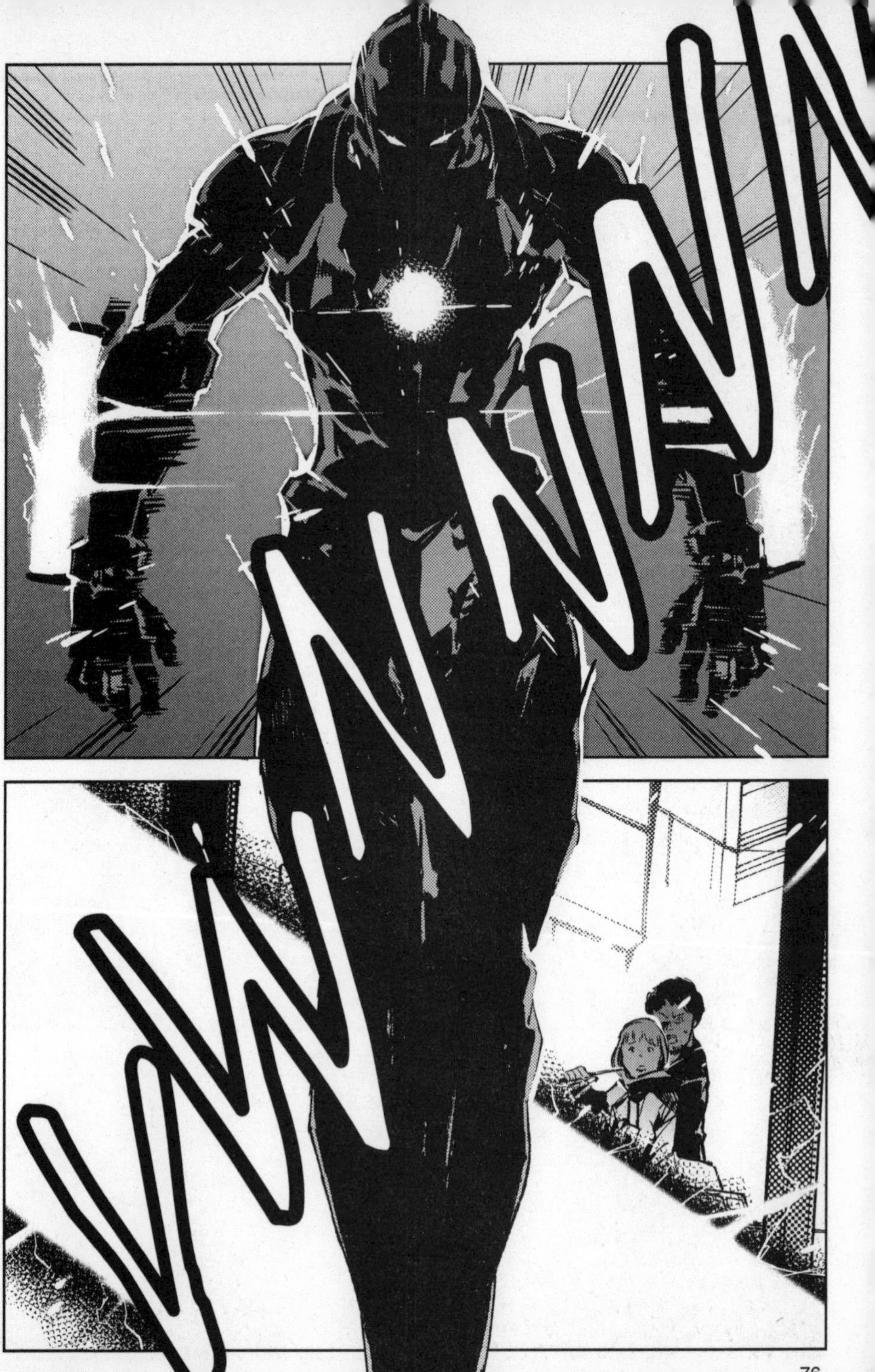

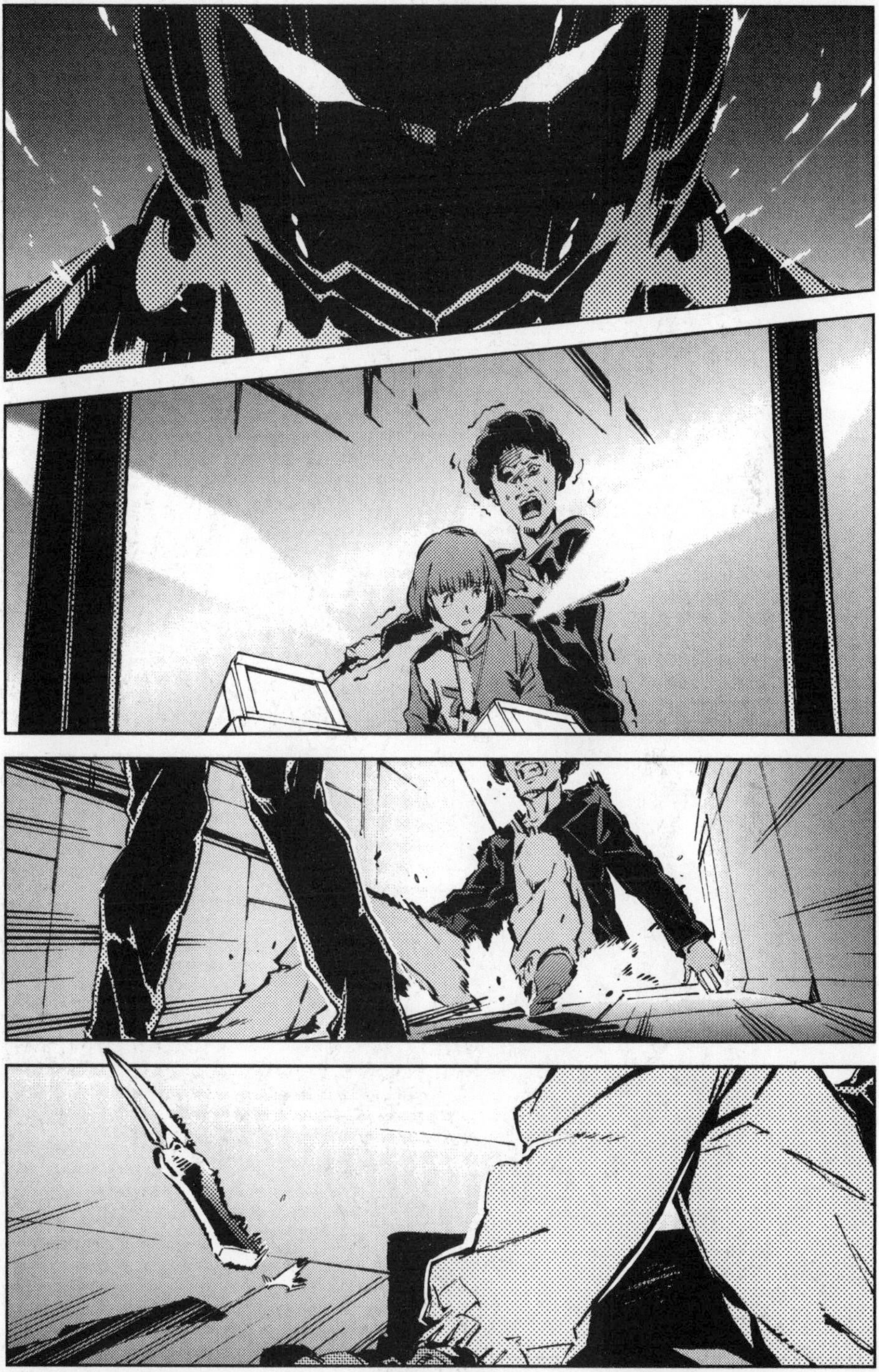

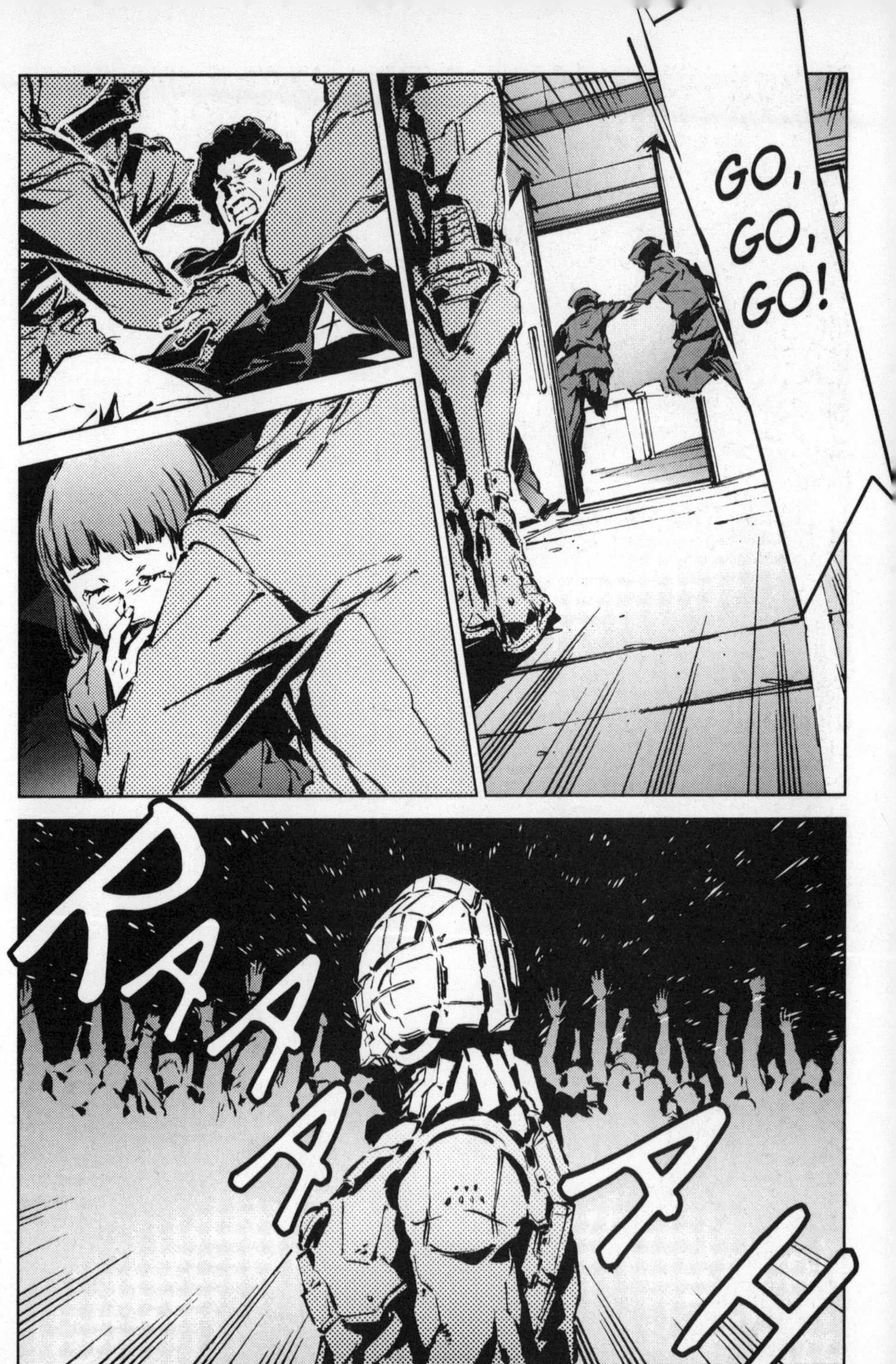
GO, GO, GO!
RAAAAAH

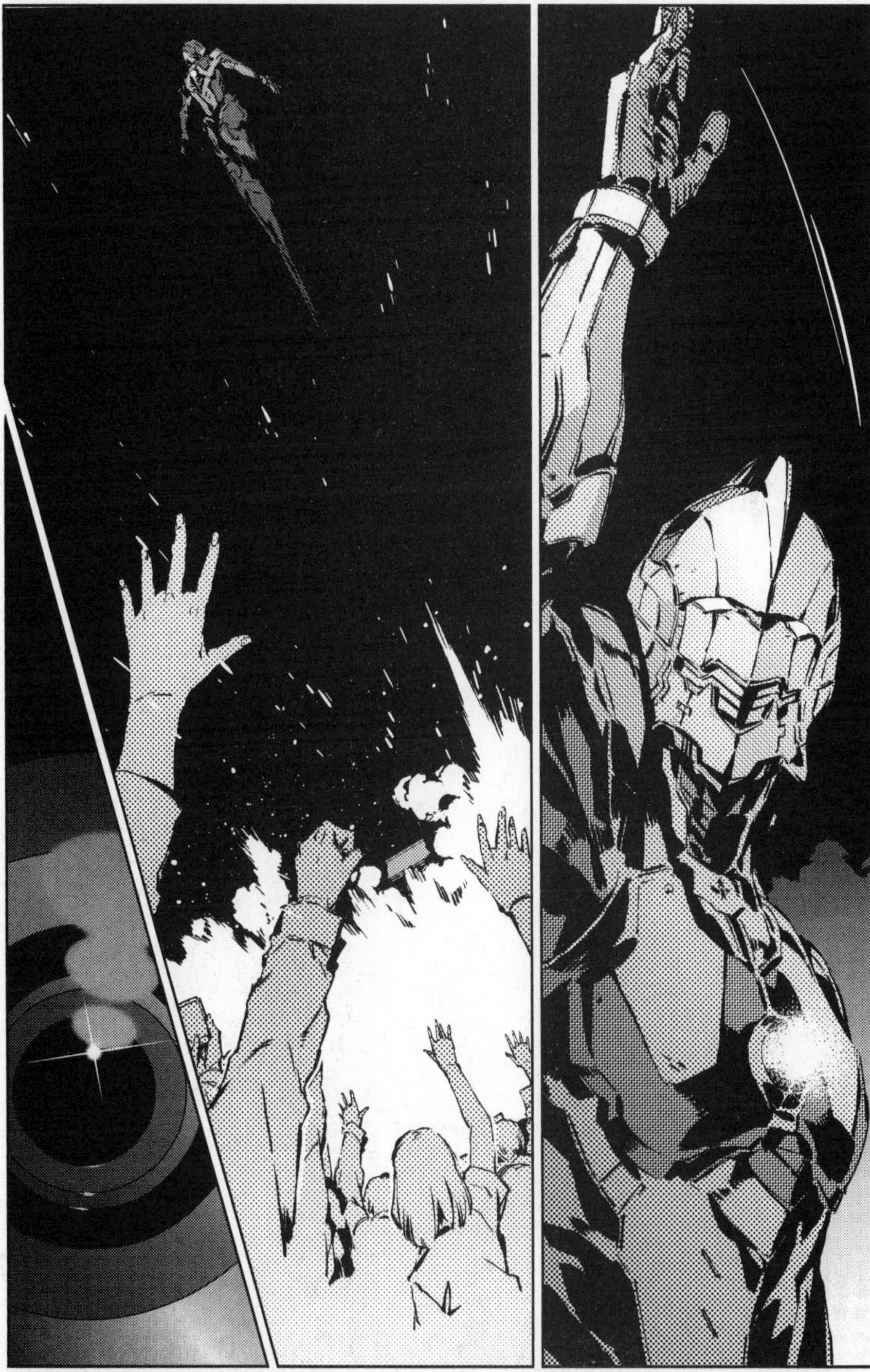

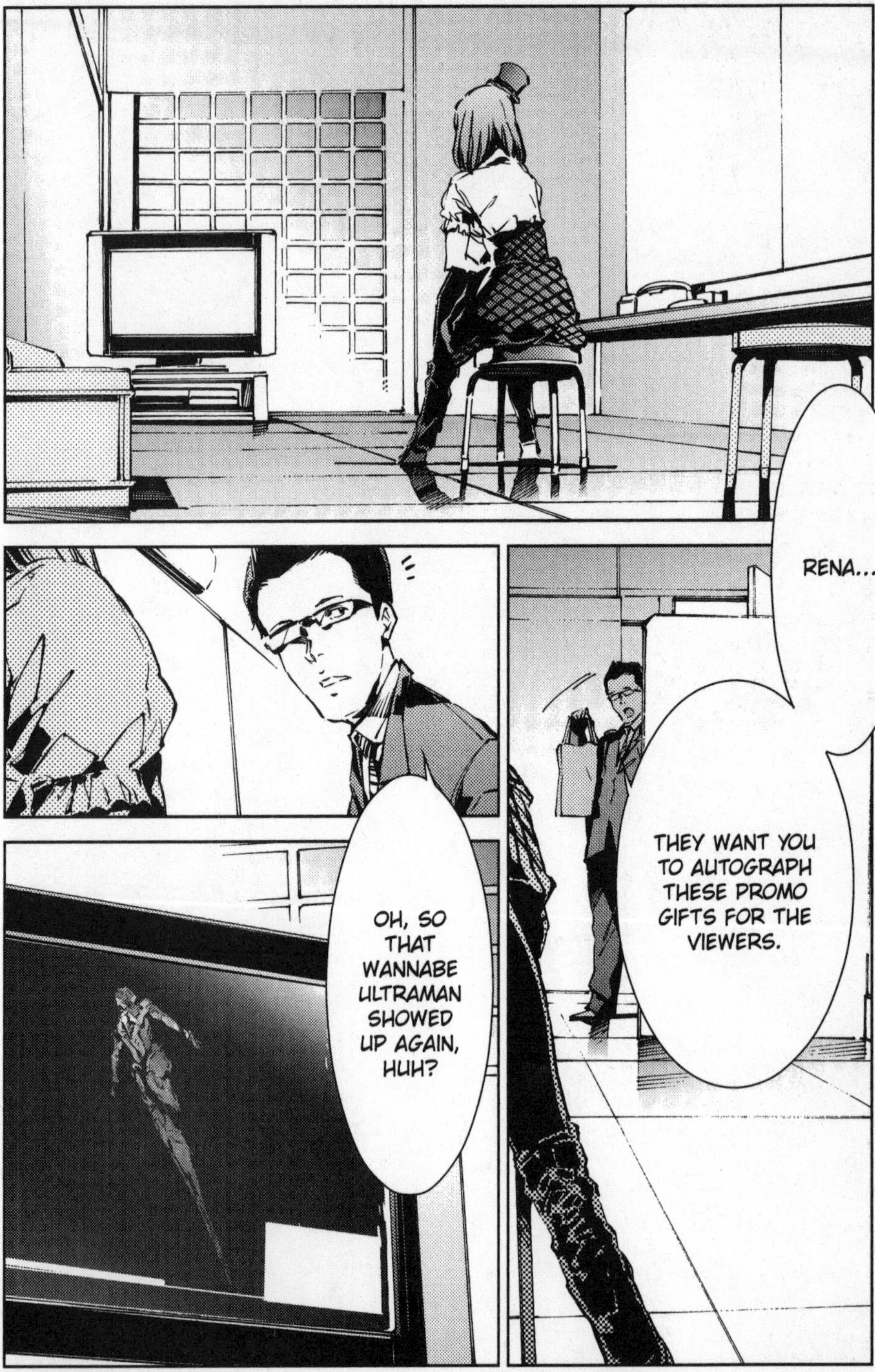
RENA...
THEY WANT YOU TO AUTOGRAPH THESE PROMO GIFTS FOR THE VIEWERS.
OH, SO THAT WANNABE ULTRAMAN SHOWED UP AGAIN, HUH?

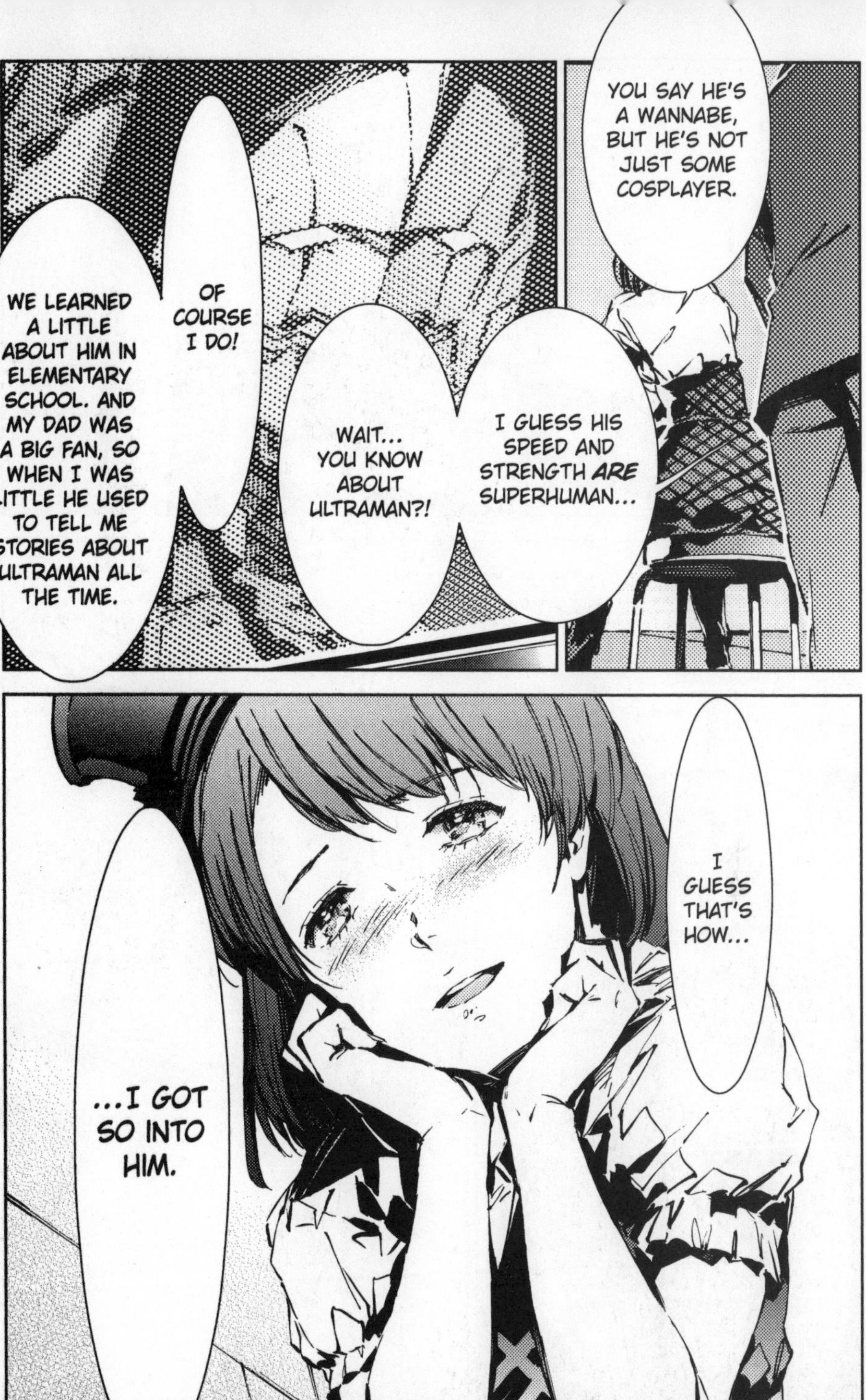
YOU SAY HE'S A WANNABE, BUT HE'S NOT JUST SOME COSPLAYER.
I GUESS HIS SPEED AND STRENGTH *ARE* SUPERHUMAN...
WAIT... YOU KNOW ABOUT ULTRAMAN?!
OF COURSE I DO!
WE LEARNED A LITTLE ABOUT HIM IN ELEMENTARY SCHOOL. AND MY DAD WAS A BIG FAN, SO WHEN I WAS LITTLE HE USED TO TELL ME STORIES ABOUT ULTRAMAN ALL THE TIME.
I GUESS THAT'S HOW...
...I GOT SO INTO HIM.

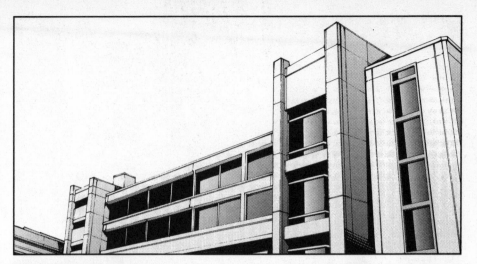

THAT'S JUST A FANCY ULTRAMAN COSTUME, ISN'T IT?

BUT CHECK THIS OUT—A COSPLAYER WOULDN'T BE ABLE TO MOVE LIKE THAT! AND THE WEAPONS ON HIS ARMS—THOSE'RE FOR REAL!

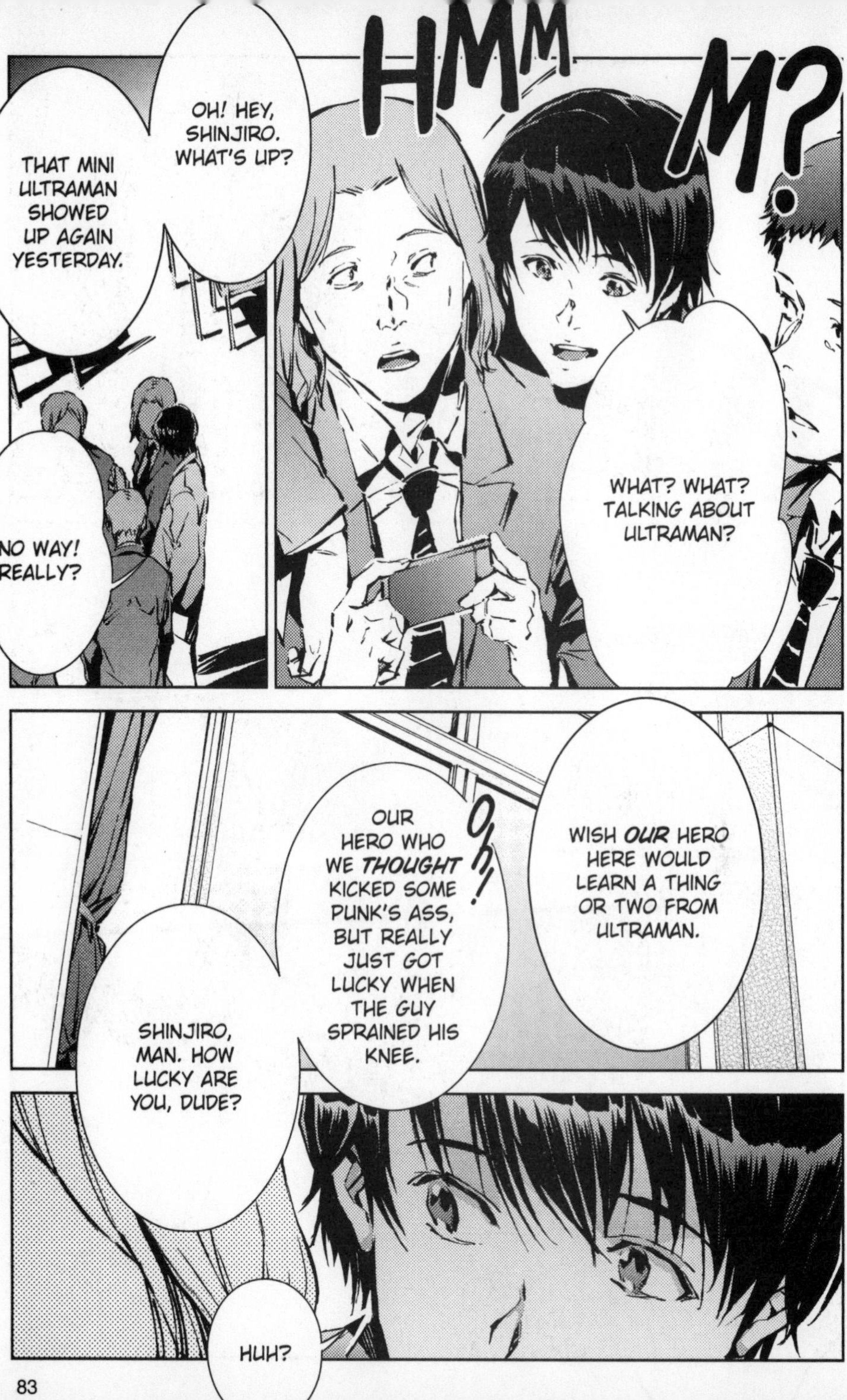
HMMM?
OH! HEY, SHINJIRO. WHAT'S UP?
WHAT? WHAT? TALKING ABOUT ULTRAMAN?
THAT MINI ULTRAMAN SHOWED UP AGAIN YESTERDAY.
NO WAY! REALLY?
WISH *OUR* HERO HERE WOULD LEARN A THING OR TWO FROM ULTRAMAN.
OH!
OUR HERO WHO WE *THOUGHT* KICKED SOME PUNK'S ASS, BUT REALLY JUST GOT LUCKY WHEN THE GUY SPRAINED HIS KNEE.
SHINJIRO, MAN. HOW LUCKY ARE YOU, DUDE?
HUH?

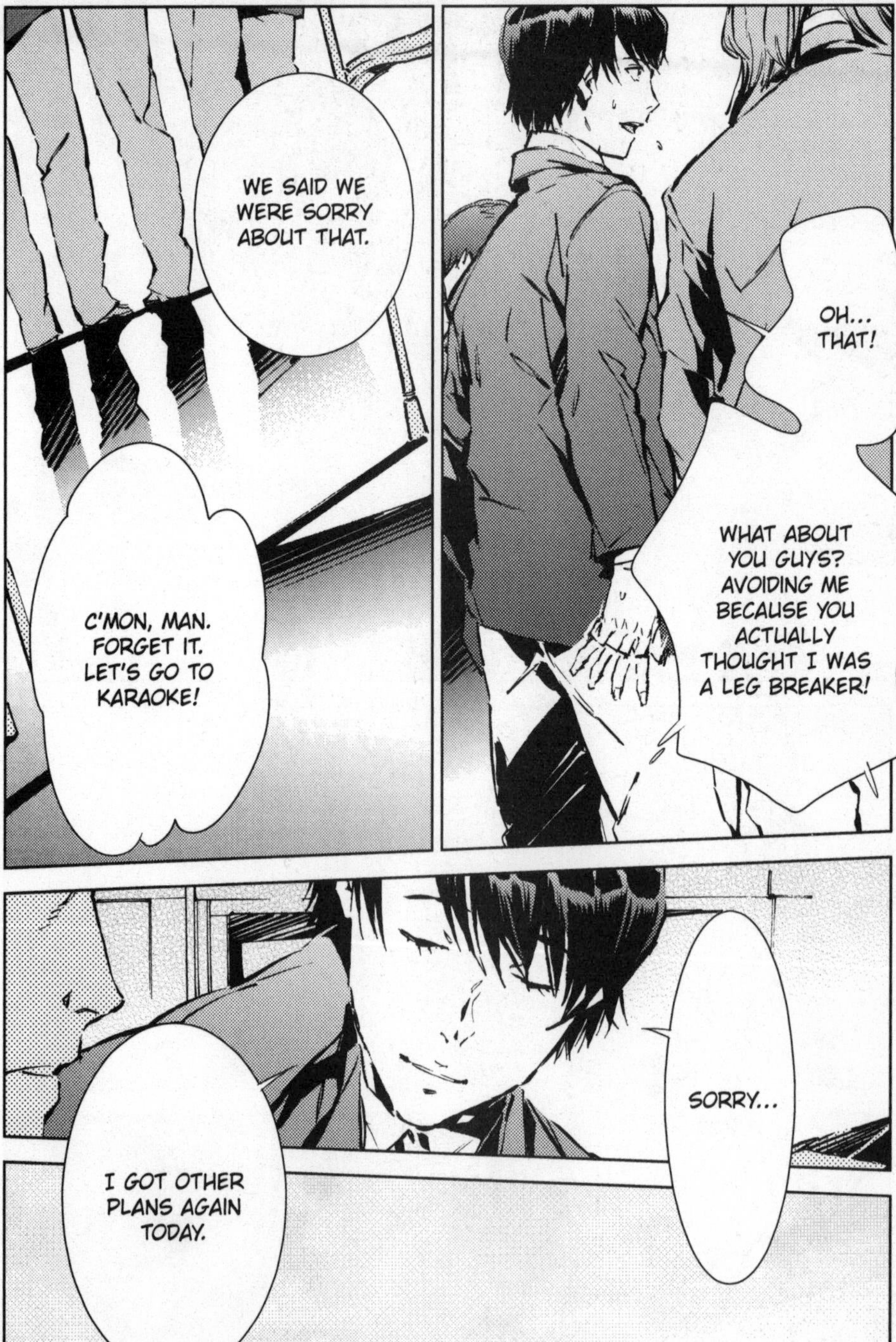
OH... THAT!
WHAT ABOUT YOU GUYS? AVOIDING ME BECAUSE YOU ACTUALLY THOUGHT I WAS A LEG BREAKER!
WE SAID WE WERE SORRY ABOUT THAT.
C'MON, MAN. FORGET IT. LET'S GO TO KARAOKE!
SORRY...
I GOT OTHER PLANS AGAIN TODAY.

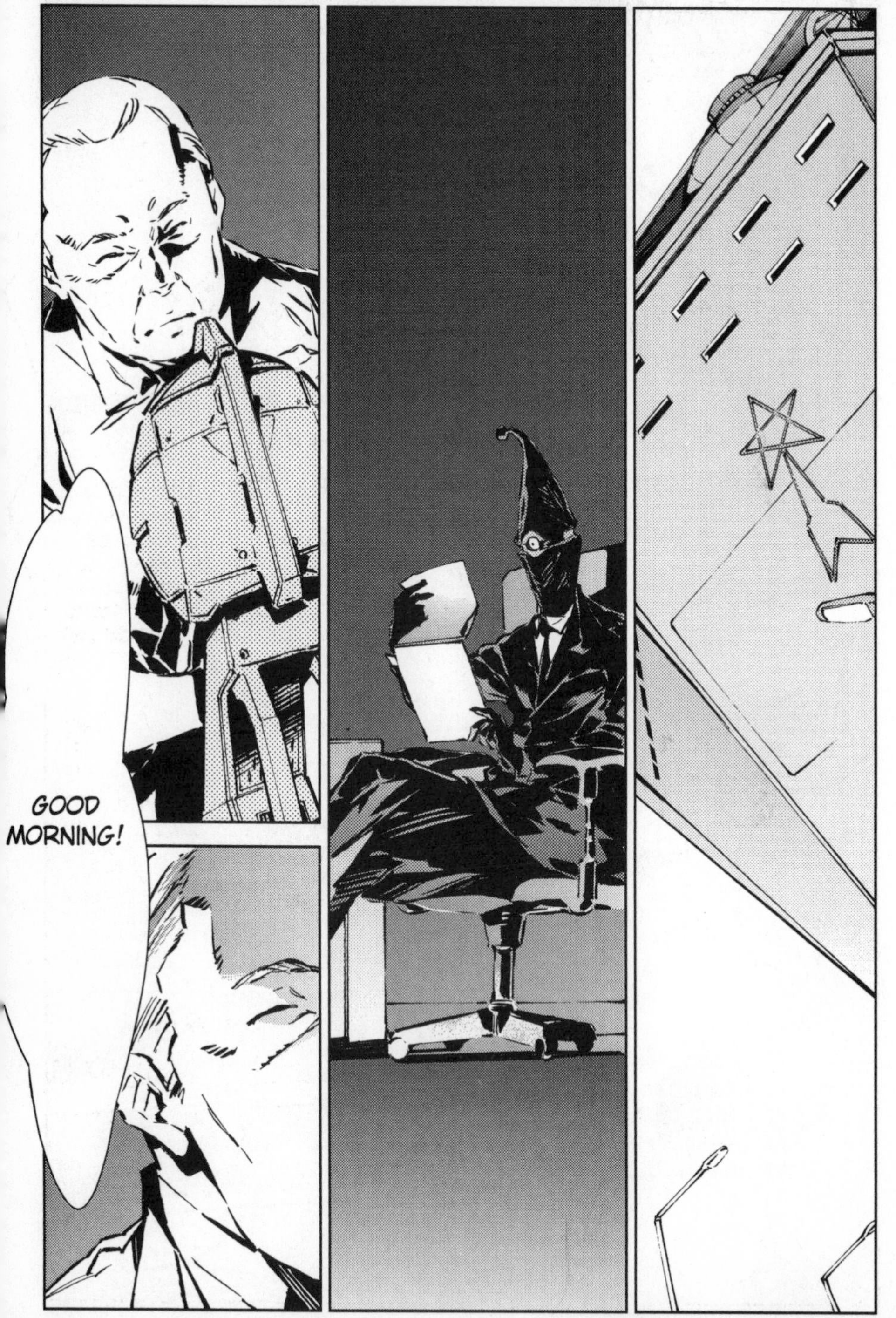
GOOD
MORNING!

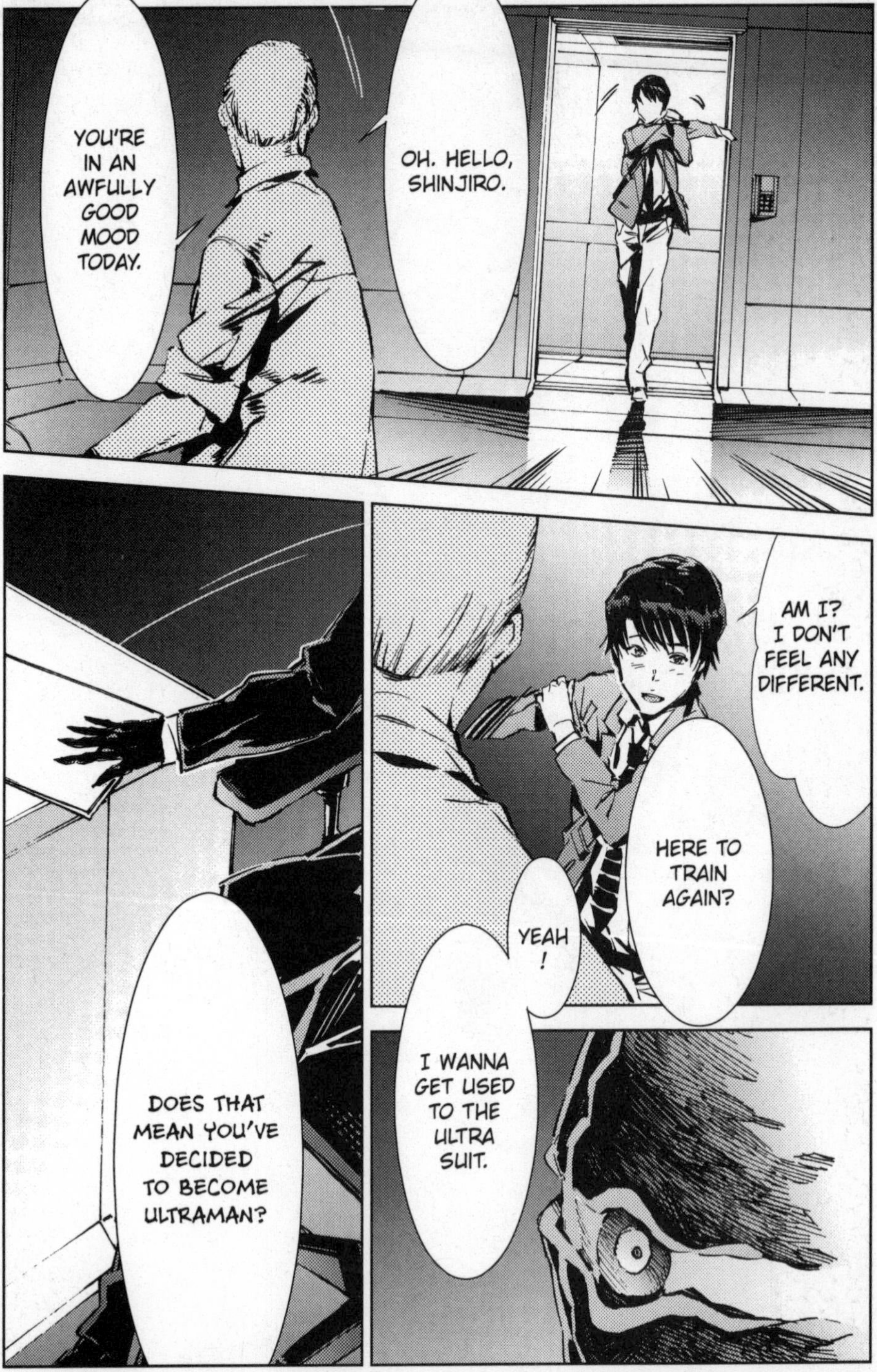
OH. HELLO, SHINJIRO.
YOU'RE IN AN AWFULLY GOOD MOOD TODAY.
AM I? I DON'T FEEL ANY DIFFERENT.
HERE TO TRAIN AGAIN?
YEAH!
I WANNA GET USED TO THE ULTRA SUIT.
DOES THAT MEAN YOU'VE DECIDED TO BECOME ULTRAMAN?

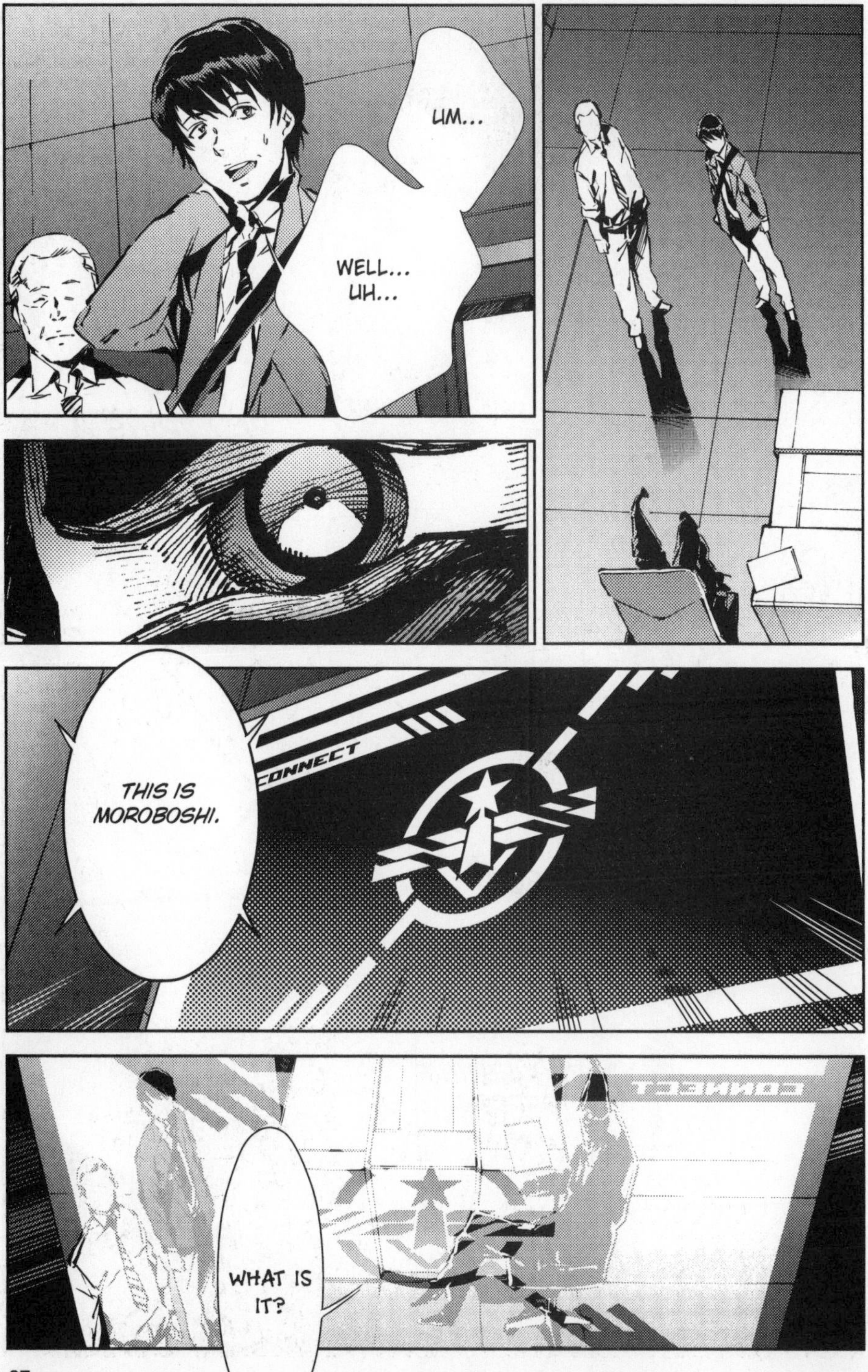
UM...
WELL... UH...
THIS IS MOROBOSHI.
CONNECT
WHAT IS IT?

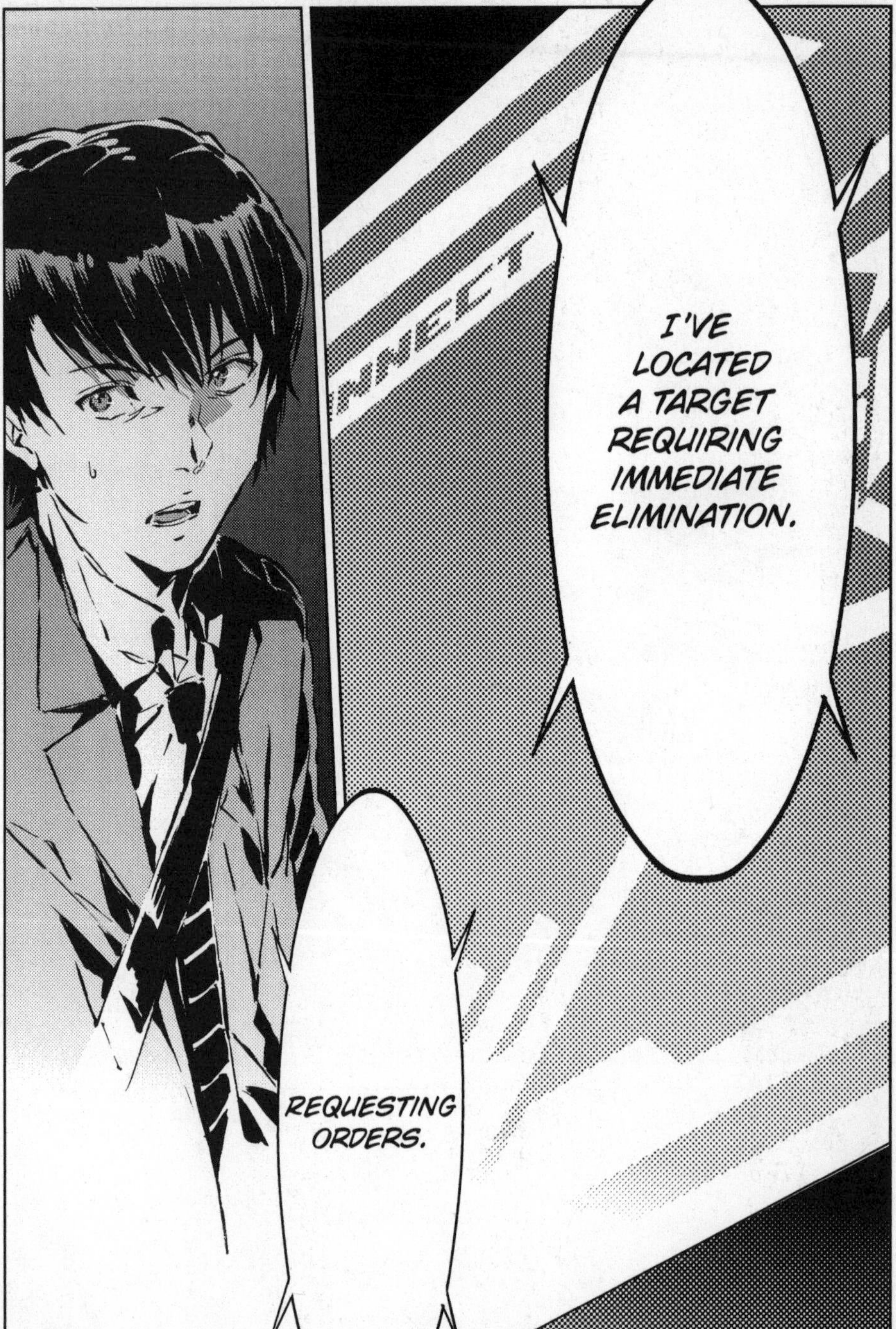
I'VE LOCATED A TARGET REQUIRING IMMEDIATE ELIMINATION.
REQUESTING ORDERS.

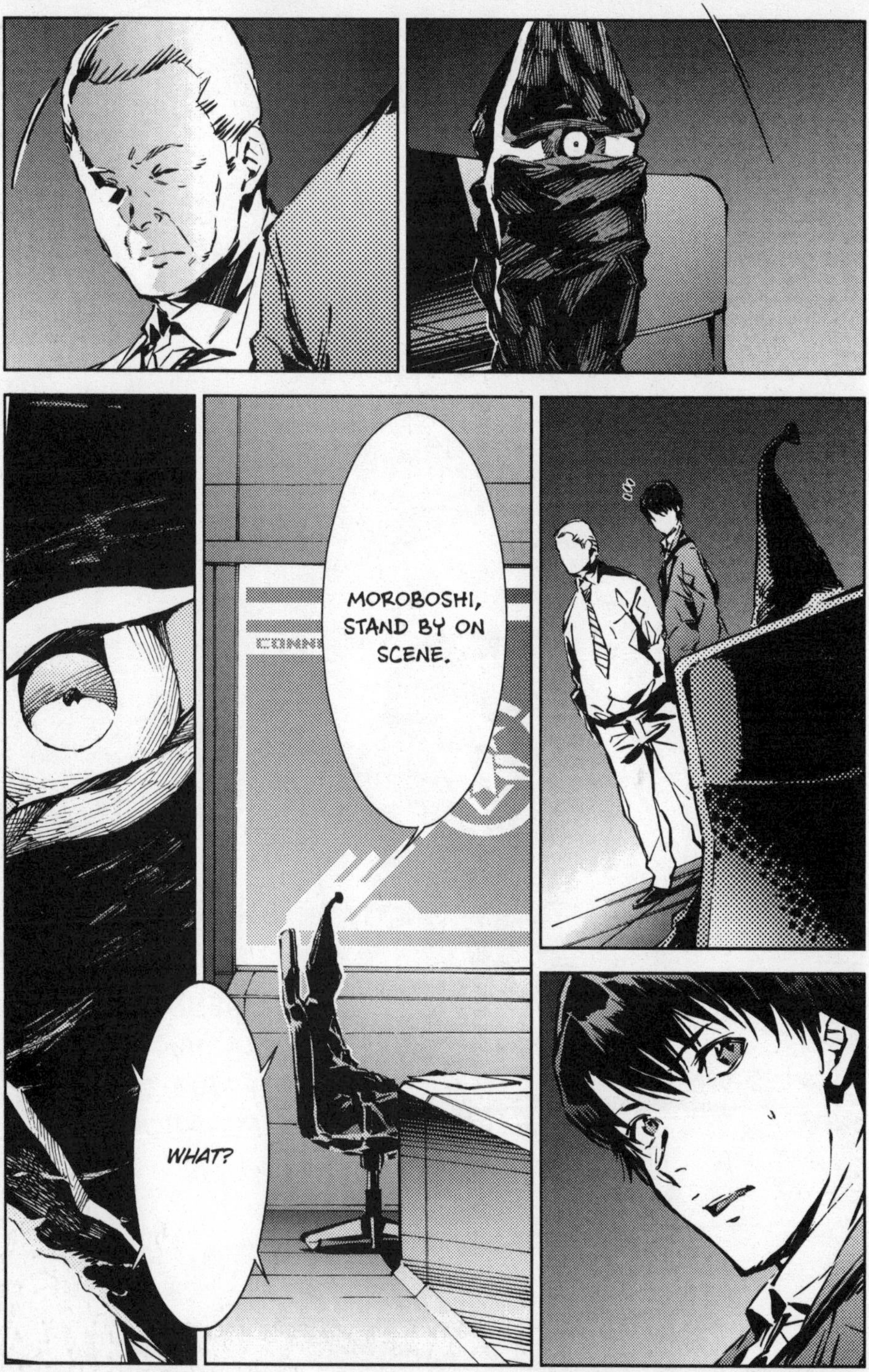
MOROBOSHI, STAND BY ON SCENE.
WHAT?

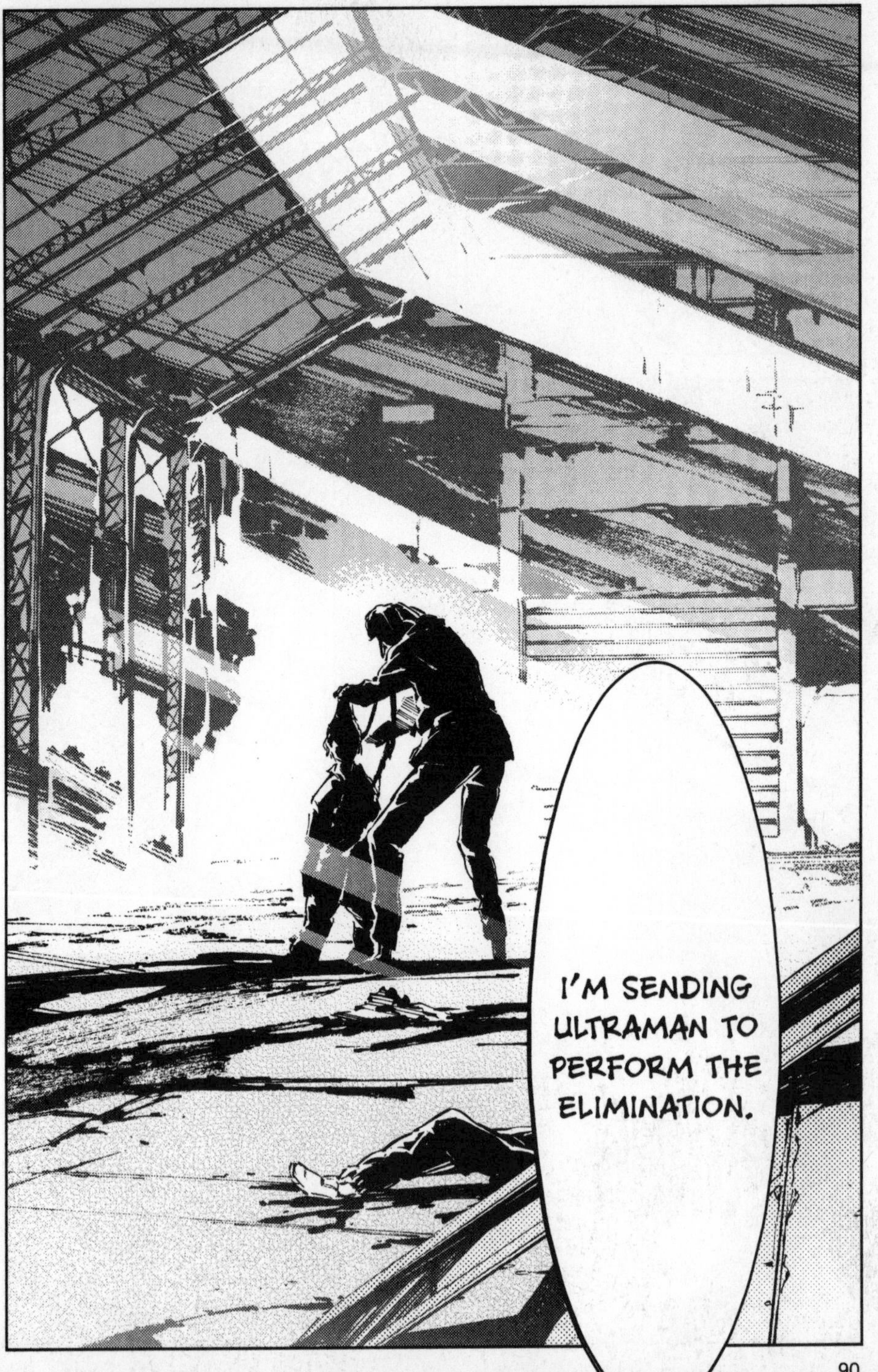
I'M SENDING ULTRAMAN TO PERFORM THE ELIMINATION.

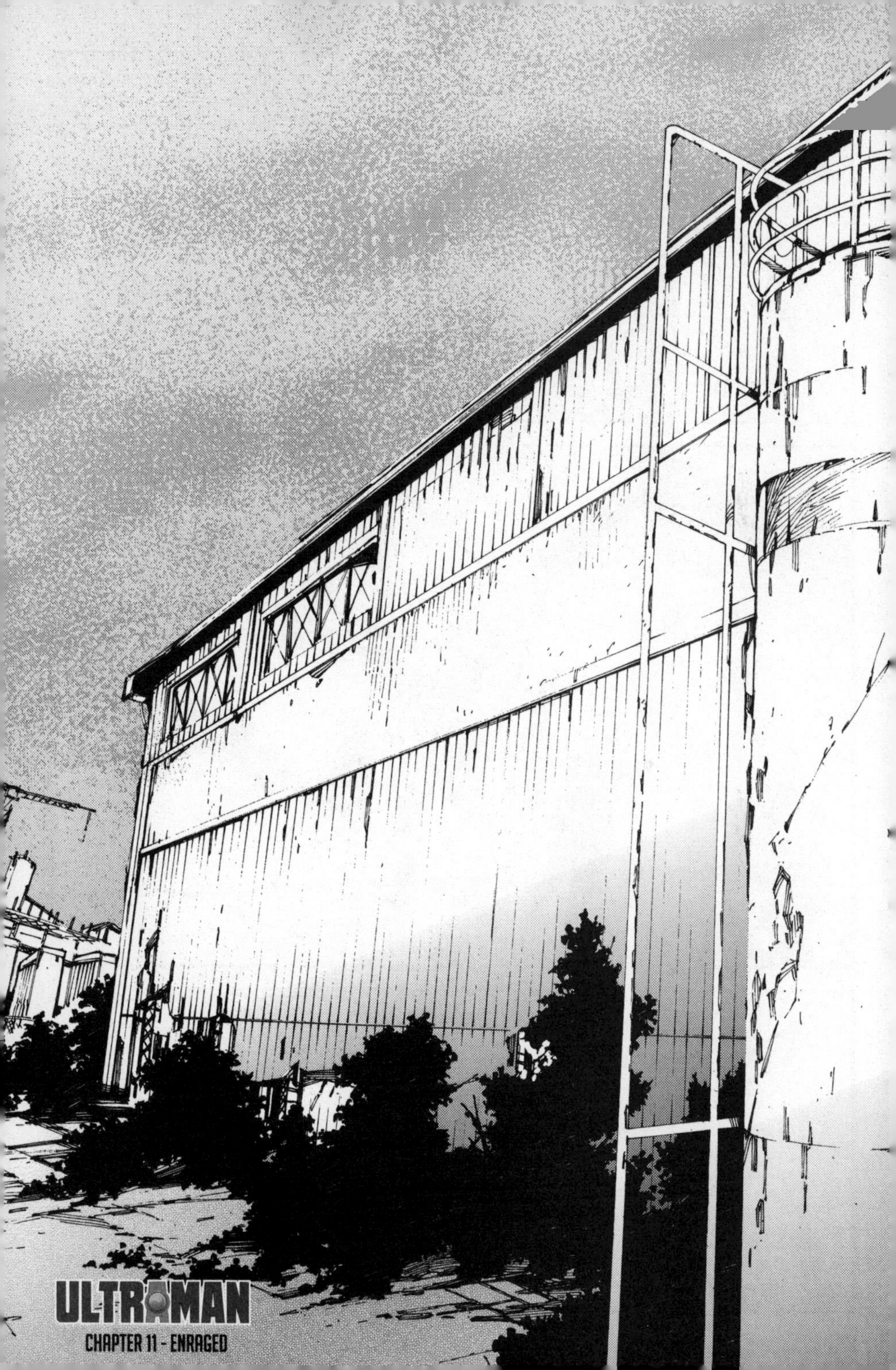
ULTRAMAN
CHAPTER 11 - ENRAGED

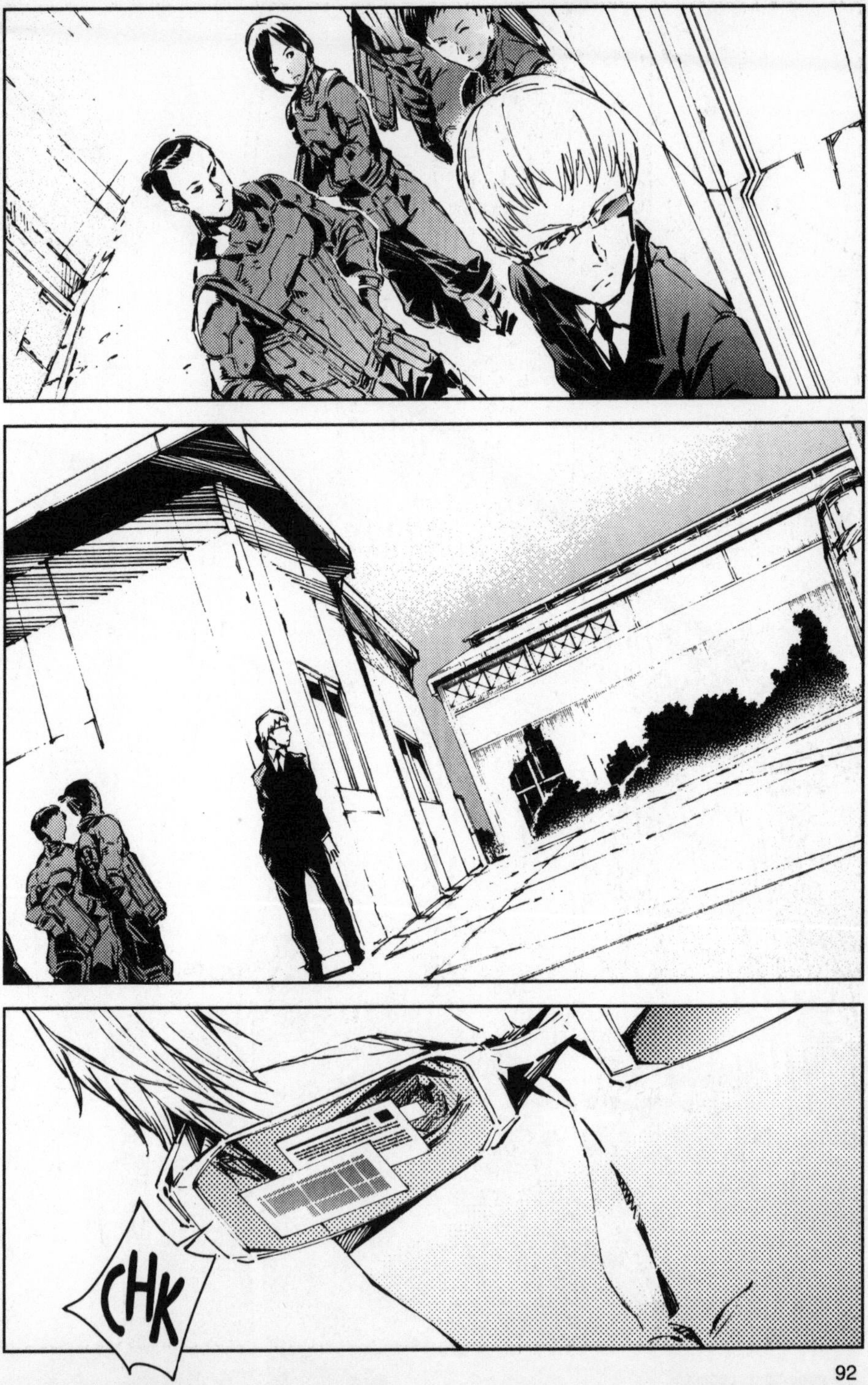
CHK

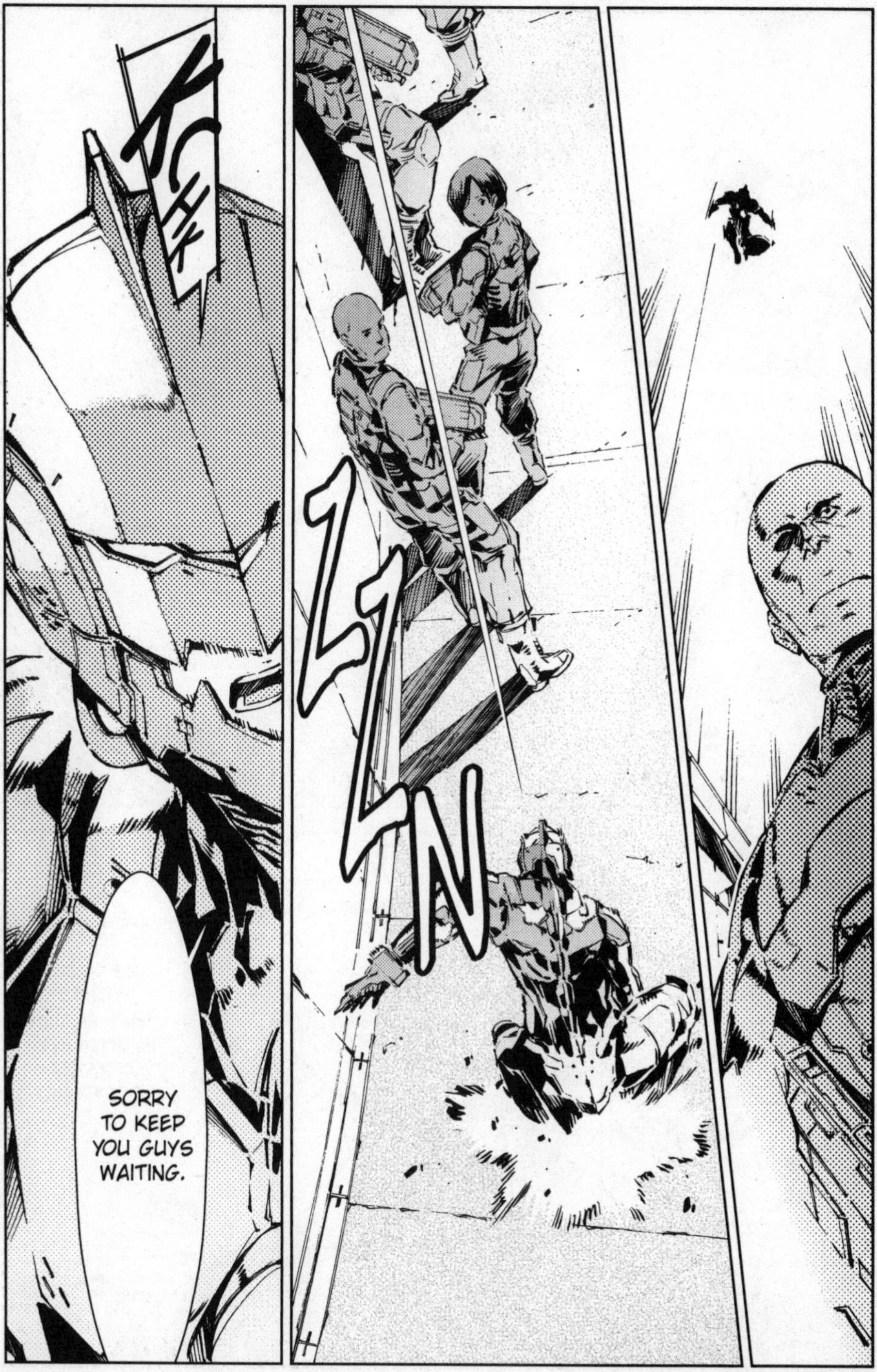
KCHK
ZZN
SORRY TO KEEP YOU GUYS WAITING.

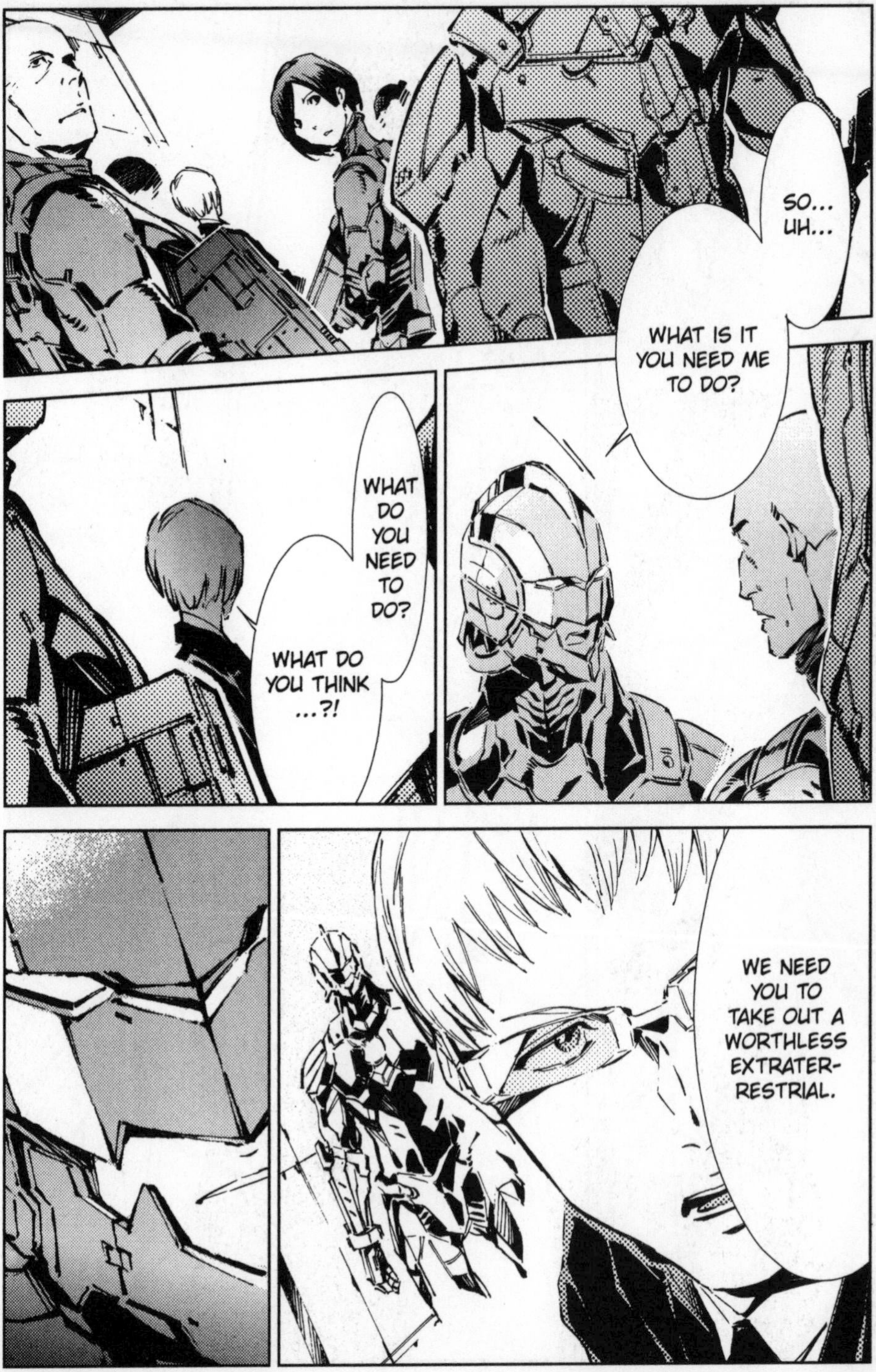
SO... UH...
WHAT IS IT YOU NEED ME TO DO?
WHAT DO YOU NEED TO DO?
WHAT DO YOU THINK ...?!
WE NEED YOU TO TAKE OUT A WORTHLESS EXTRATER-RESTRIAL.

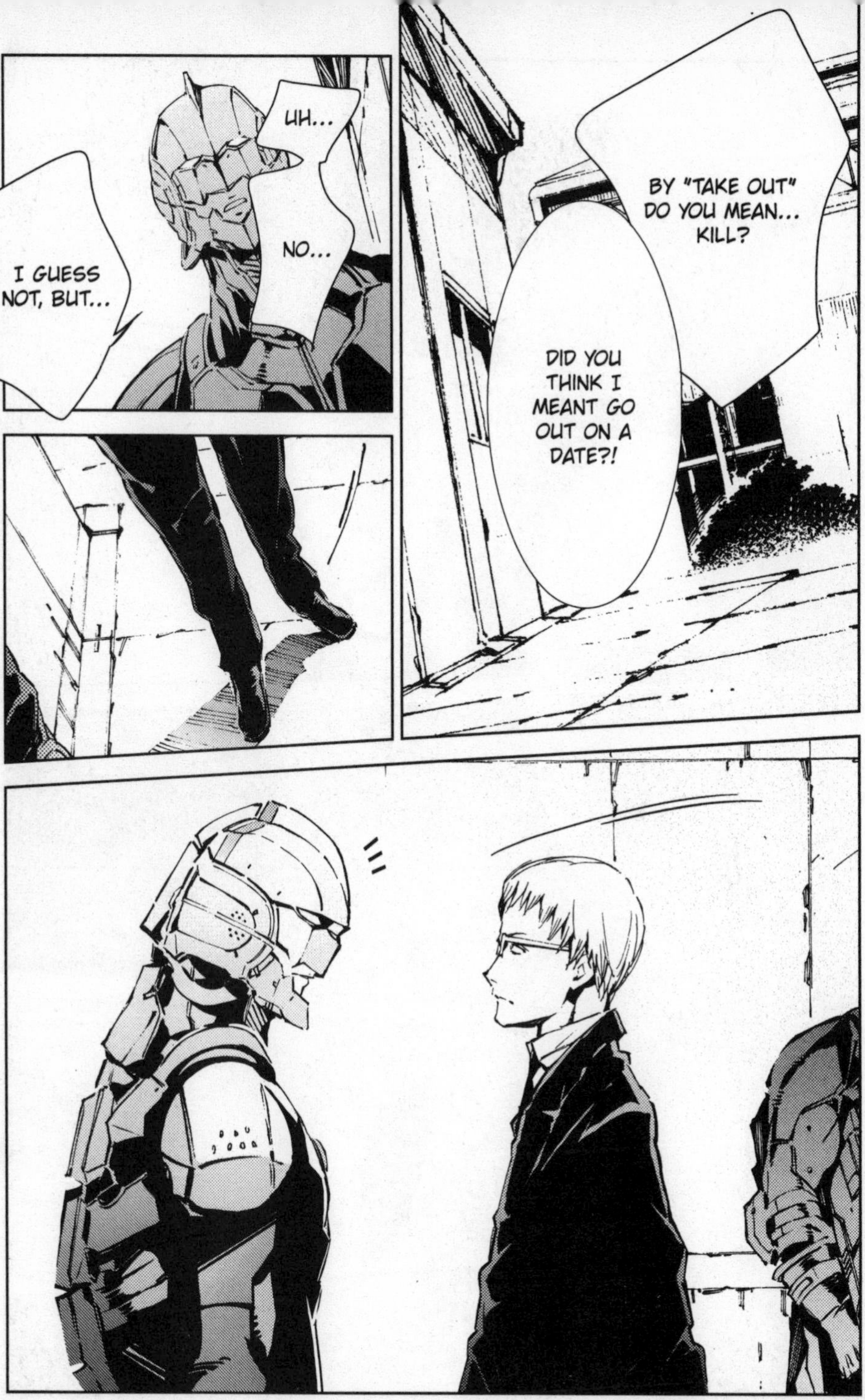
BY "TAKE OUT" DO YOU MEAN... KILL?
DID YOU THINK I MEANT GO OUT ON A DATE?!
UH...
NO...
I GUESS NOT, BUT...

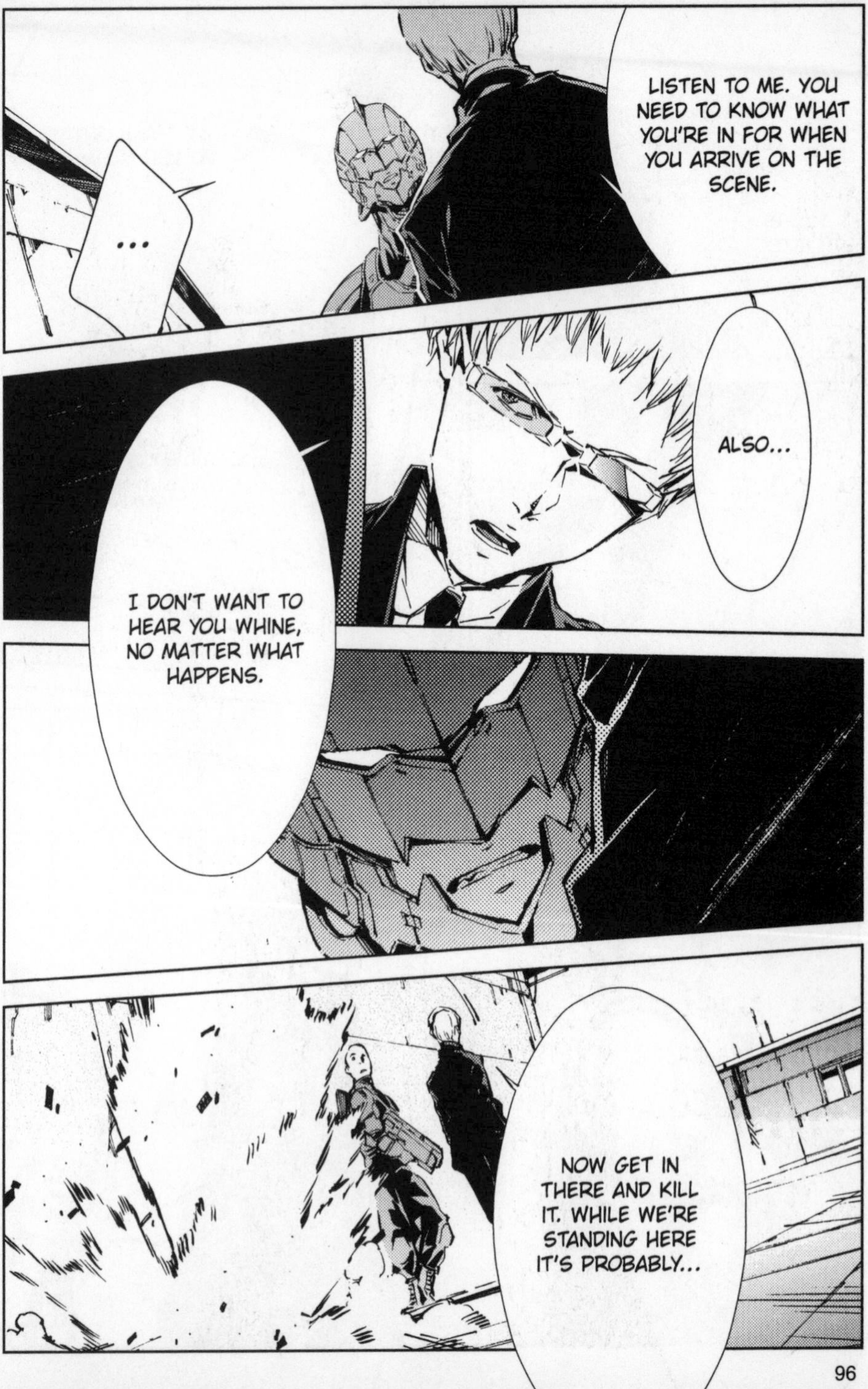
LISTEN TO ME. YOU NEED TO KNOW WHAT YOU'RE IN FOR WHEN YOU ARRIVE ON THE SCENE.
...
ALSO...
I DON'T WANT TO HEAR YOU WHINE, NO MATTER WHAT HAPPENS.
NOW GET IN THERE AND KILL IT. WHILE WE'RE STANDING HERE IT'S PROBABLY...

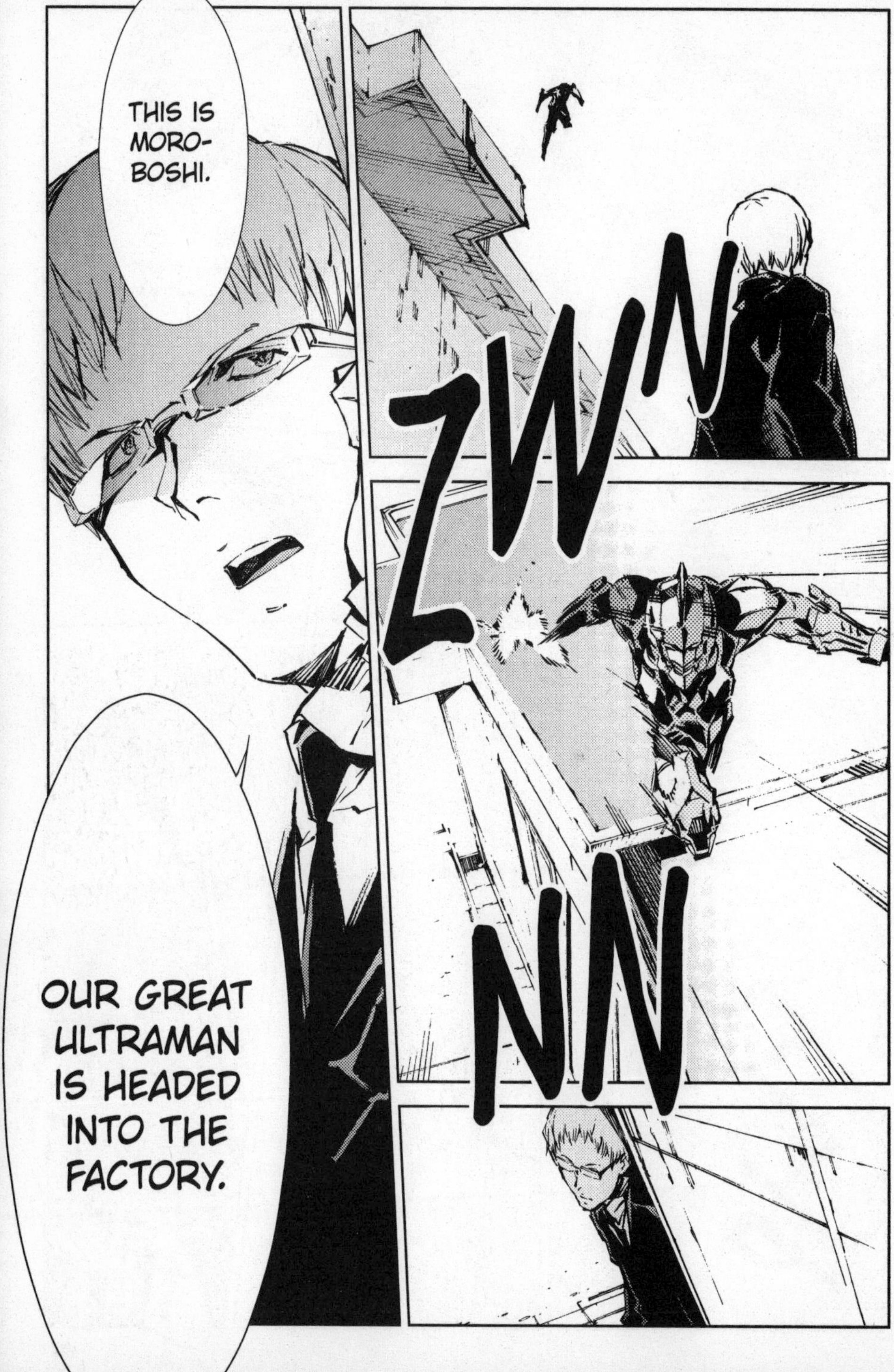
THIS IS MORO-BOSHI.
ZWN
NN
OUR GREAT ULTRAMAN IS HEADED INTO THE FACTORY.

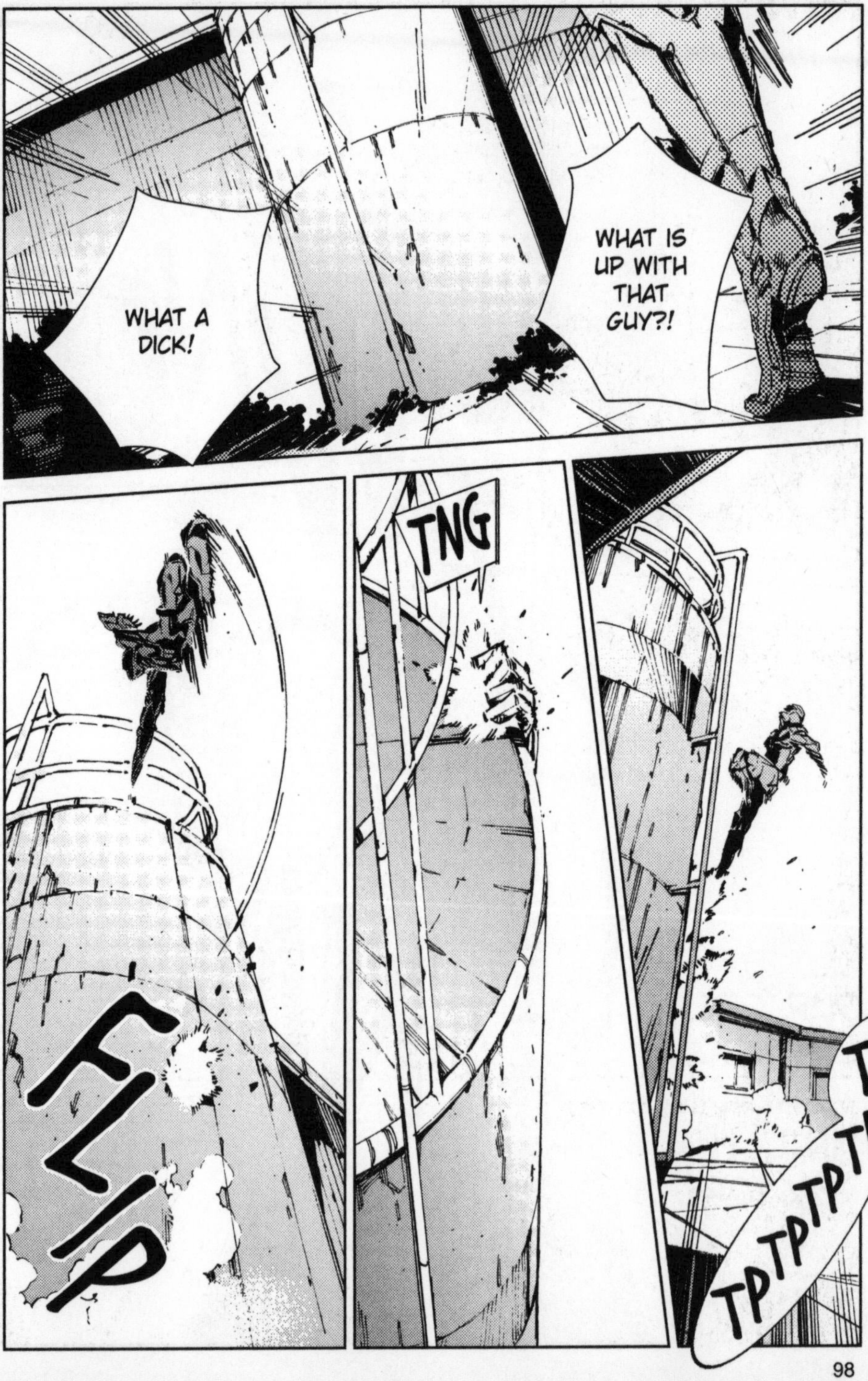
WHAT IS UP WITH THAT GUY?!
WHAT A DICK!
TNG
FLIP
TPTPTPTPTP

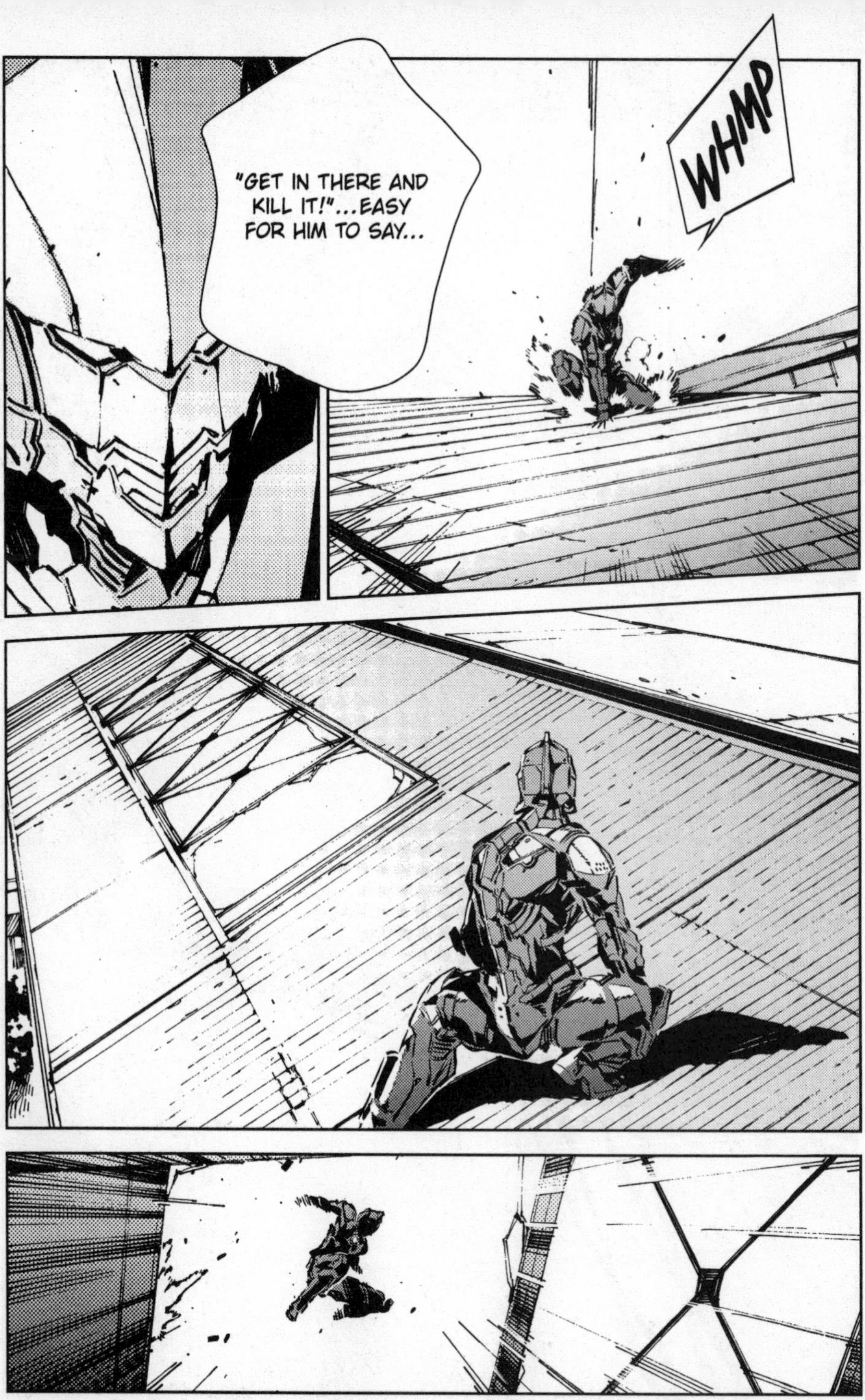
"GET IN THERE AND KILL IT!"...EASY FOR HIM TO SAY...
WHMP

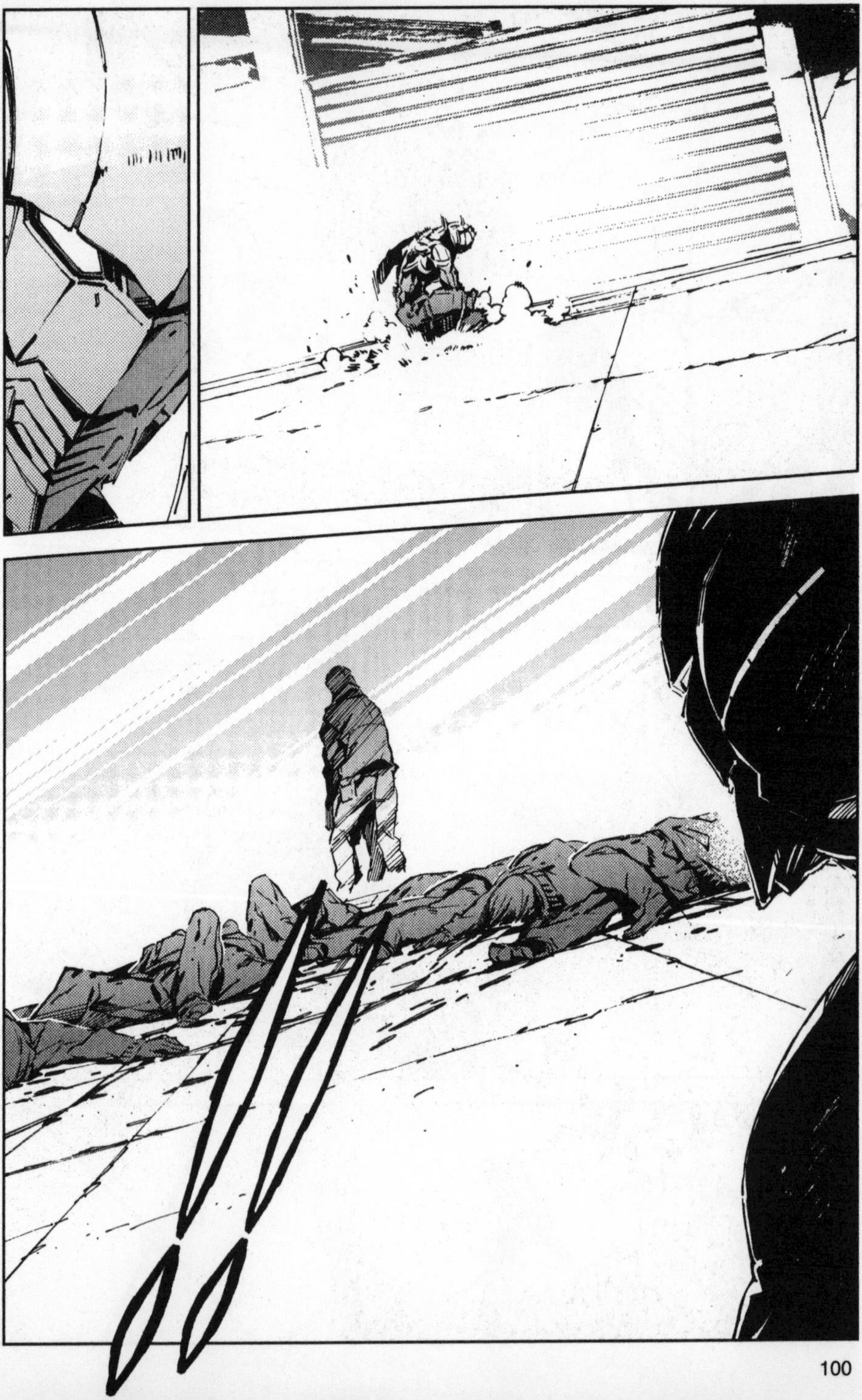

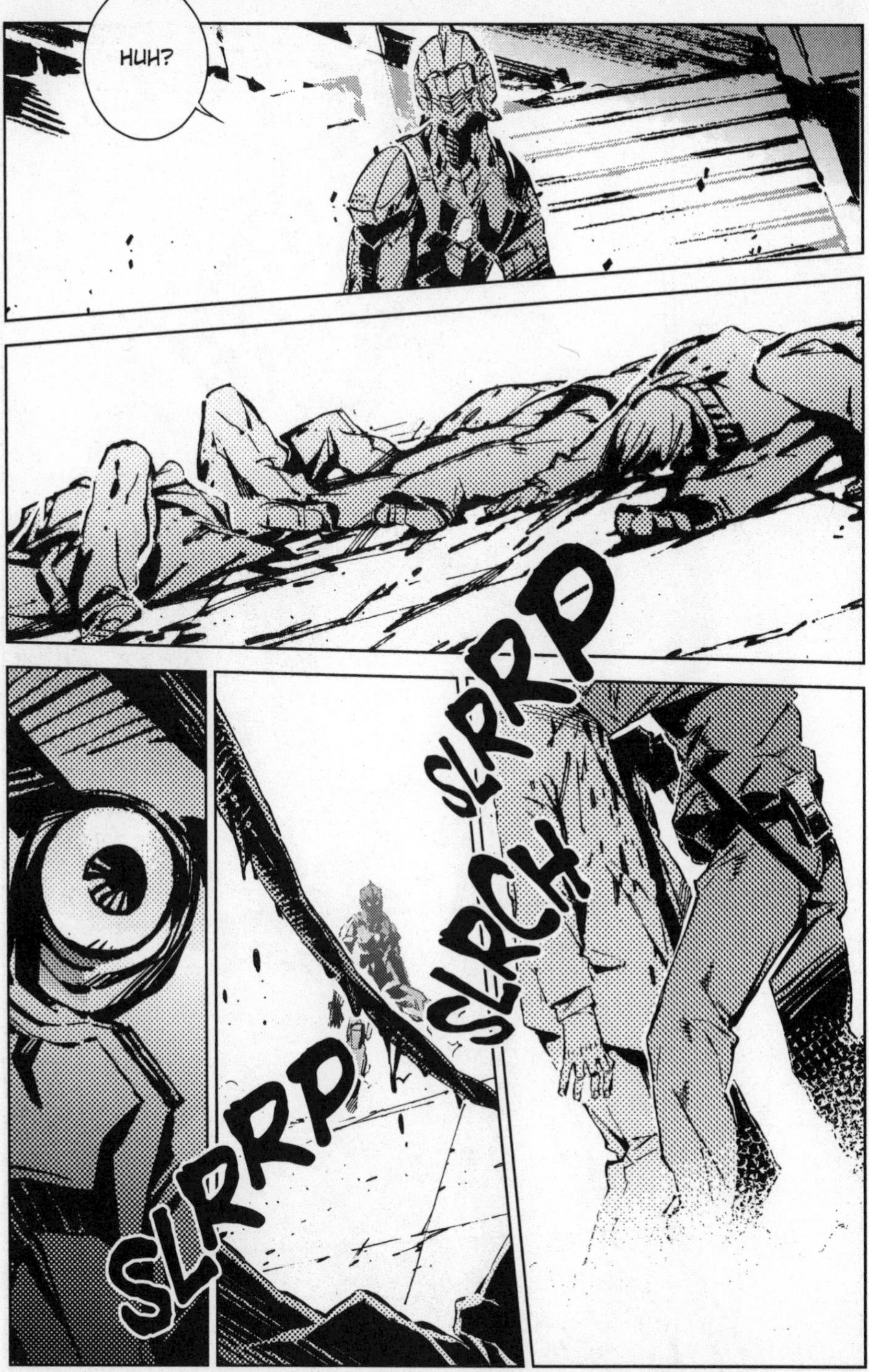
HUH?
SLRRP
SLRCH
SLRRP

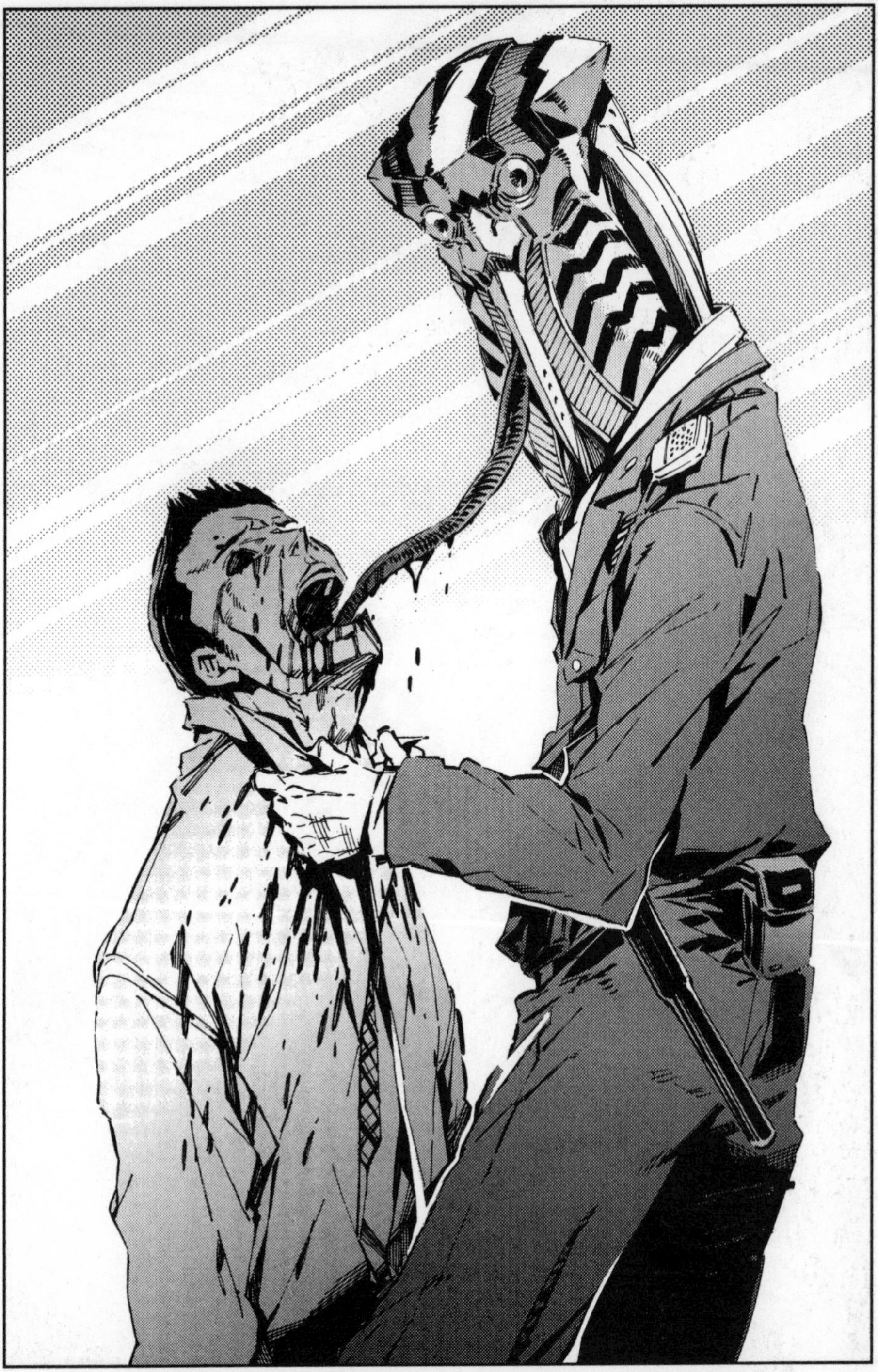

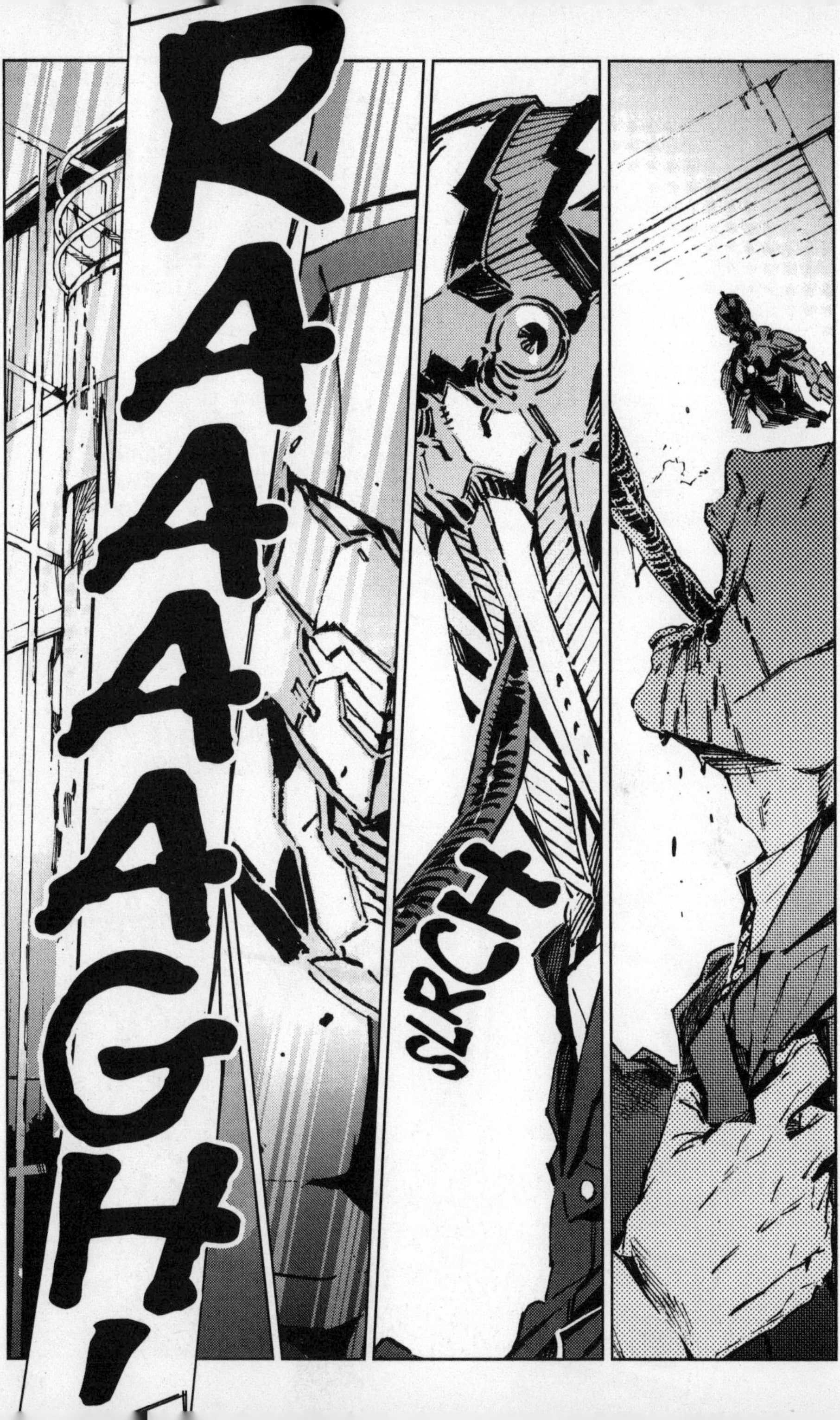
RAAAAGH!
SLRCH

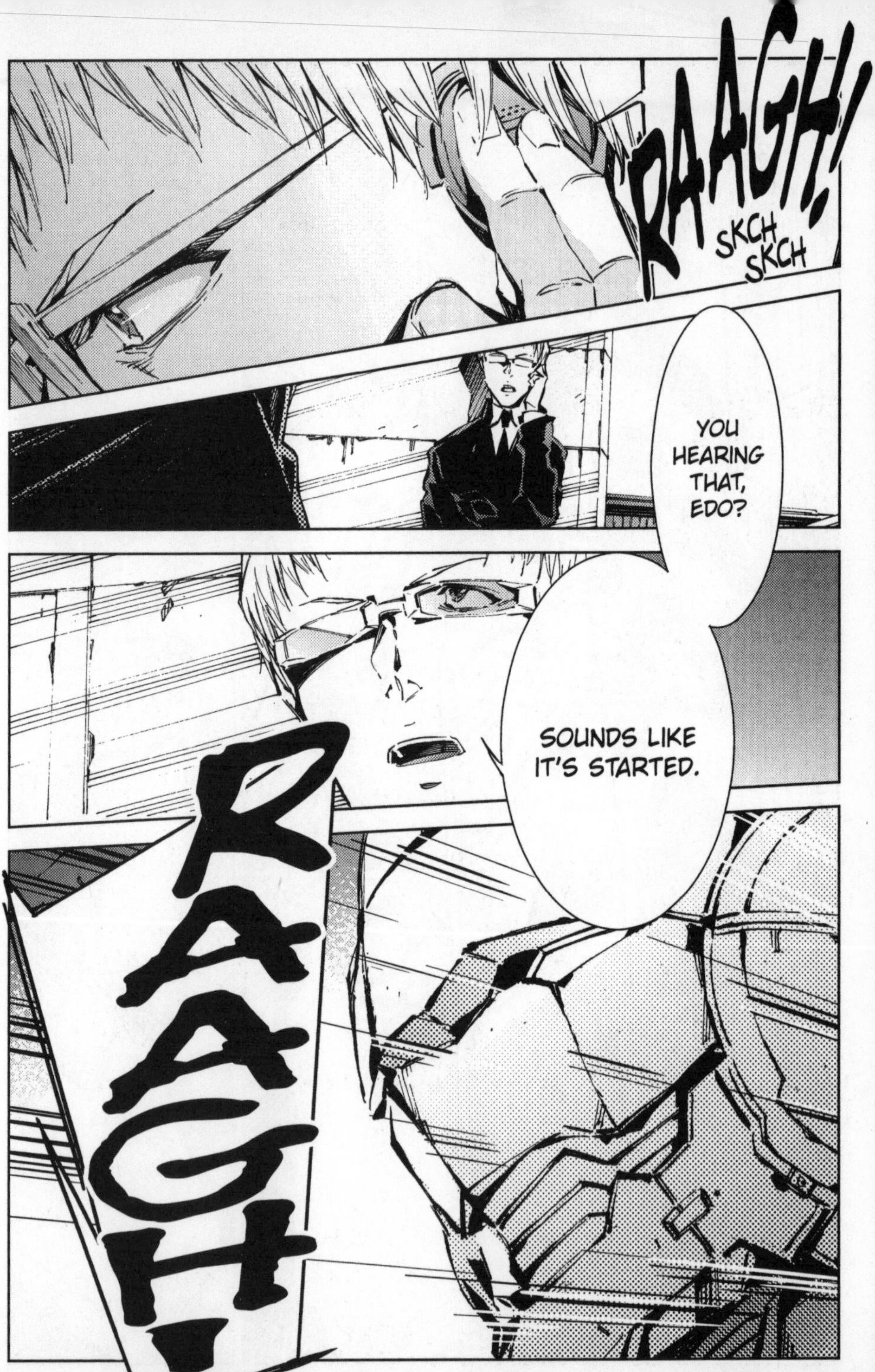
RAAGH!
SKCH SKCH
YOU HEARING THAT, EDO?
SOUNDS LIKE IT'S STARTED.
RAAGH!

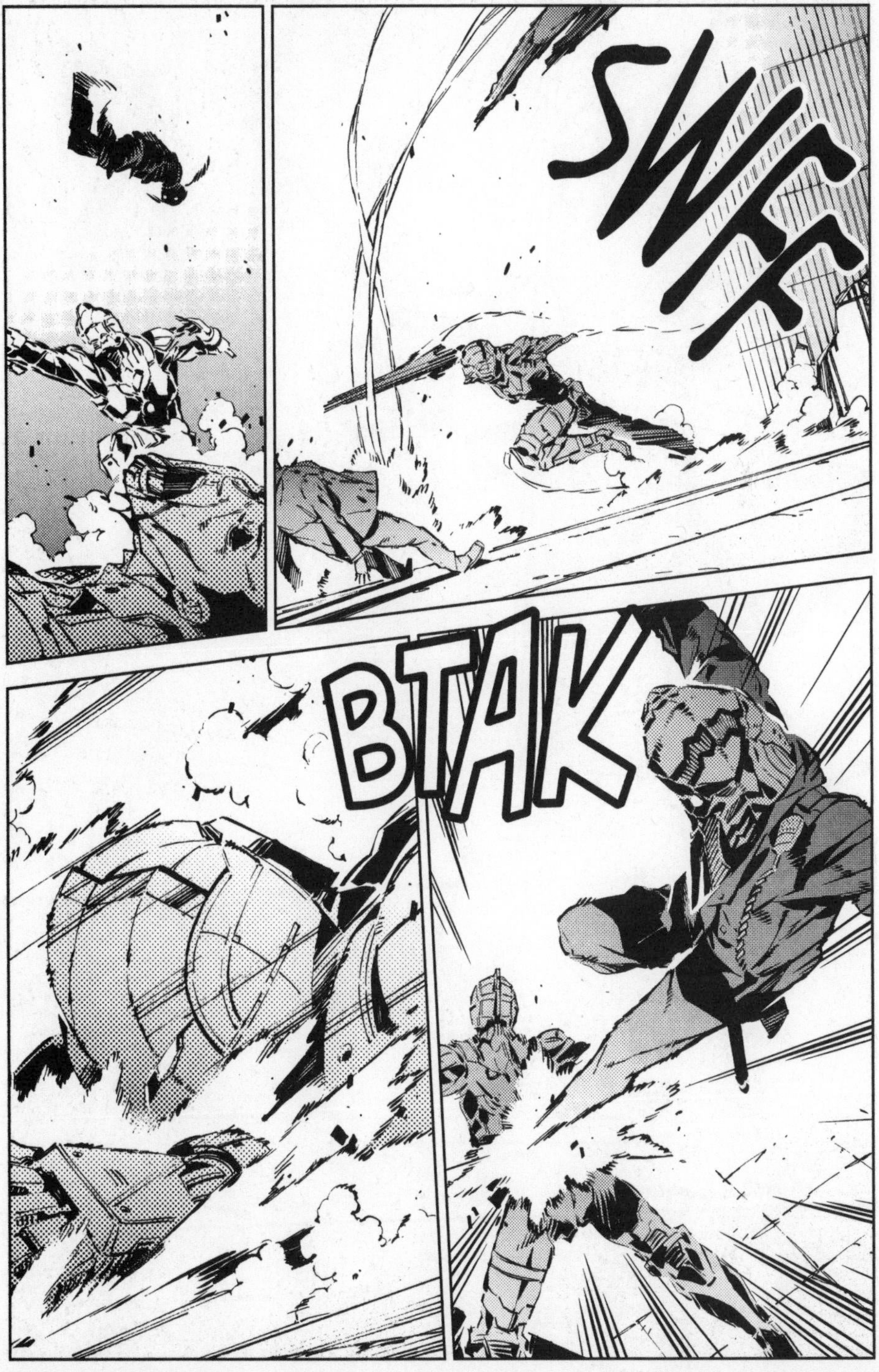
SWFF
BTAK

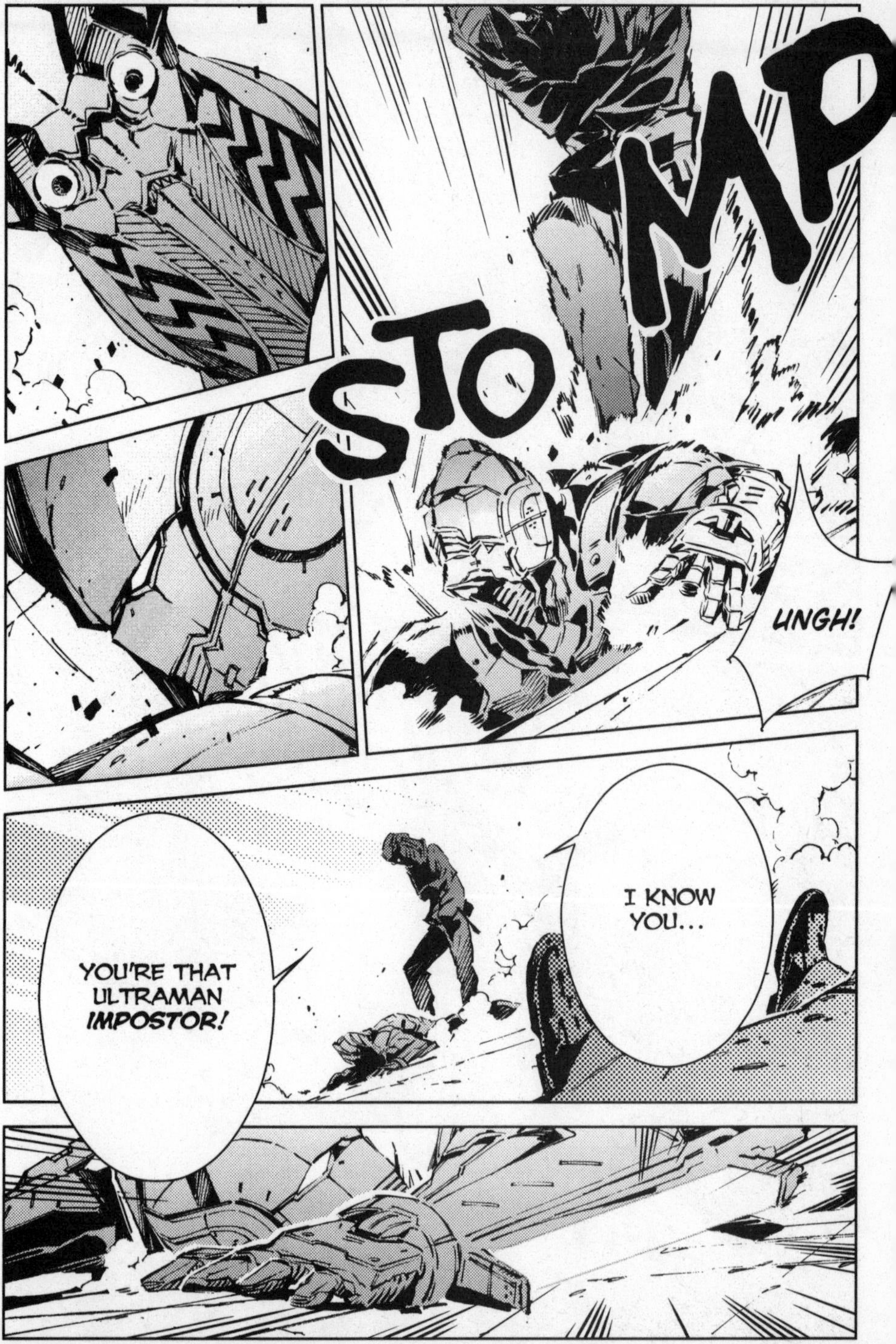
STOMP
UNGH!
I KNOW YOU...
YOU'RE THAT ULTRAMAN IMPOSTOR!

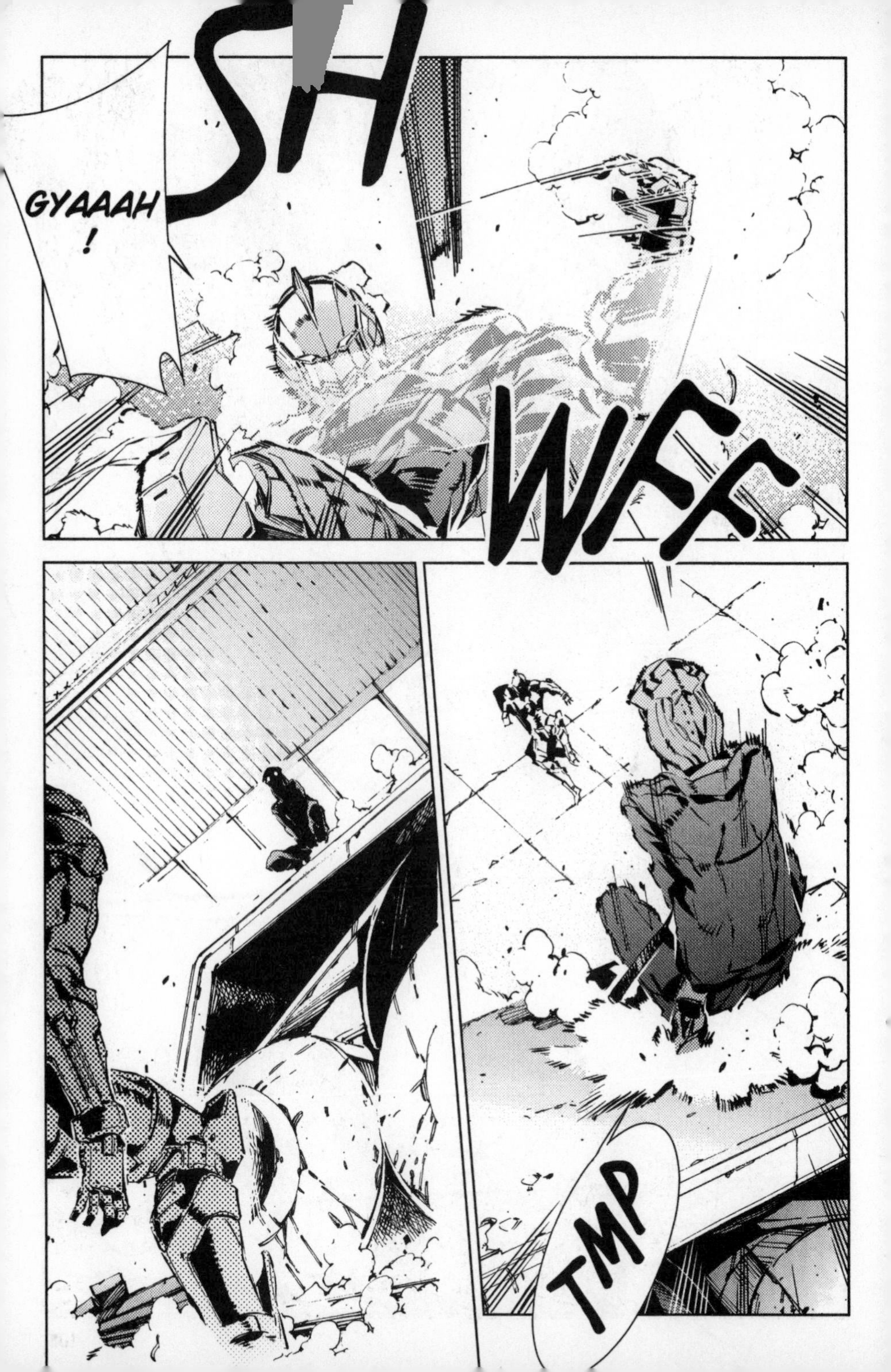
SH
GYAAAH!
WIFF
TMP

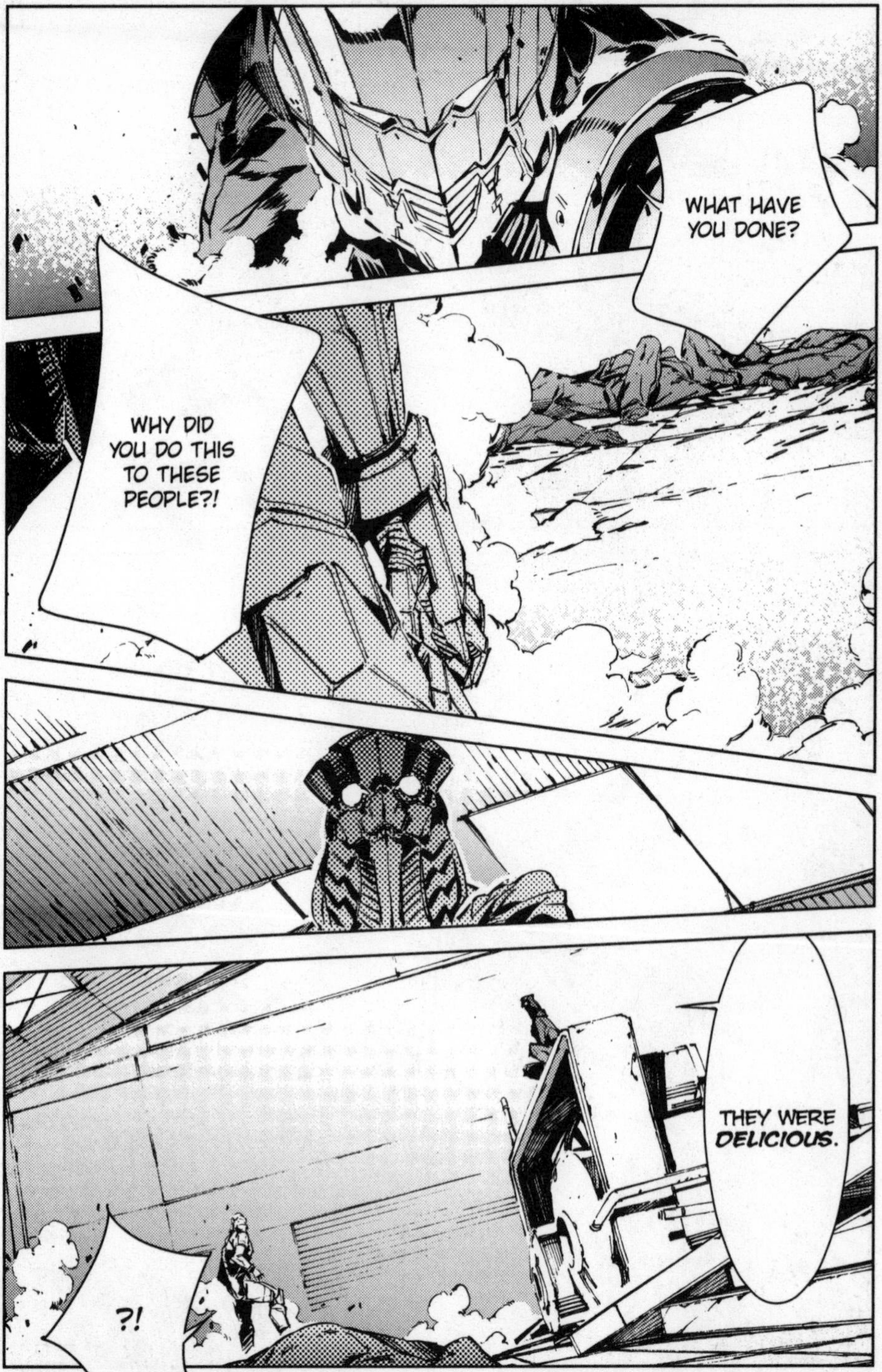
WHAT HAVE YOU DONE?
WHY DID YOU DO THIS TO THESE PEOPLE?!
THEY WERE *DELICIOUS*.
?!

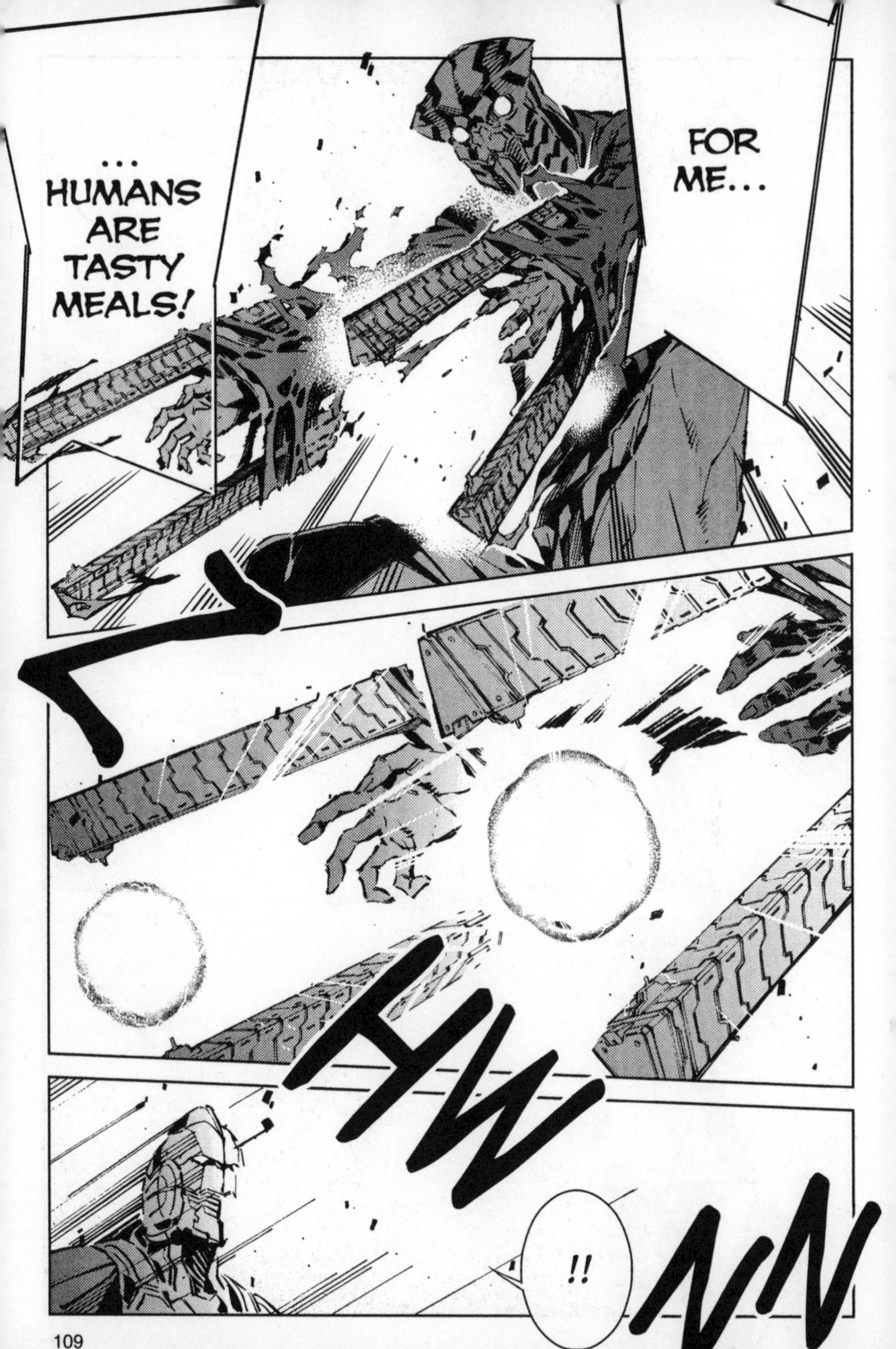
FOR ME...
... HUMANS ARE TASTY MEALS!
!!

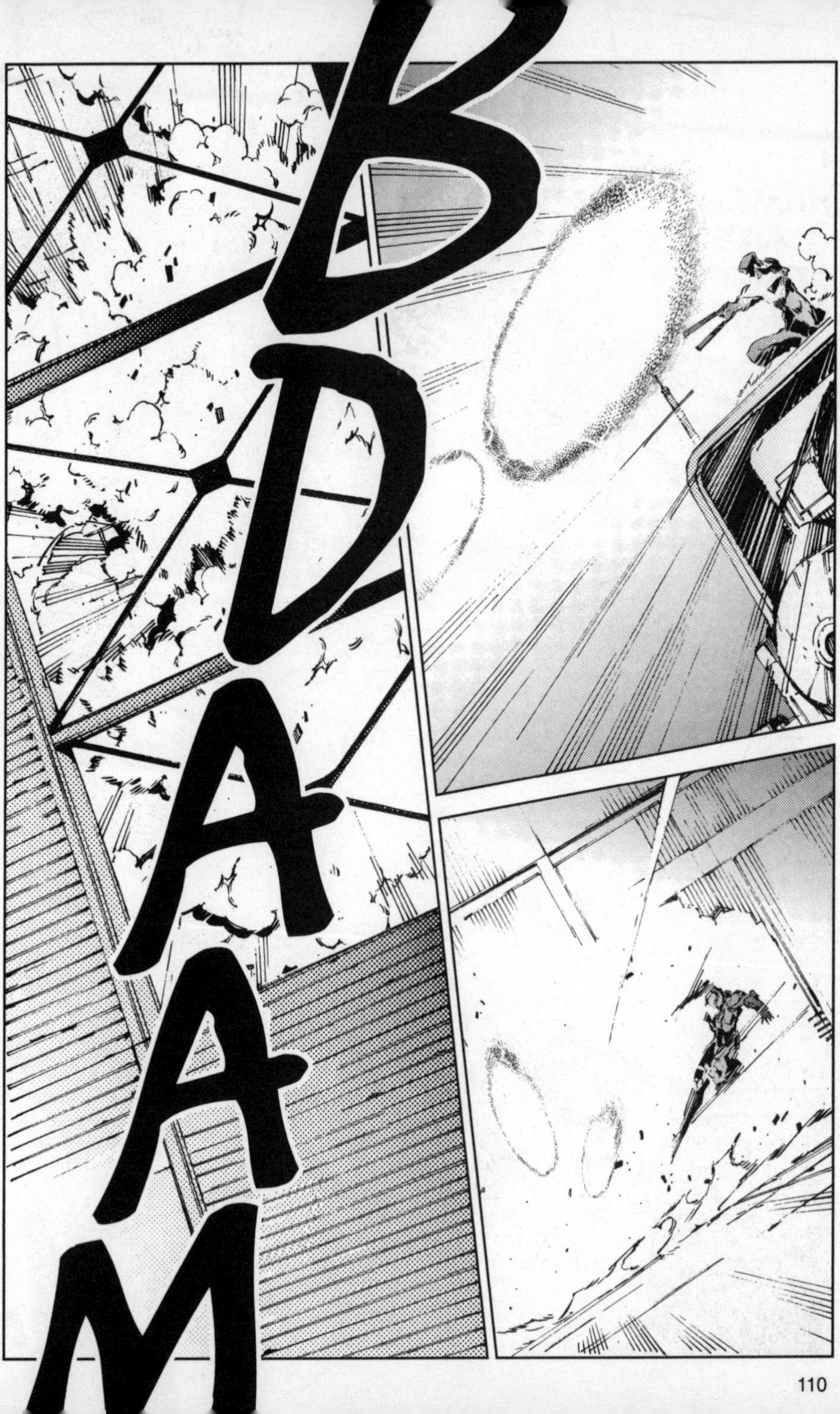
BDAAAM

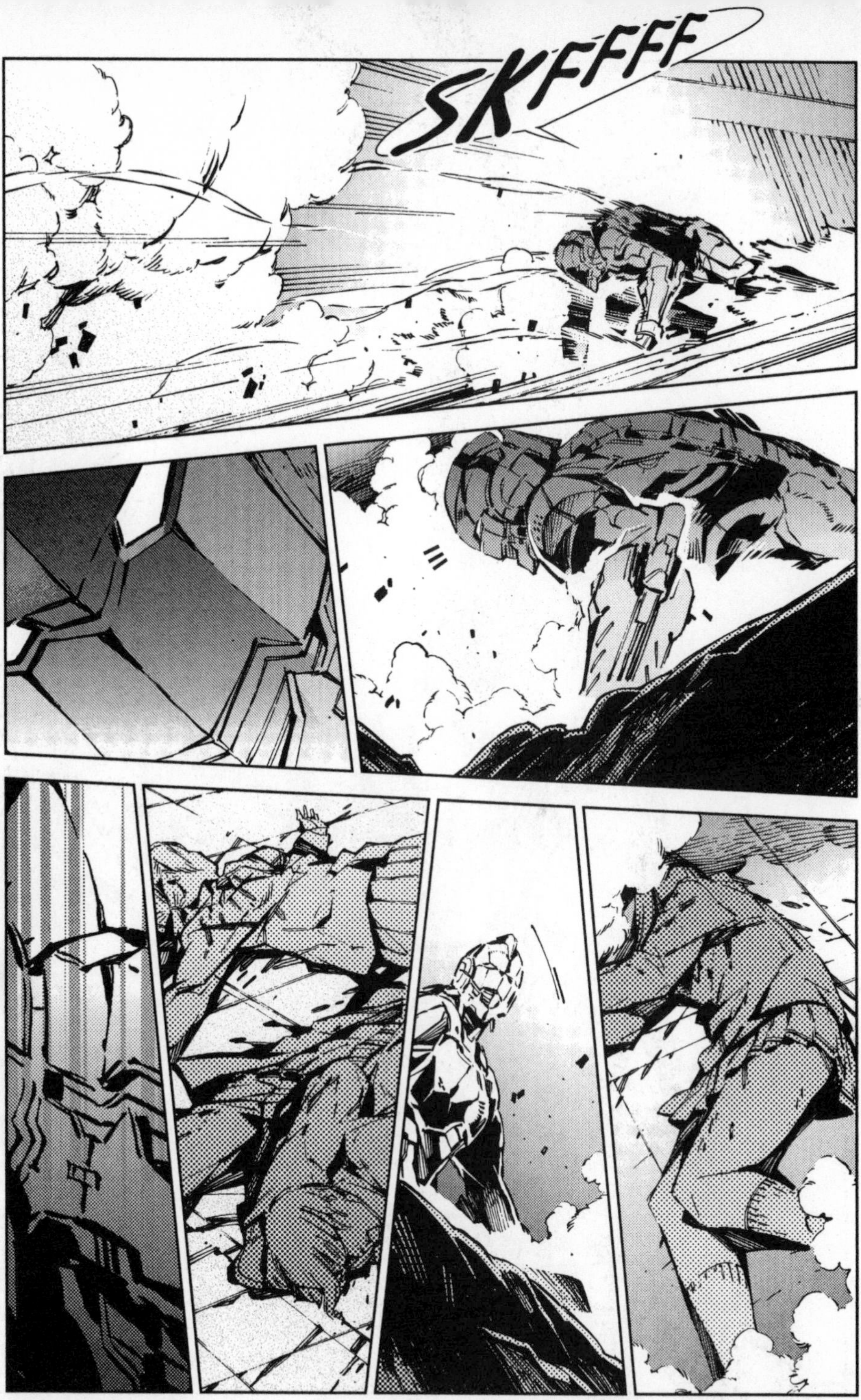
SKFFFF

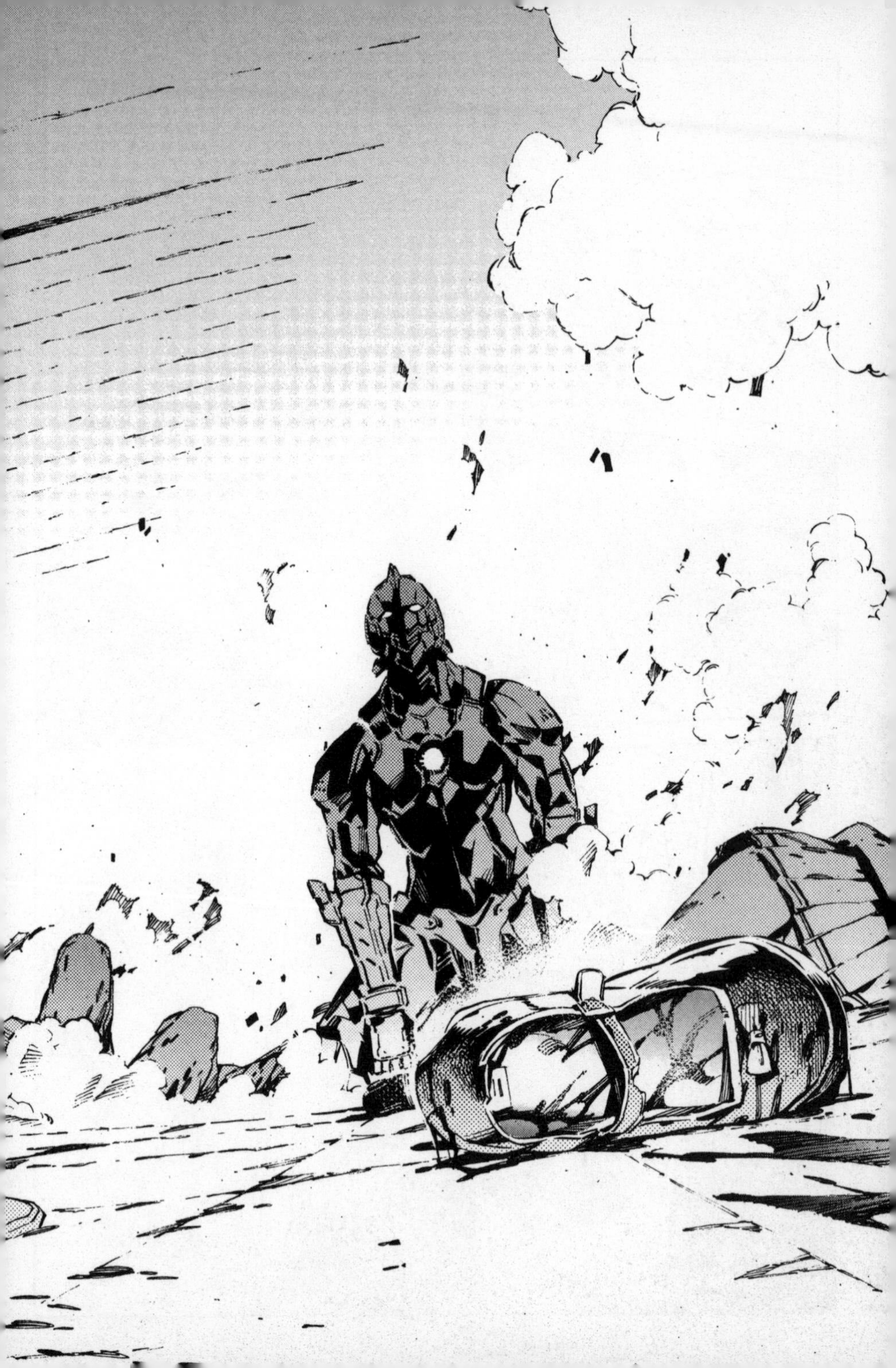

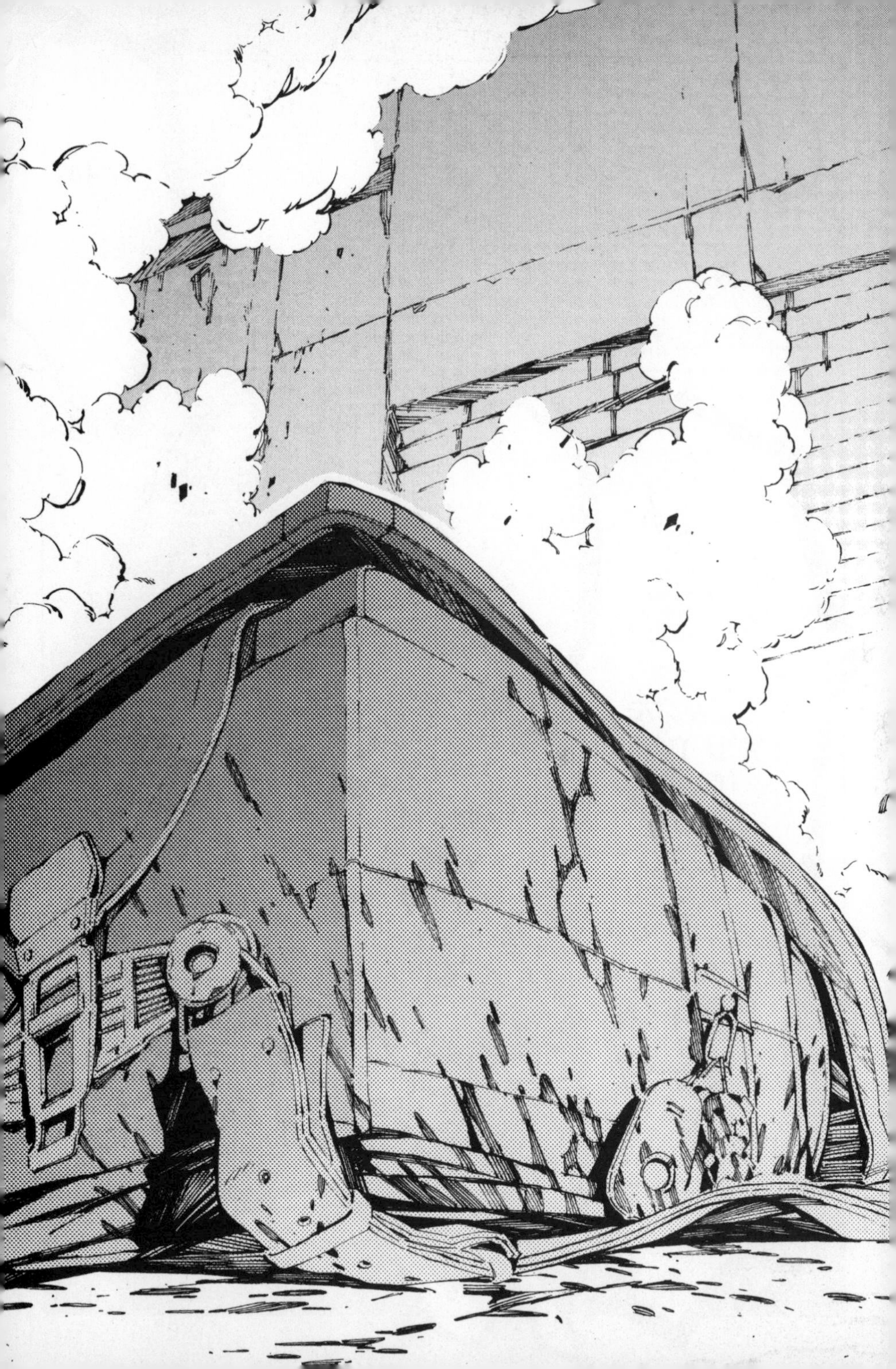

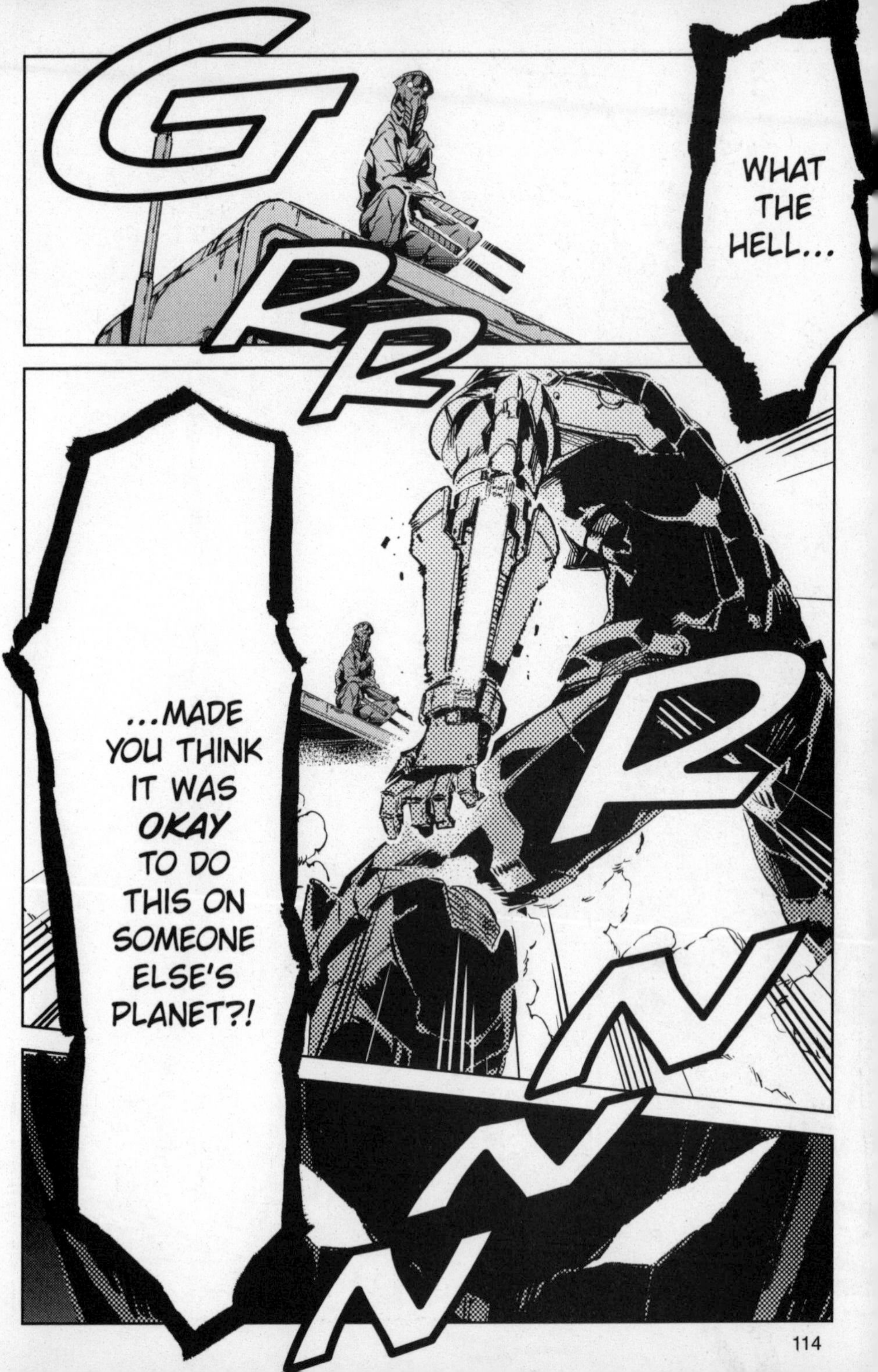
GRRR
WHAT THE HELL...
...MADE YOU THINK IT WAS OKAY TO DO THIS ON SOMEONE ELSE'S PLANET?!
NNN

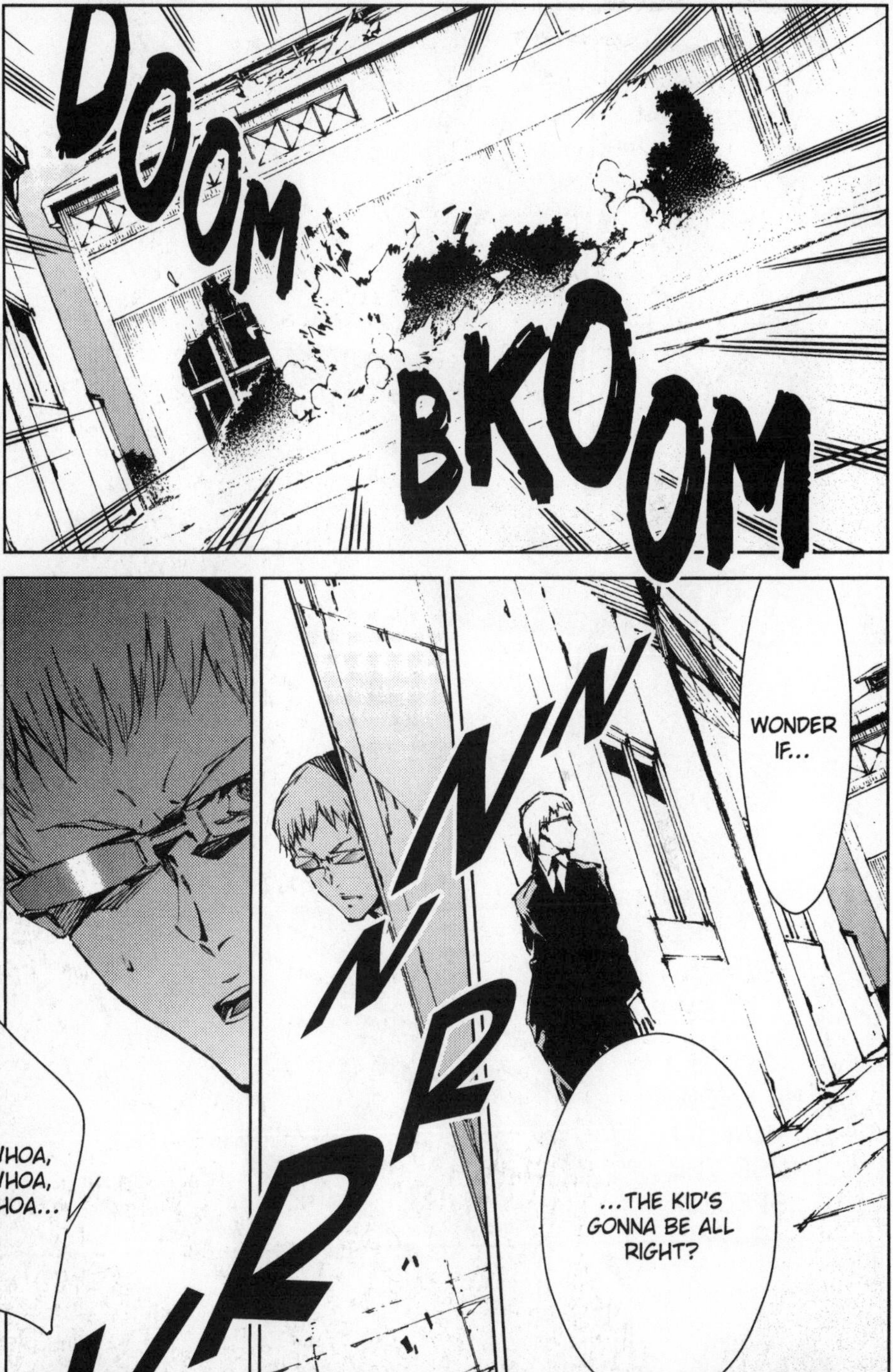
DOOM
BKOOM
WONDER IF...
...THE KID'S GONNA BE ALL RIGHT?
VRRNNNN
WHOA, WHOA, WHOA...

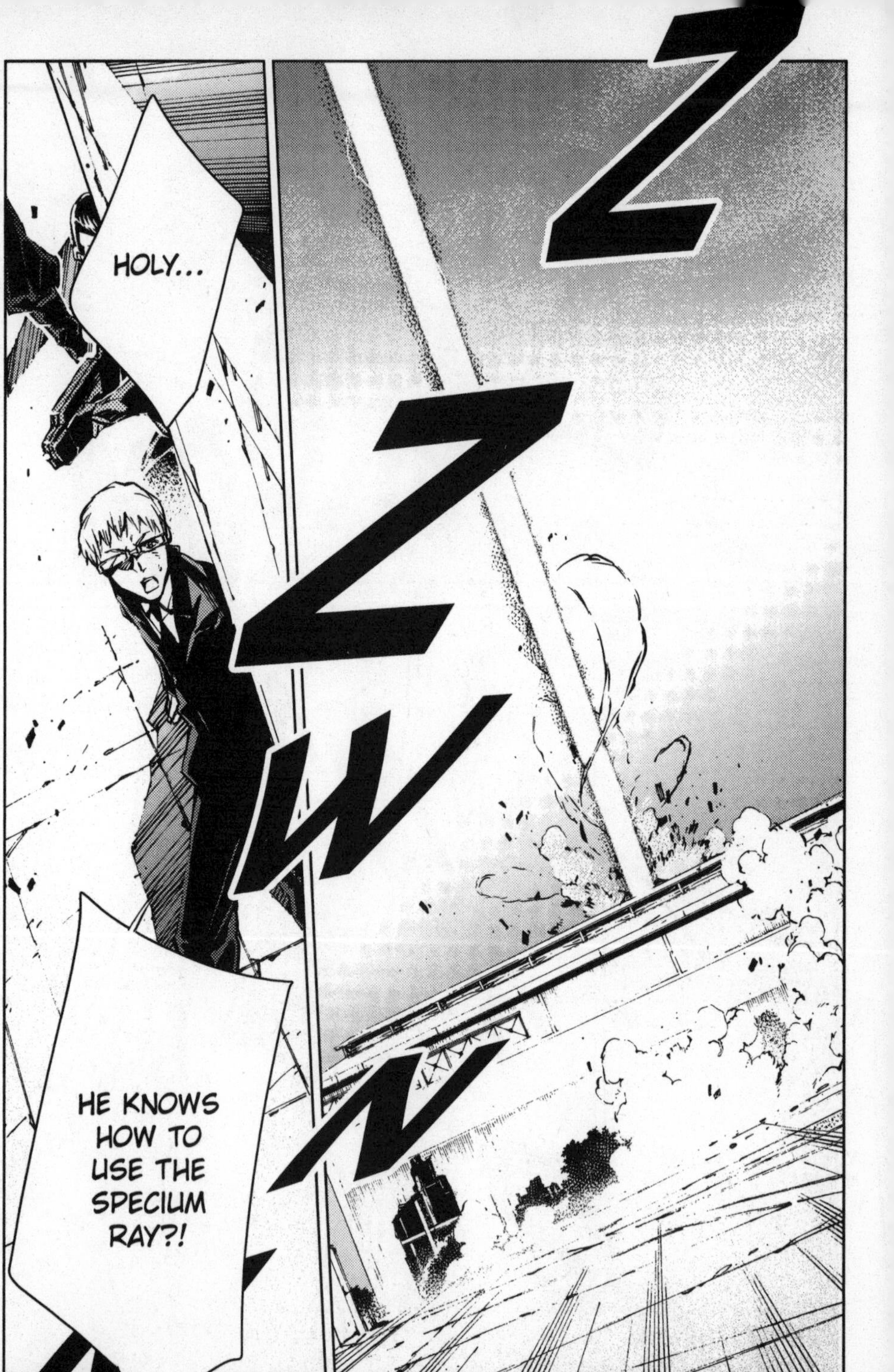
HOLY...
HE KNOWS HOW TO USE THE SPECIUM RAY?!
ZZZWN

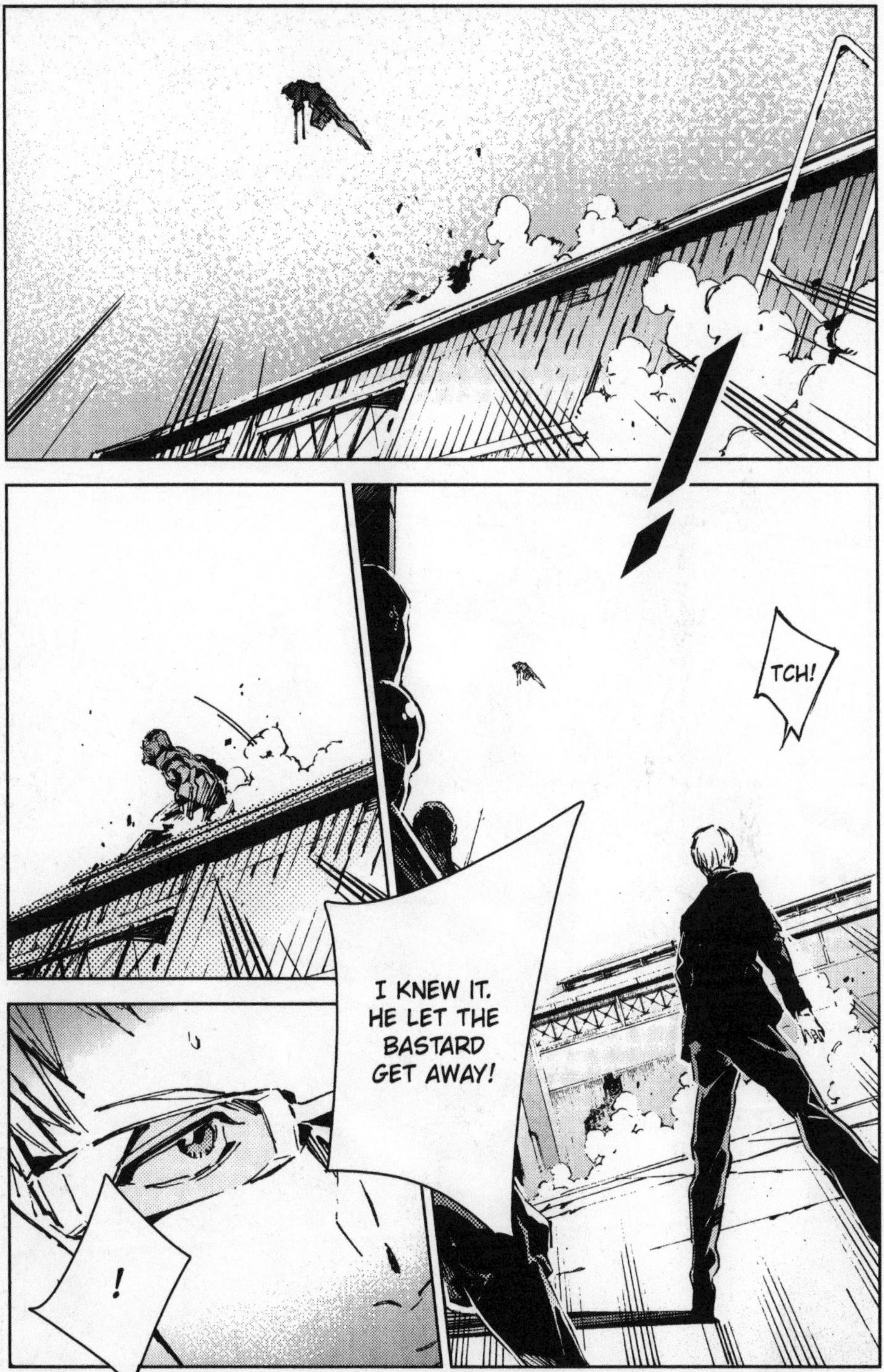
TCH!
I KNEW IT. HE LET THE BASTARD GET AWAY!
!

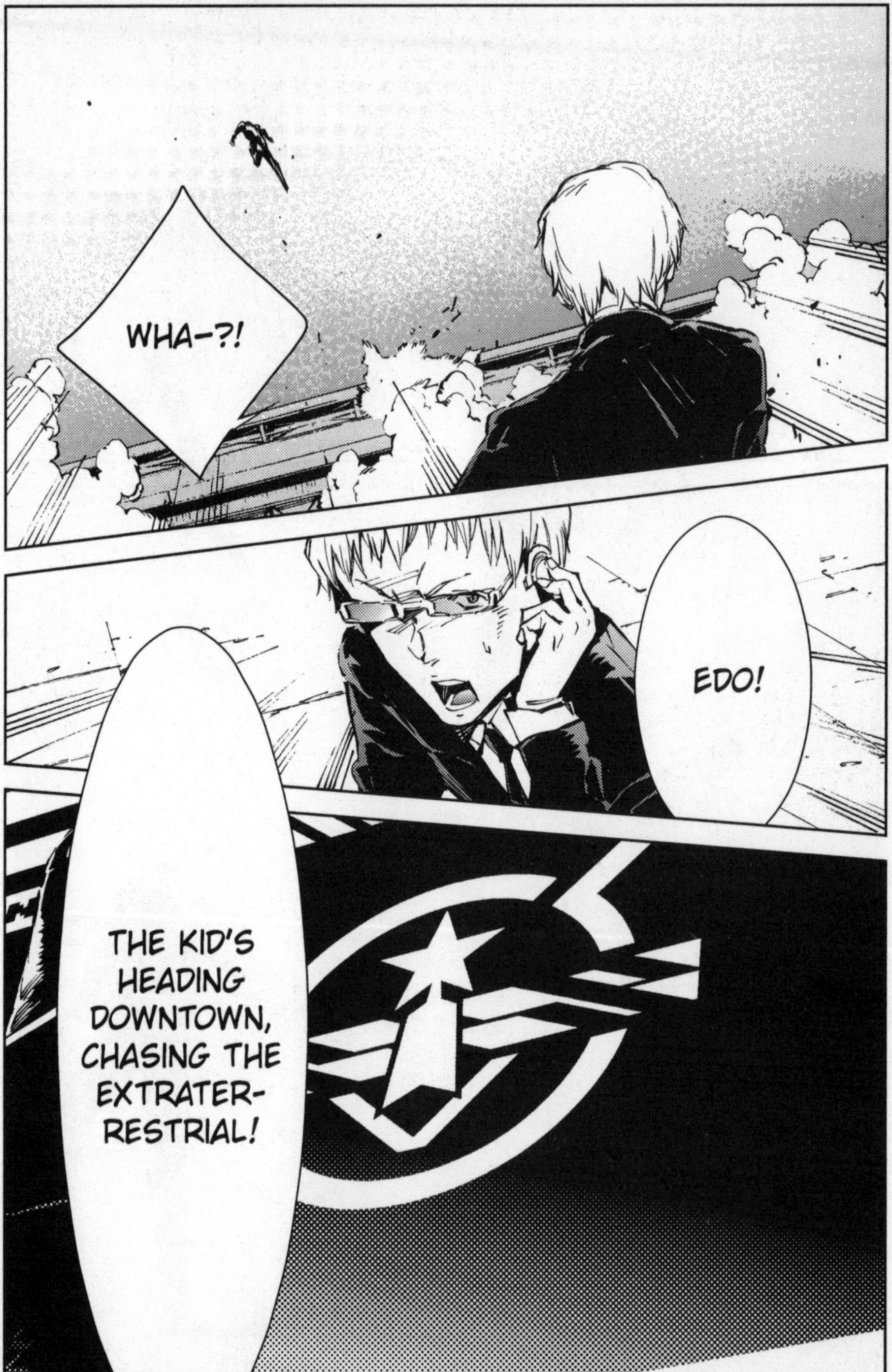
WHA-?!
EDO!
THE KID'S HEADING DOWNTOWN, CHASING THE EXTRATER-RESTRIAL!

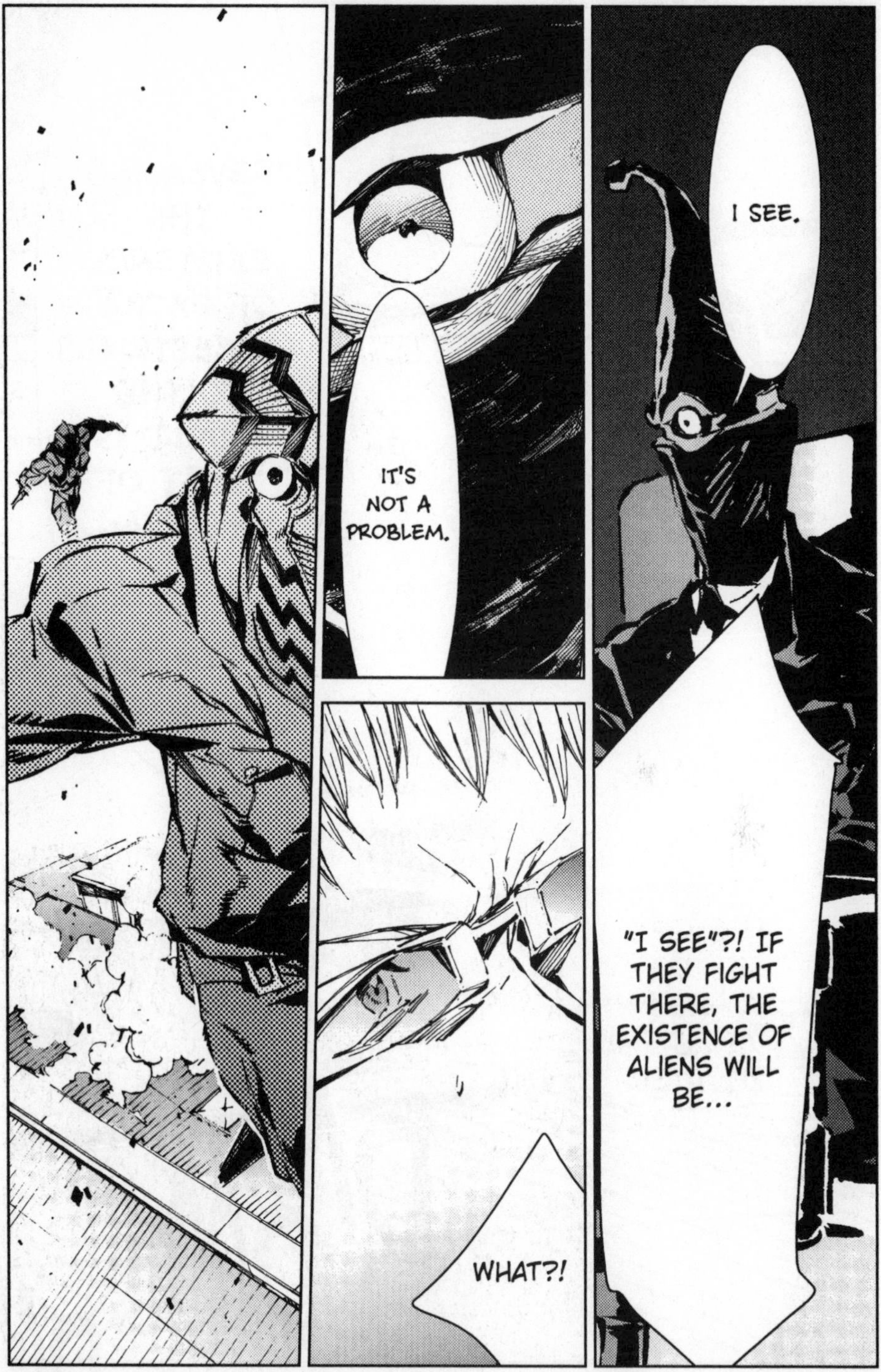
I SEE.
IT'S NOT A PROBLEM.
"I SEE"?! IF THEY FIGHT THERE, THE EXISTENCE OF ALIENS WILL BE...
WHAT?!

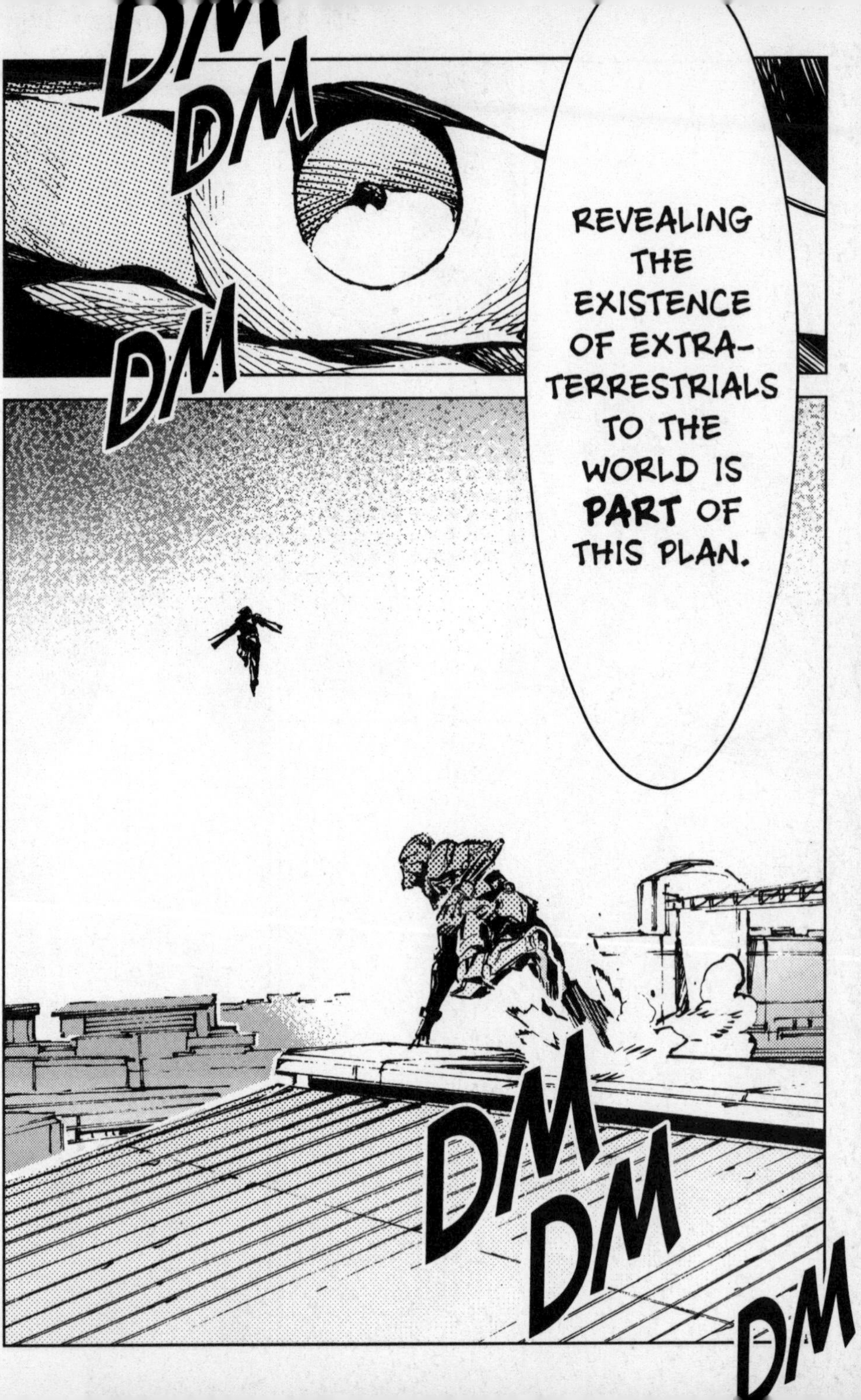
DM
DM
DM
REVEALING THE EXISTENCE OF EXTRA-TERRESTRIALS TO THE WORLD IS **PART** OF THIS PLAN.
DM
DM
DM

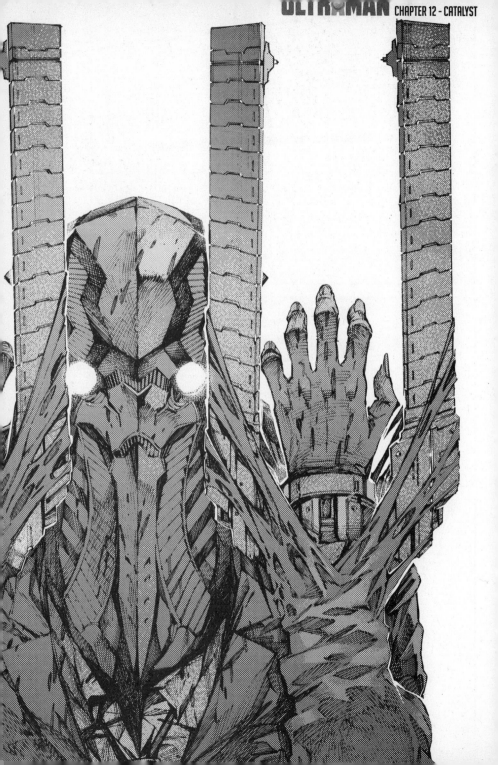

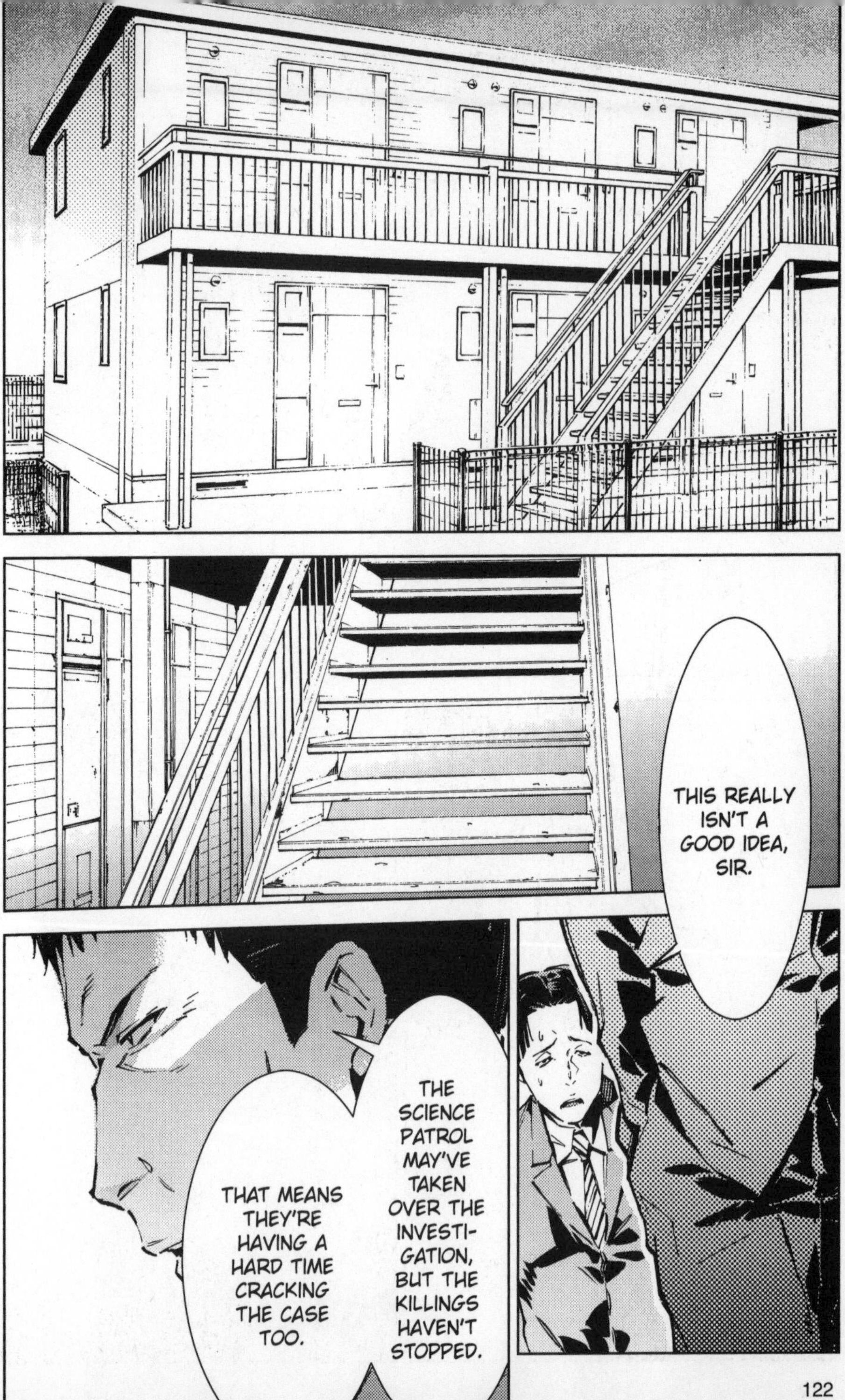
THIS REALLY ISN'T A GOOD IDEA, SIR.
THE SCIENCE PATROL MAY'VE TAKEN OVER THE INVESTI-GATION, BUT THE KILLINGS HAVEN'T STOPPED.
THAT MEANS THEY'RE HAVING A HARD TIME CRACKING THE CASE TOO.

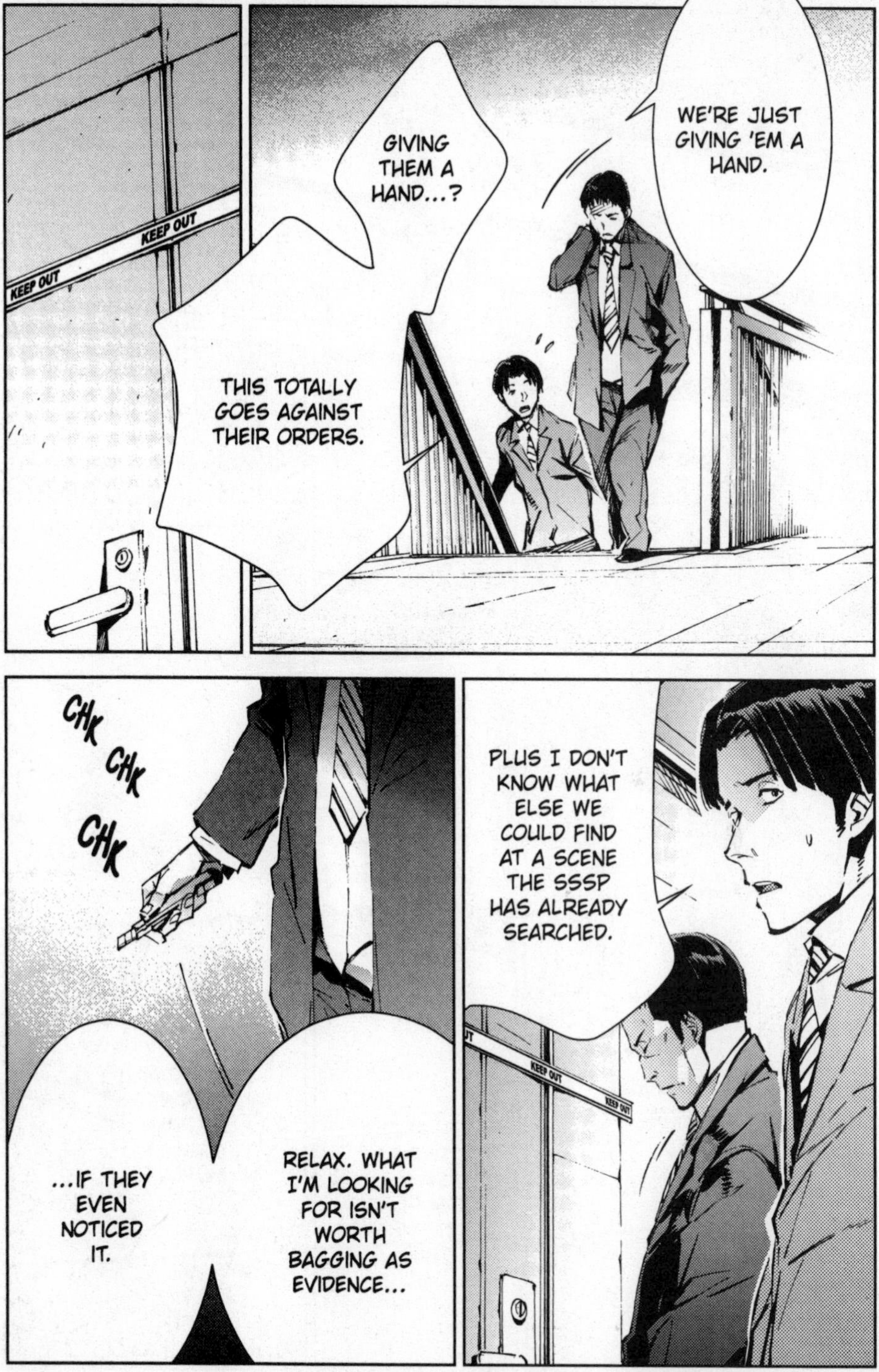
WE'RE JUST GIVING 'EM A HAND.
GIVING THEM A HAND...?
THIS TOTALLY GOES AGAINST THEIR ORDERS.
KEEP OUT
KEEP OUT
PLUS I DON'T KNOW WHAT ELSE WE COULD FIND AT A SCENE THE SSSP HAS ALREADY SEARCHED.
KEEP OUT
KEEP OUT
CHK CHK CHK
RELAX. WHAT I'M LOOKING FOR ISN'T WORTH BAGGING AS EVIDENCE...
...IF THEY EVEN NOTICED IT.

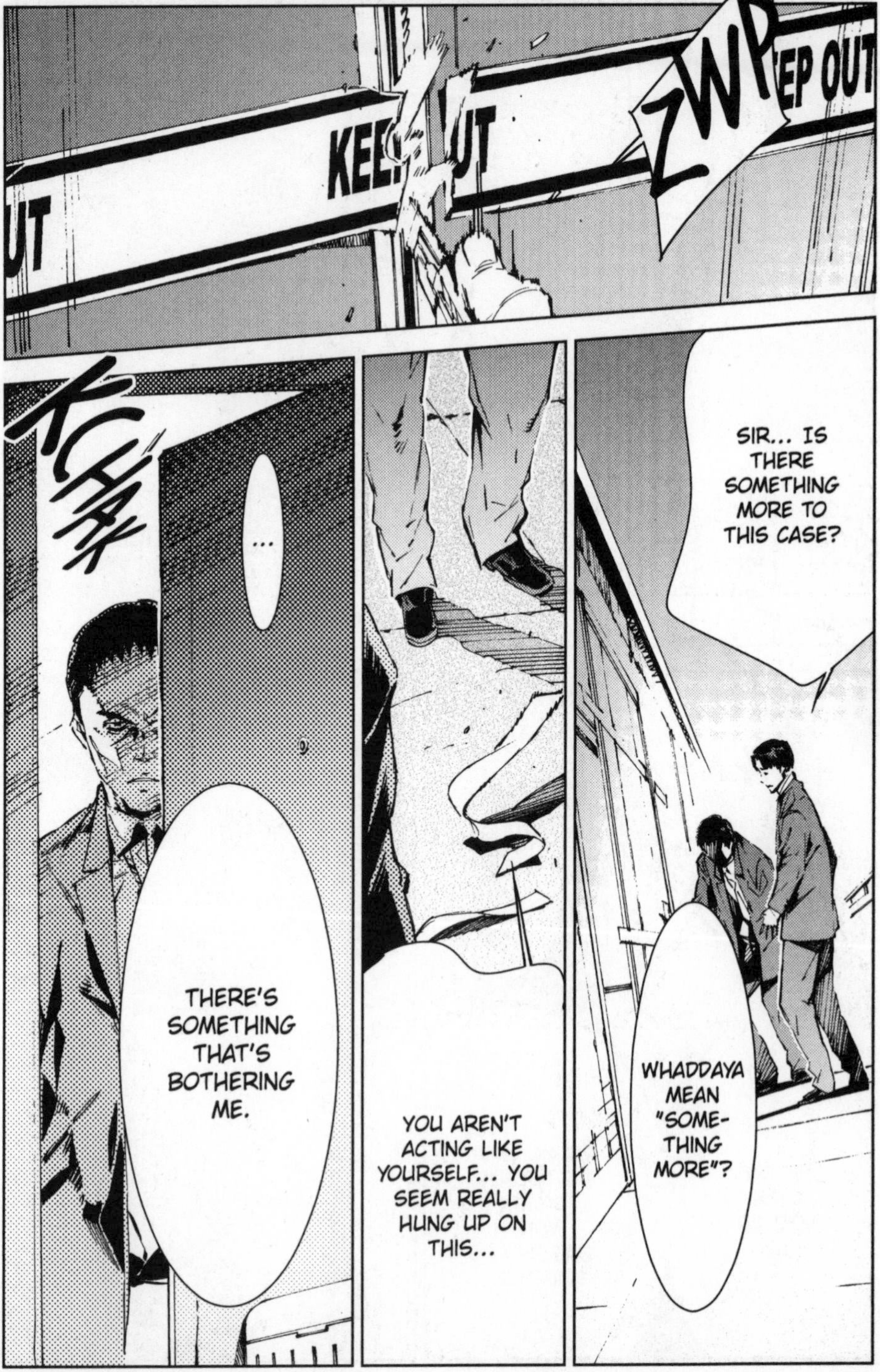
ZWP
EP OUT
KEE UT
UT
SIR... IS THERE SOMETHING MORE TO THIS CASE?
WHADDAYA MEAN "SOME-THING MORE"?
YOU AREN'T ACTING LIKE YOURSELF... YOU SEEM REALLY HUNG UP ON THIS...
K'CHAK
...
THERE'S SOMETHING THAT'S BOTHERING ME.

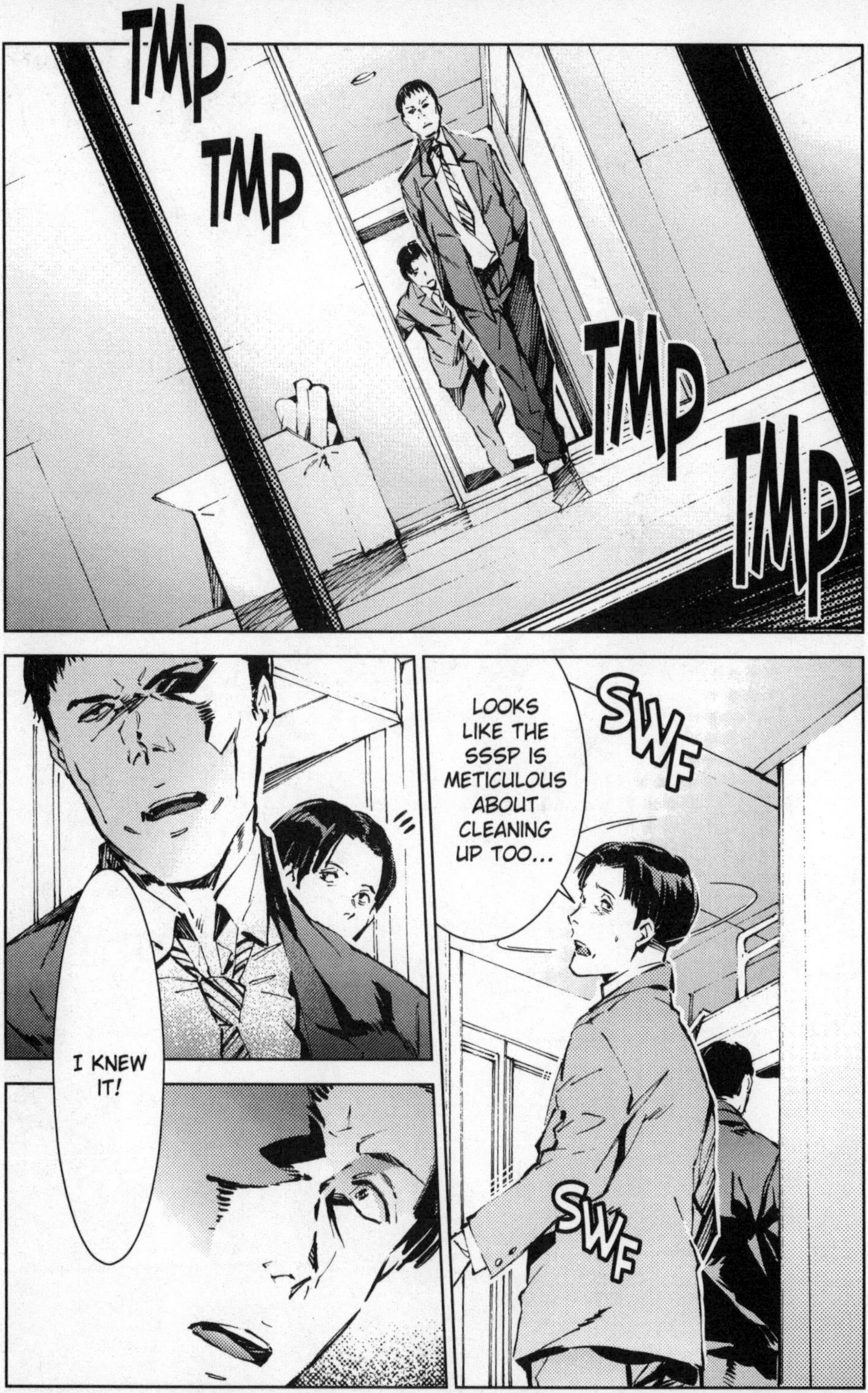
TMP
TMP
TMP
TMP
LOOKS LIKE THE SSSP IS METICULOUS ABOUT CLEANING UP TOO...
SWF
SWF
SWF
I KNEW IT!

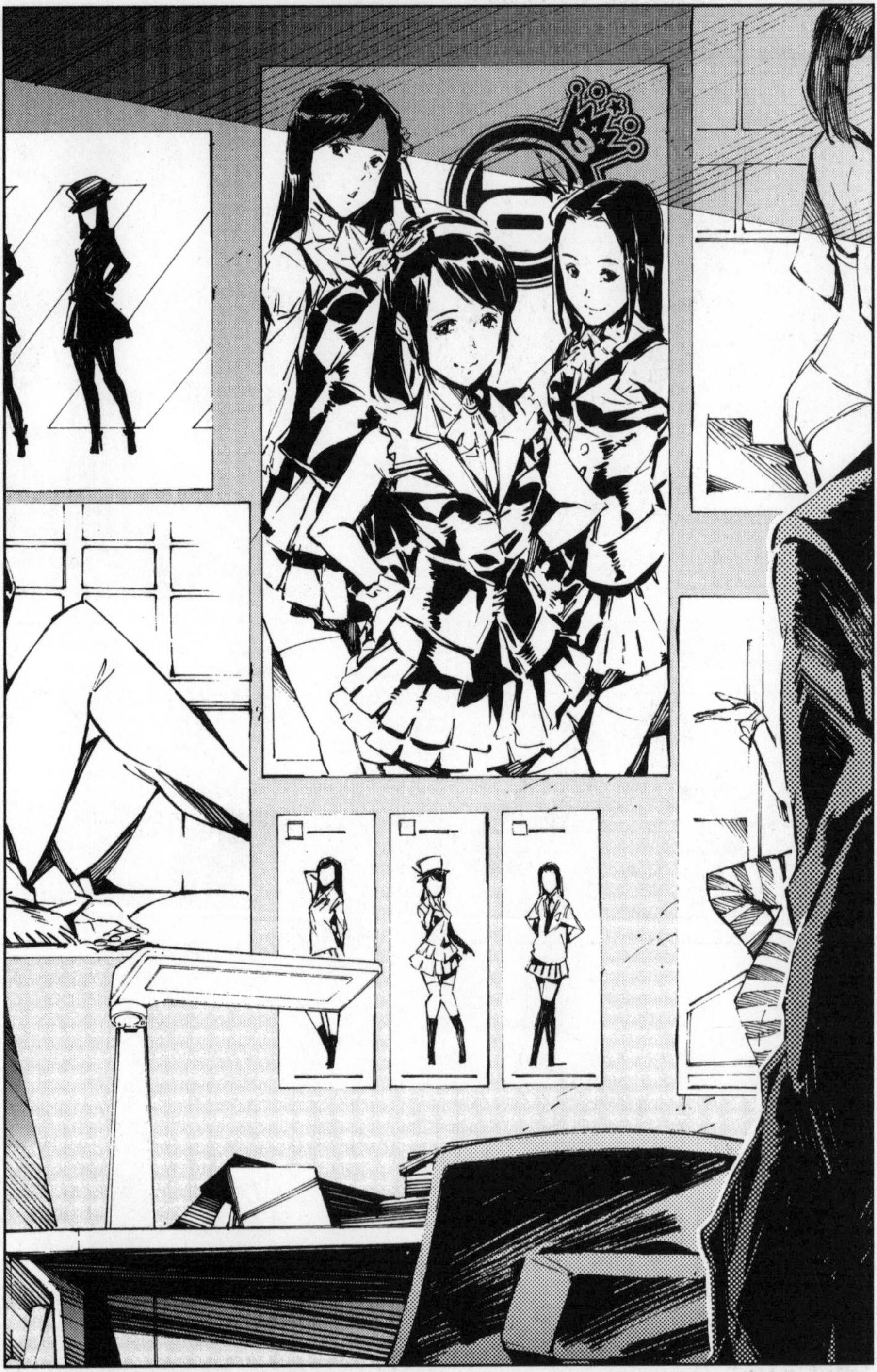

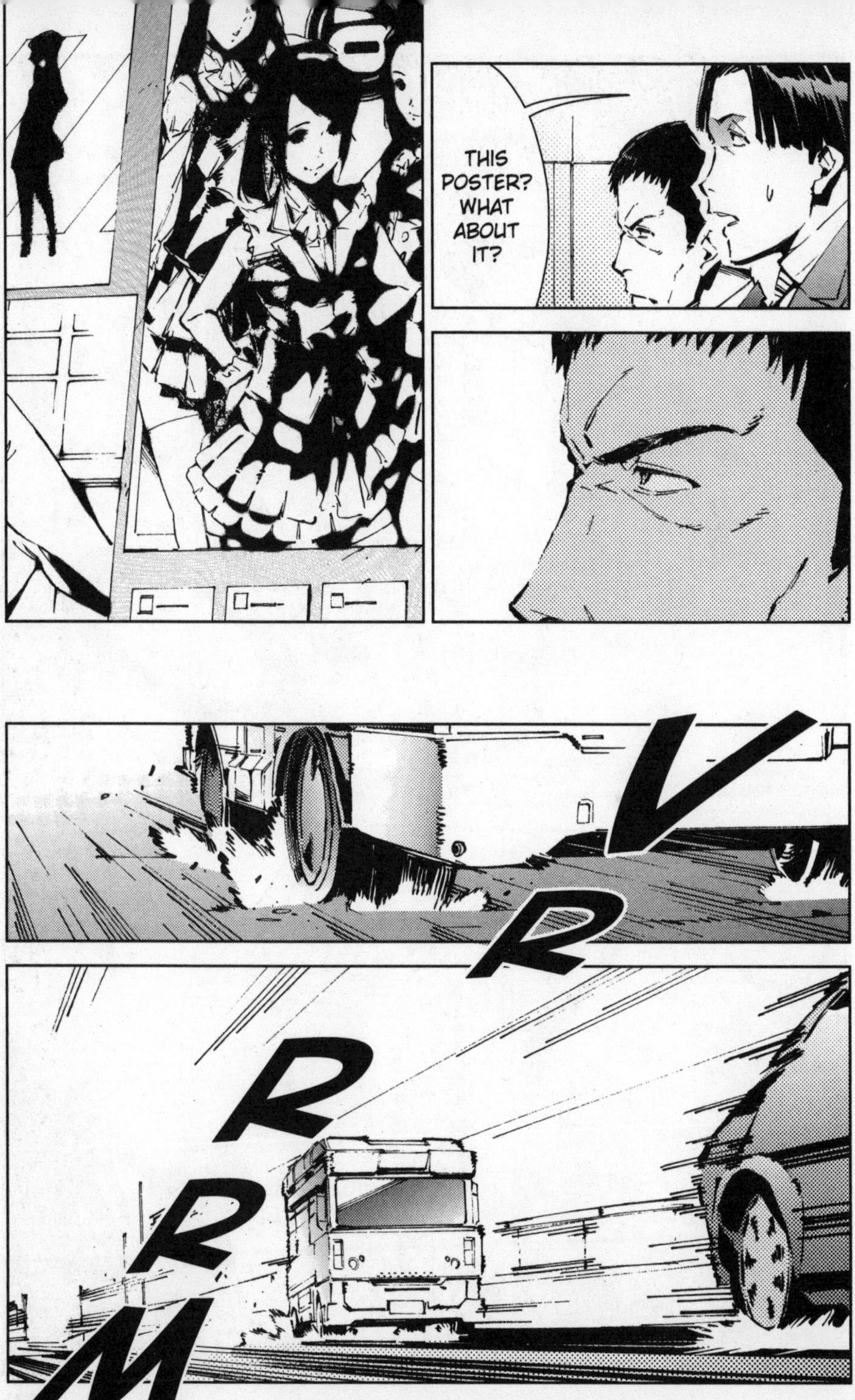
THIS POSTER? WHAT ABOUT IT?
VRRRM

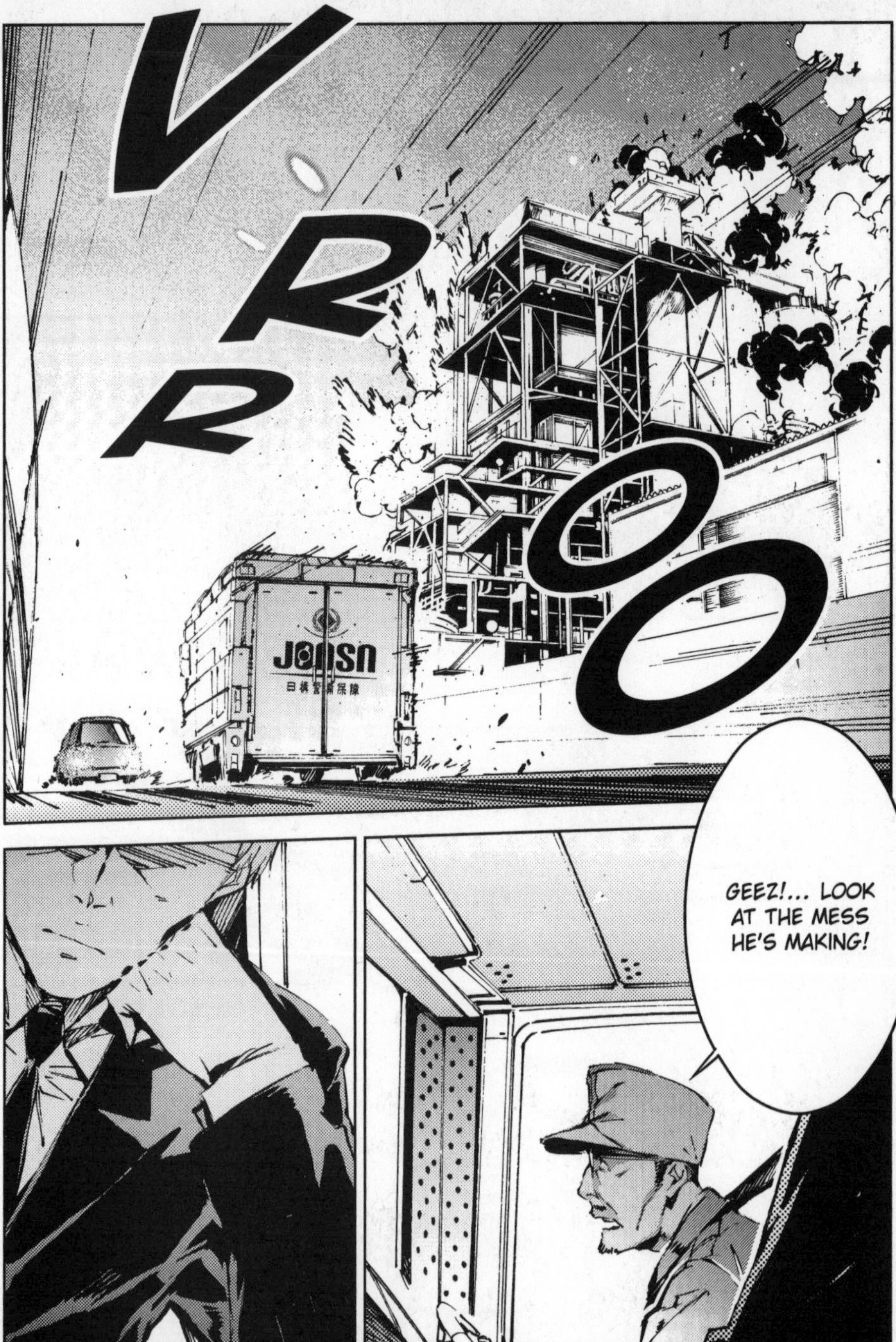
VRROO
GEEZ!... LOOK AT THE MESS HE'S MAKING!

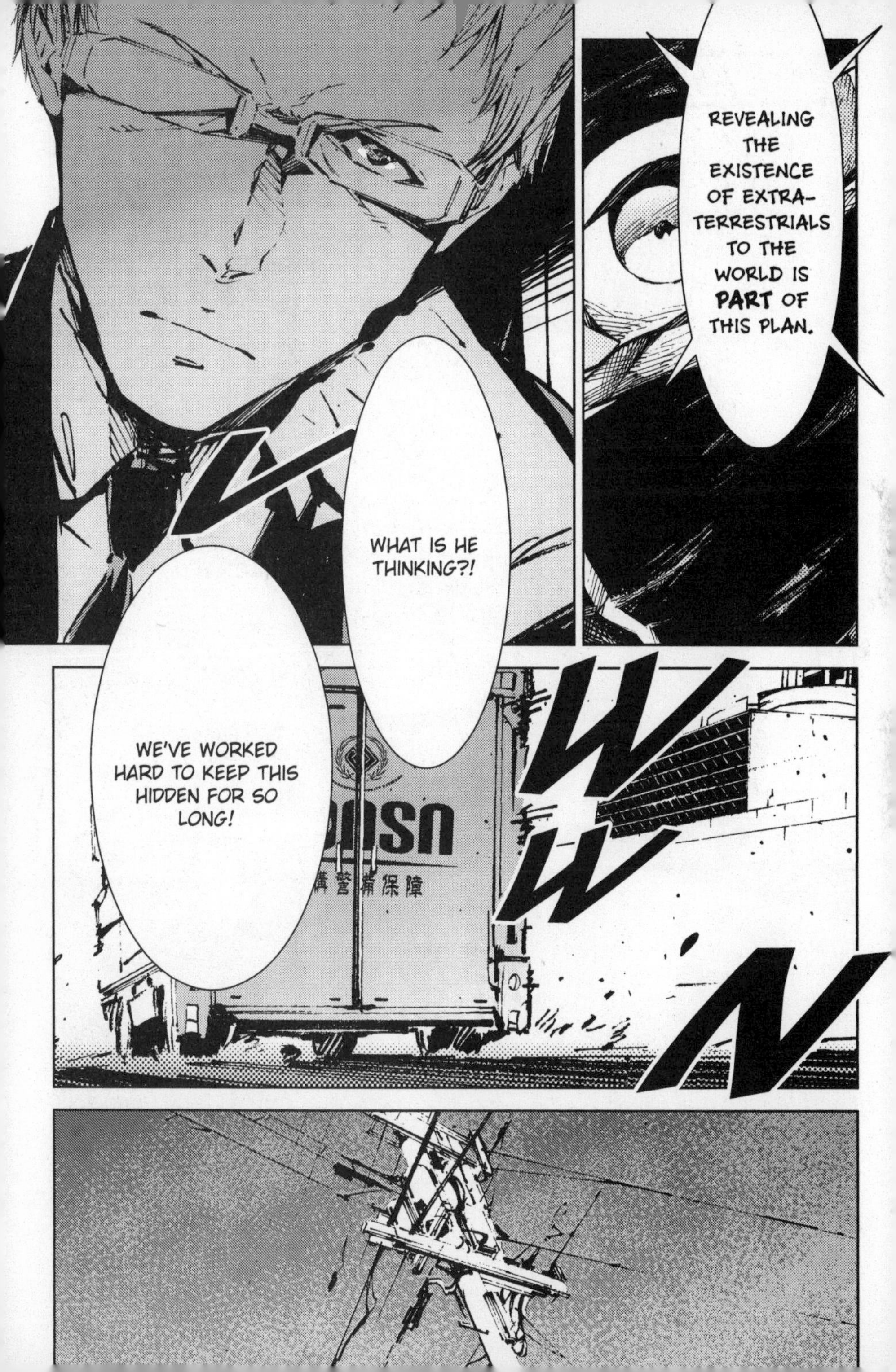
REVEALING THE EXISTENCE OF EXTRA-TERRESTRIALS TO THE WORLD IS **PART** OF THIS PLAN.
WHAT IS HE THINKING?!
WE'VE WORKED HARD TO KEEP THIS HIDDEN FOR SO LONG!

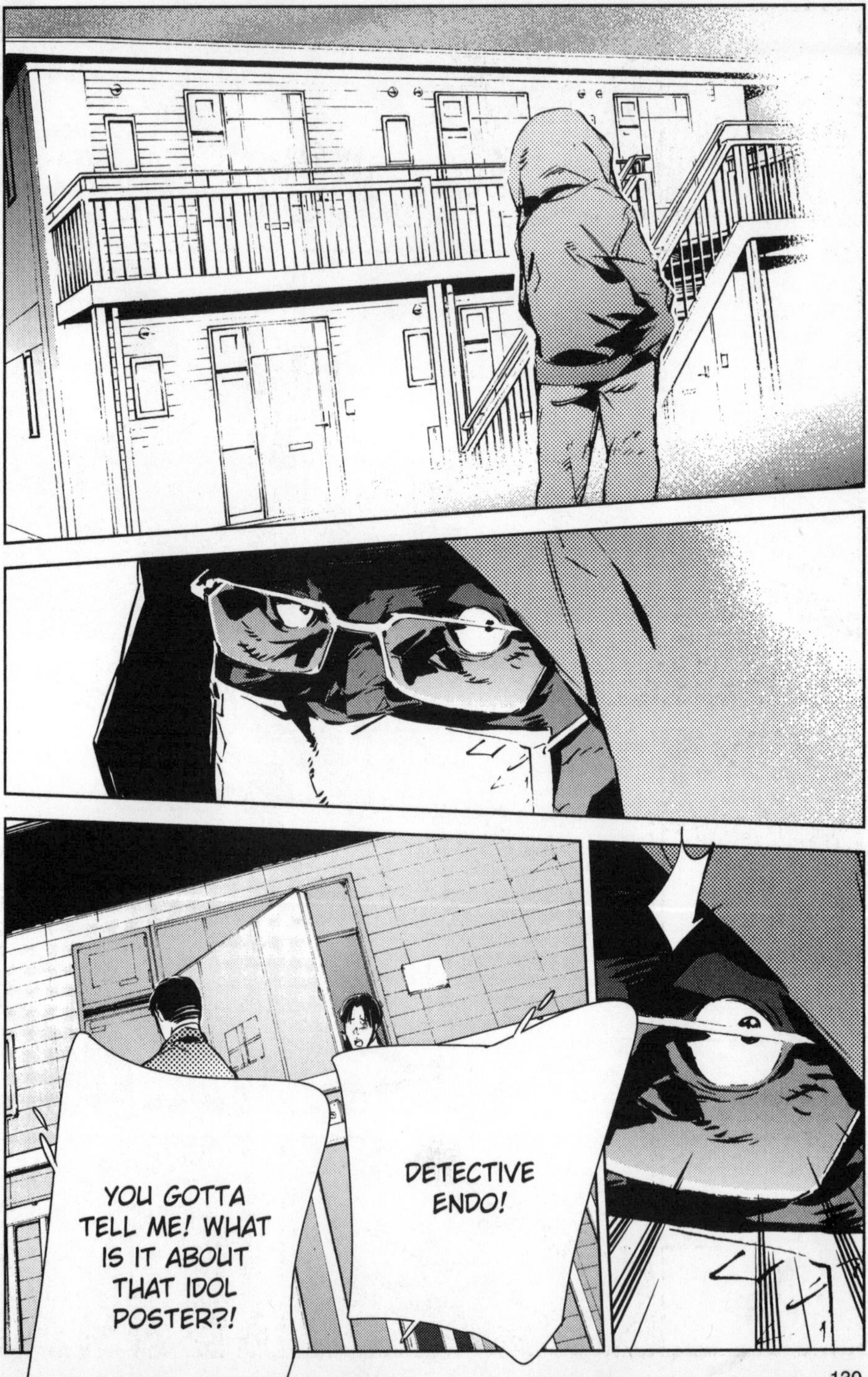
DETECTIVE ENDO!
YOU GOTTA TELL ME! WHAT IS IT ABOUT THAT IDOL POSTER?!

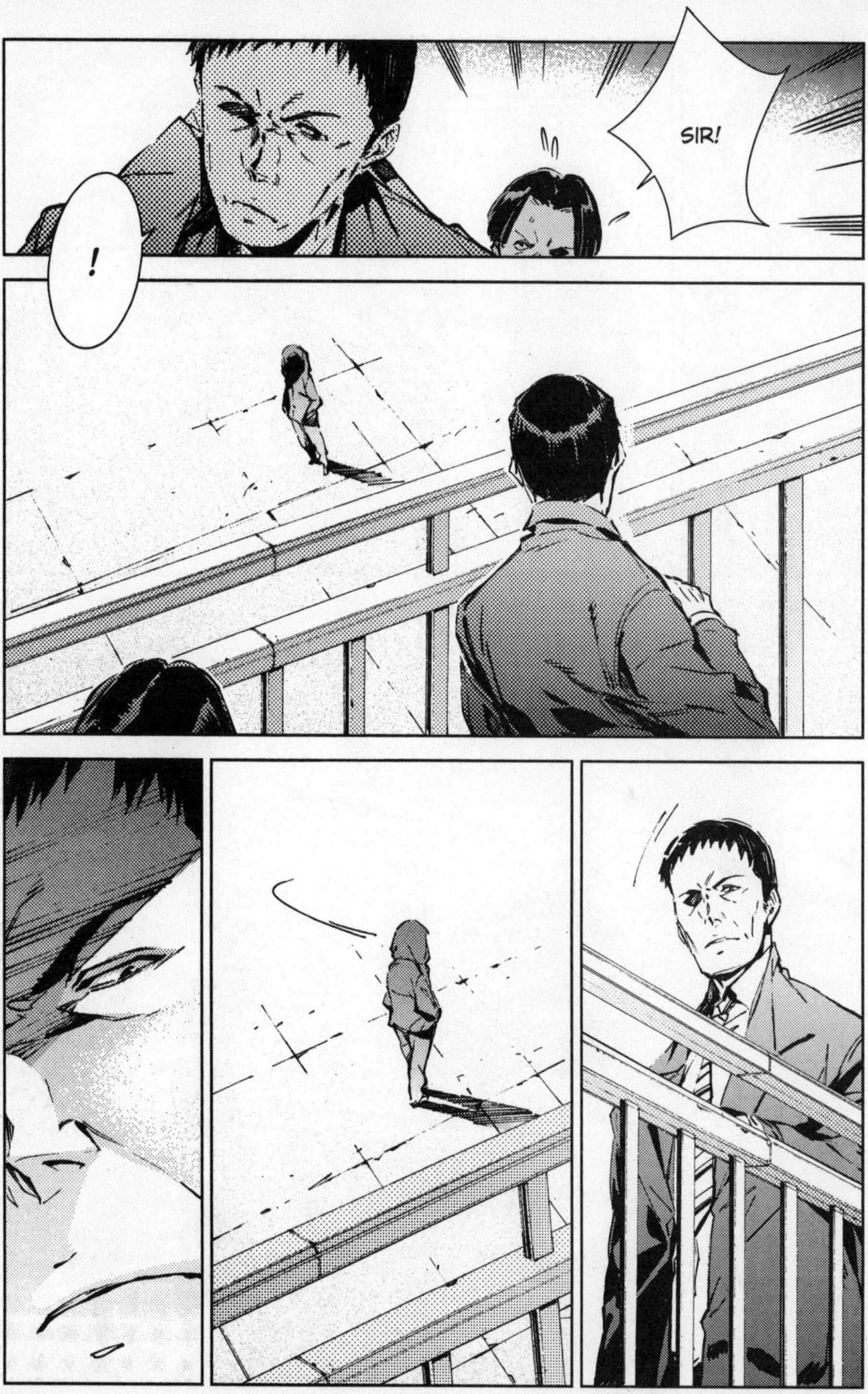
SIR!
!

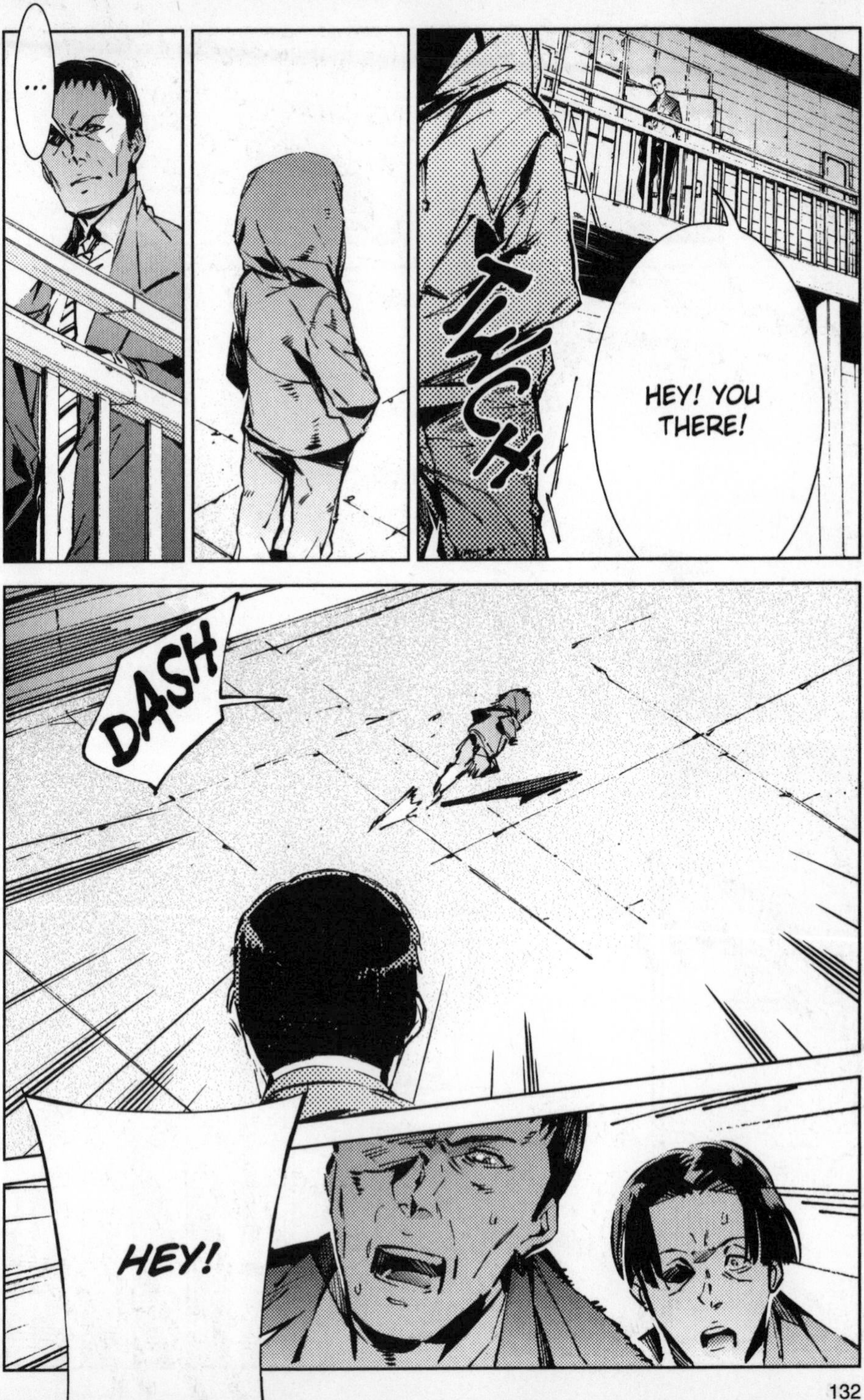
...
TWITCH
HEY! YOU THERE!
DASH
HEY!

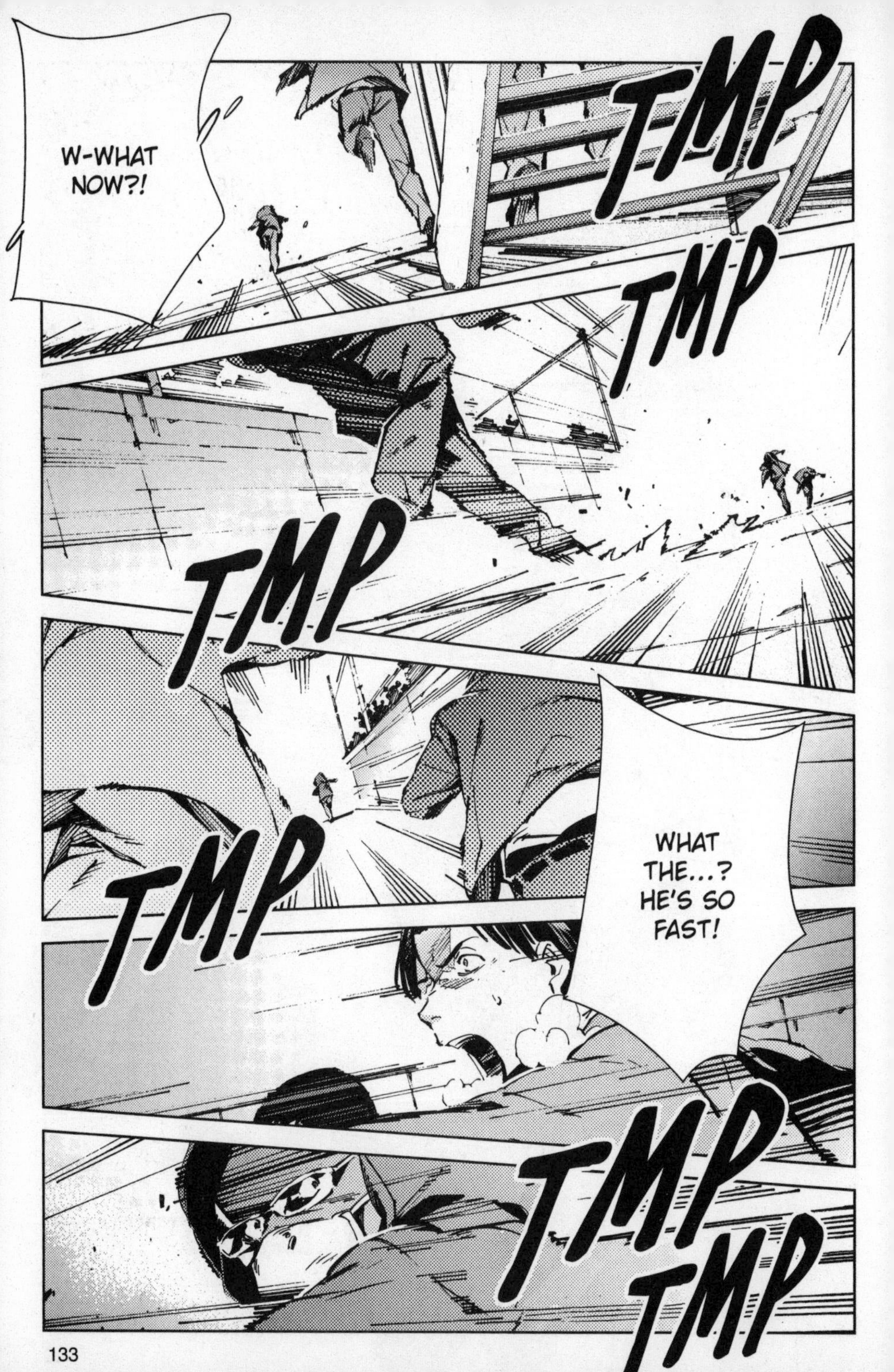

TMP
TMP
W-WHAT NOW?!
TMP
TMP
WHAT THE...? HE'S SO FAST!
TMP
TMP

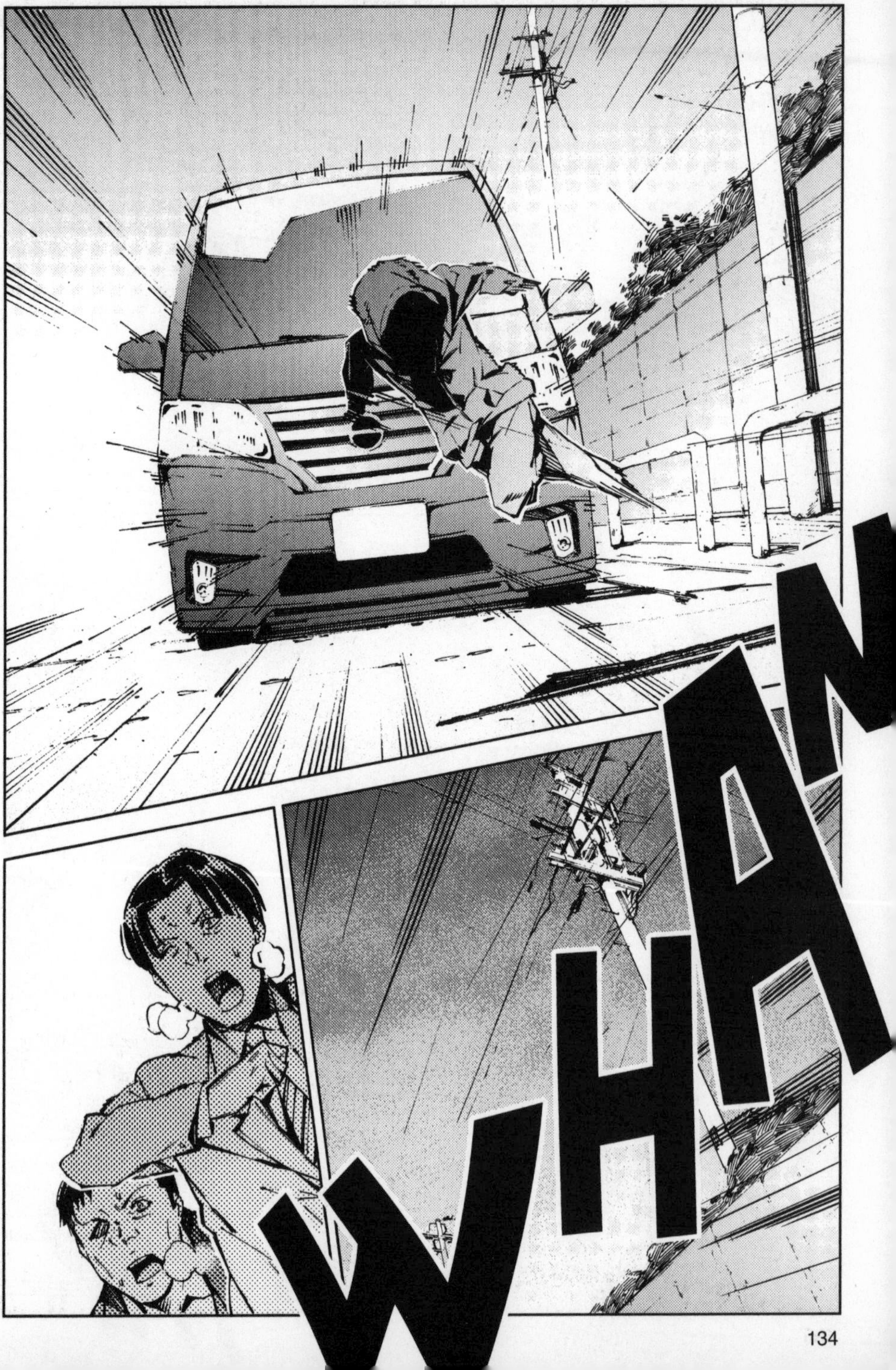
WHAM

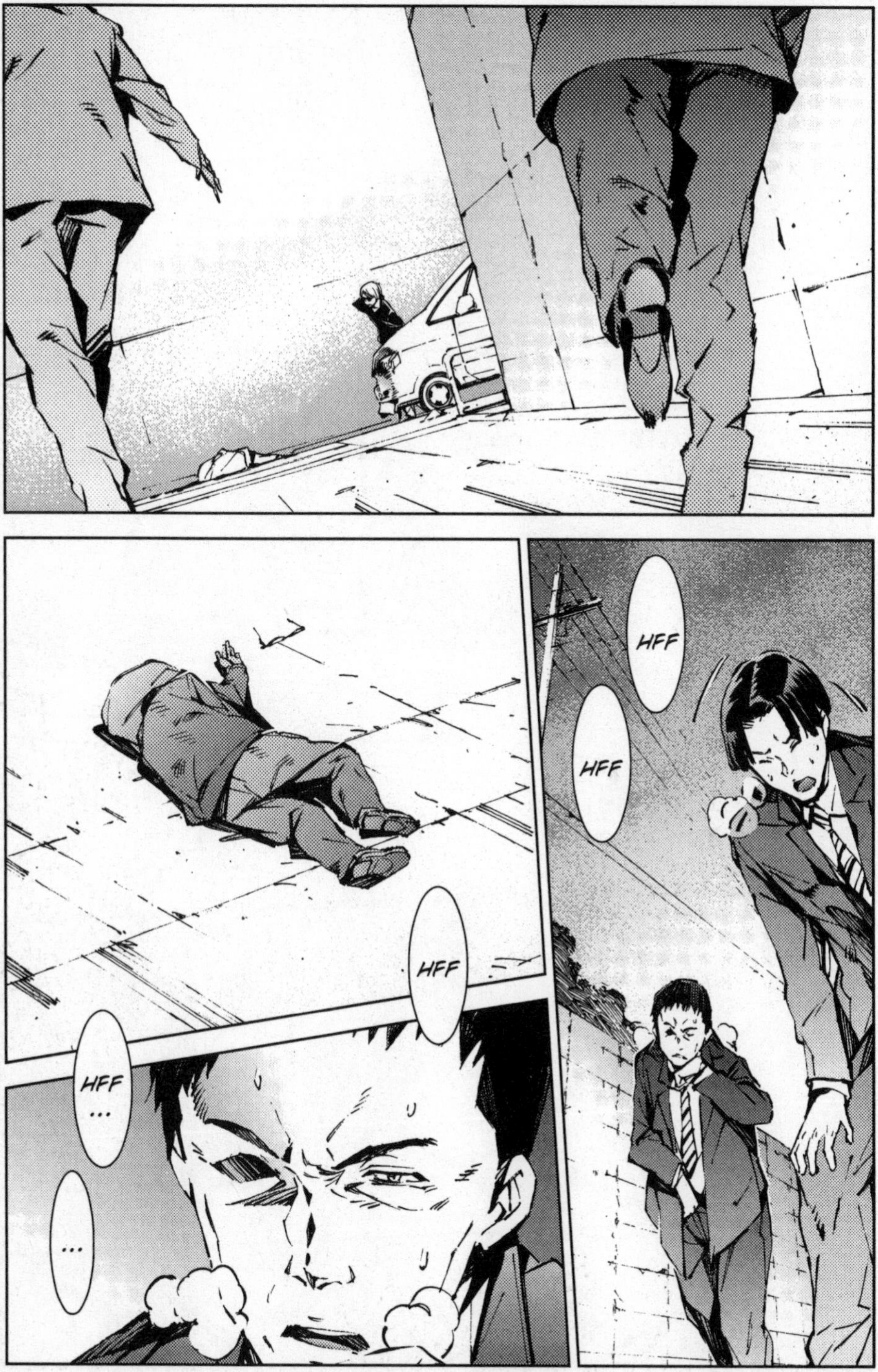
HFF
HFF
HFF
HFF ...
...

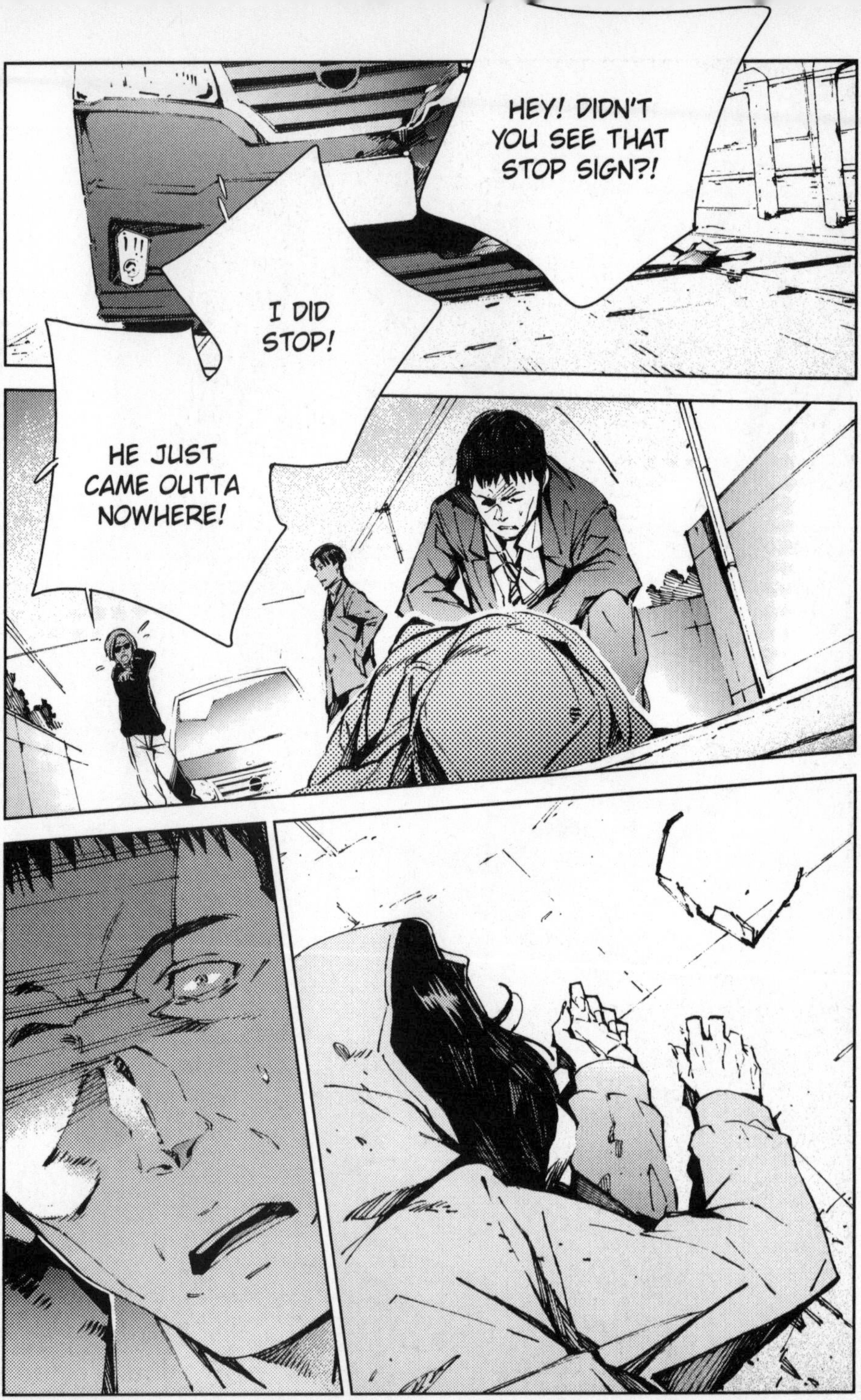
HEY! DIDN'T YOU SEE THAT STOP SIGN?!
I DID STOP!
HE JUST CAME OUTTA NOWHERE!

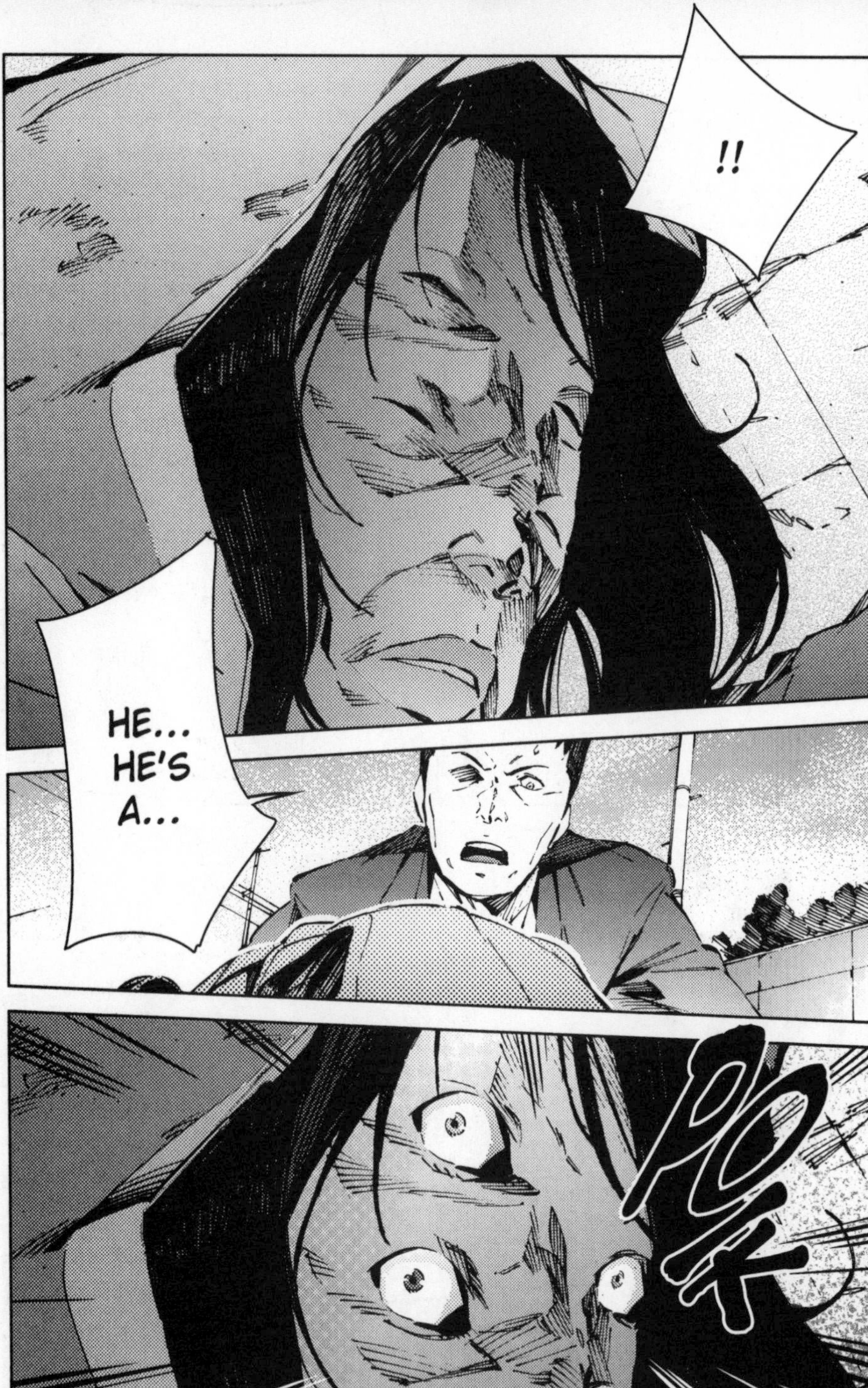
!!
HE... HE'S A...
POK

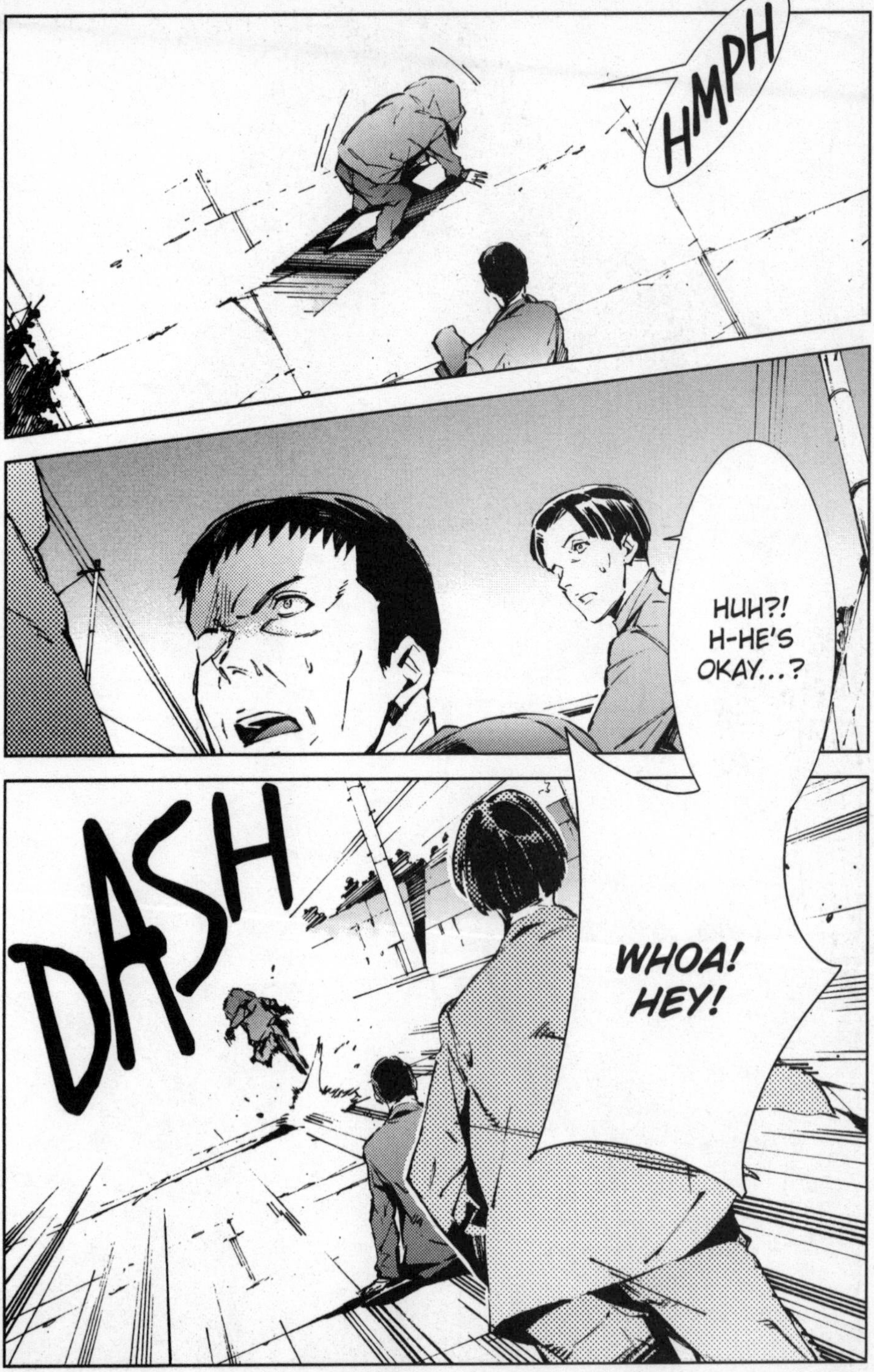
HMPH
HUH?! H-HE'S OKAY...?
DASH
WHOA! HEY!

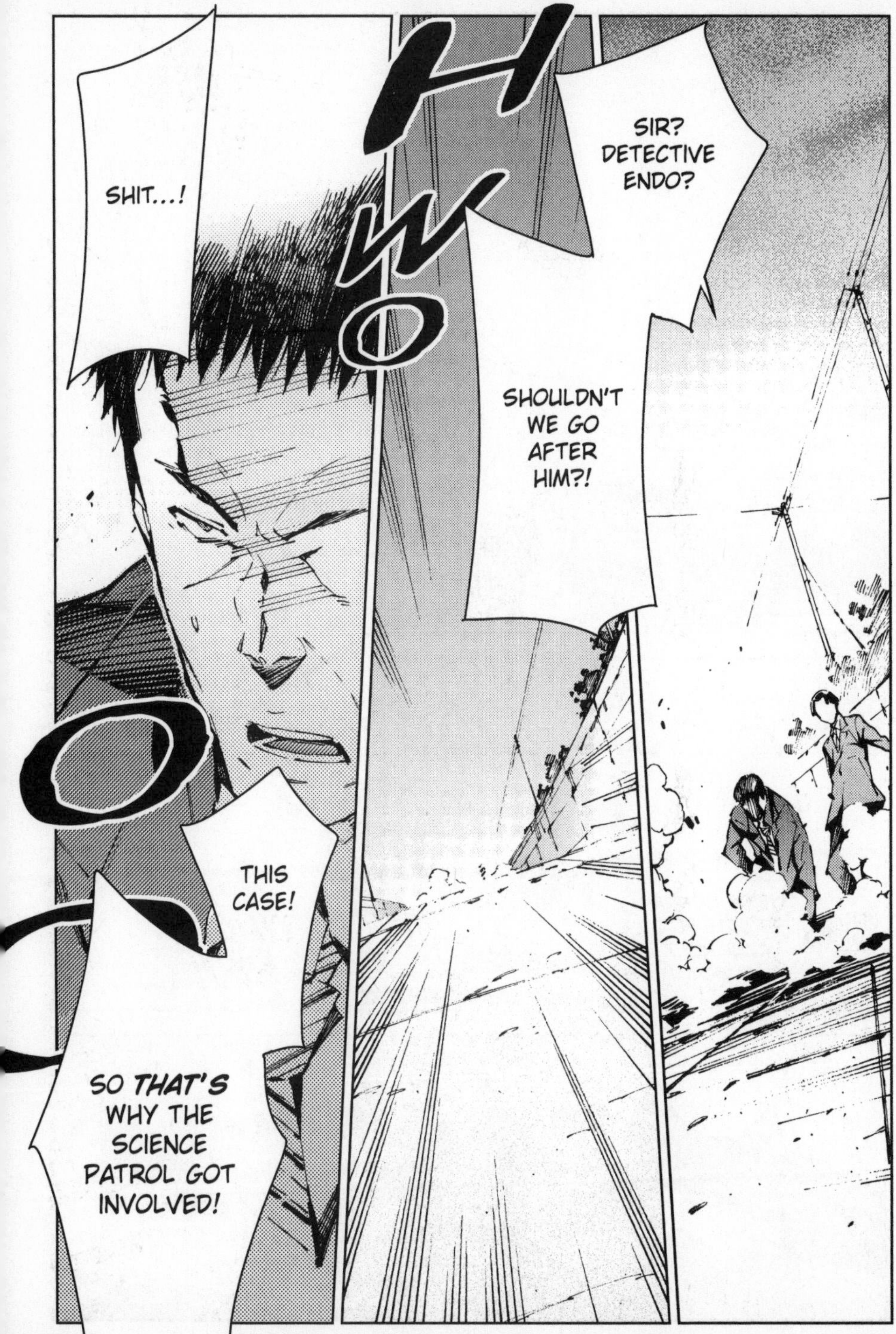
SIR? DETECTIVE ENDO?
SHOULDN'T WE GO AFTER HIM?!
SHIT...!
THIS CASE!
SO THAT'S WHY THE SCIENCE PATROL GOT INVOLVED!

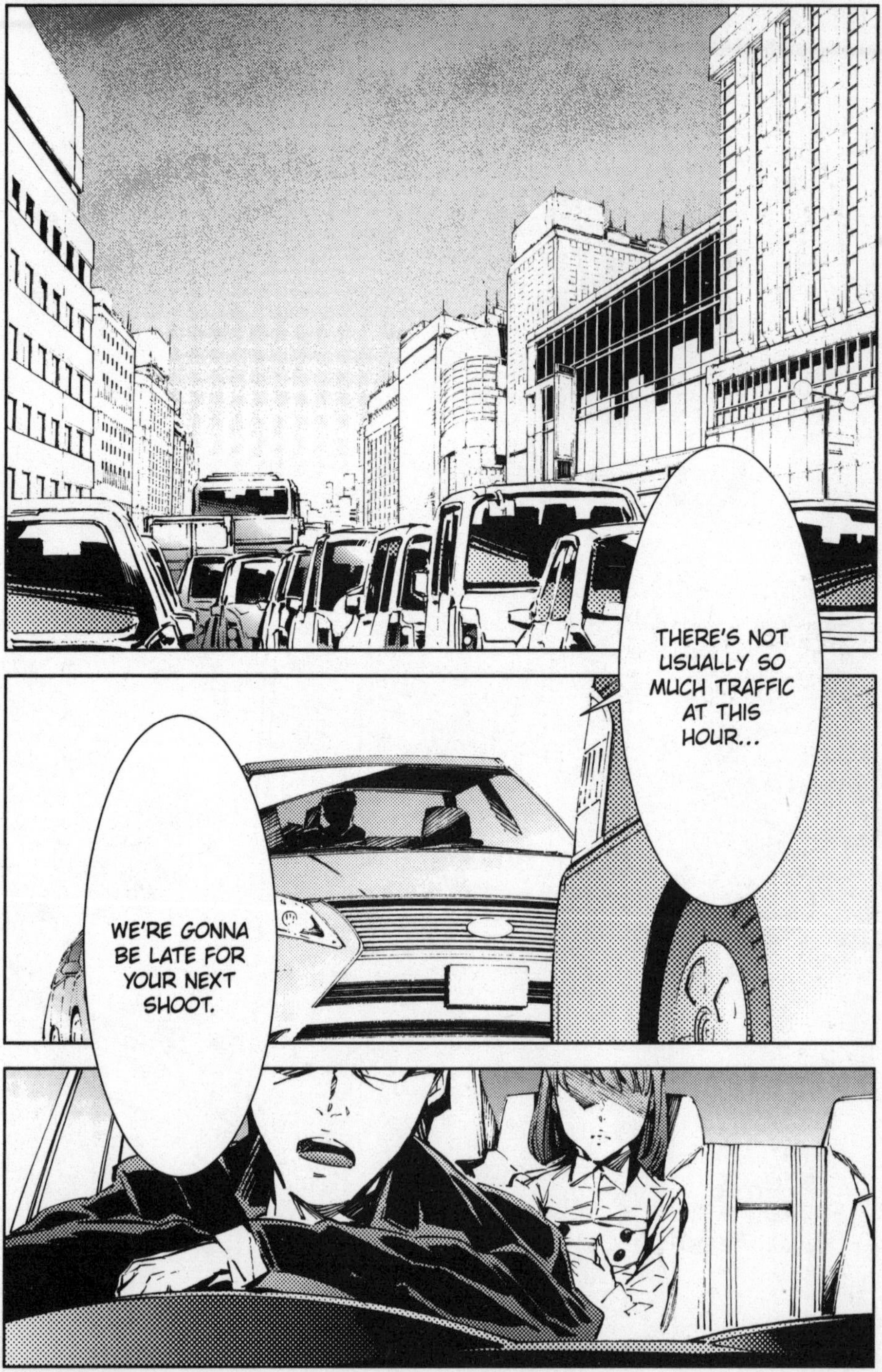
THERE'S NOT USUALLY SO MUCH TRAFFIC AT THIS HOUR...
WE'RE GONNA BE LATE FOR YOUR NEXT SHOOT.

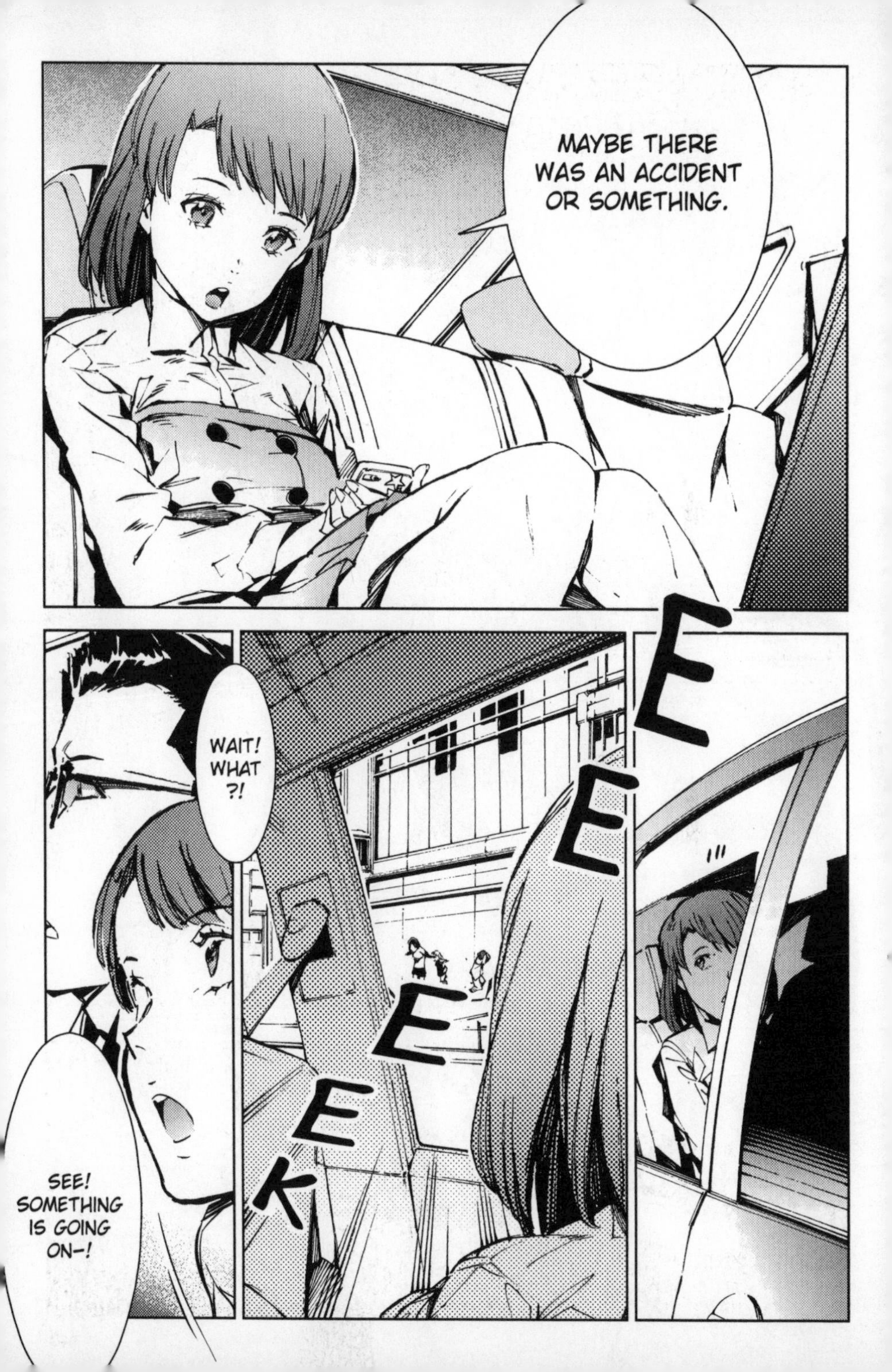
MAYBE THERE WAS AN ACCIDENT OR SOMETHING.
EEEEEK"
WAIT! WHAT ?!
SEE! SOMETHING IS GOING ON-!

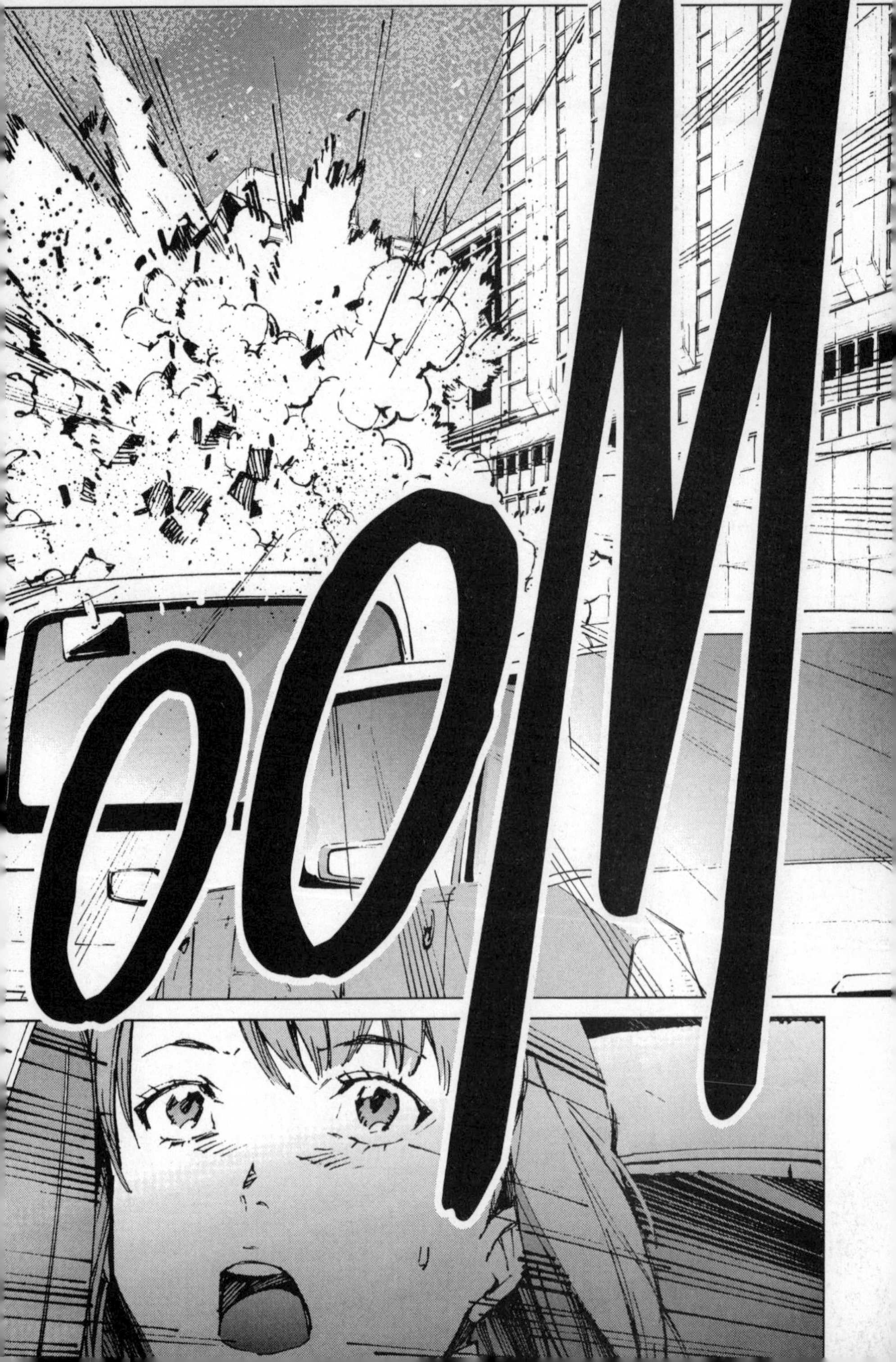
OOM

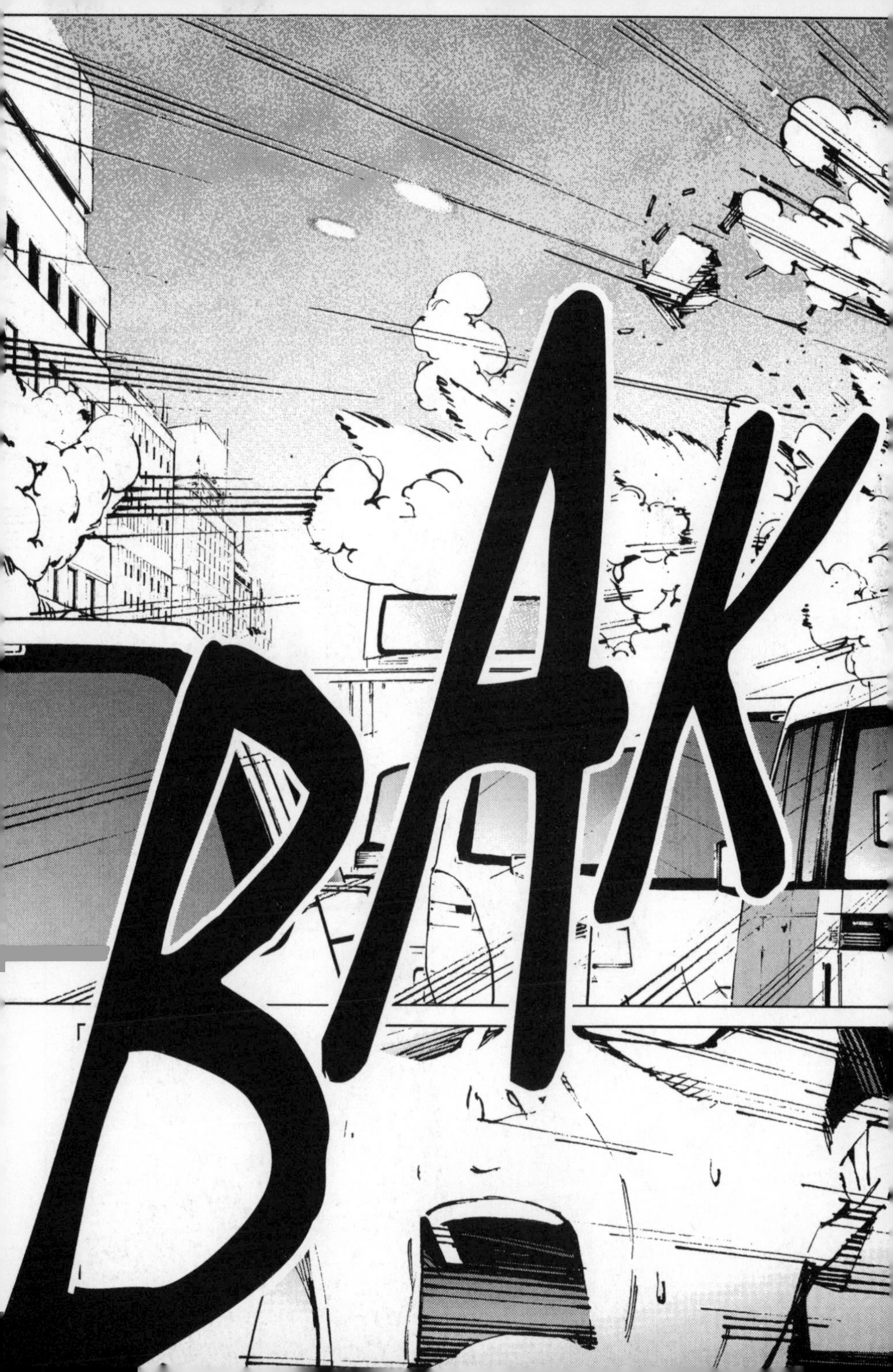
BAK

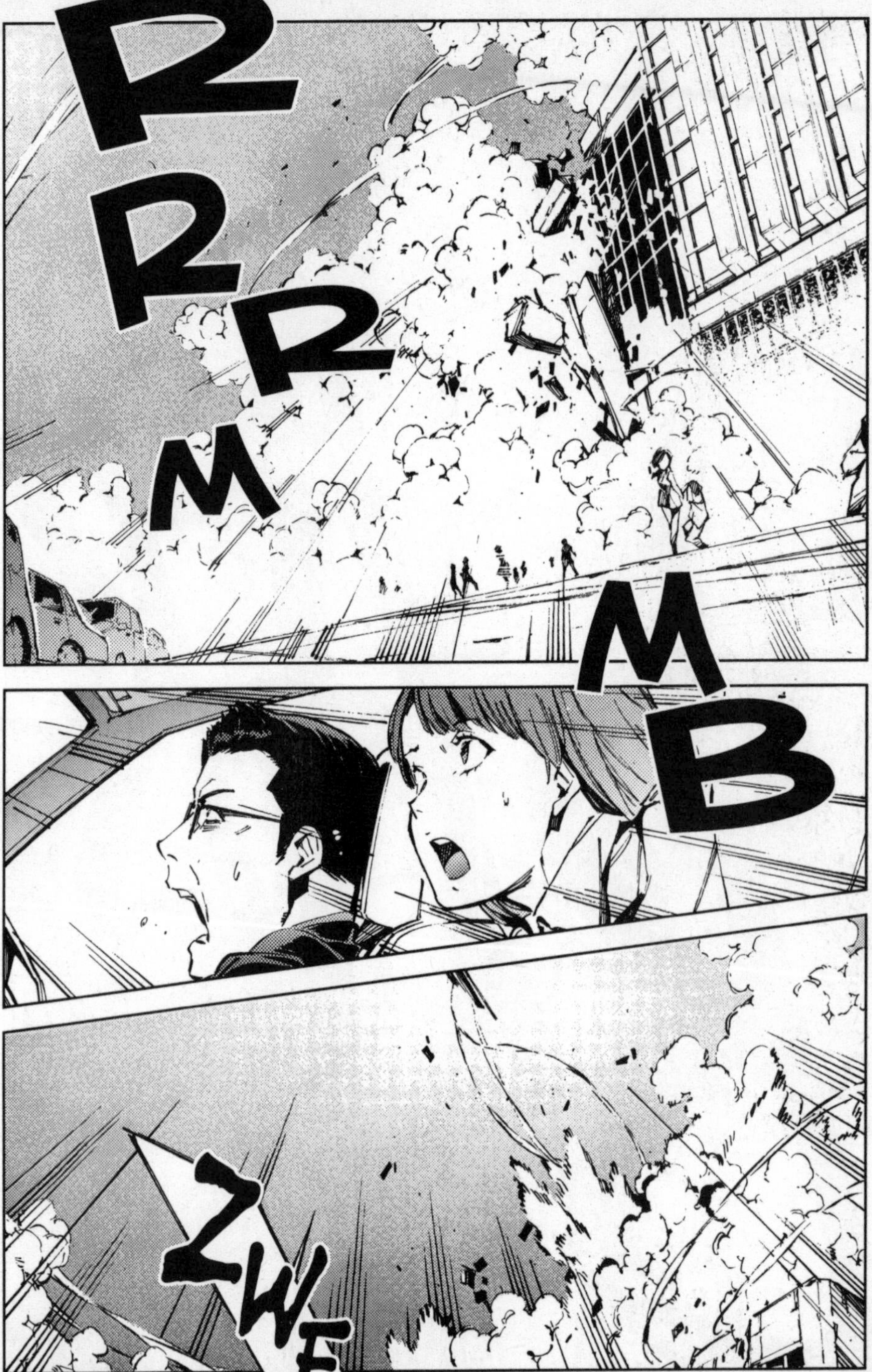
RRRMMB
ZWF

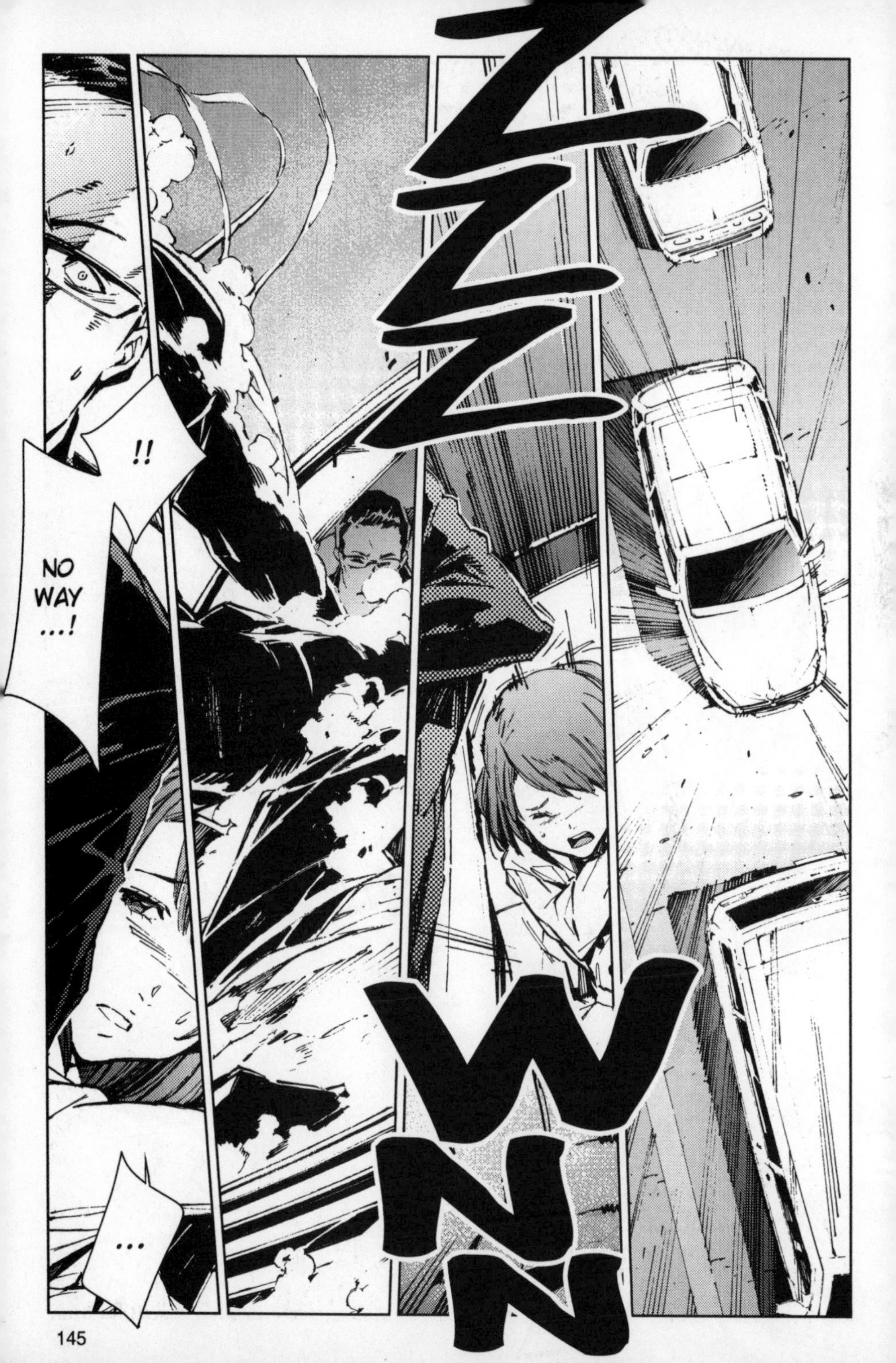
!!
NO WAY ...!
...
ZZZZ
WNN

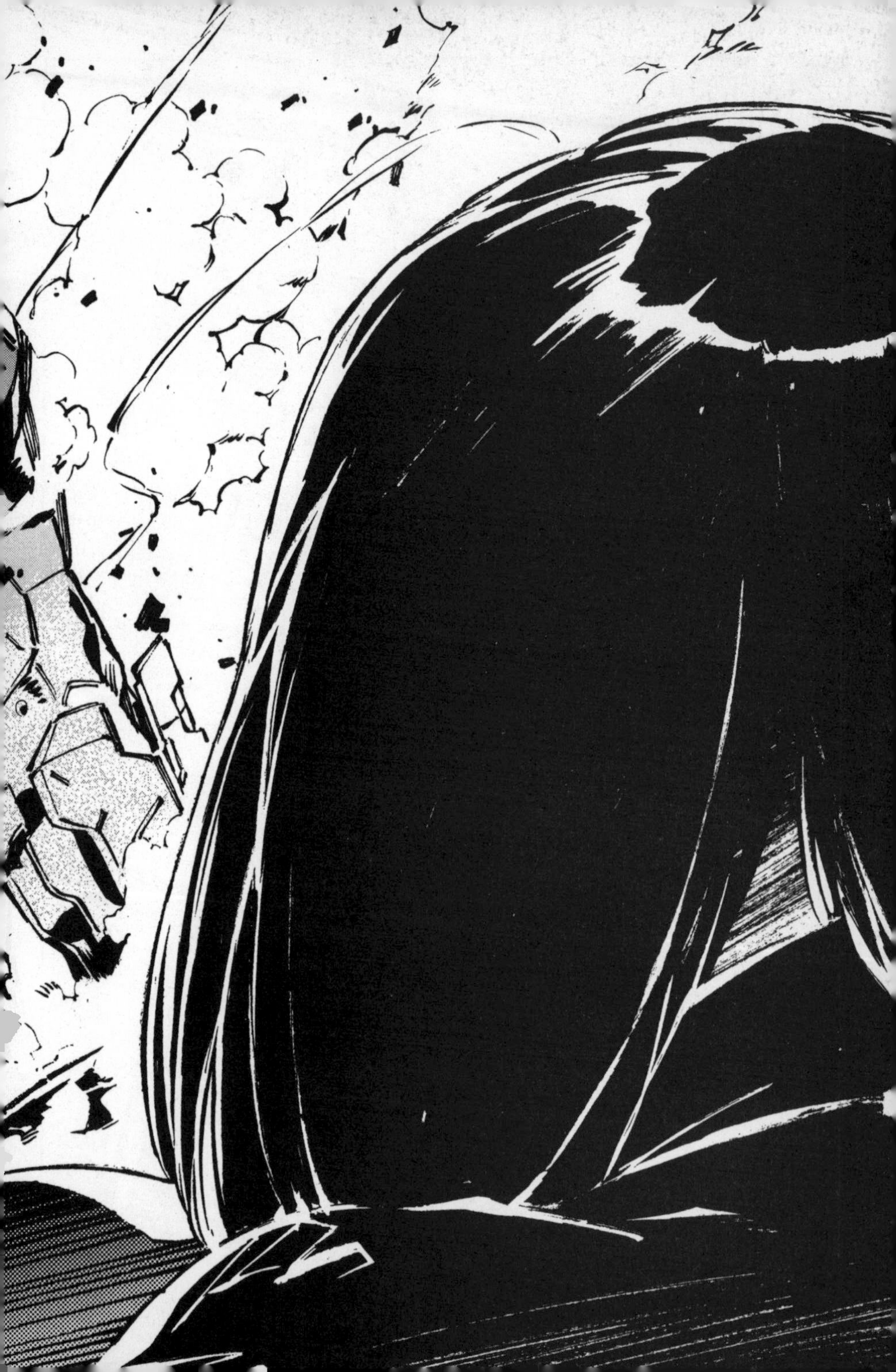

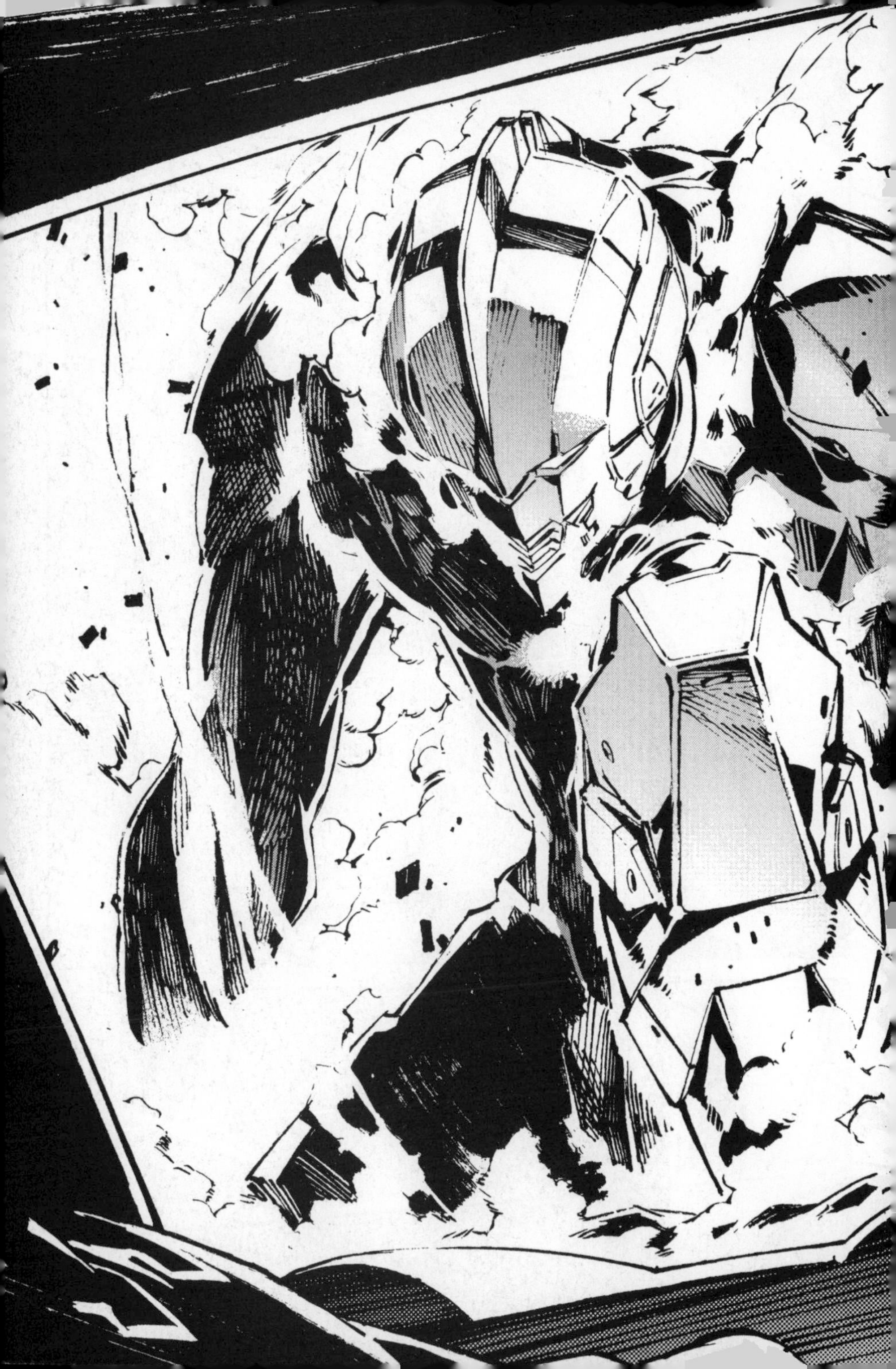

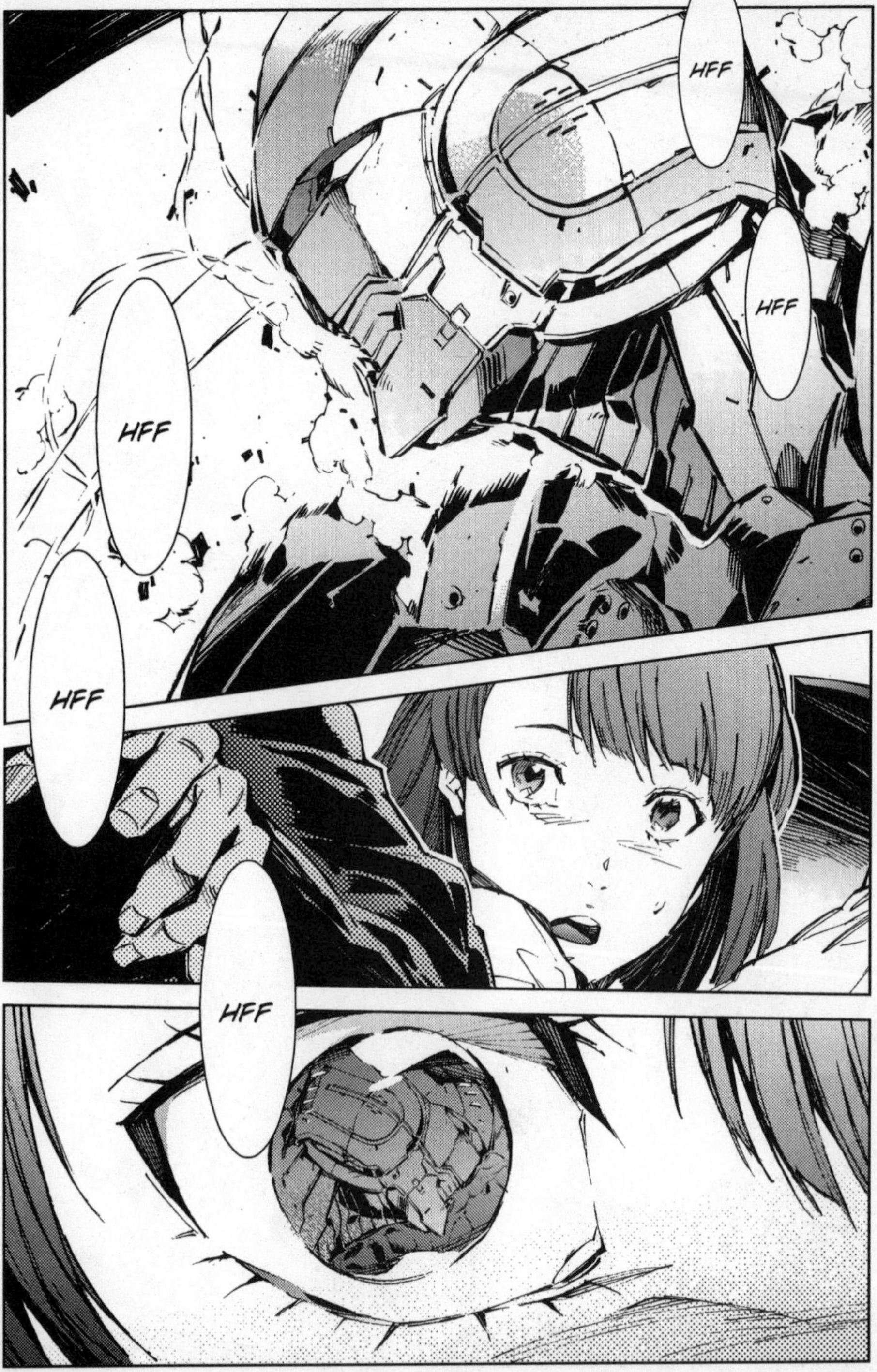
HFF
HFF
HFF
HFF
HFF

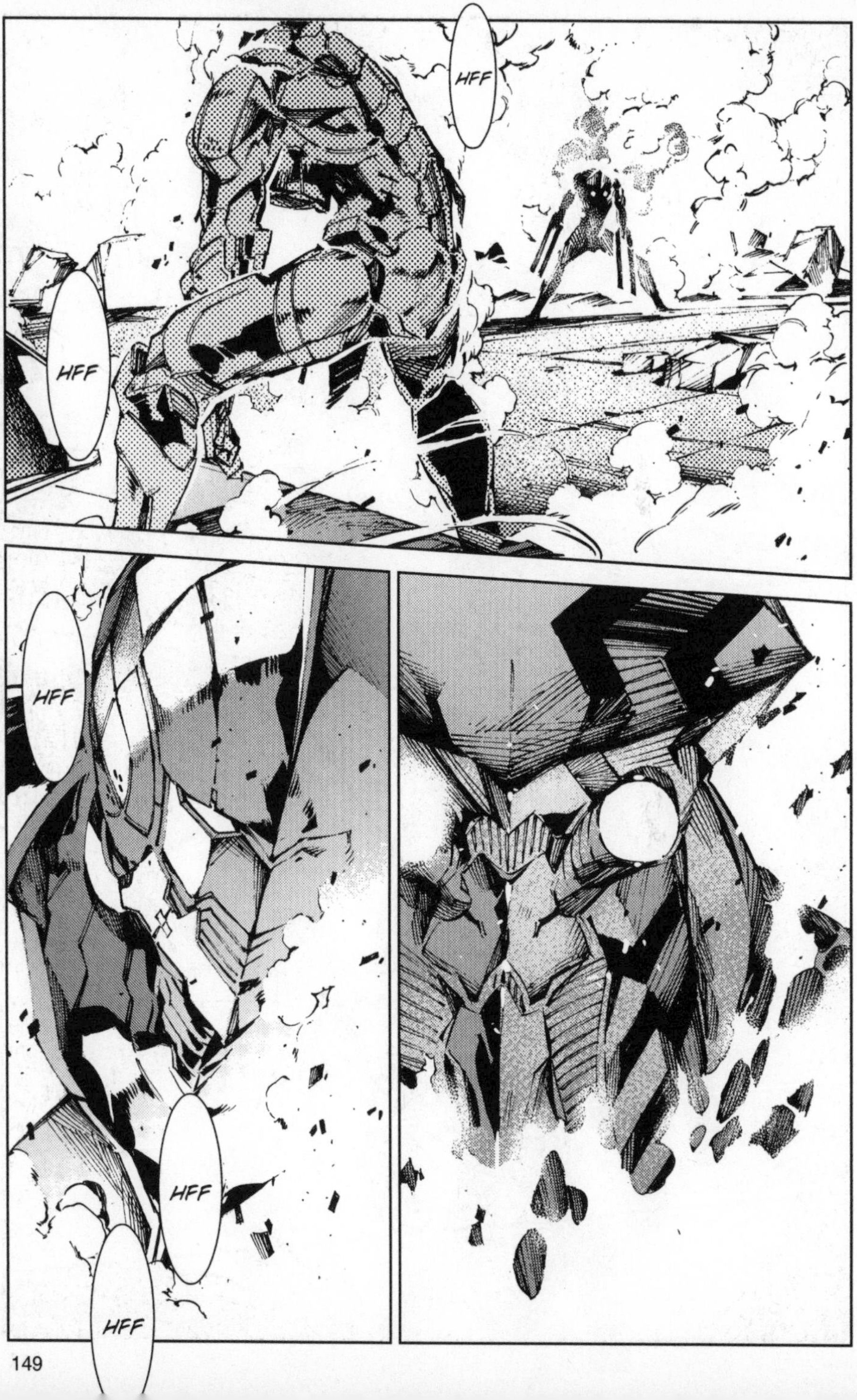
HFF
HFF
HFF
HFF
HFF

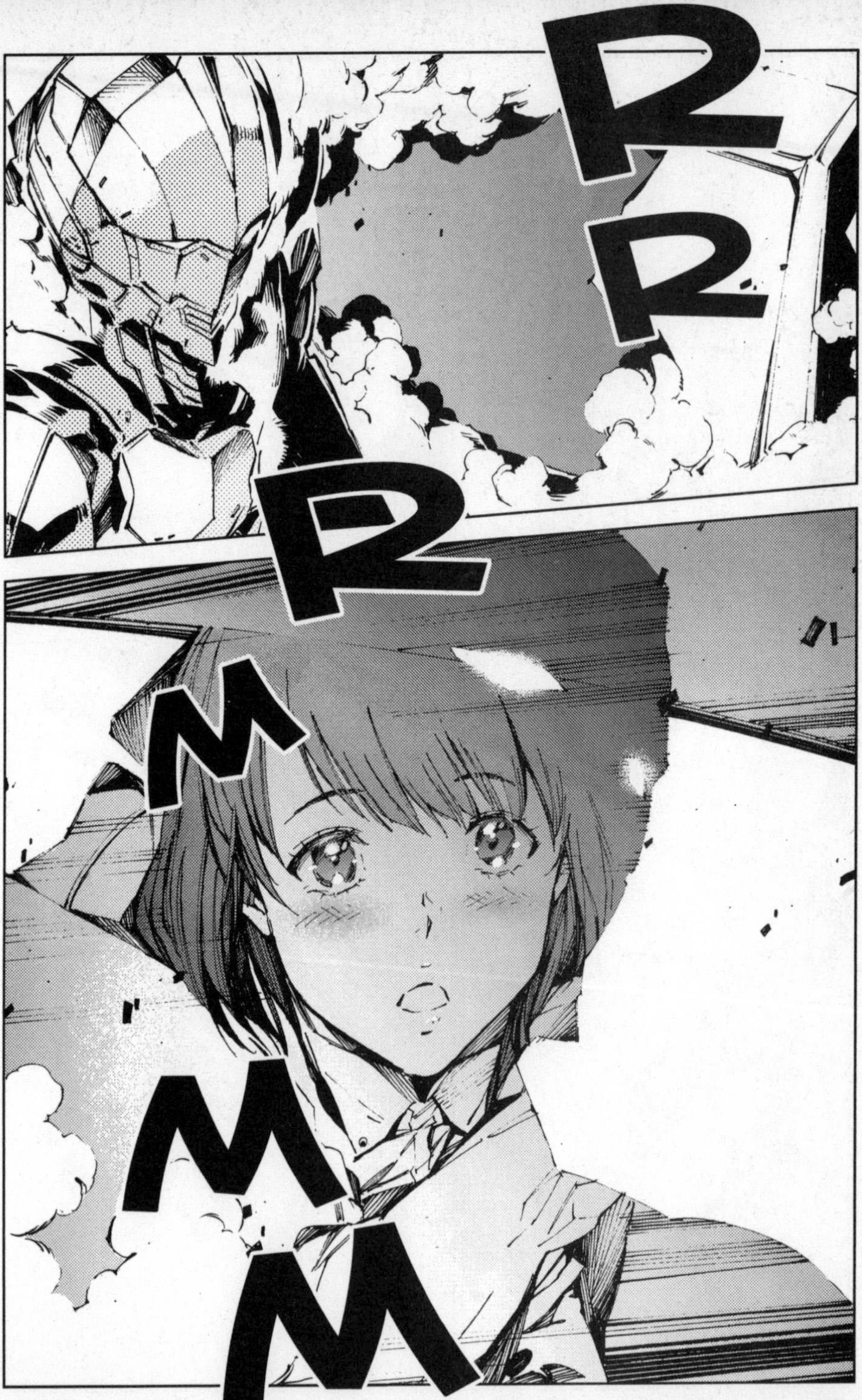
RRRMMM

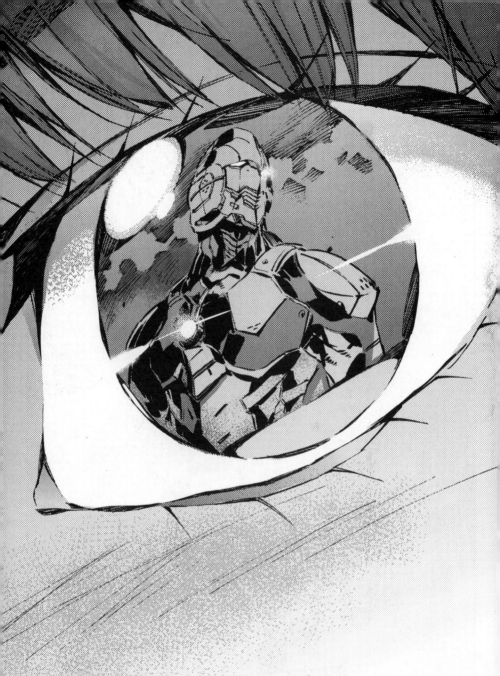

ULTRAMAN
CHAPTER 13 - RHYTHMIC

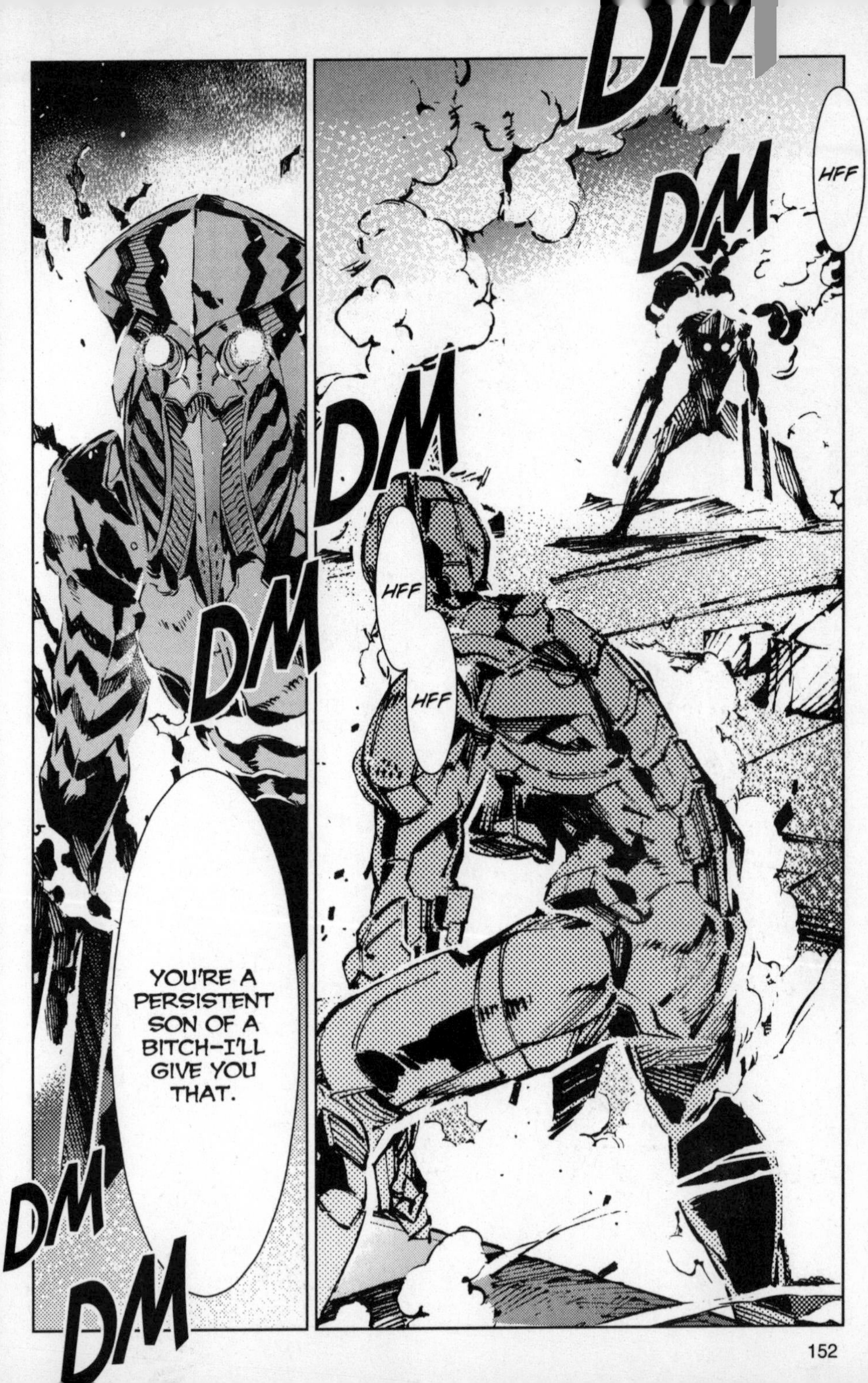
DM
DM
HFF
DM
HFF
HFF
DM
YOU'RE A PERSISTENT SON OF A BITCH—I'LL GIVE YOU THAT.
DM
DM

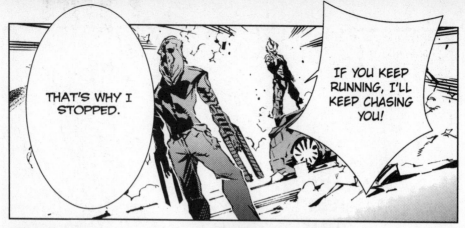

IF YOU KEEP RUNNING, I'LL KEEP CHASING YOU!
THAT'S WHY I STOPPED.
HUH?
IT'S STRANGE. THE SCIENCE PATROL AND THE GOVERNMENT HAVE SPENT A LOT OF TIME KEEPING OUR EXISTENCE A SECRET. THAT'S WHY I'VE BEEN FEEDING ON HUMANS SECRETLY... SO I WOULDN'T BE DISCOVERED.
...
THEN YOU SHOW UP AND CHASE ME RIGHT INTO THE MIDDLE OF THE CITY. I COULDN'T FIGURE OUT WHY YOU'D DO THAT.
BUT I THINK I KNOW WHY NOW.
SSLCH

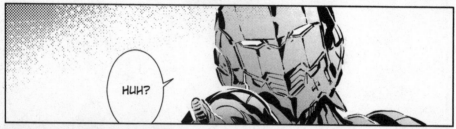

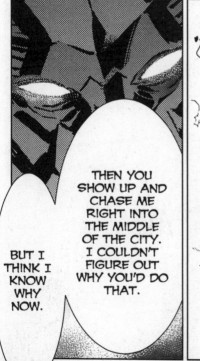

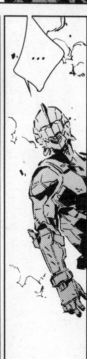

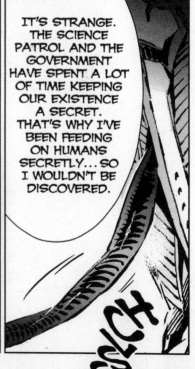

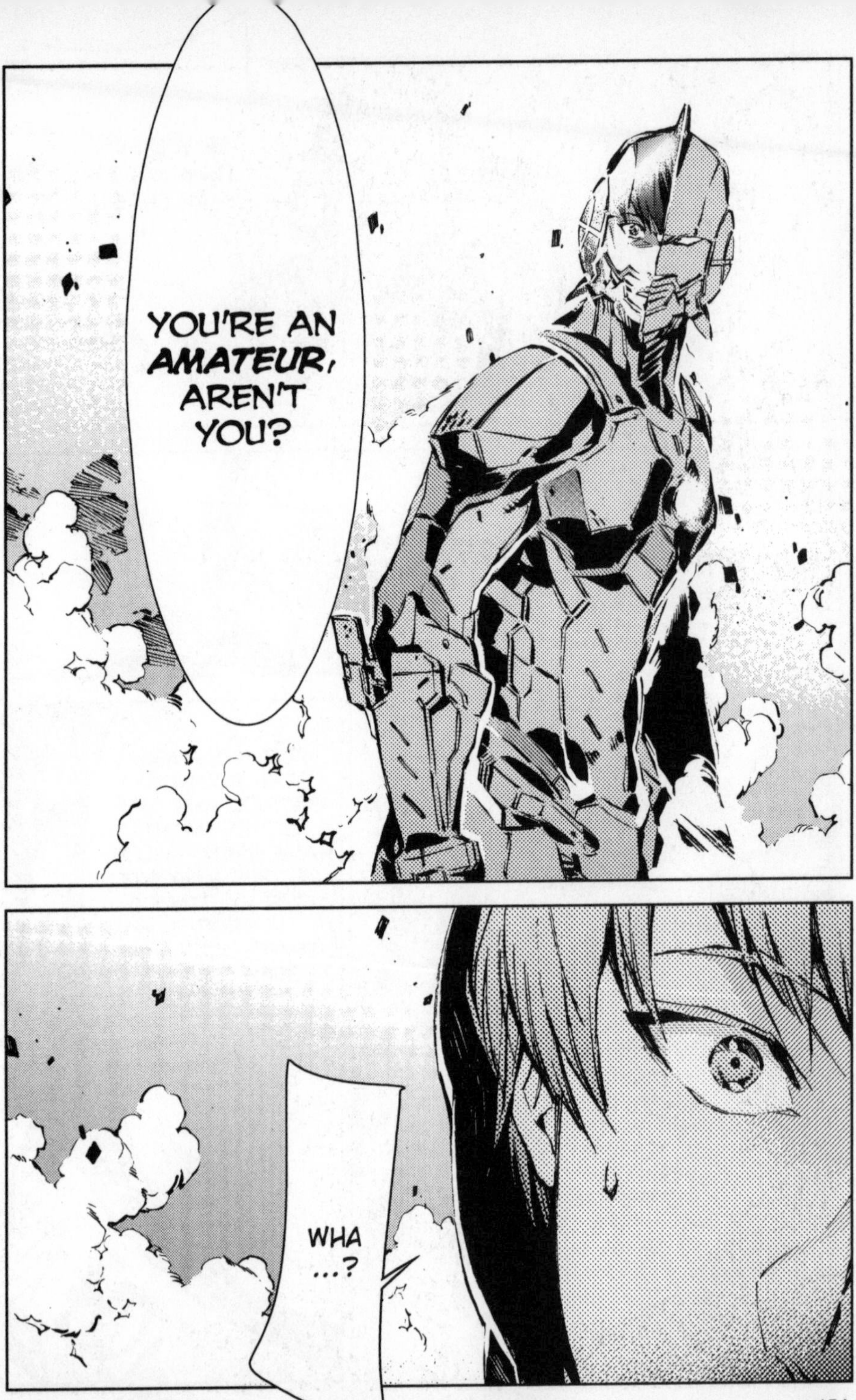
YOU'RE AN AMATEUR, AREN'T YOU?
WHA ...?

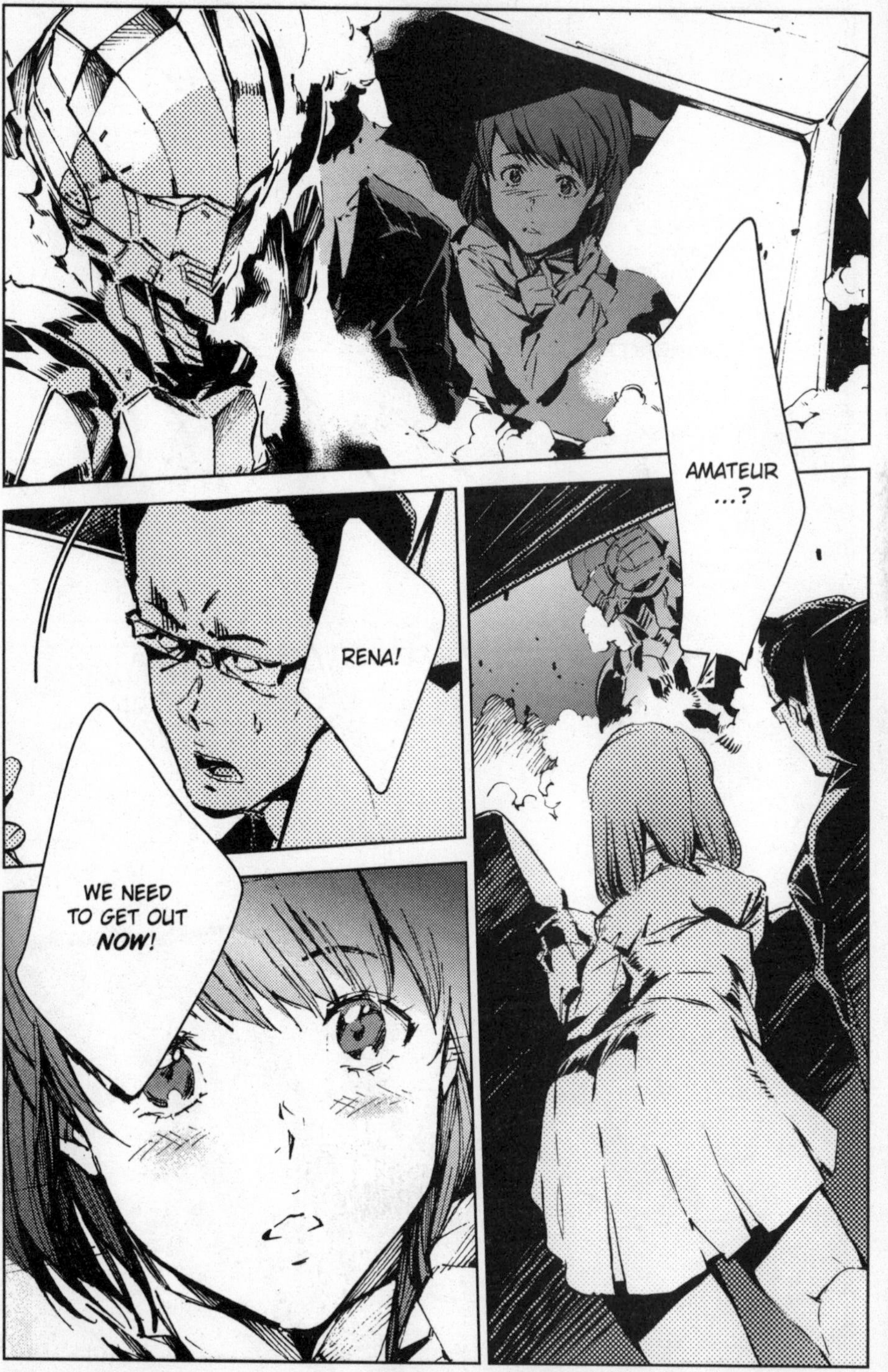
AMATEUR ...?
RENA!
WE NEED TO GET OUT NOW!

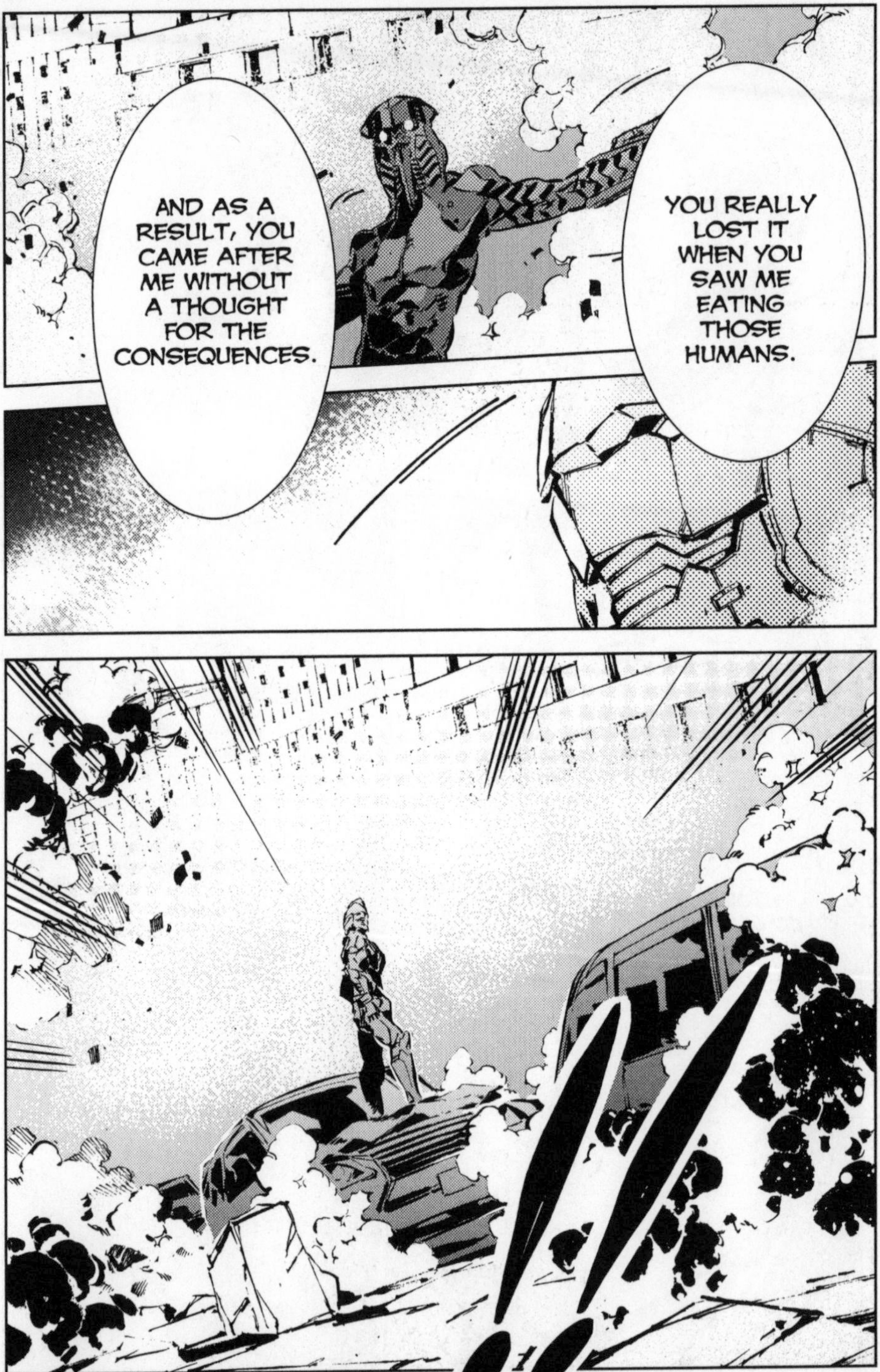
YOU REALLY LOST IT WHEN YOU SAW ME EATING THOSE HUMANS.
AND AS A RESULT, YOU CAME AFTER ME WITHOUT A THOUGHT FOR THE CONSEQUENCES.
!!

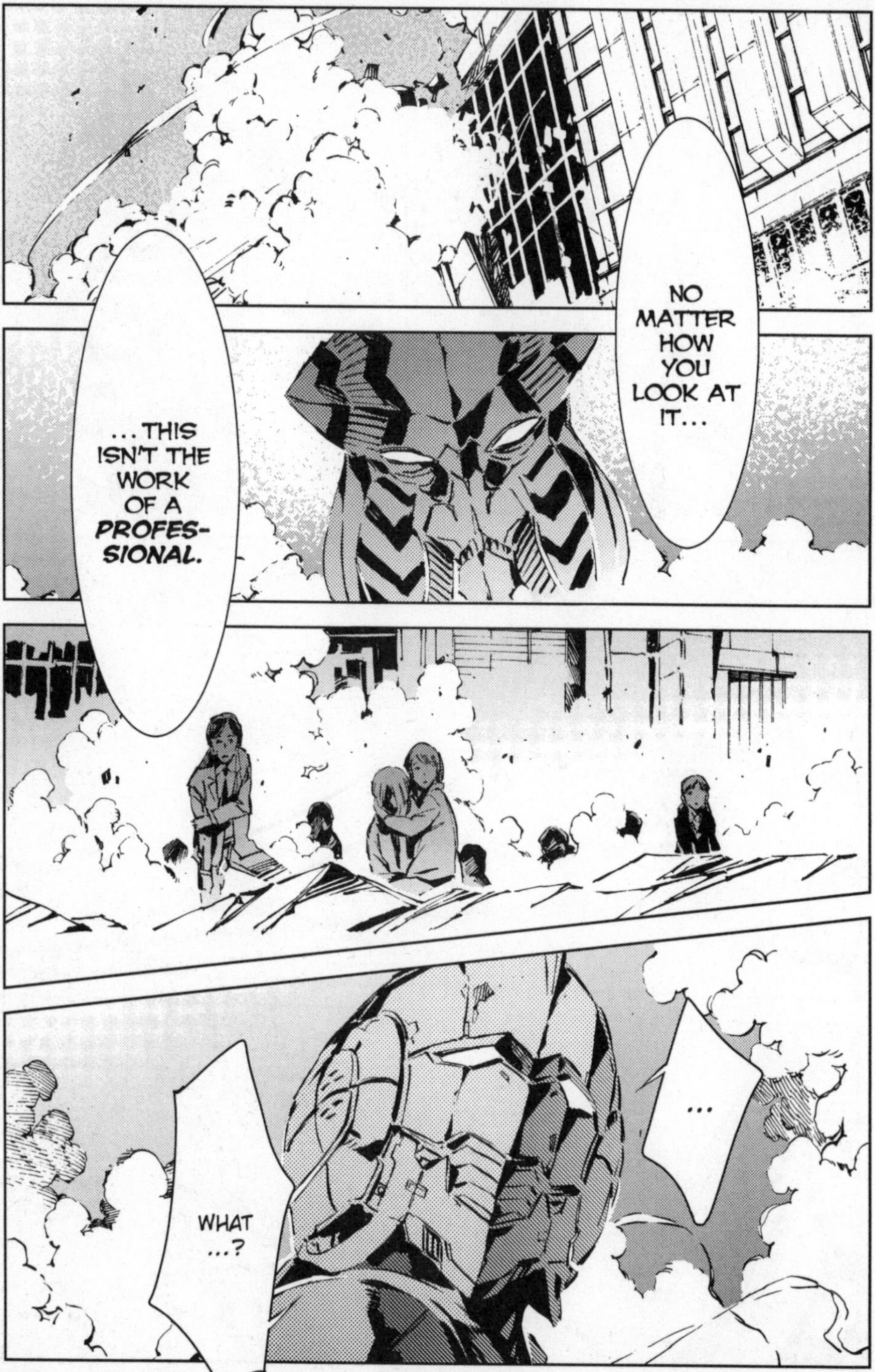
NO MATTER HOW YOU LOOK AT IT...
...THIS ISN'T THE WORK OF A PROFESSIONAL.
...
WHAT ...?

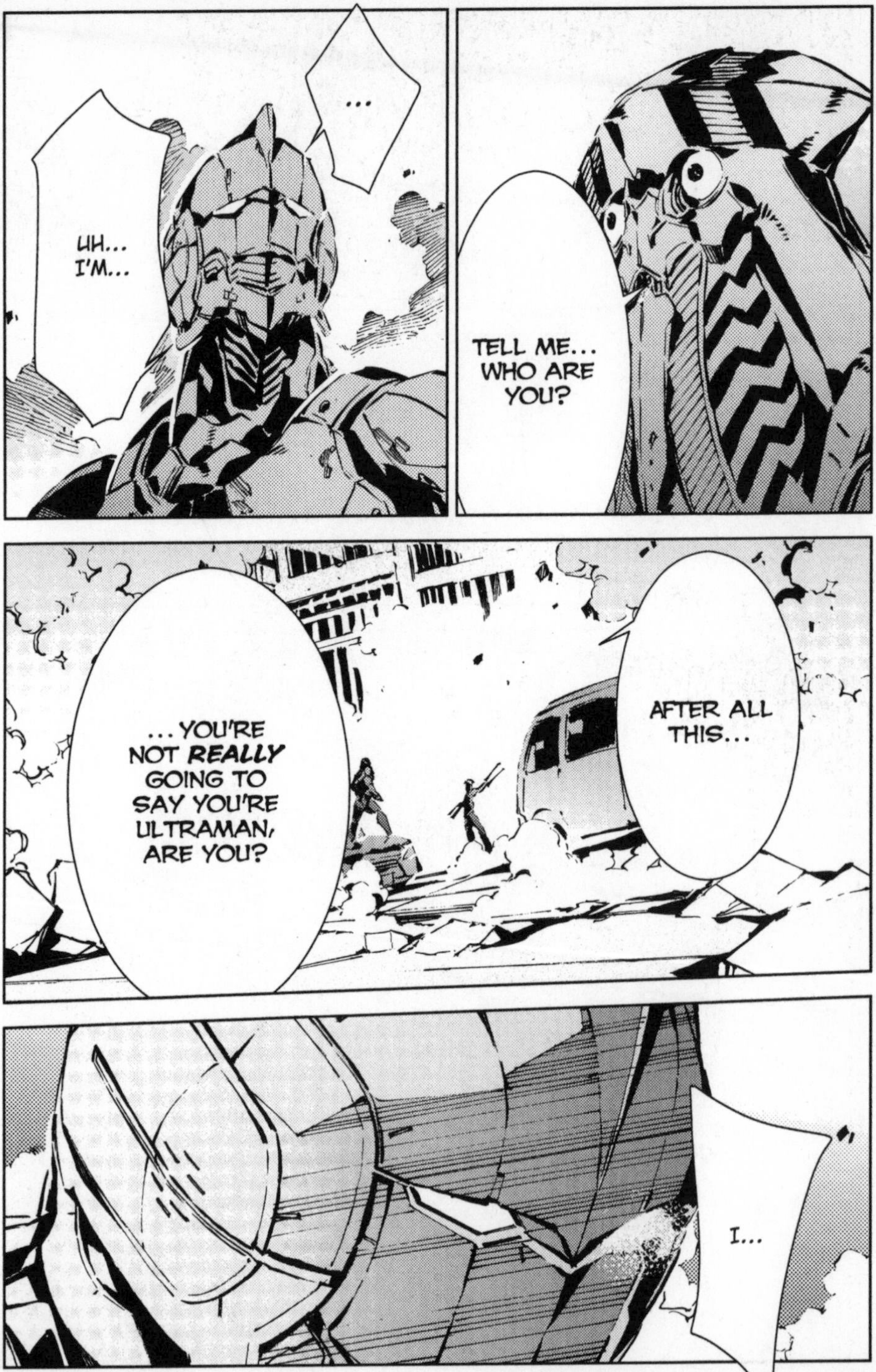
TELL ME... WHO ARE YOU?
...
UH... I'M...
AFTER ALL THIS...
...YOU'RE NOT REALLY GOING TO SAY YOU'RE ULTRAMAN, ARE YOU?
I...

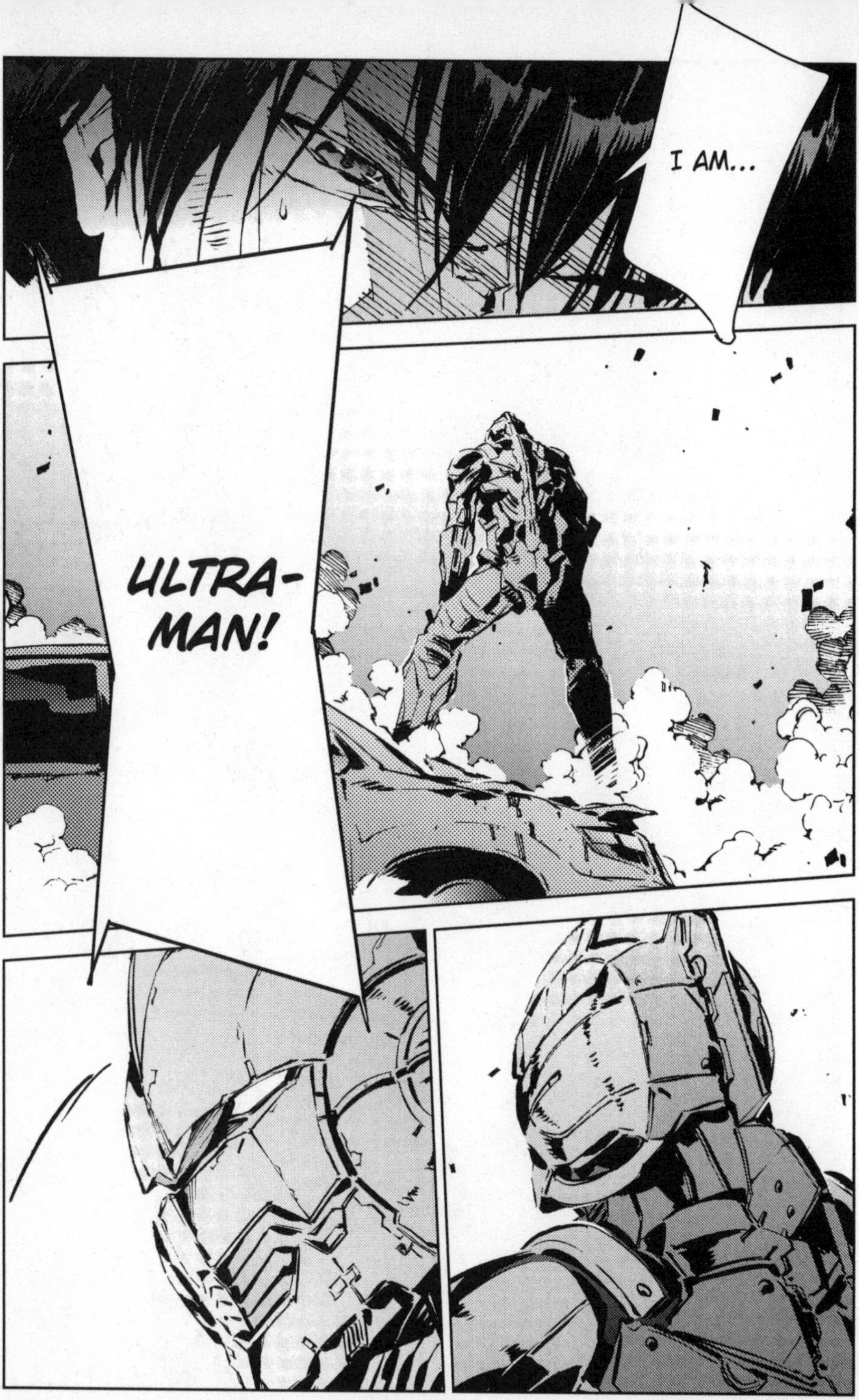
I AM...
ULTRA-
MAN!

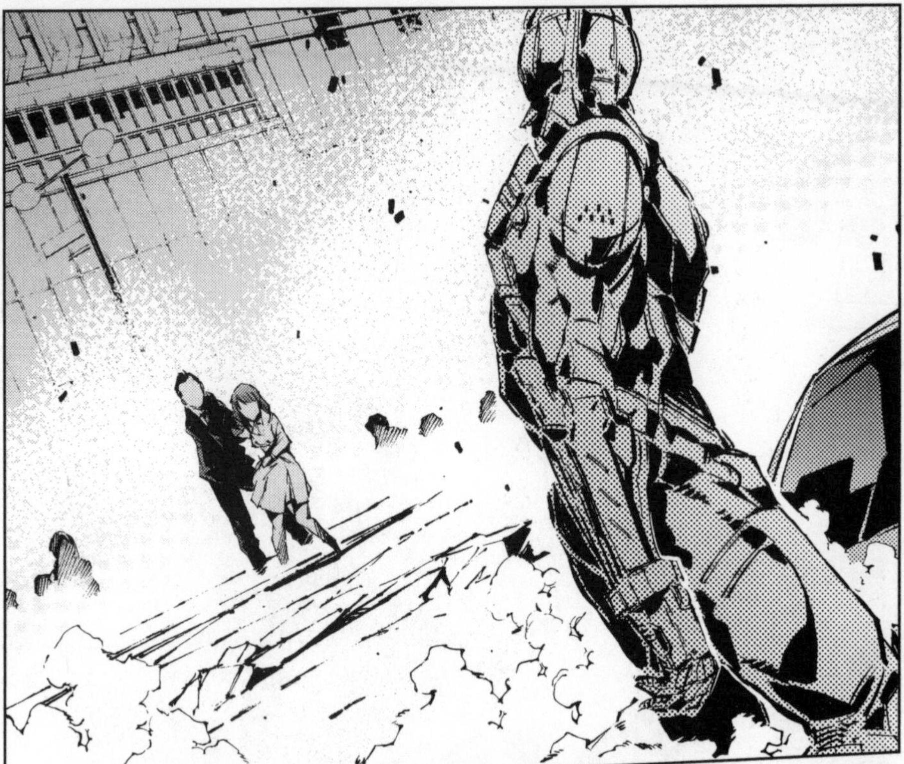
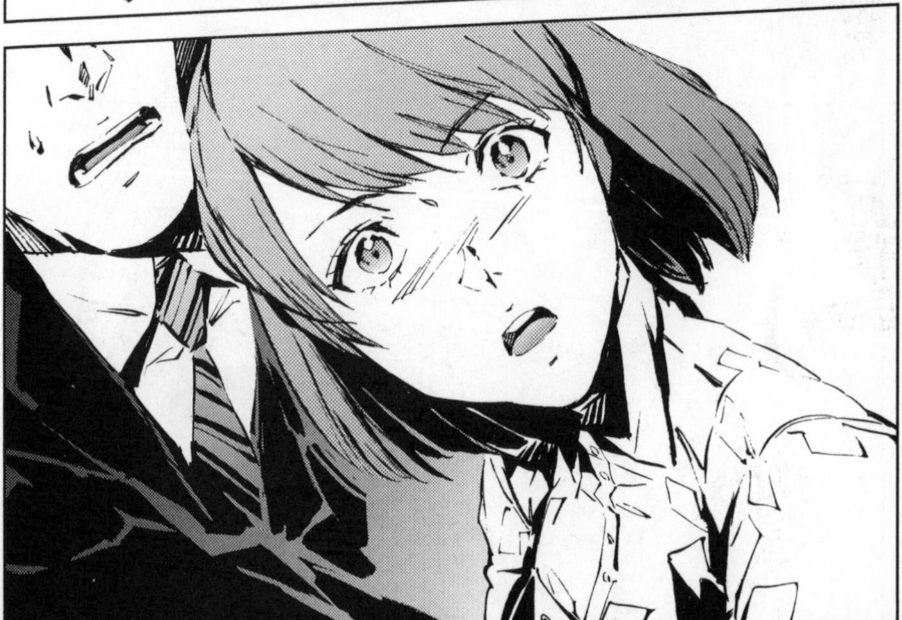

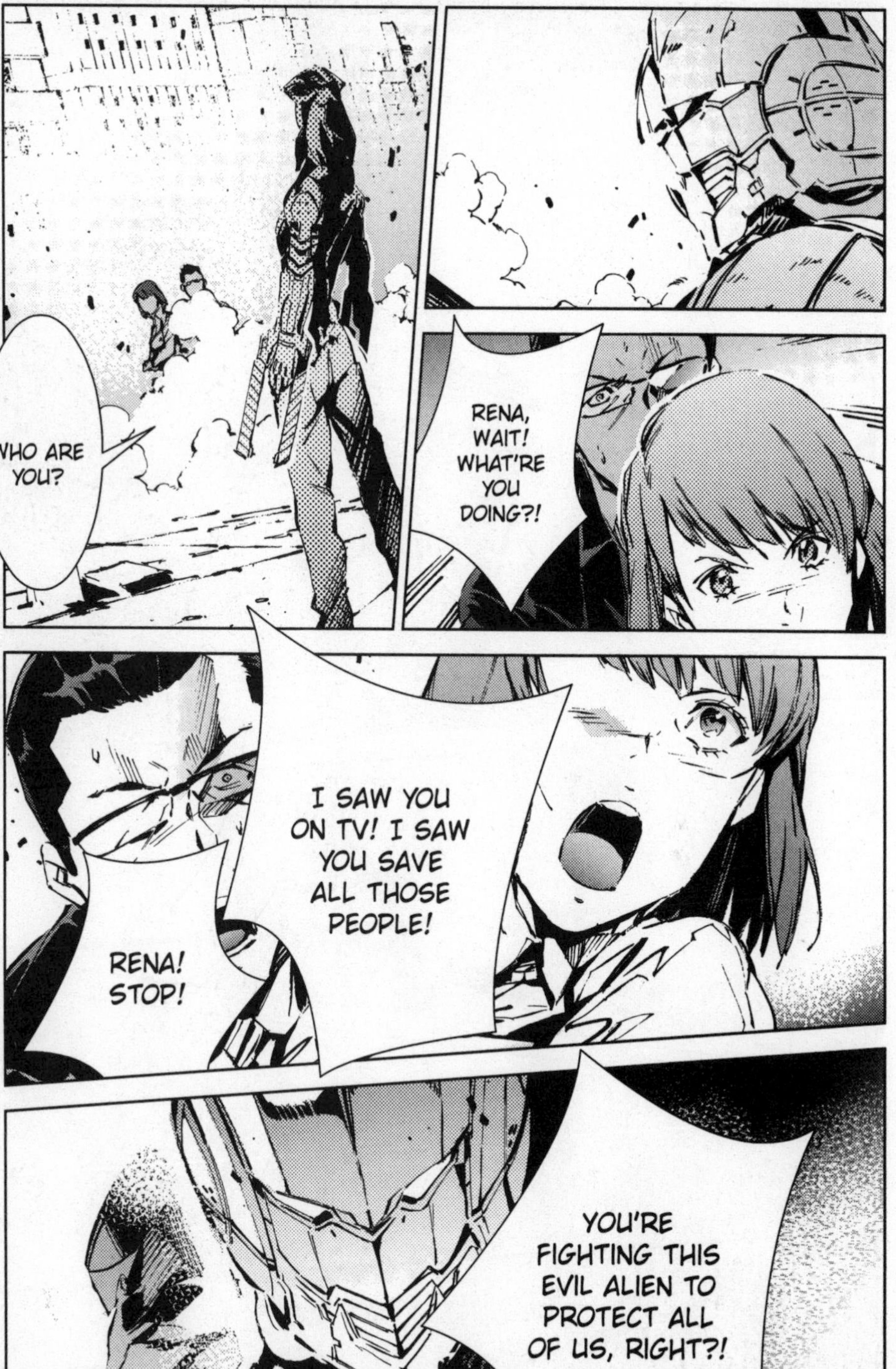
WHO ARE YOU?
RENA, WAIT! WHAT'RE YOU DOING?!
I SAW YOU ON TV! I SAW YOU SAVE ALL THOSE PEOPLE!
RENA! STOP!
YOU'RE FIGHTING THIS EVIL ALIEN TO PROTECT ALL OF US, RIGHT?!

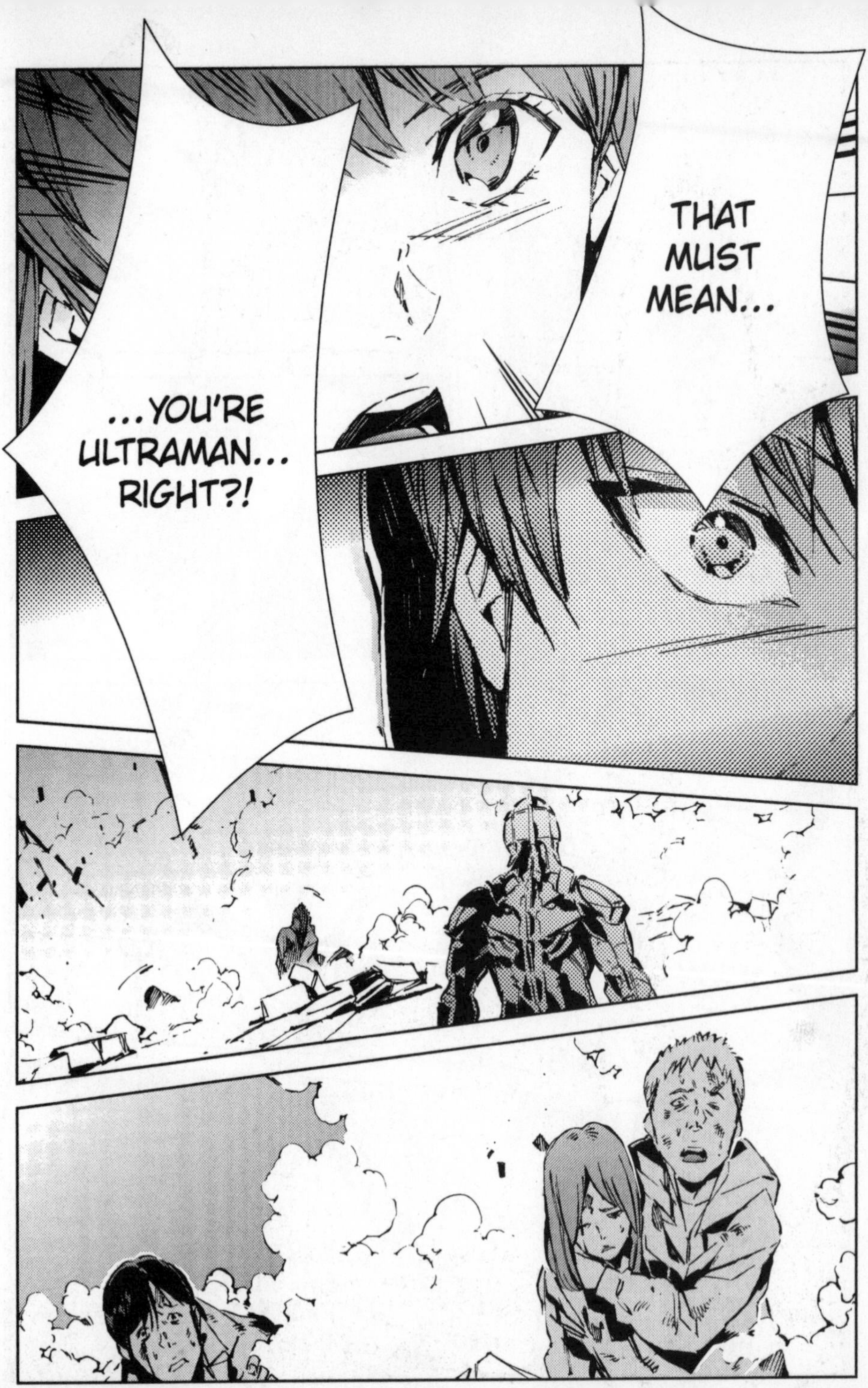
THAT MUST MEAN...
...YOU'RE ULTRAMAN... RIGHT?!

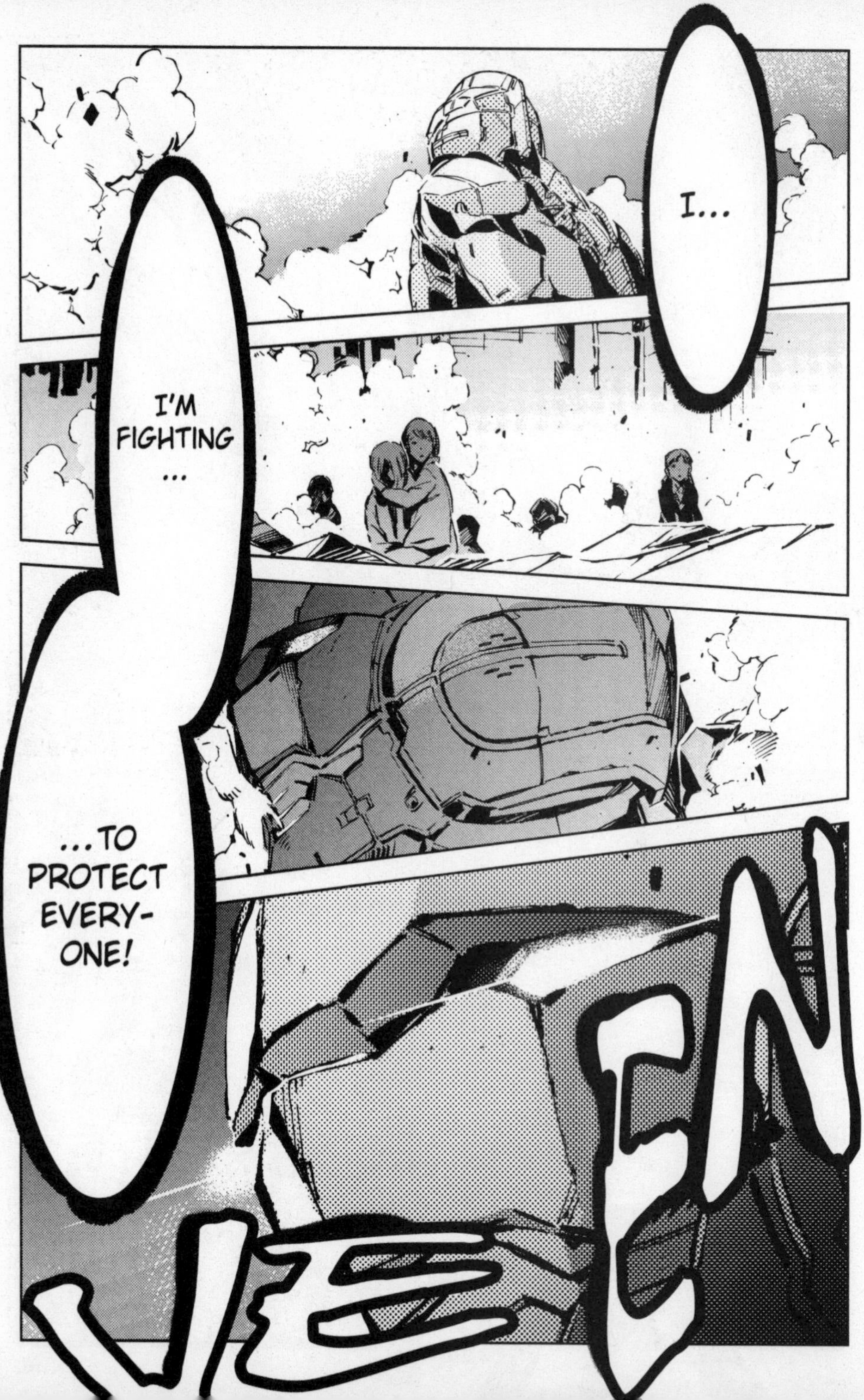
I...
I'M FIGHTING ...
...TO PROTECT EVERY-ONE!

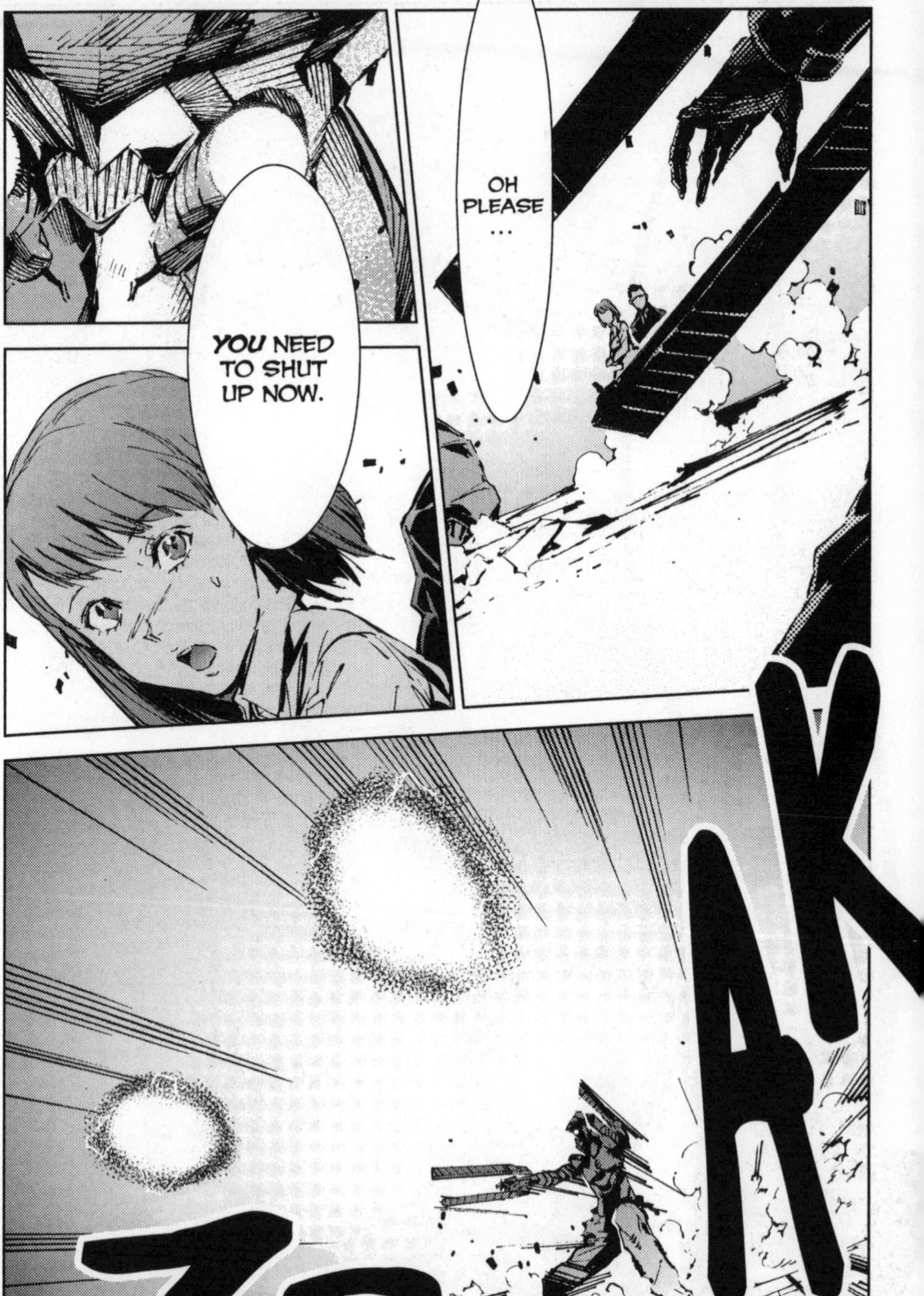
OH PLEASE ...
YOU NEED TO SHUT UP NOW.
TRAK

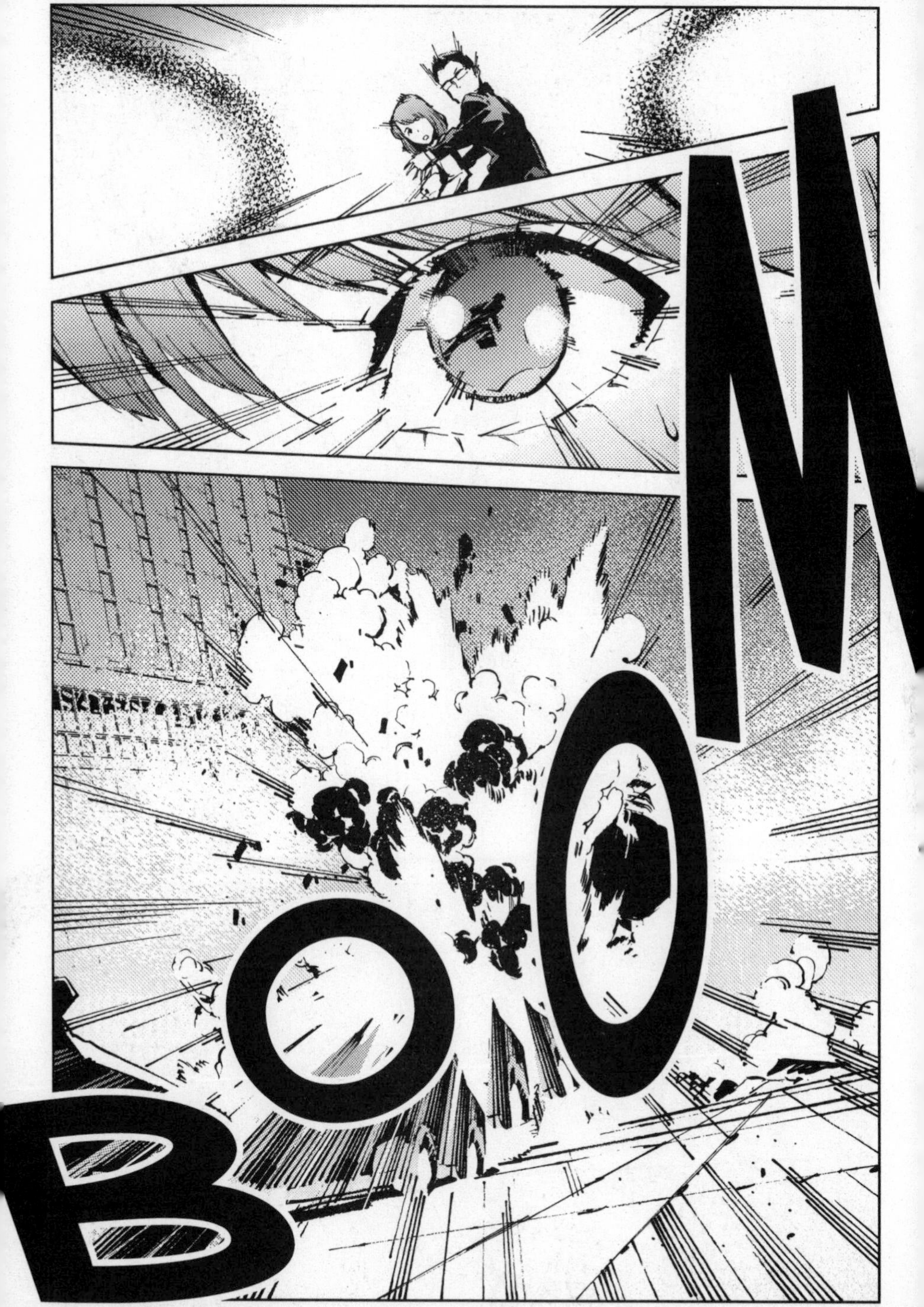
BOOM

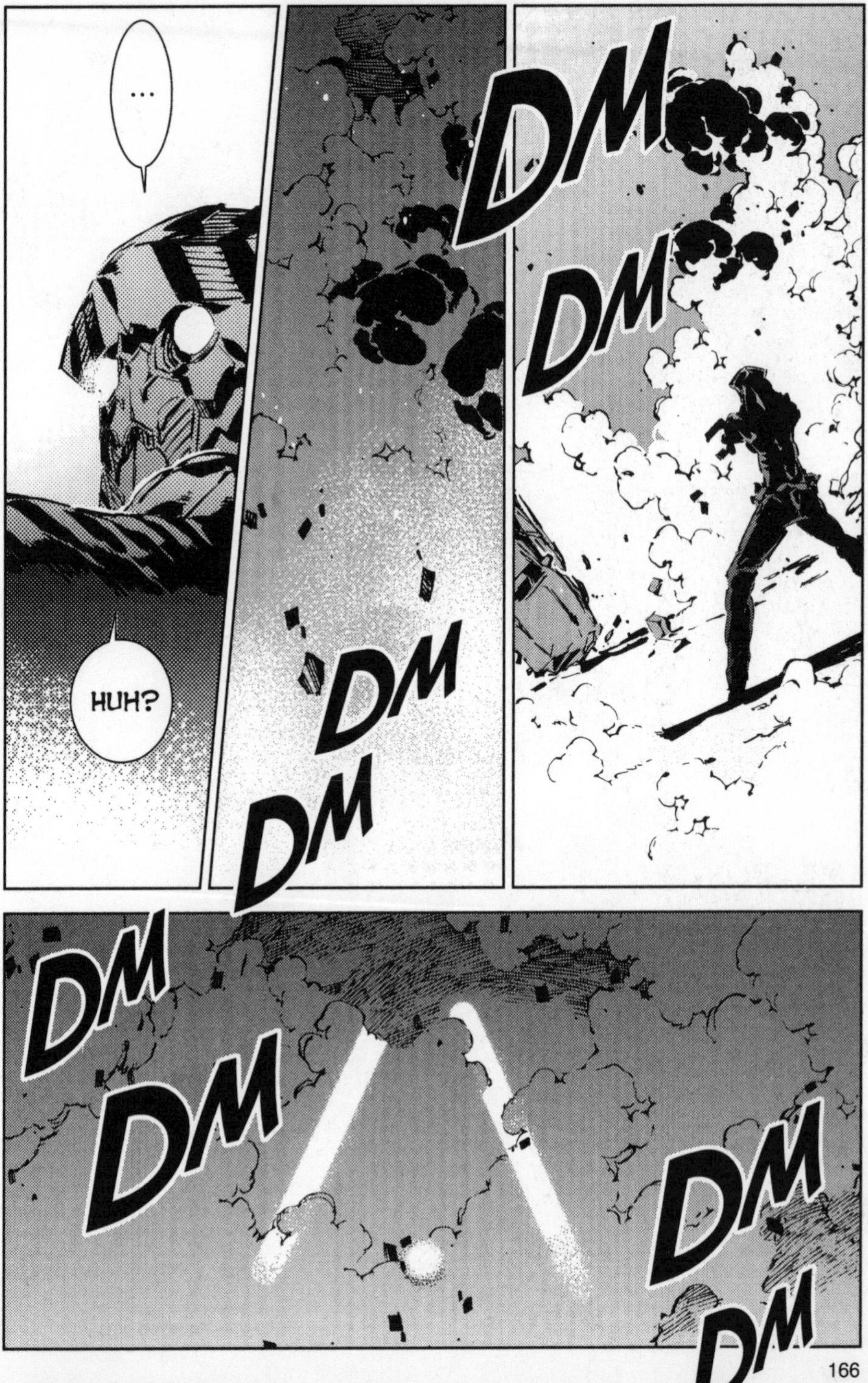
DM
DM
DM
DM
...
HUH?
DM
DM
DM
DM

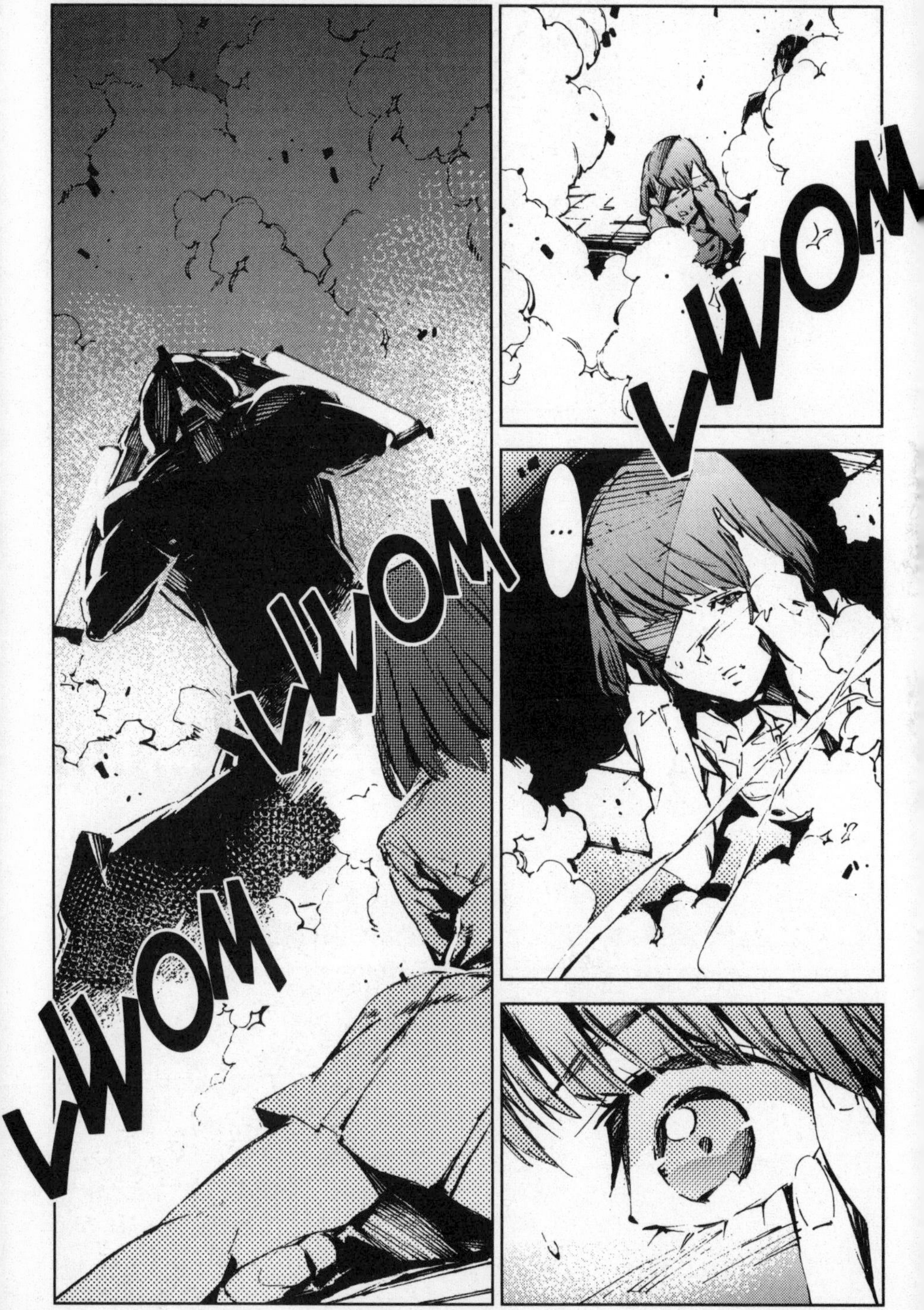
VWOM
VWOM
VWOM
VWOM
...

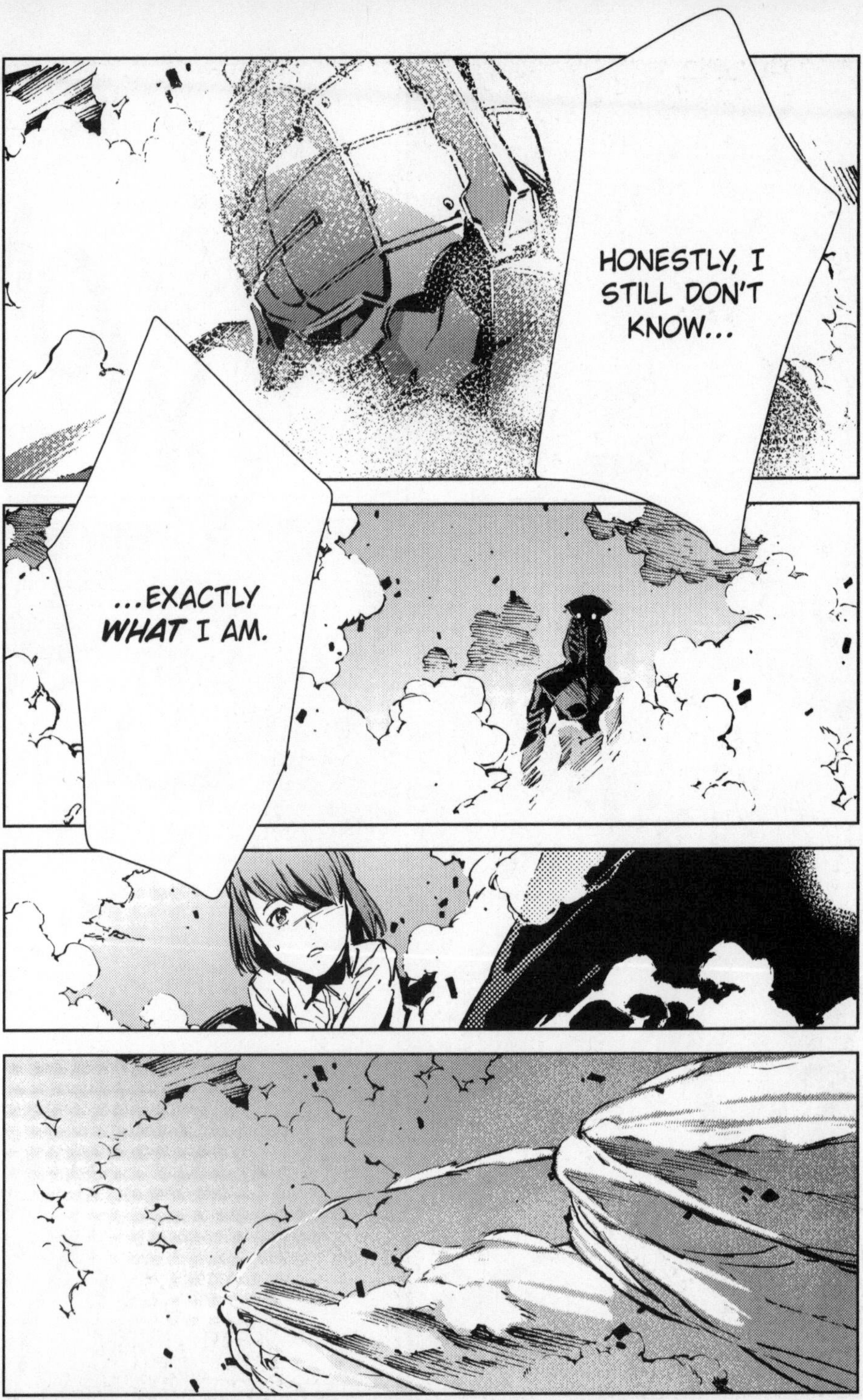

HONESTLY, I STILL DON'T KNOW...
...EXACTLY *WHAT* I AM.

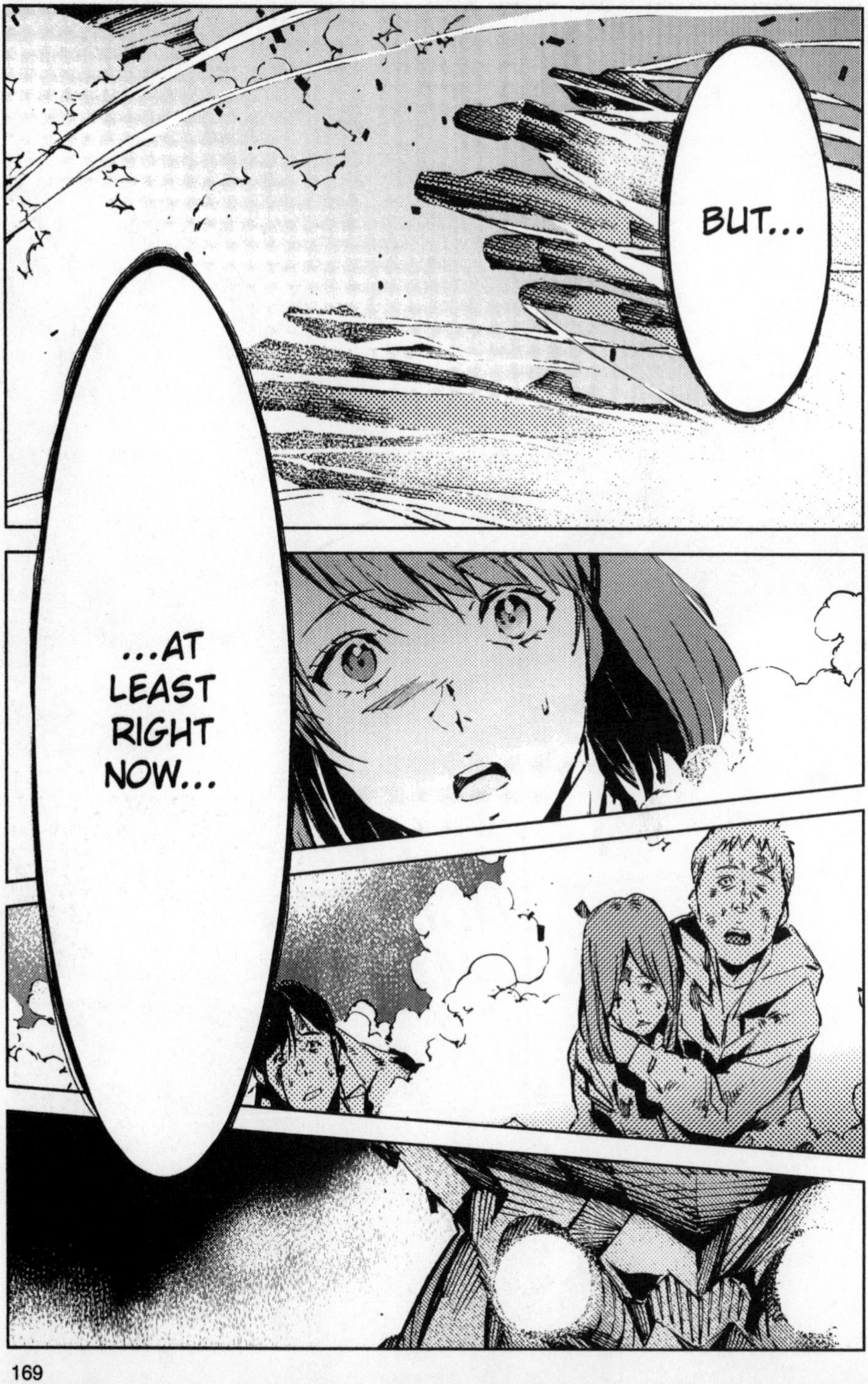
BUT...
...AT LEAST RIGHT NOW...

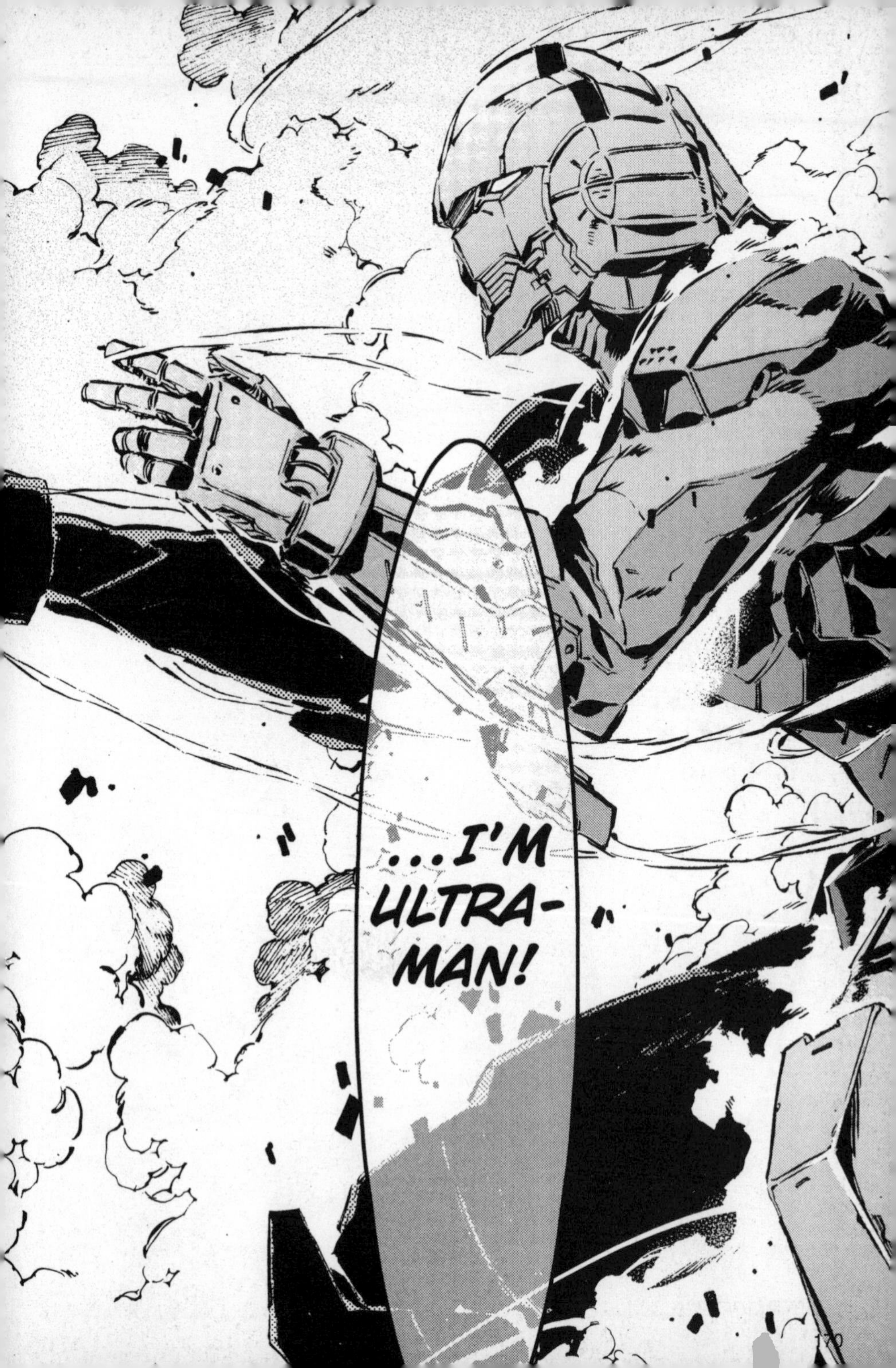
...I'M ULTRA-MAN!

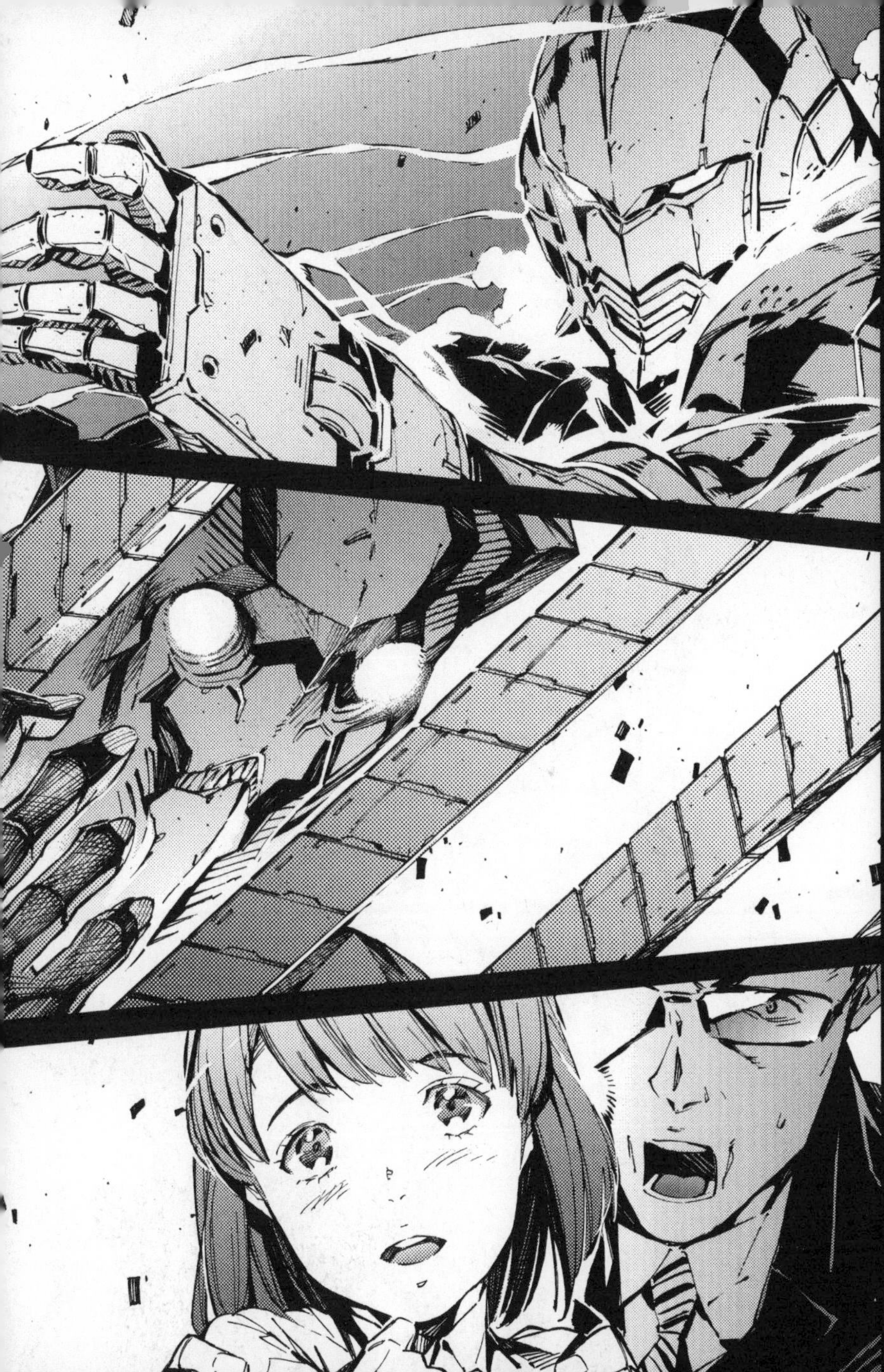

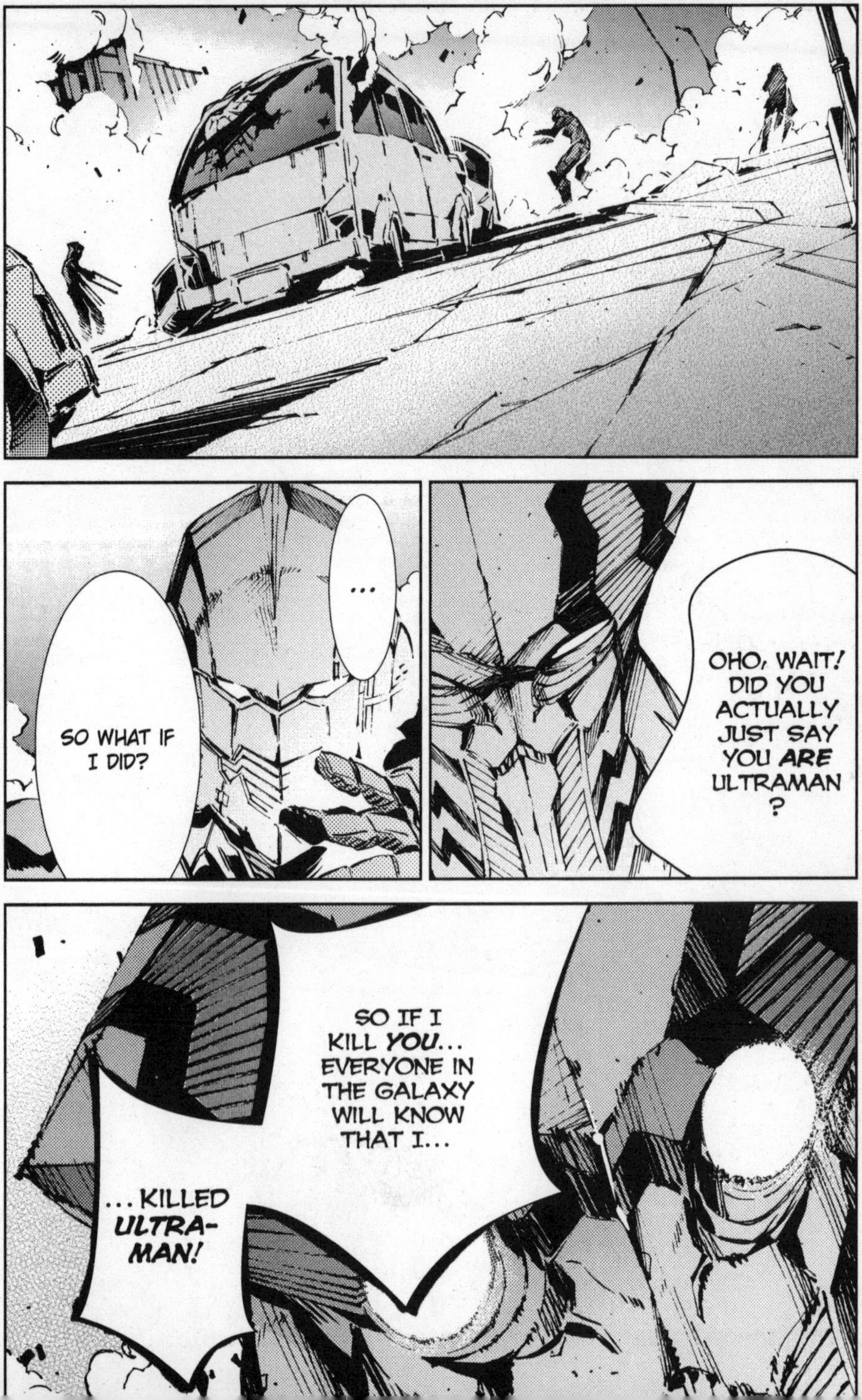
OHO, WAIT! DID YOU ACTUALLY JUST SAY YOU ARE ULTRAMAN ?
...
SO WHAT IF I DID?
SO IF I KILL YOU... EVERYONE IN THE GALAXY WILL KNOW THAT I...
...KILLED ULTRA-MAN!

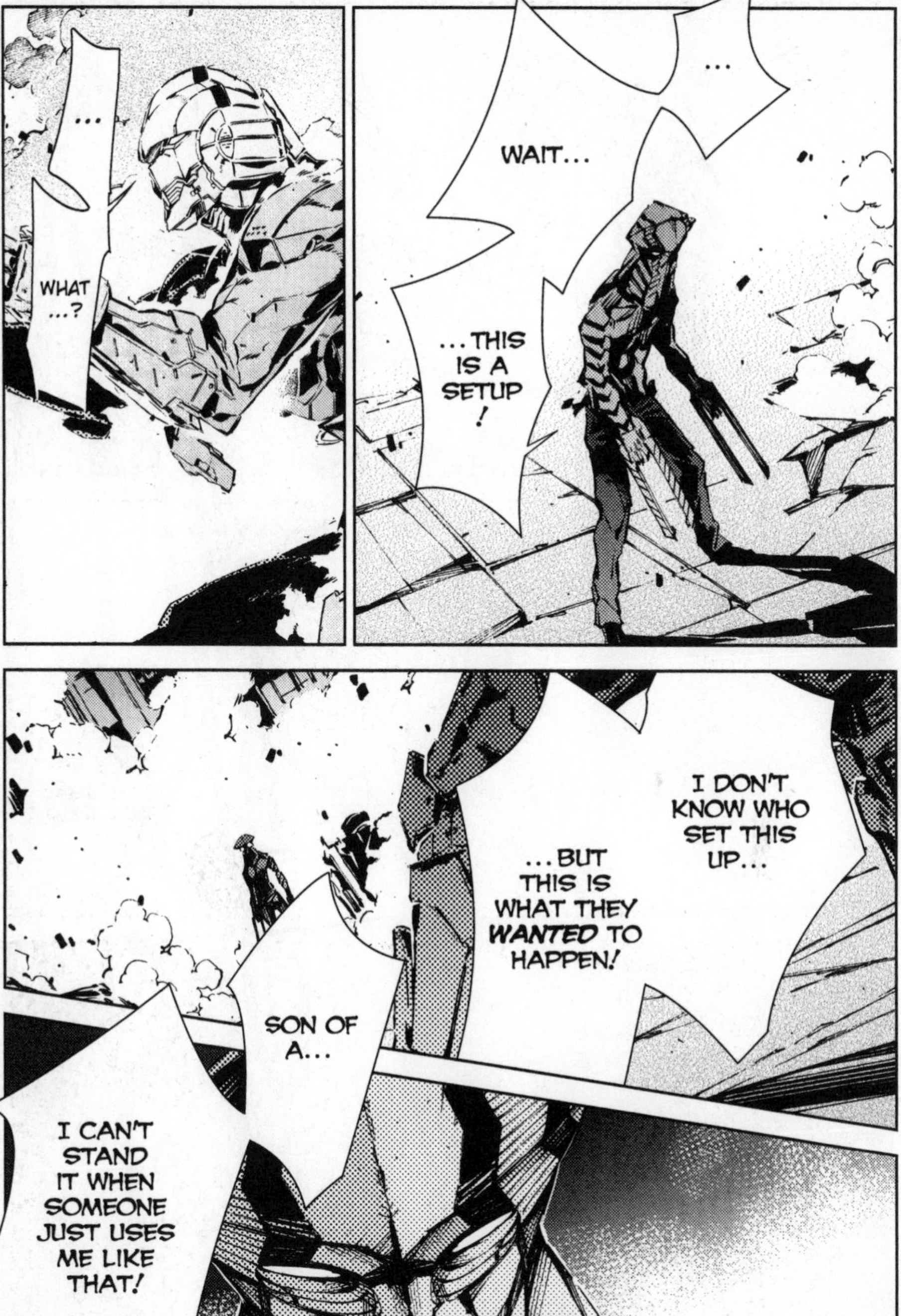
...
WAIT...
...THIS IS A SETUP!
...
WHAT...?
I DON'T KNOW WHO SET THIS UP...
...BUT THIS IS WHAT THEY WANTED TO HAPPEN!
SON OF A...
I CAN'T STAND IT WHEN SOMEONE JUST USES ME LIKE THAT!

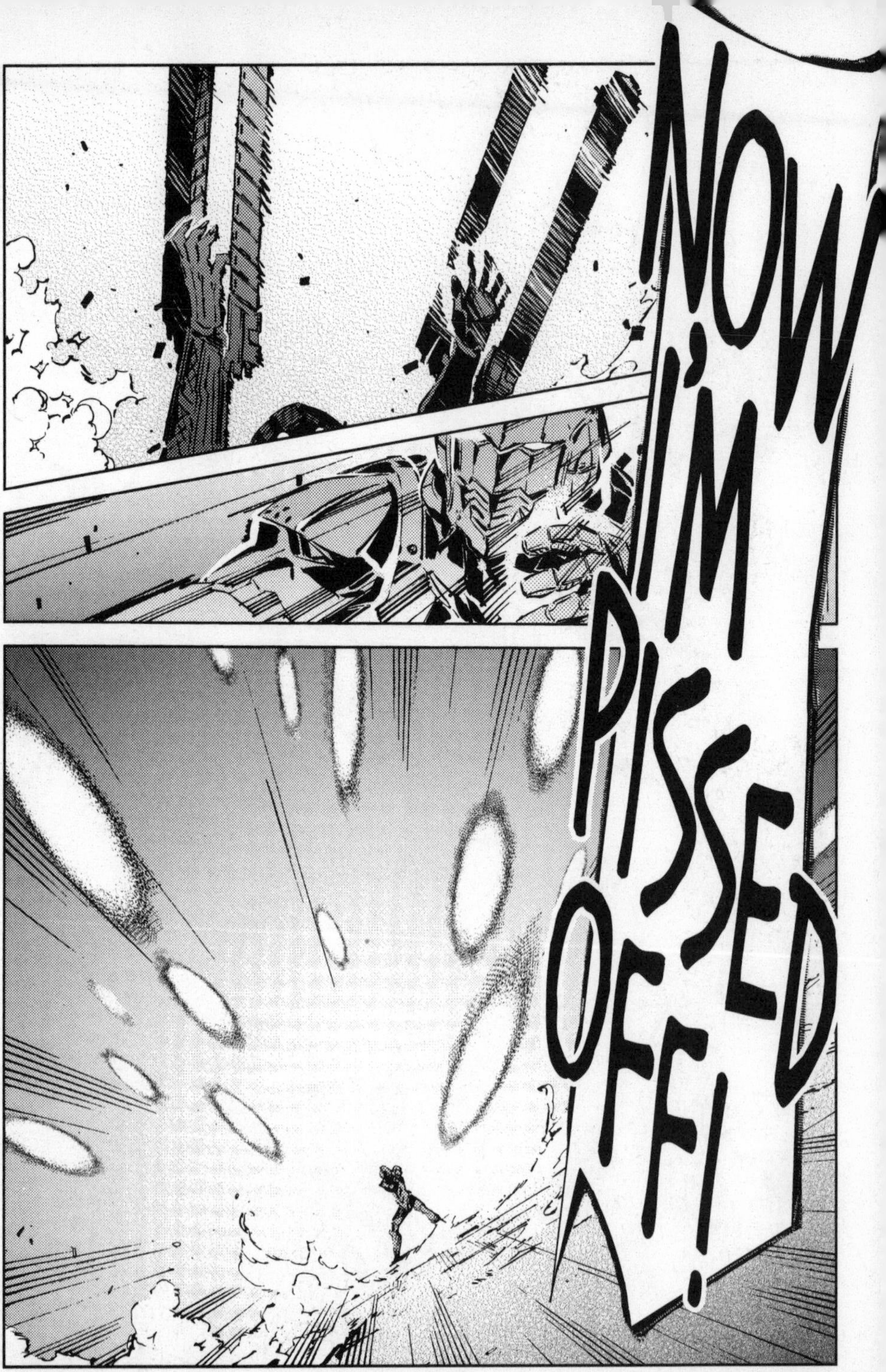
NOW I'M PISSED OFF!

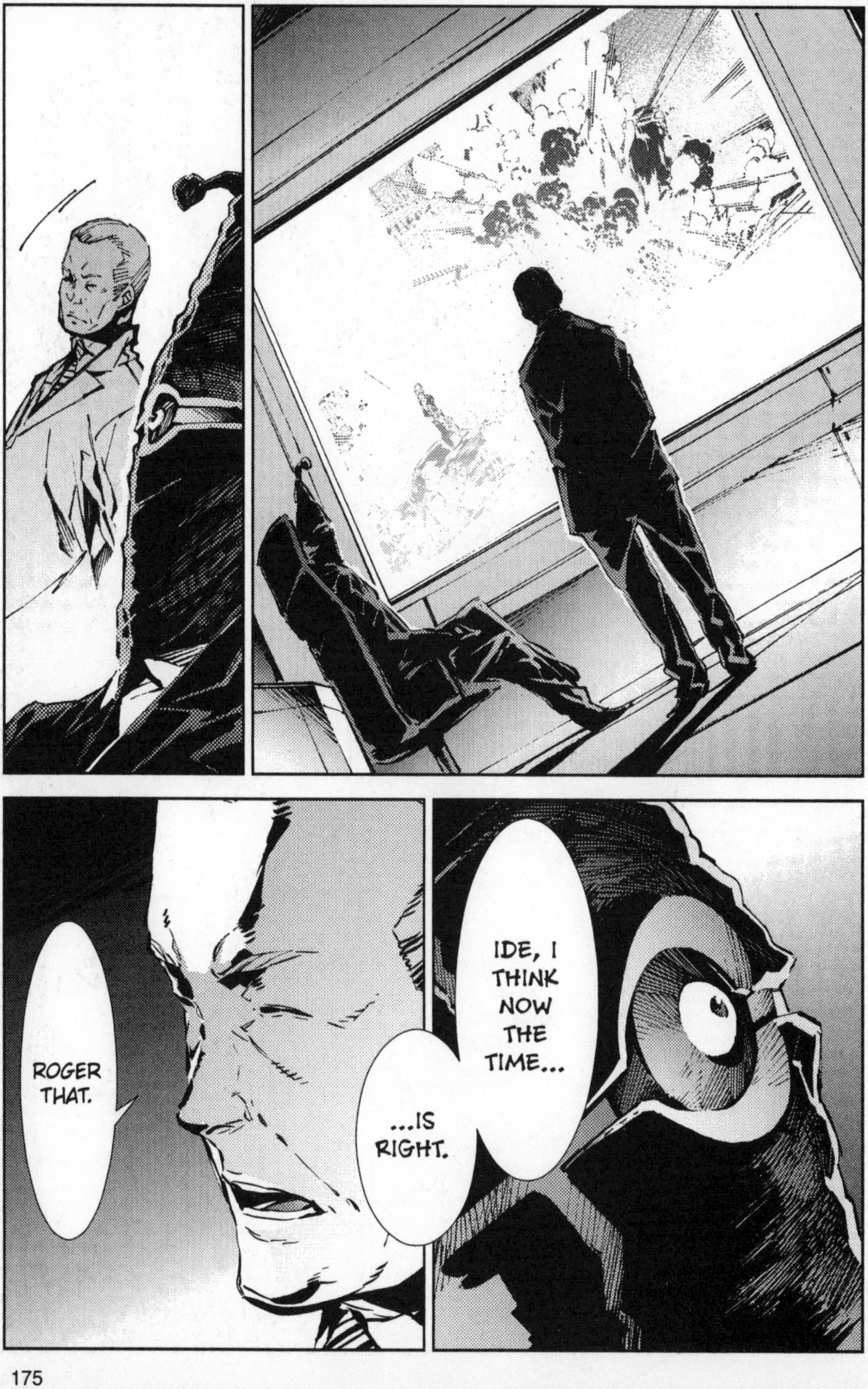
IDE, I THINK NOW THE TIME...
...IS RIGHT.
ROGER THAT.

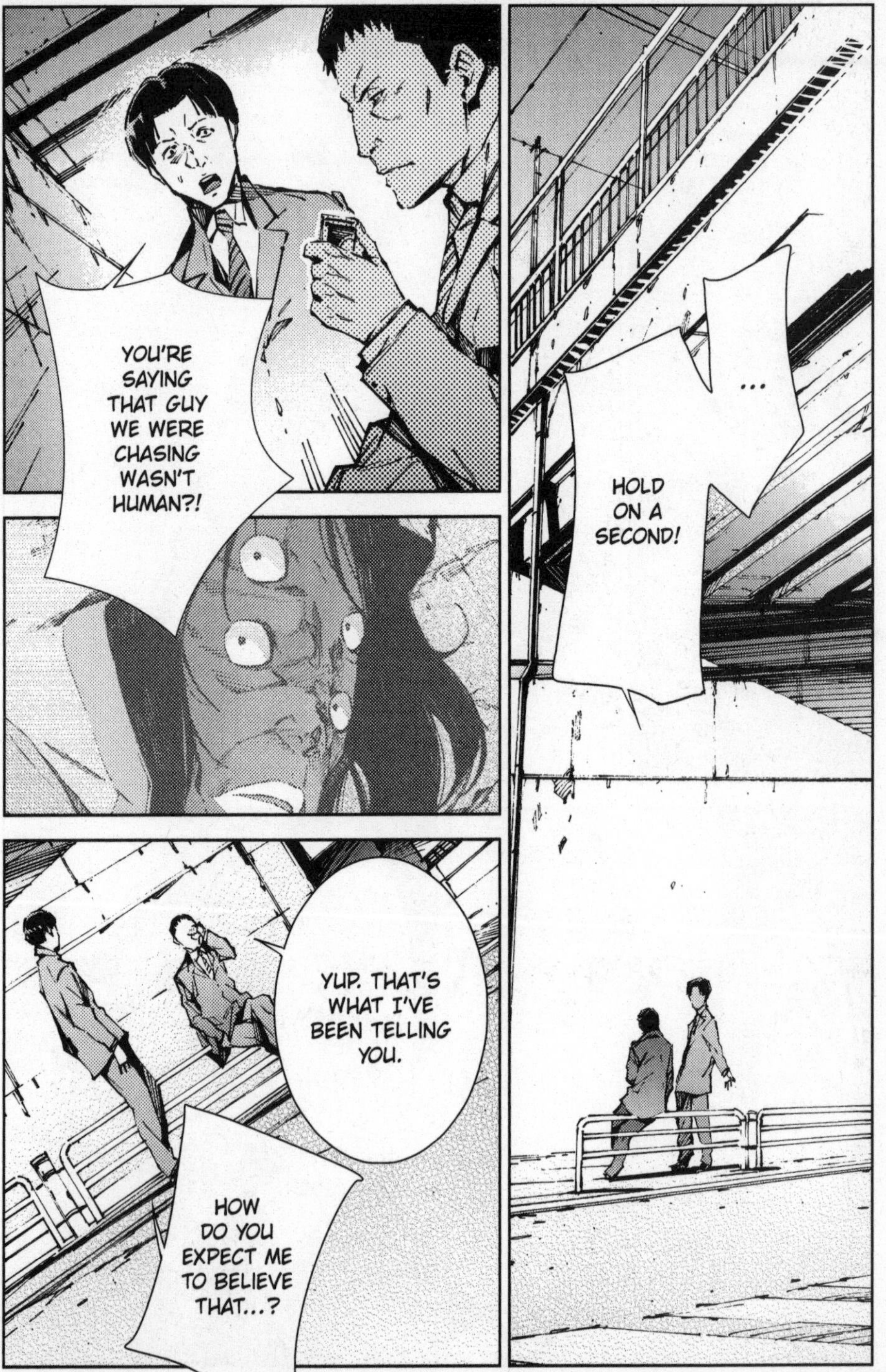
...
HOLD ON A SECOND!
YOU'RE SAYING THAT GUY WE WERE CHASING WASN'T HUMAN?!
YUP. THAT'S WHAT I'VE BEEN TELLING YOU.
HOW DO YOU EXPECT ME TO BELIEVE THAT...?

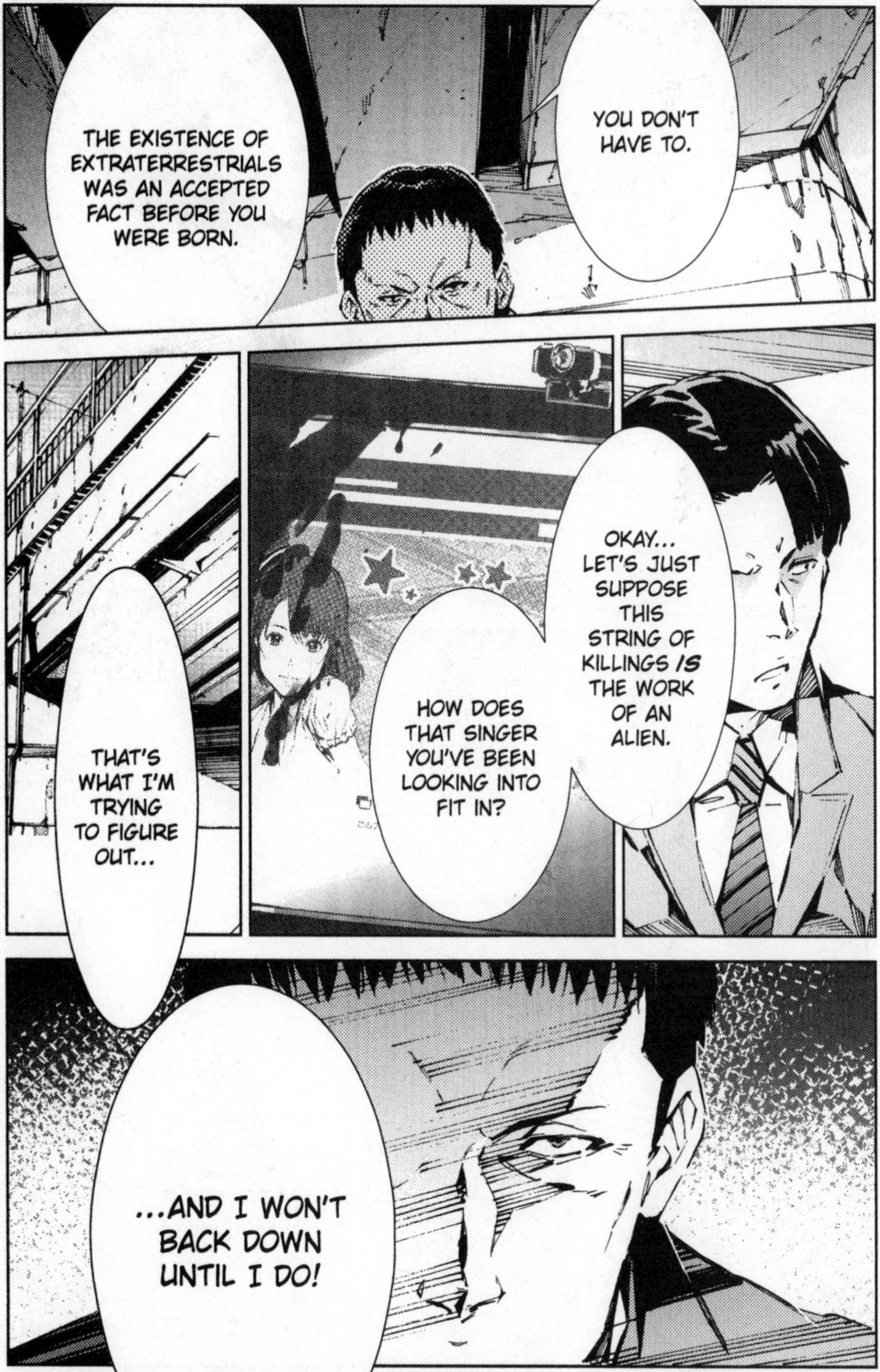
YOU DON'T HAVE TO.
THE EXISTENCE OF EXTRATERRESTRIALS WAS AN ACCEPTED FACT BEFORE YOU WERE BORN.
OKAY... LET'S JUST SUPPOSE THIS STRING OF KILLINGS *IS* THE WORK OF AN ALIEN.
HOW DOES THAT SINGER YOU'VE BEEN LOOKING INTO FIT IN?
THAT'S WHAT I'M TRYING TO FIGURE OUT...
...AND I WON'T BACK DOWN UNTIL I DO!

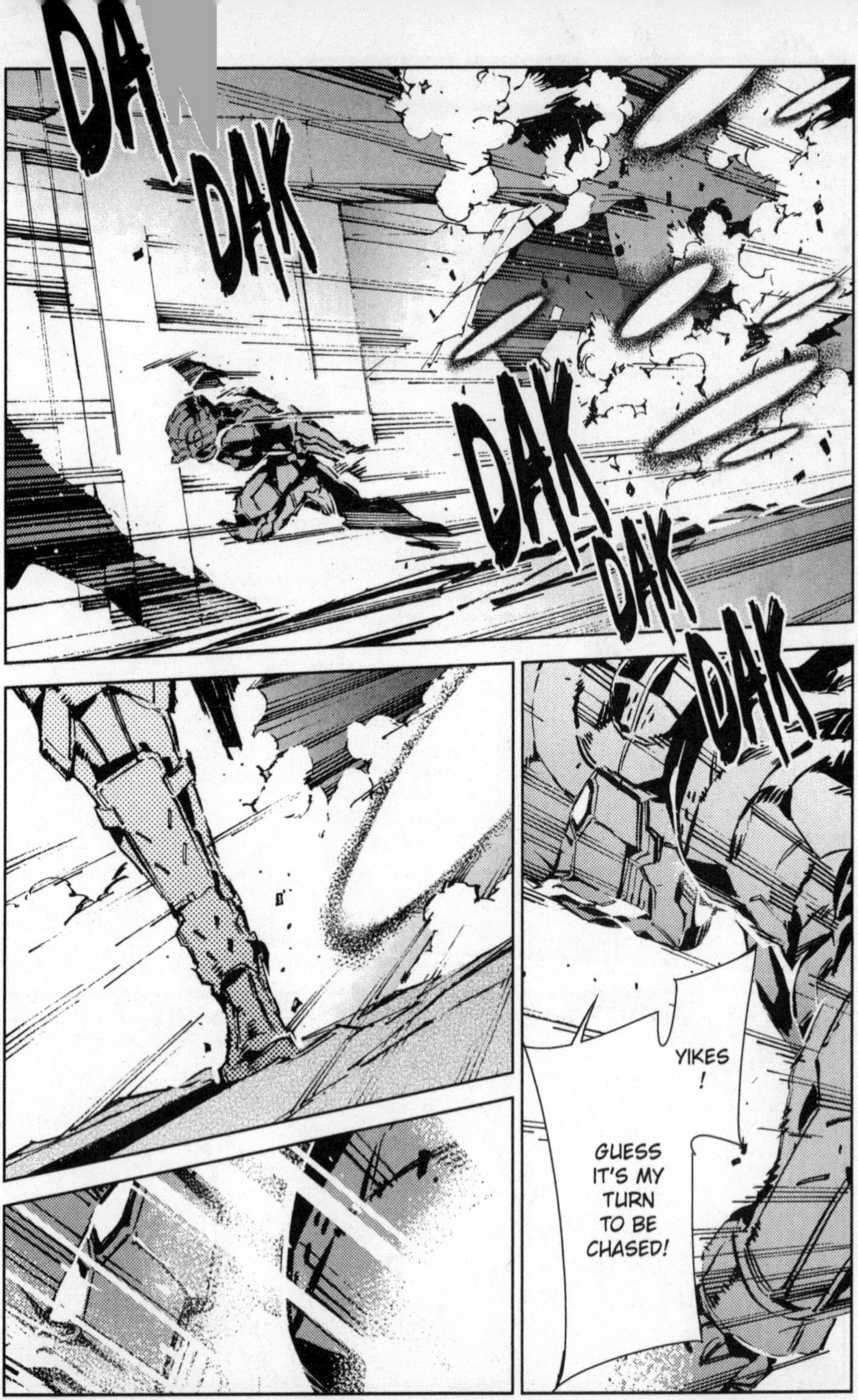
DA
DAK
DAK
DAK
DAK
YIKES!
GUESS IT'S MY TURN TO BE CHASED!

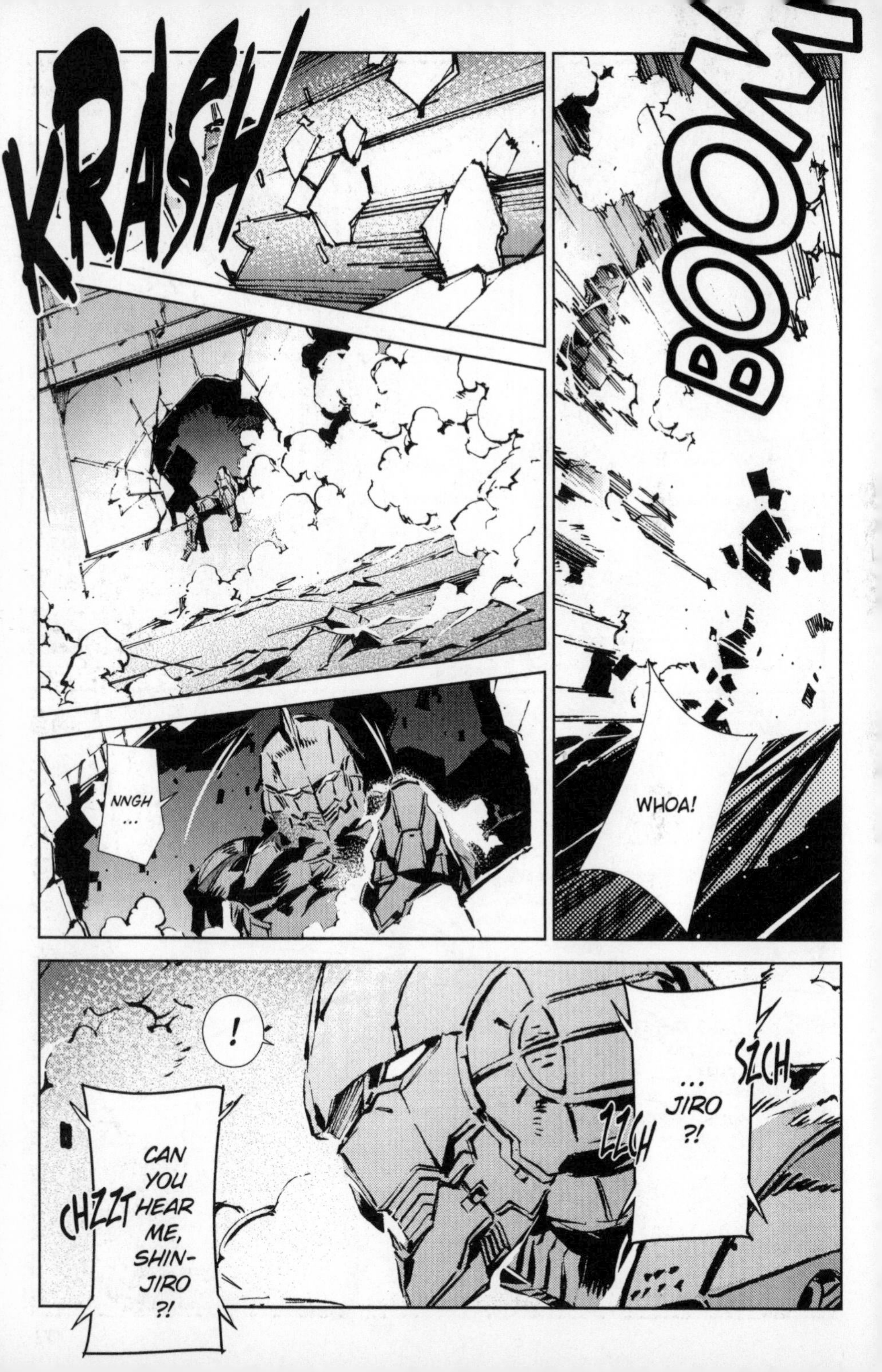
BOOM
WHOA!
KRASH!
NNGH ...
SZCH
... JIRO ?!
ZZCH
!
CHZZT
CAN YOU HEAR ME, SHIN-JIRO ?!

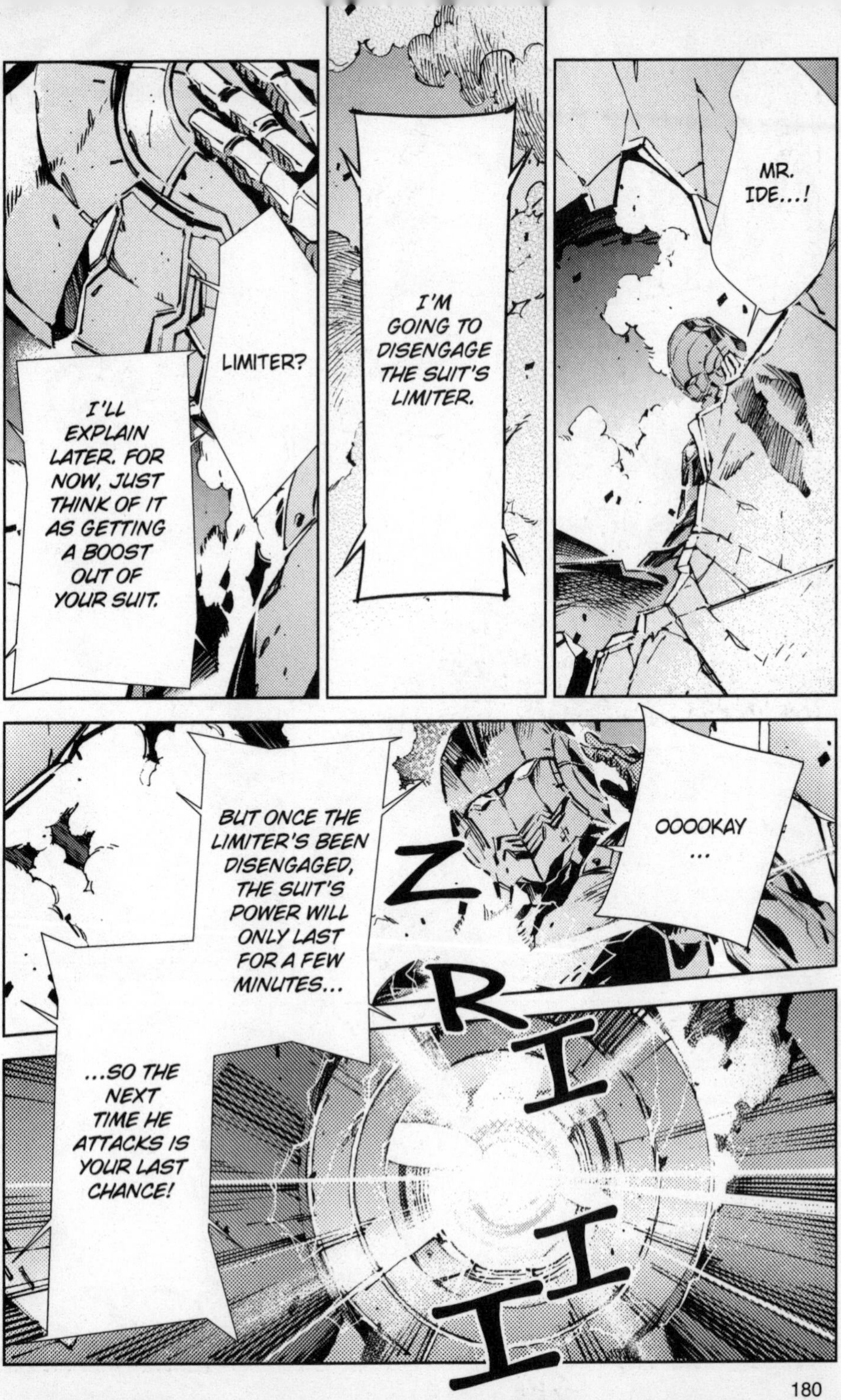
MR. IDE...!
I'M GOING TO DISENGAGE THE SUIT'S LIMITER.
LIMITER?
I'LL EXPLAIN LATER. FOR NOW, JUST THINK OF IT AS GETTING A BOOST OUT OF YOUR SUIT.
OOOOKAY ...
BUT ONCE THE LIMITER'S BEEN DISENGAGED, THE SUIT'S POWER WILL ONLY LAST FOR A FEW MINUTES...
...SO THE NEXT TIME HE ATTACKS IS YOUR LAST CHANCE!
ZRIIII

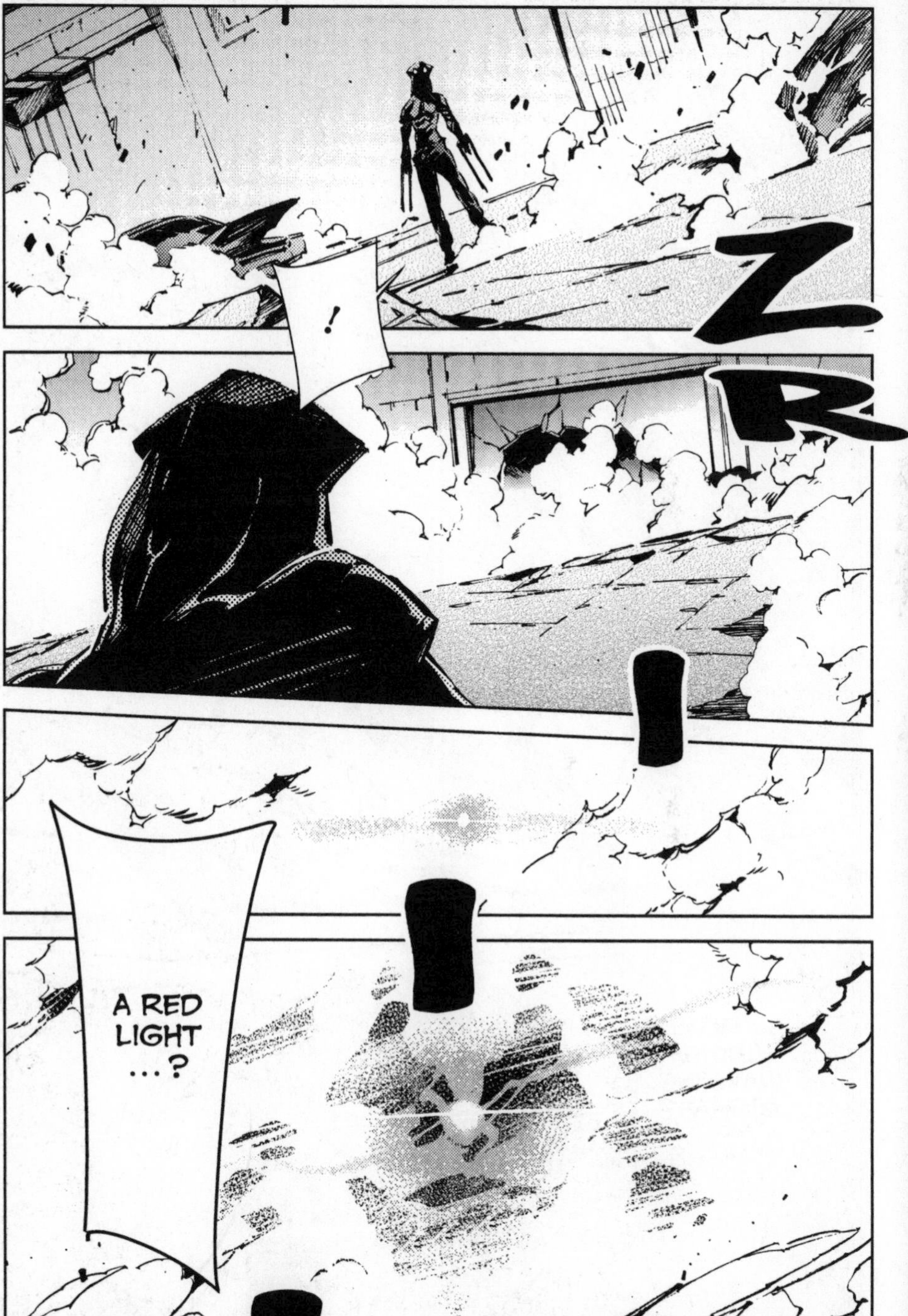
ZRR
!
A RED LIGHT ...?

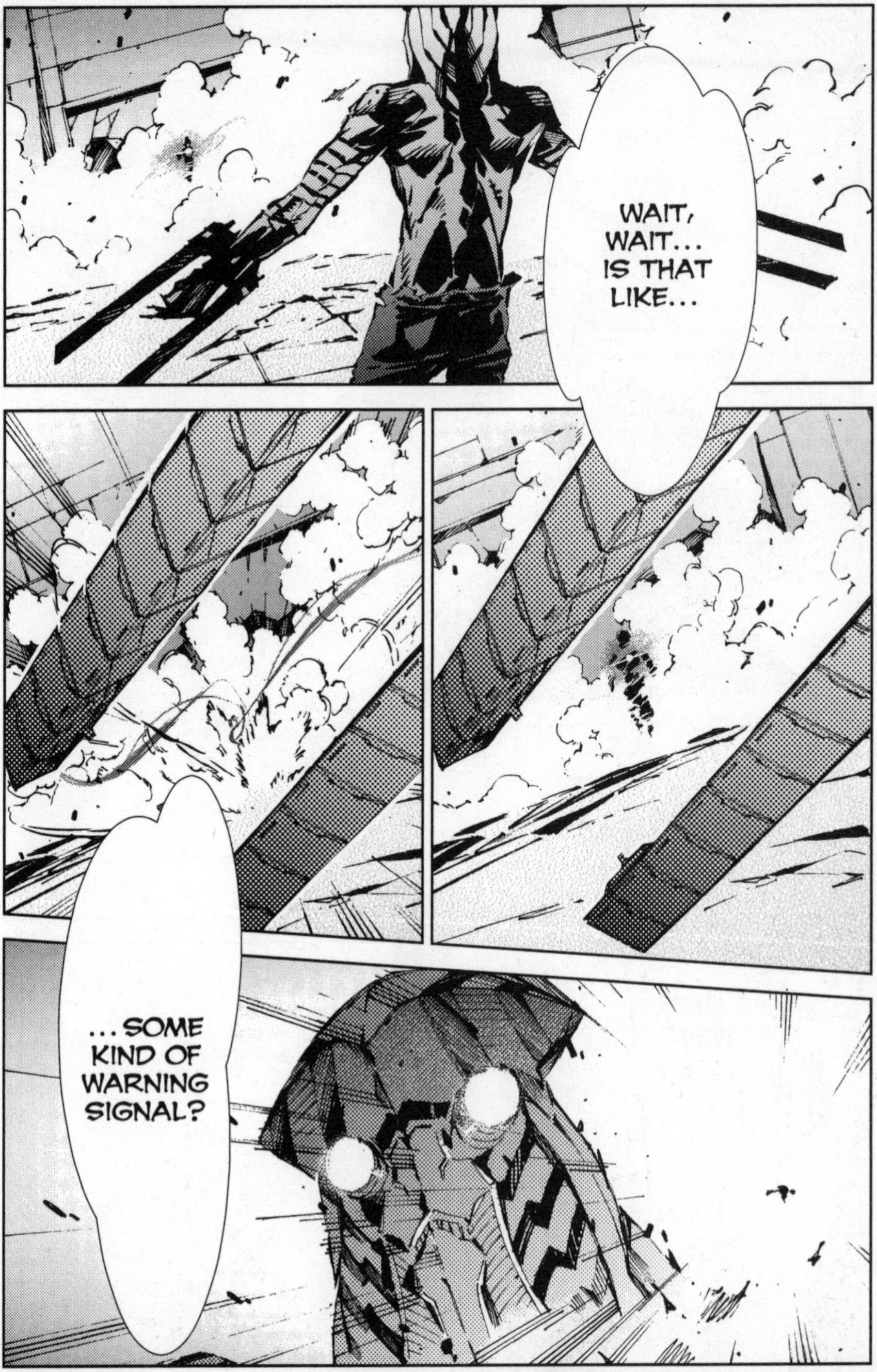
WAIT, WAIT... IS THAT LIKE...
...SOME KIND OF WARNING SIGNAL?

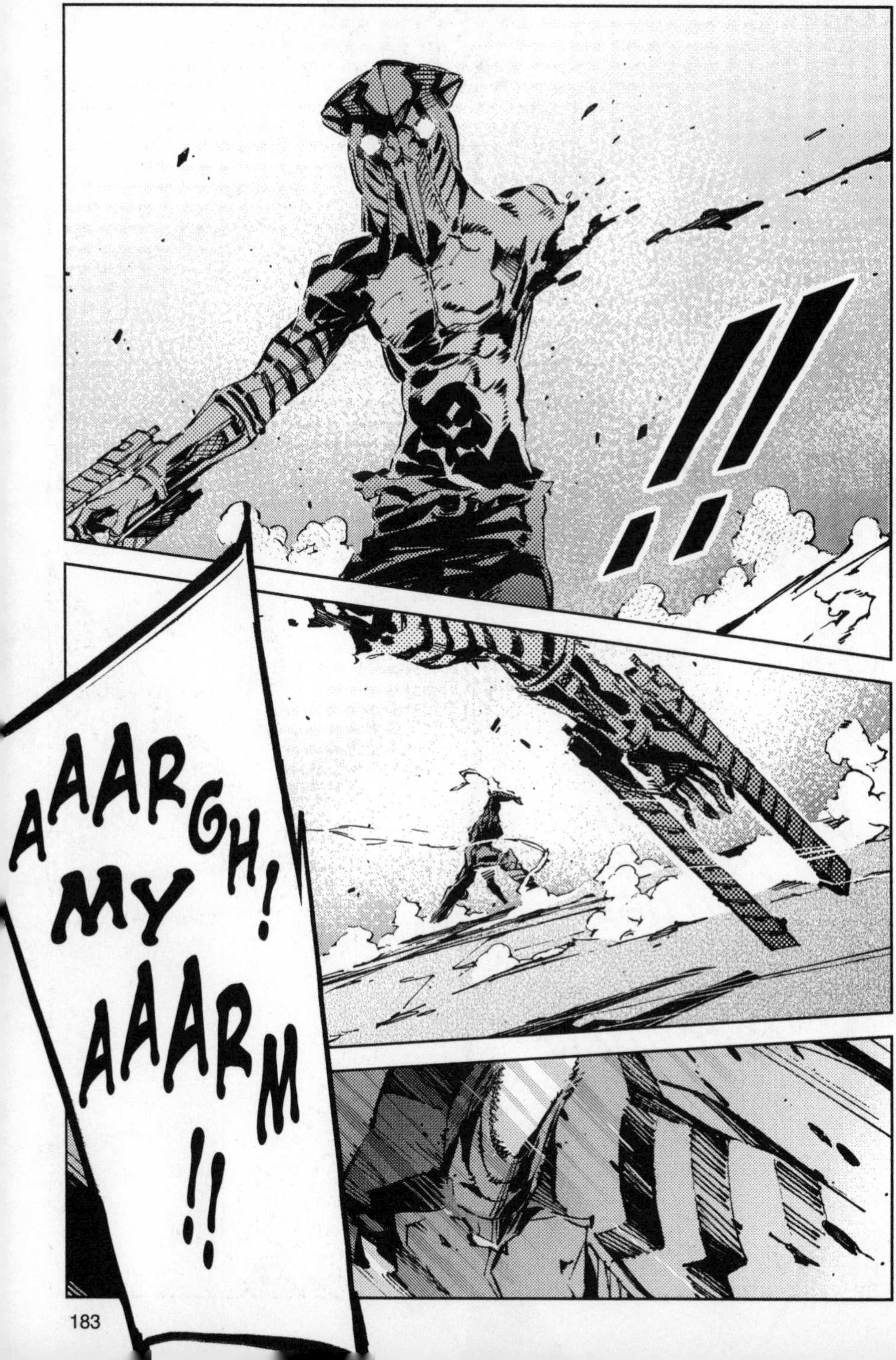
!!
AAARGH! MY AAARM!!

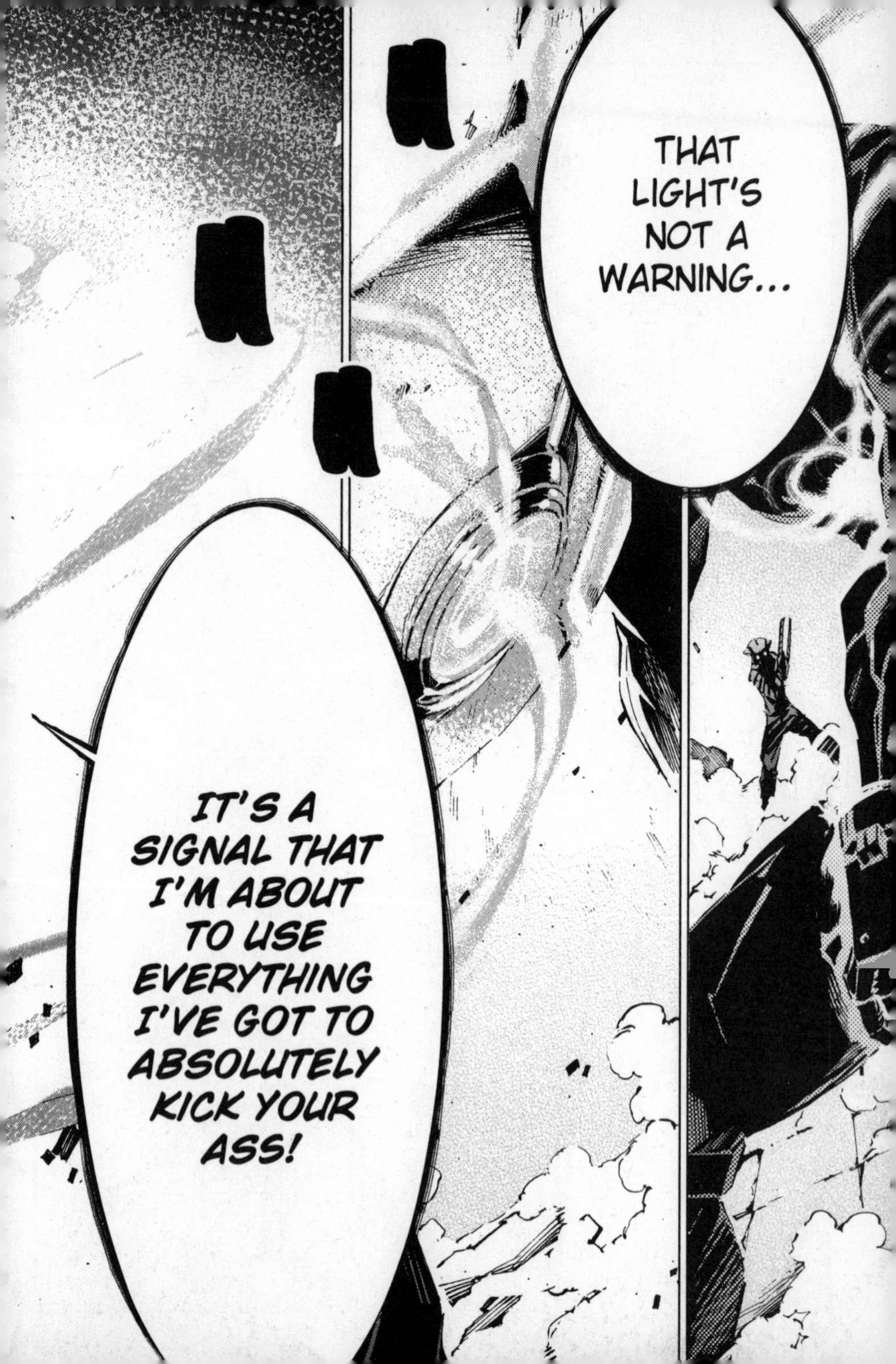
THAT LIGHT'S NOT A WARNING...
IT'S A SIGNAL THAT I'M ABOUT TO USE EVERYTHING I'VE GOT TO ABSOLUTELY KICK YOUR ASS!

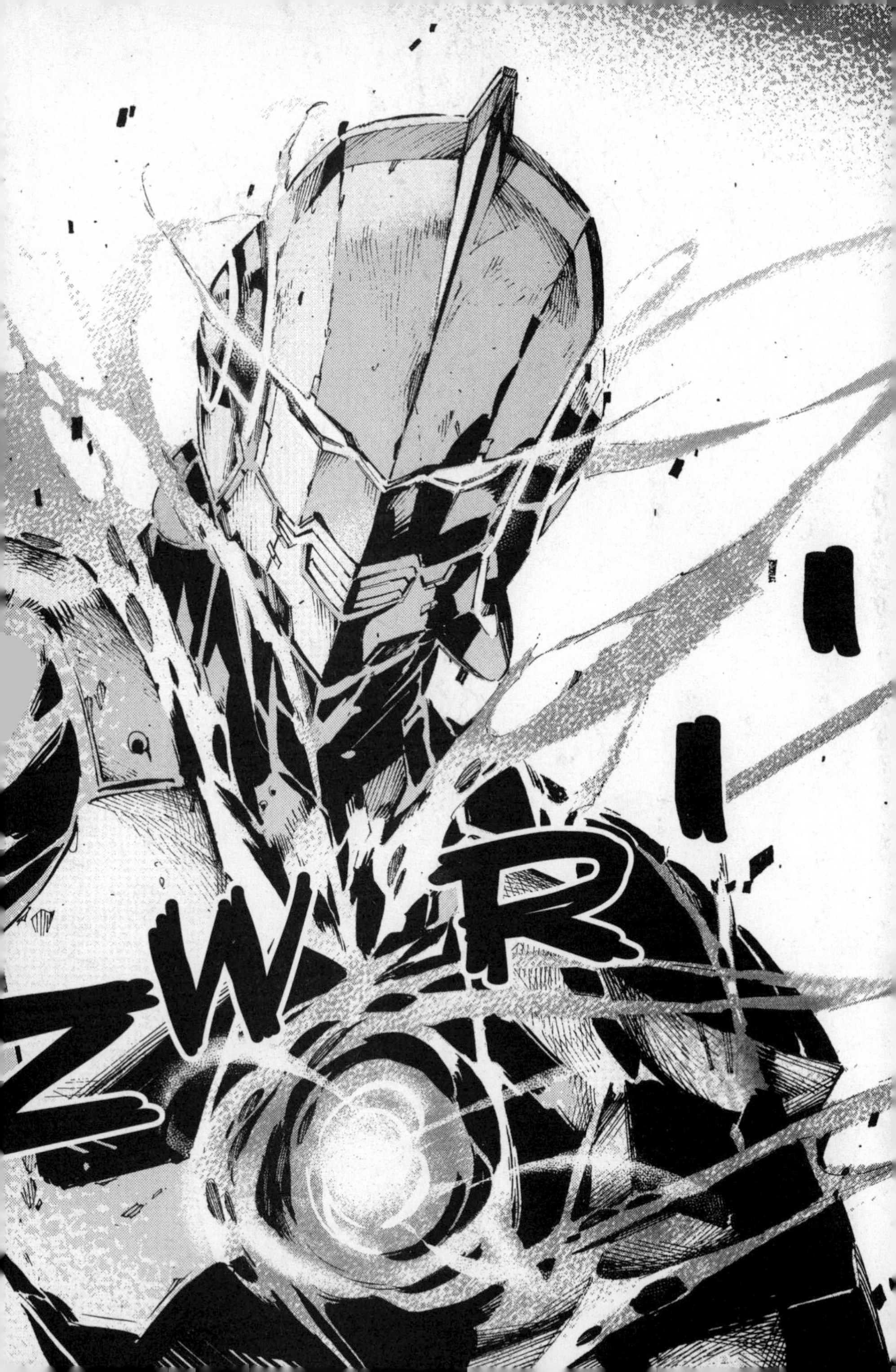
ZWR

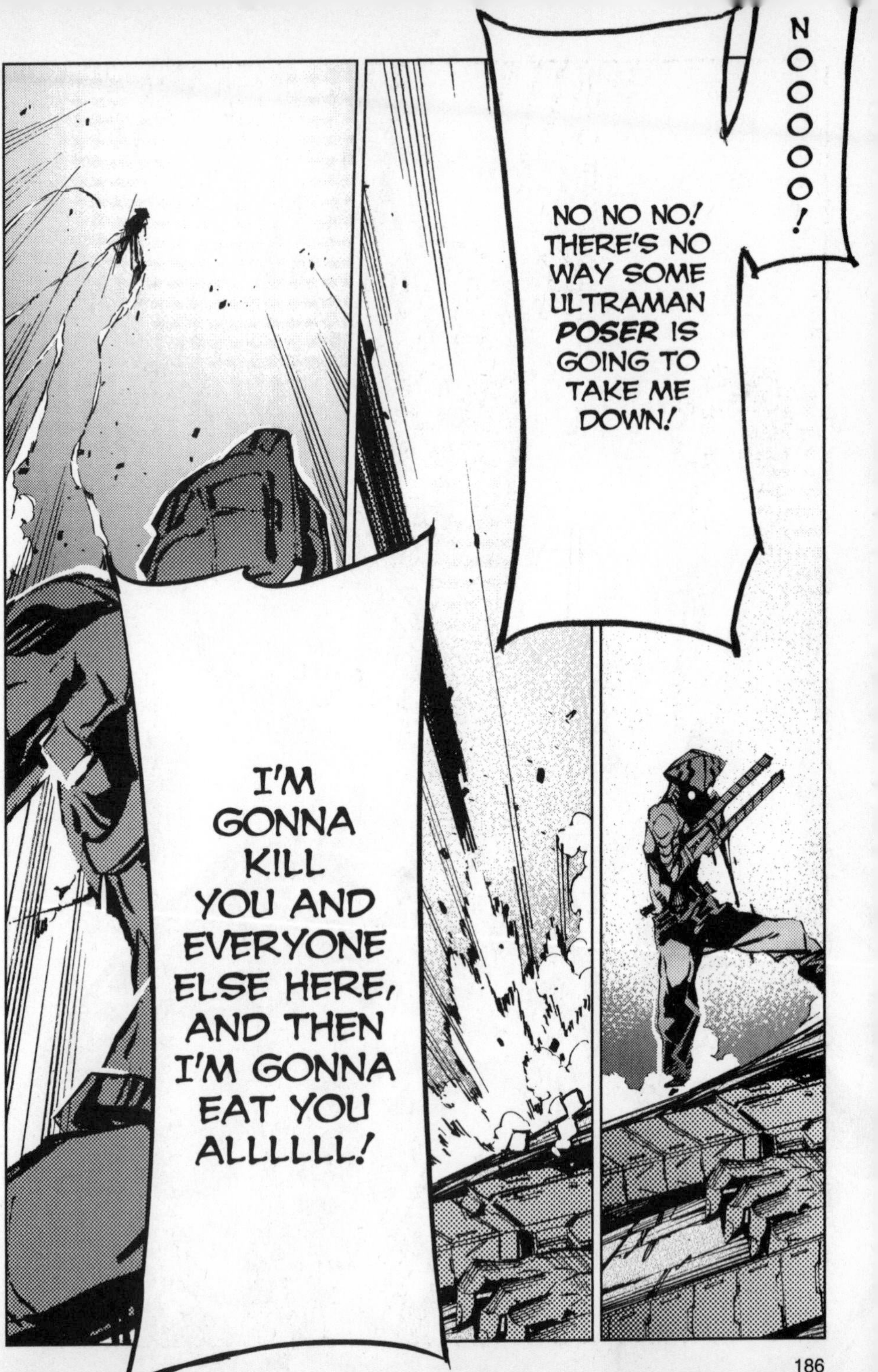
NOOOOOO!
NO NO NO! THERE'S NO WAY SOME ULTRAMAN POSER IS GOING TO TAKE ME DOWN!
I'M GONNA KILL YOU AND EVERYONE ELSE HERE, AND THEN I'M GONNA EAT YOU ALLLLLL!

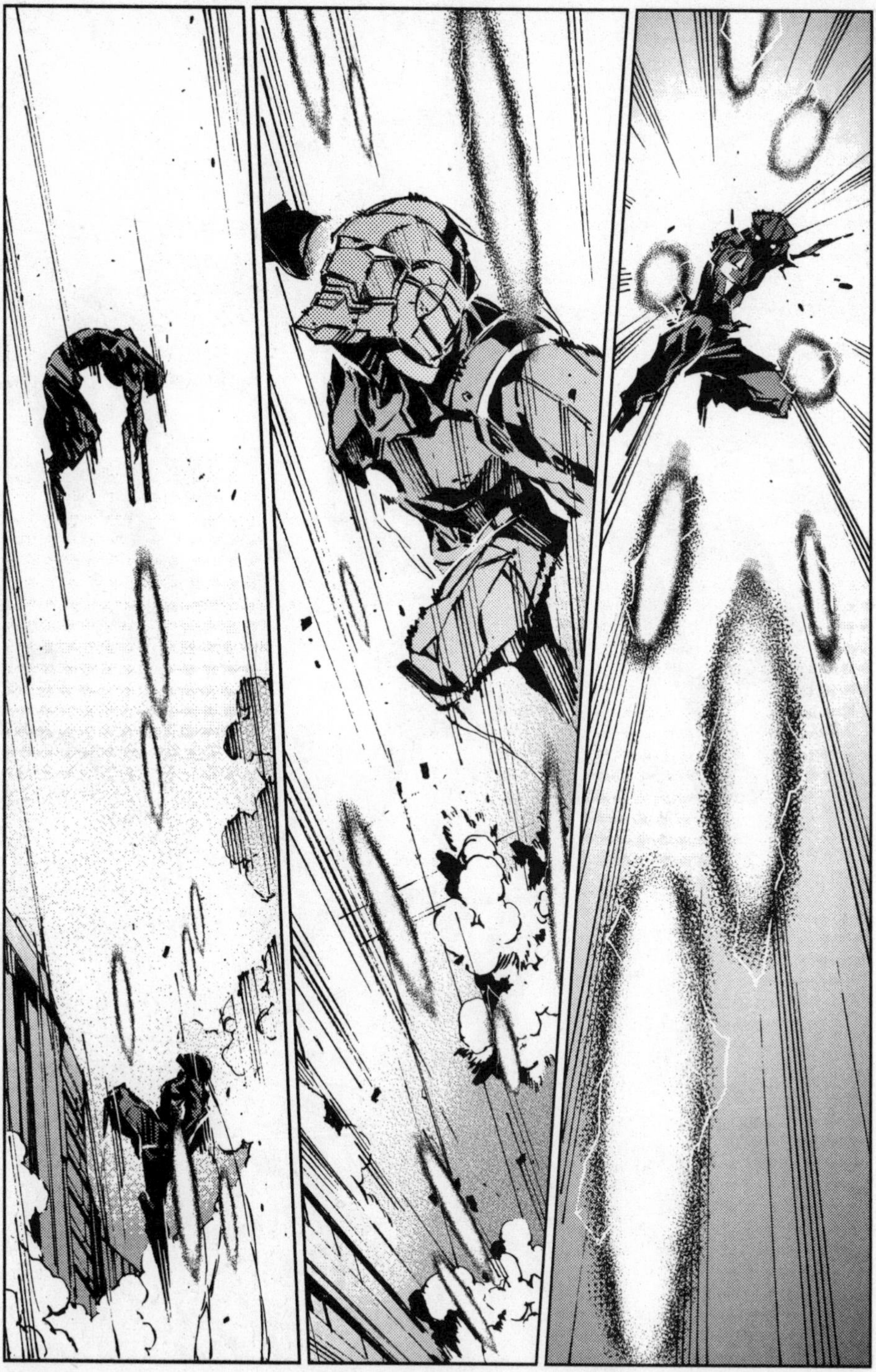

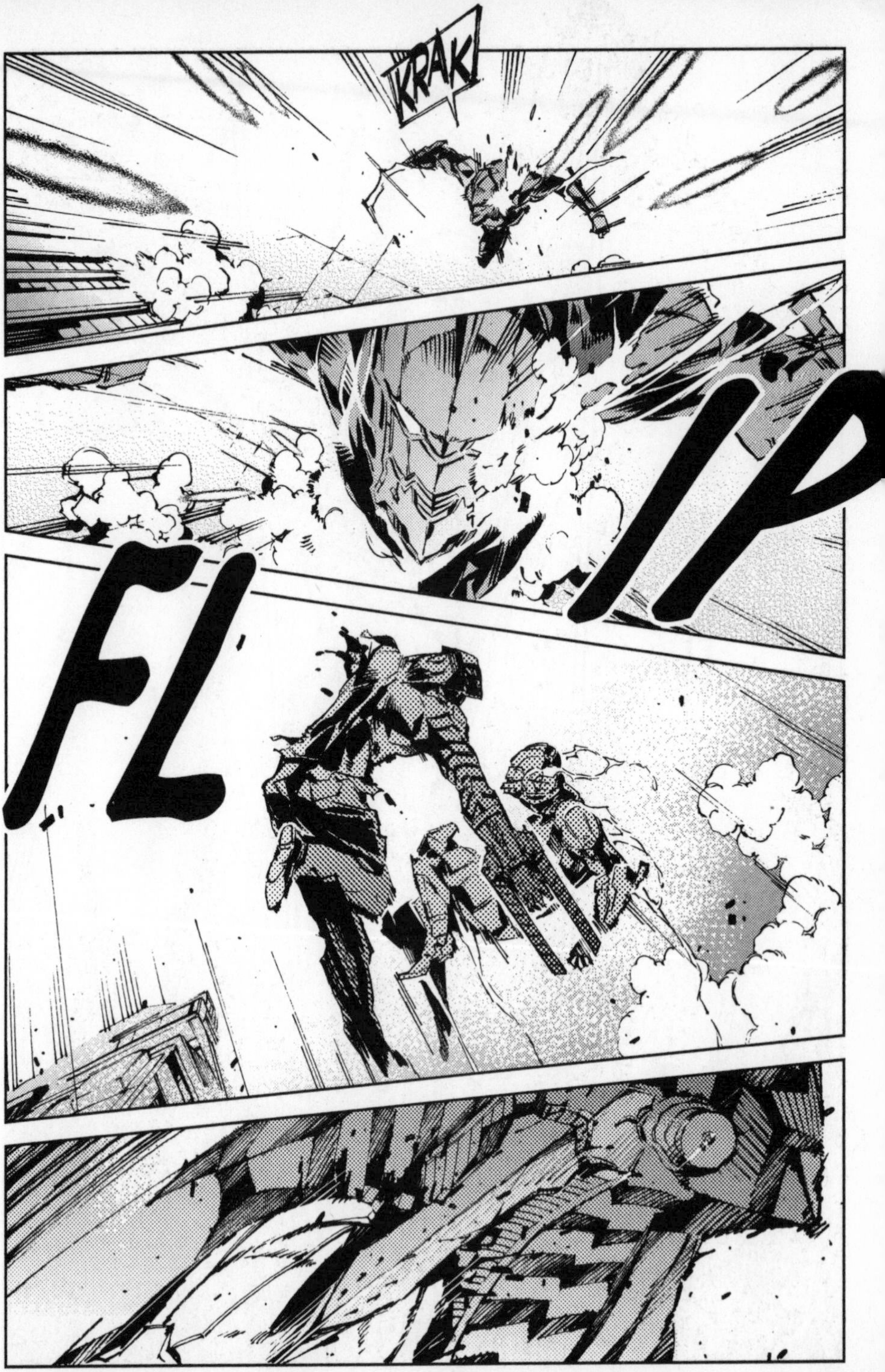
KRAK
FLIP

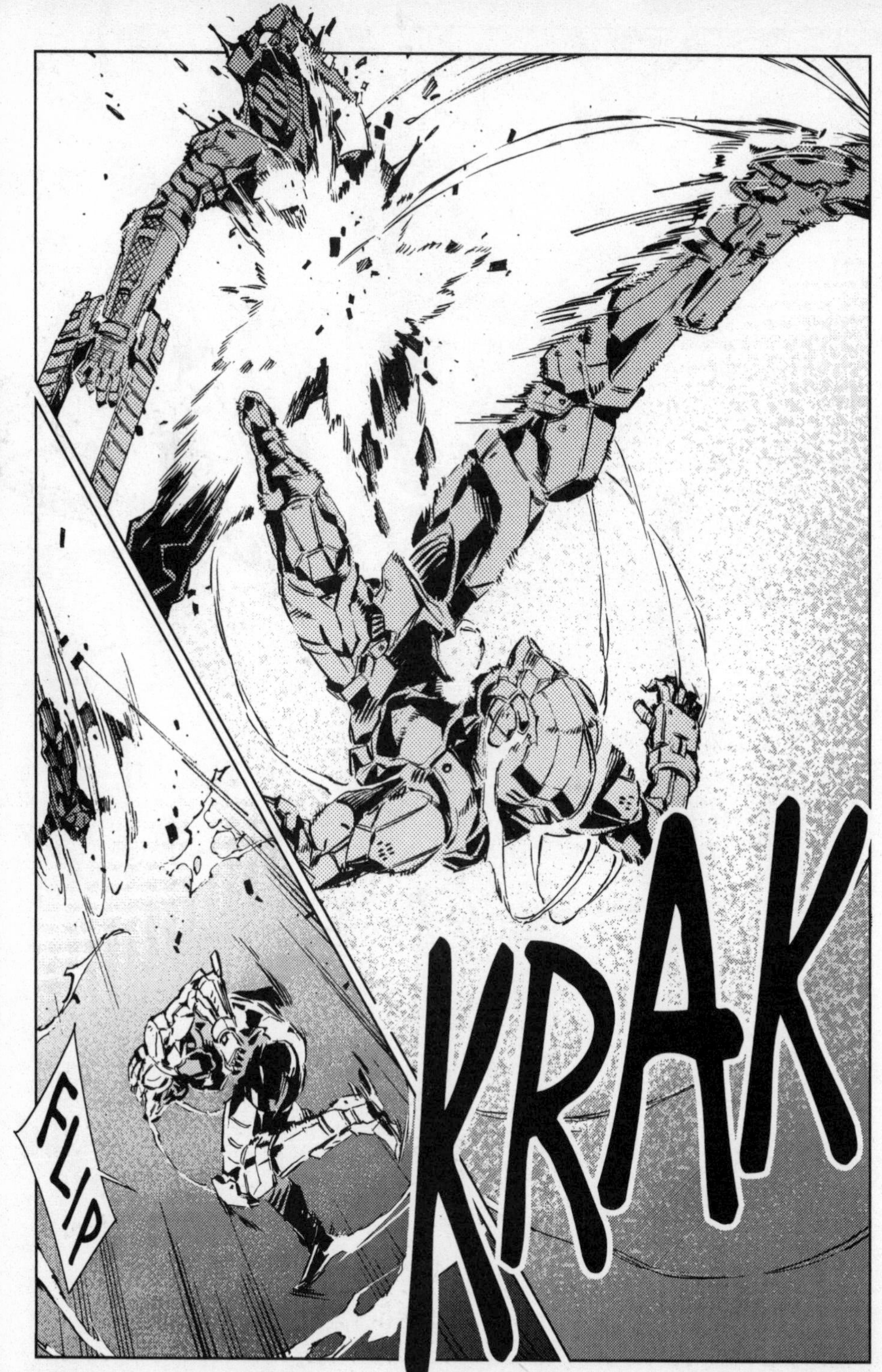
KRAK
FLIP

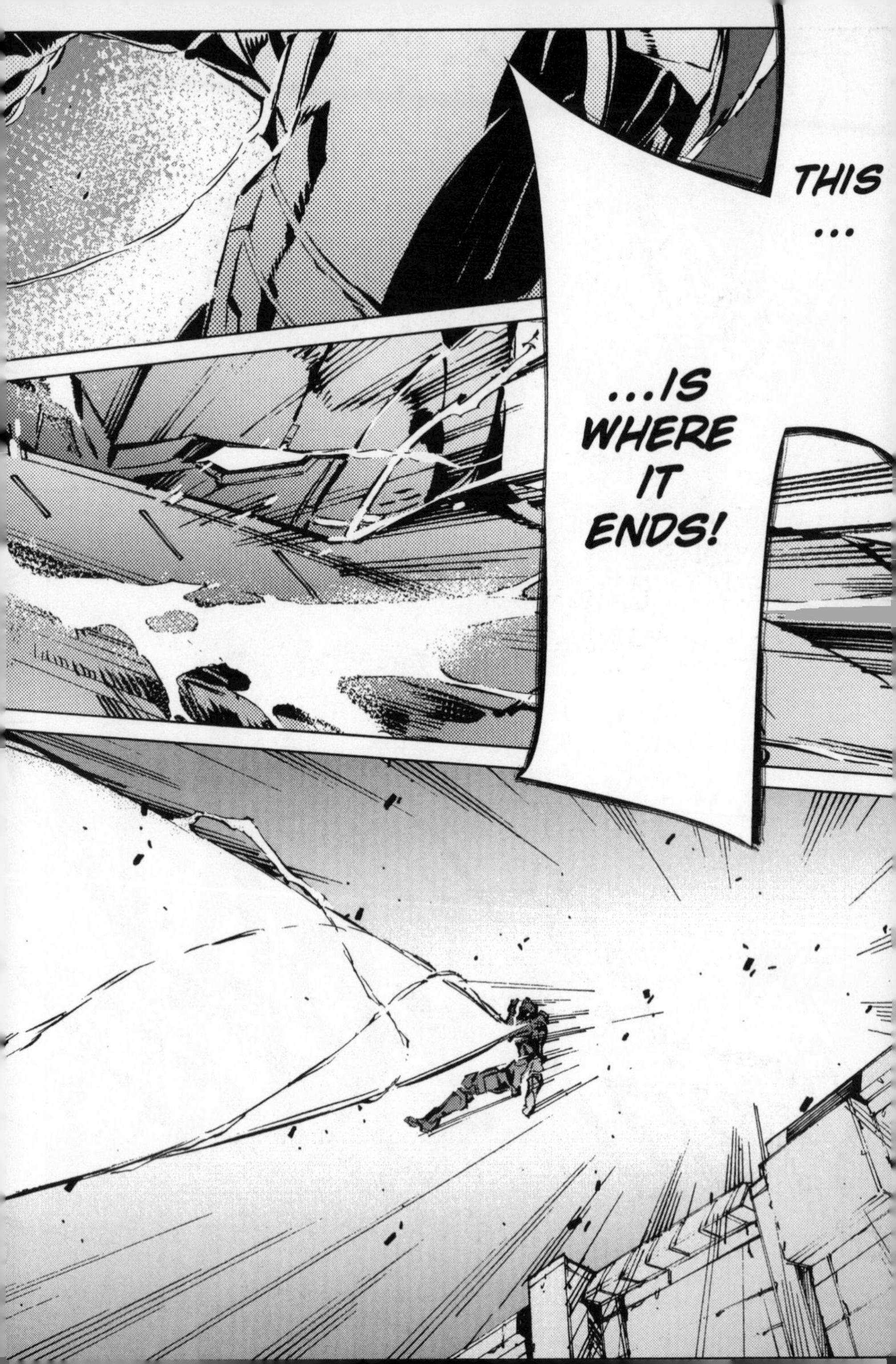
THIS ...
...IS WHERE IT ENDS!

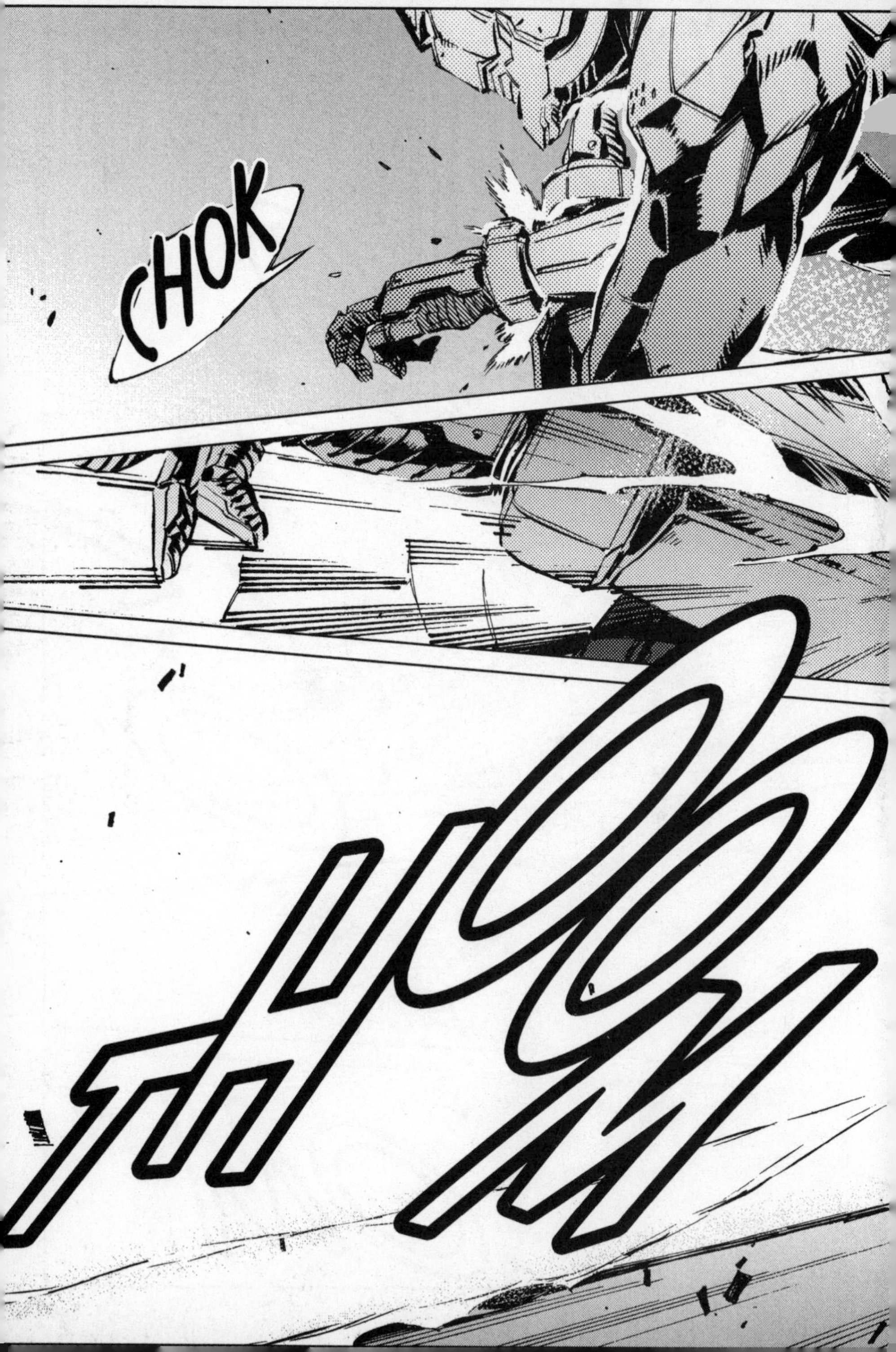
CHOK

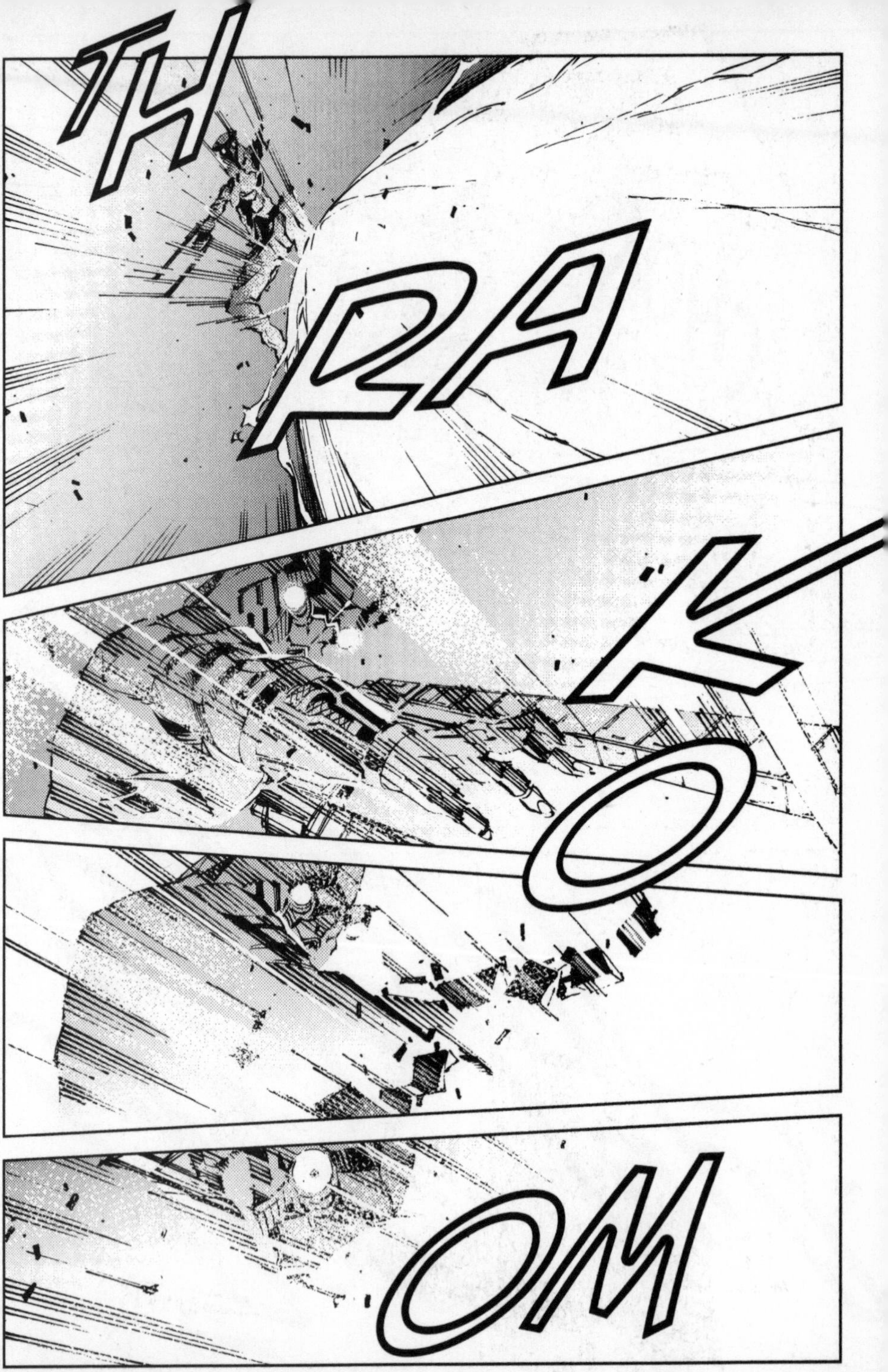
THRAKOOM

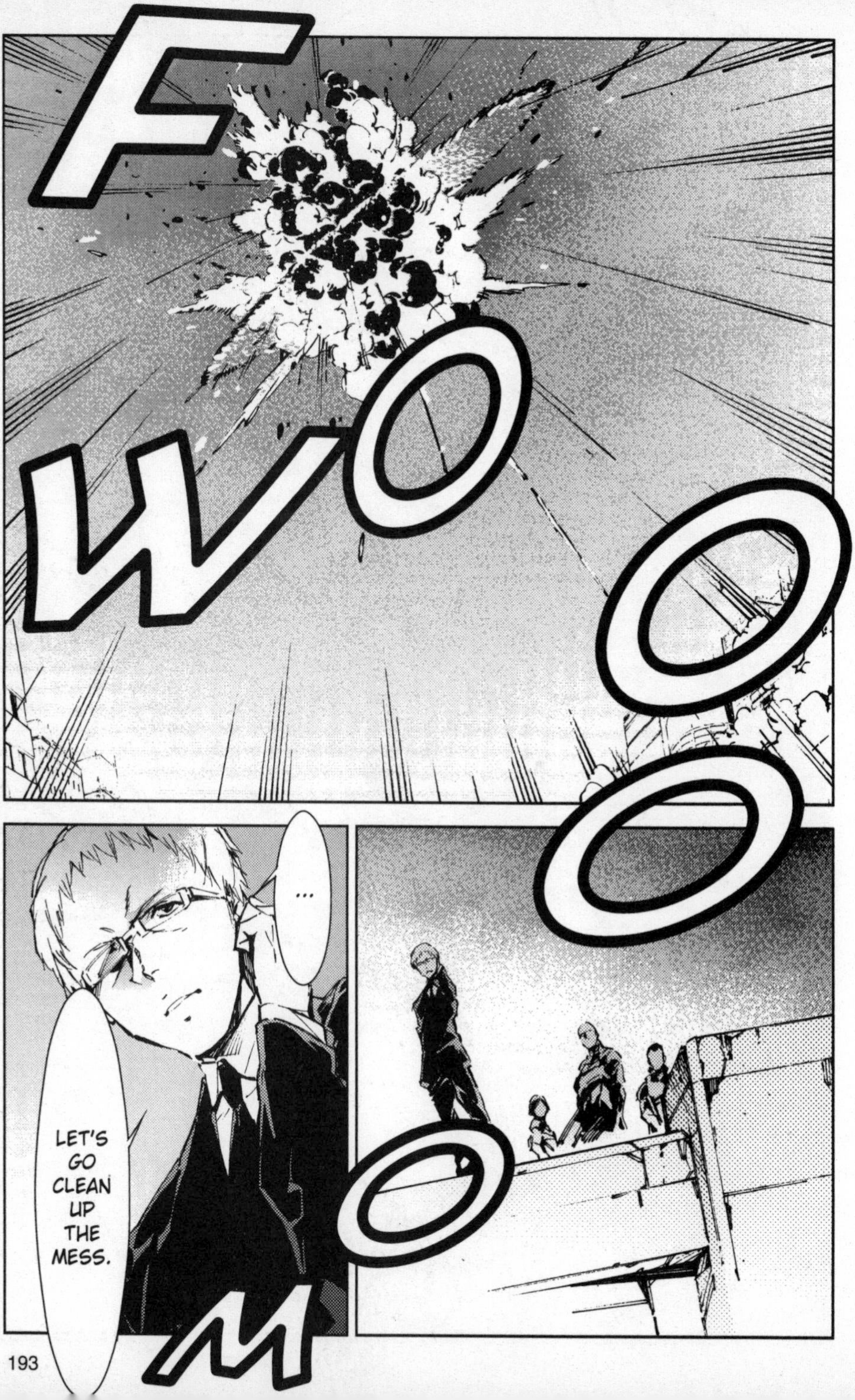
FWOOOOM
...
LET'S GO CLEAN UP THE MESS.

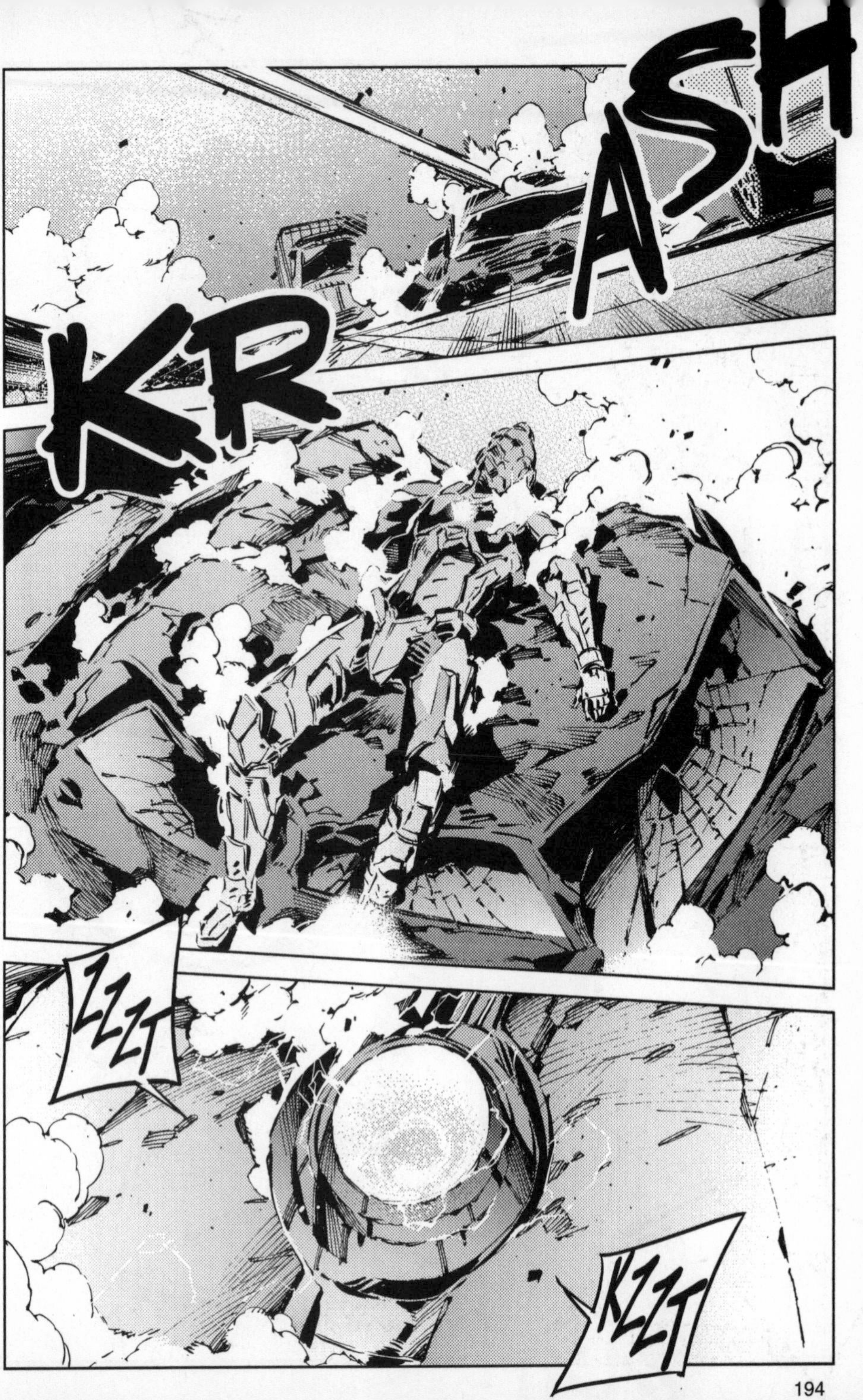
KRASH
ZZZT
KZZT

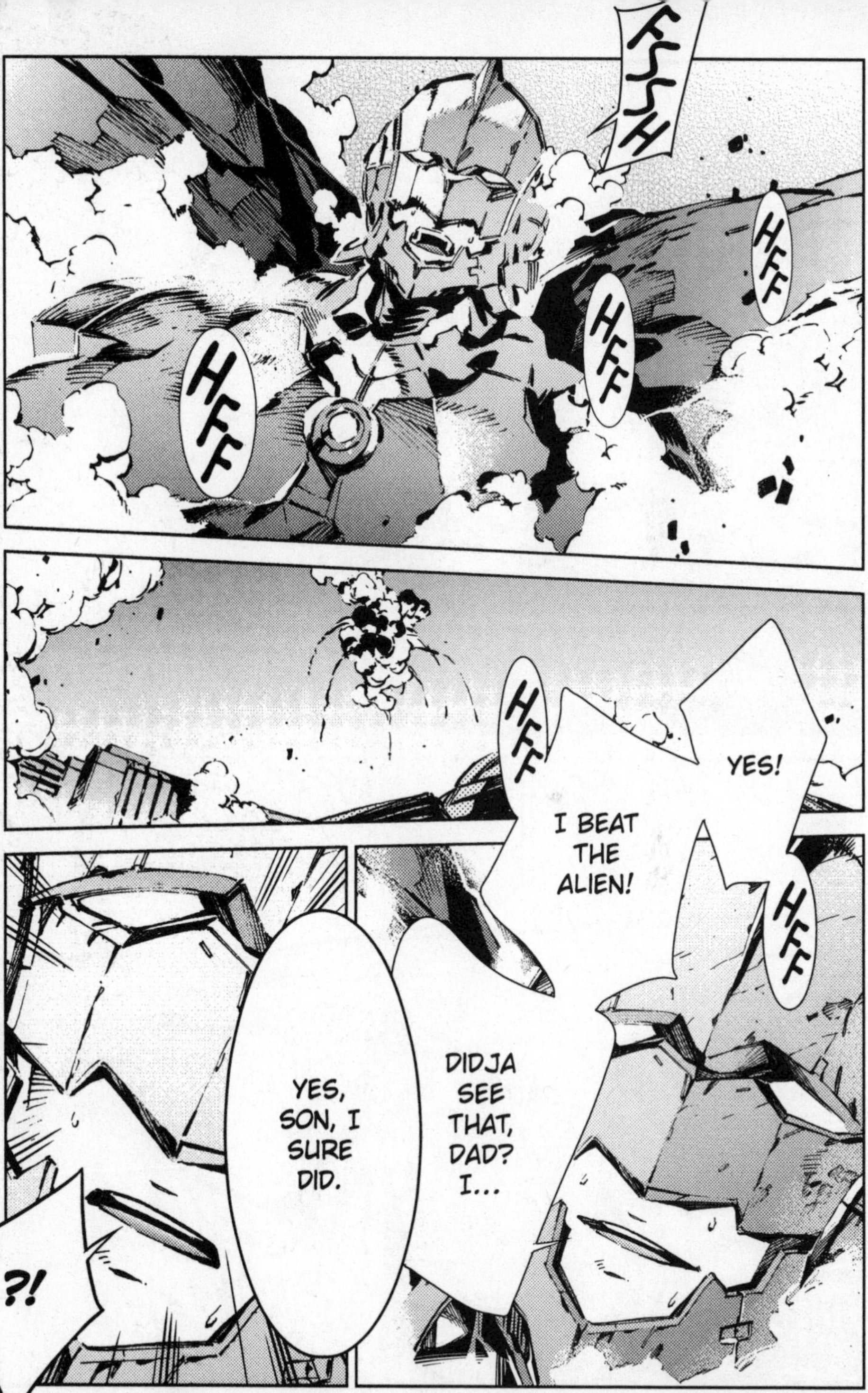
FSSH
HFF
HFF
HFF
HFF
YES!
I BEAT THE ALIEN!
HFF
DIDJA SEE THAT, DAD? I...
YES, SON, I SURE DID.
?!

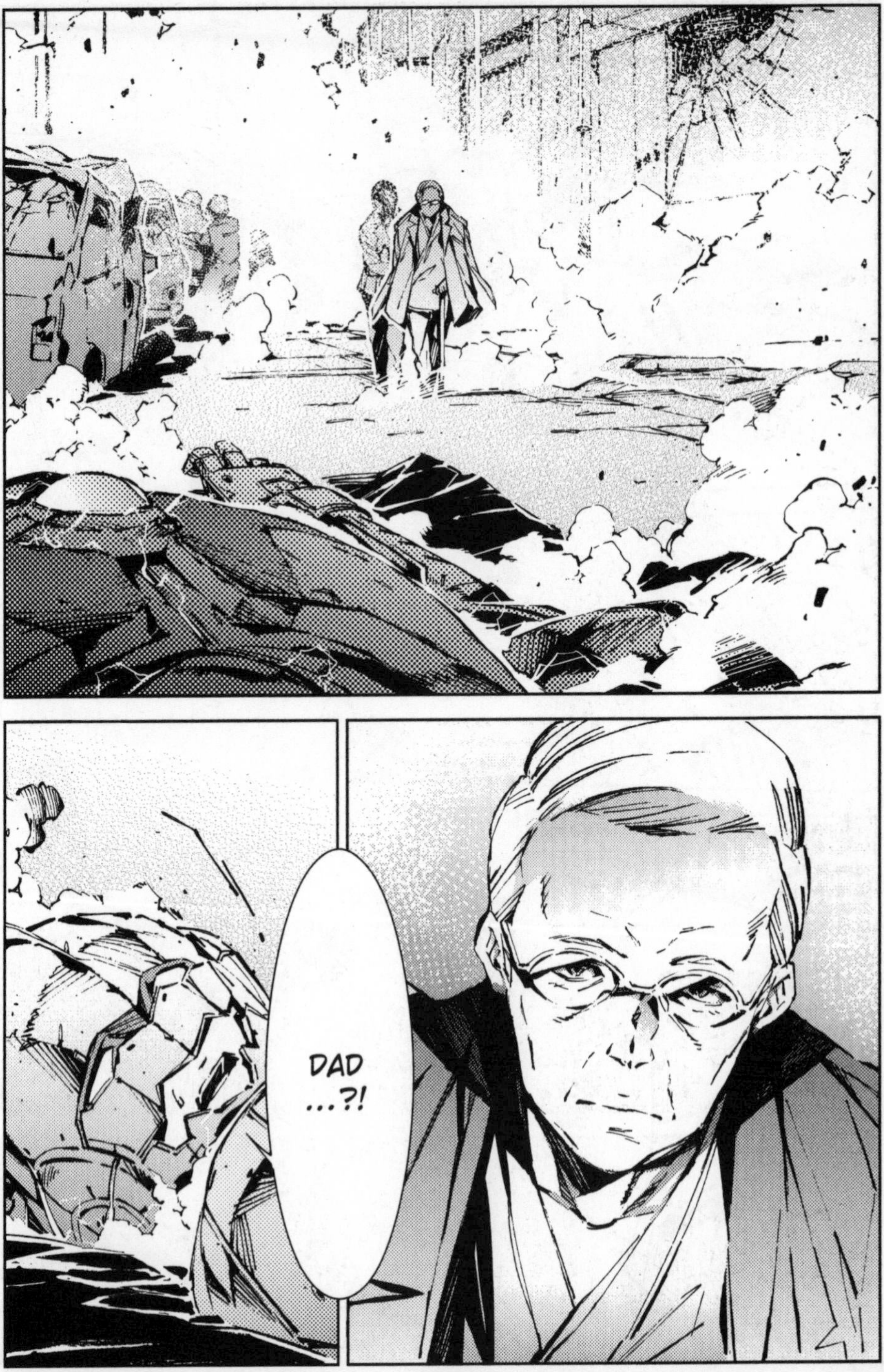
DAD
...?!

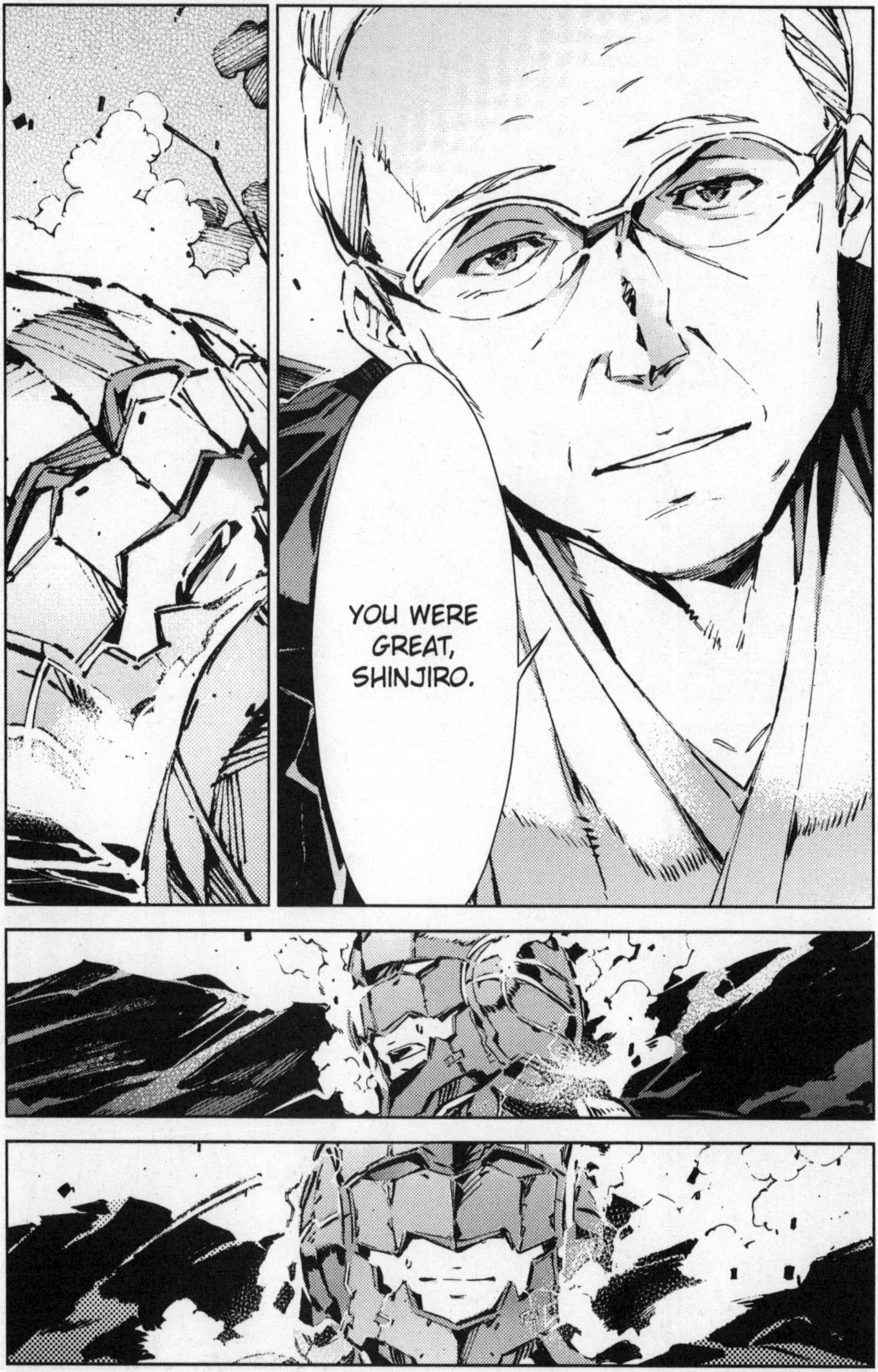
YOU WERE GREAT, SHINJIRO.

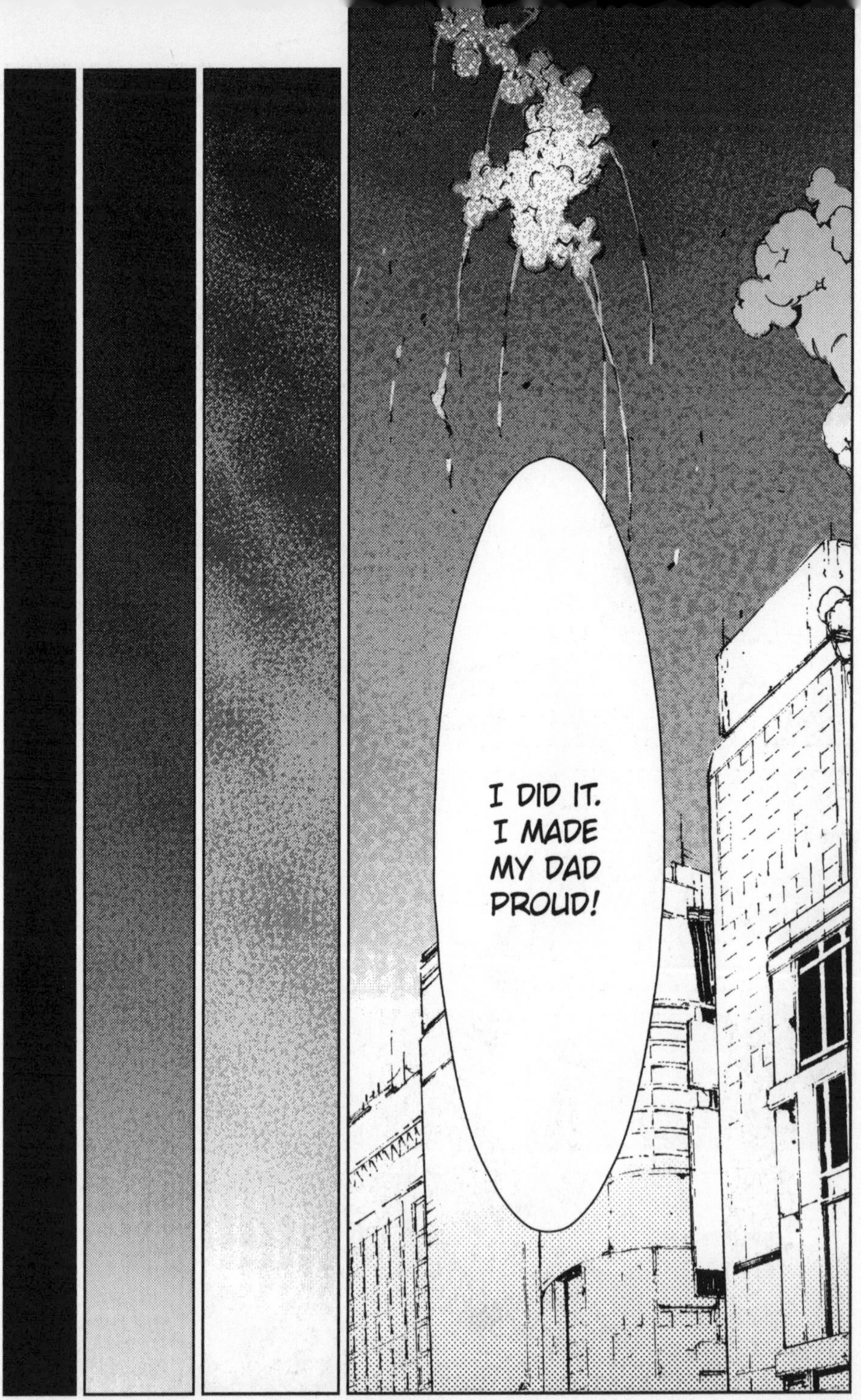
I DID IT. I MADE MY DAD PROUD!

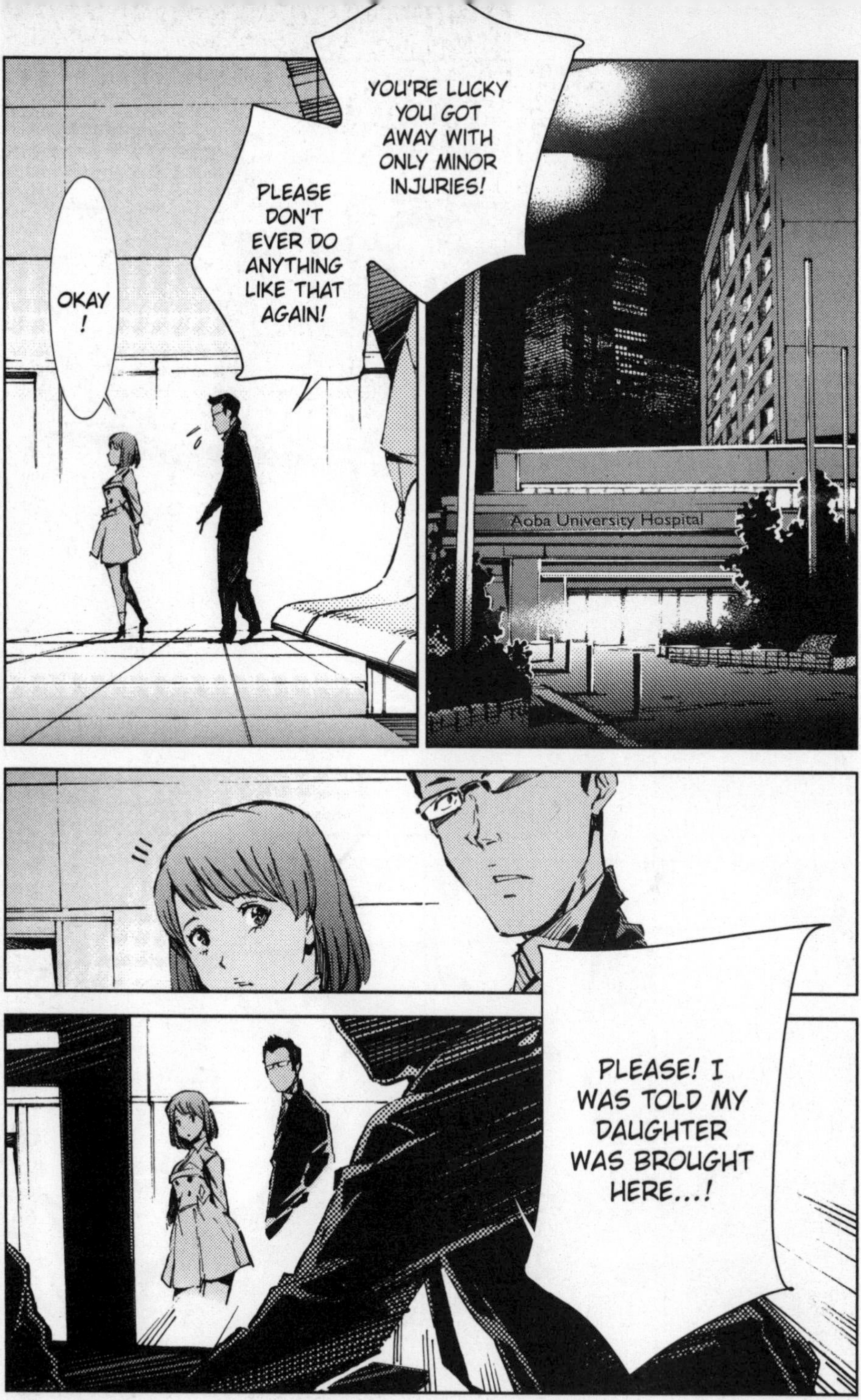
Aoba University Hospital
YOU'RE LUCKY YOU GOT AWAY WITH ONLY MINOR INJURIES!
PLEASE DON'T EVER DO ANYTHING LIKE THAT AGAIN!
OKAY!
PLEASE! I WAS TOLD MY DAUGHTER WAS BROUGHT HERE...!

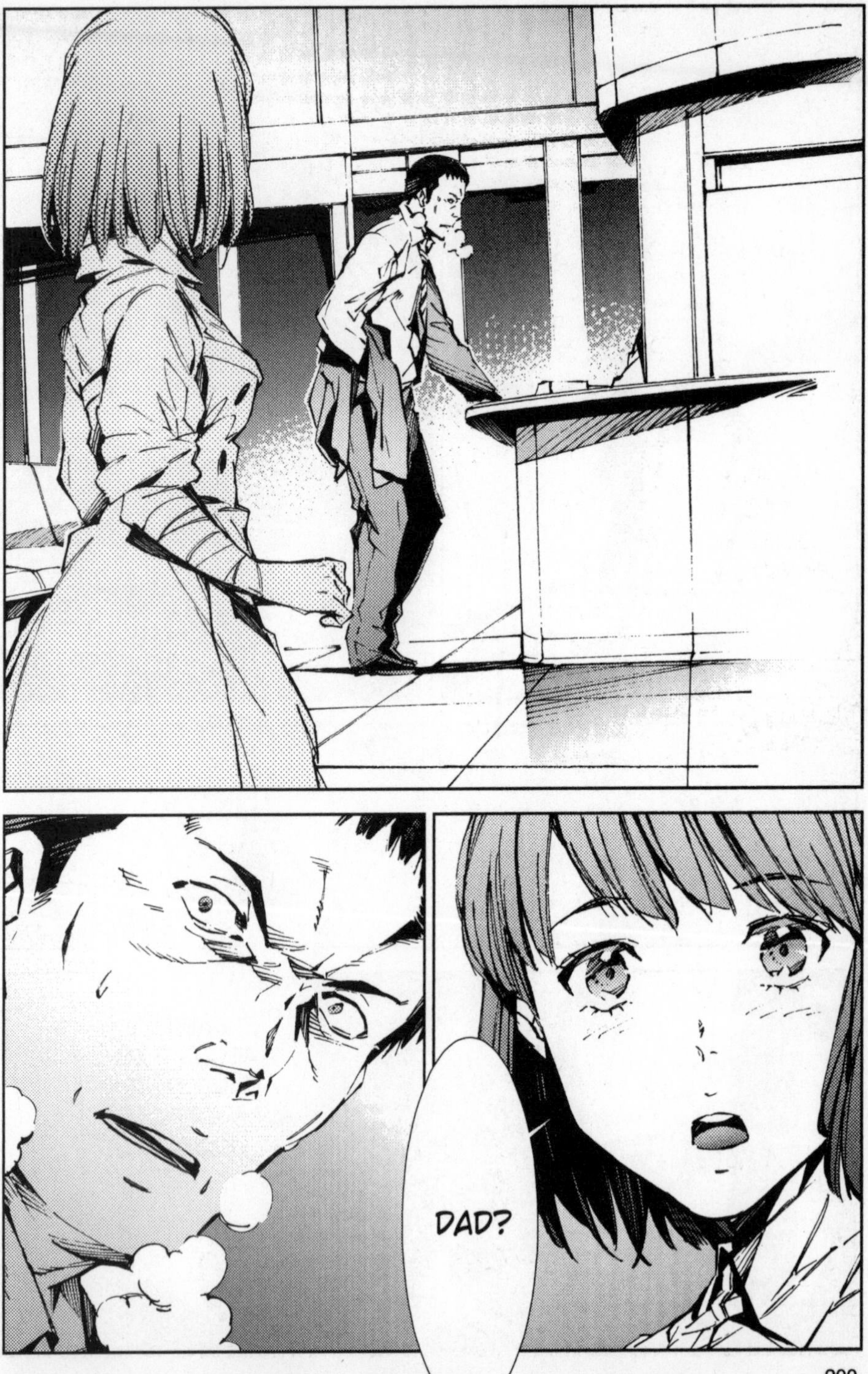
DAD?

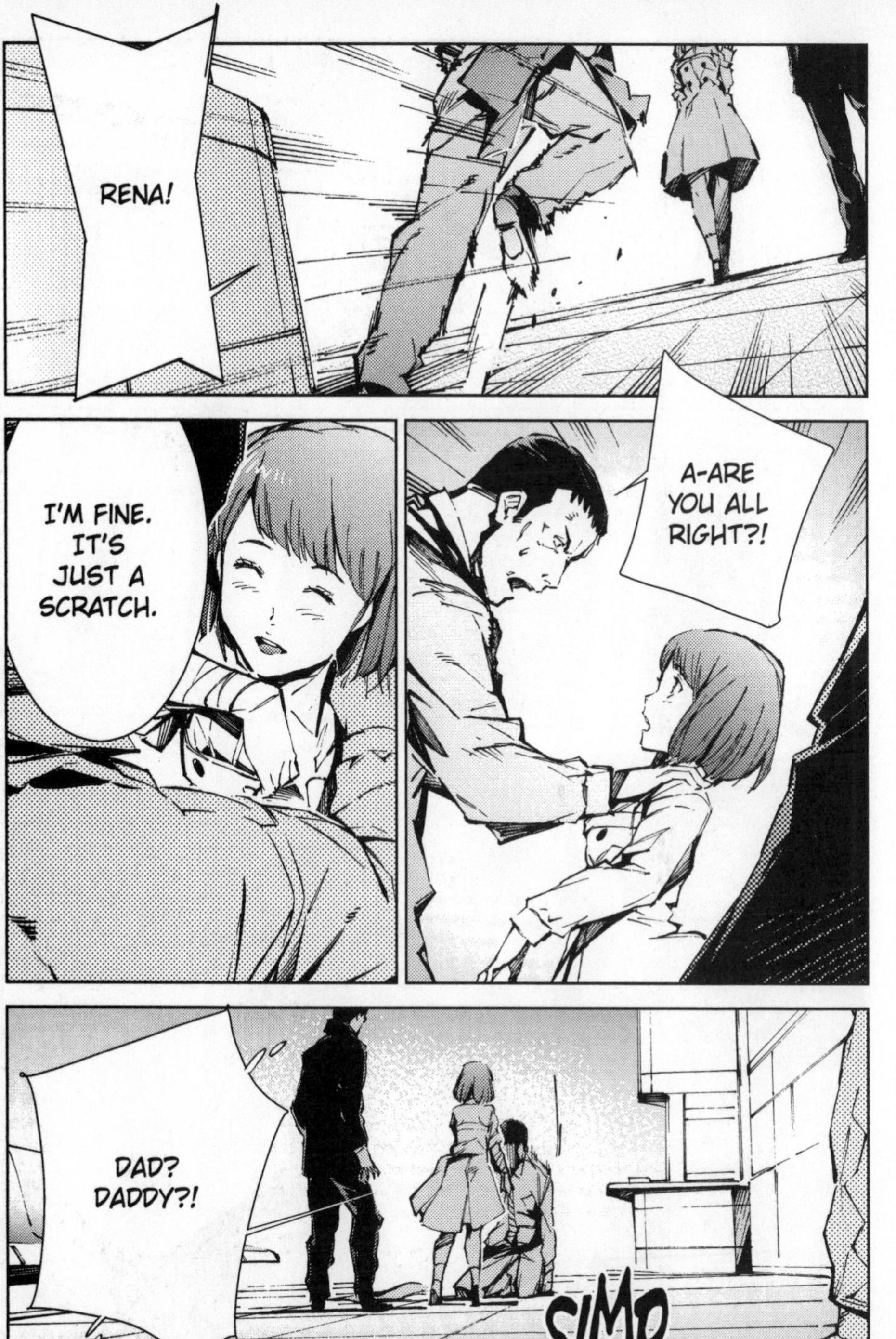
RENA!
A-ARE YOU ALL RIGHT?!
I'M FINE. IT'S JUST A SCRATCH.
DAD? DADDY?!
SLMP

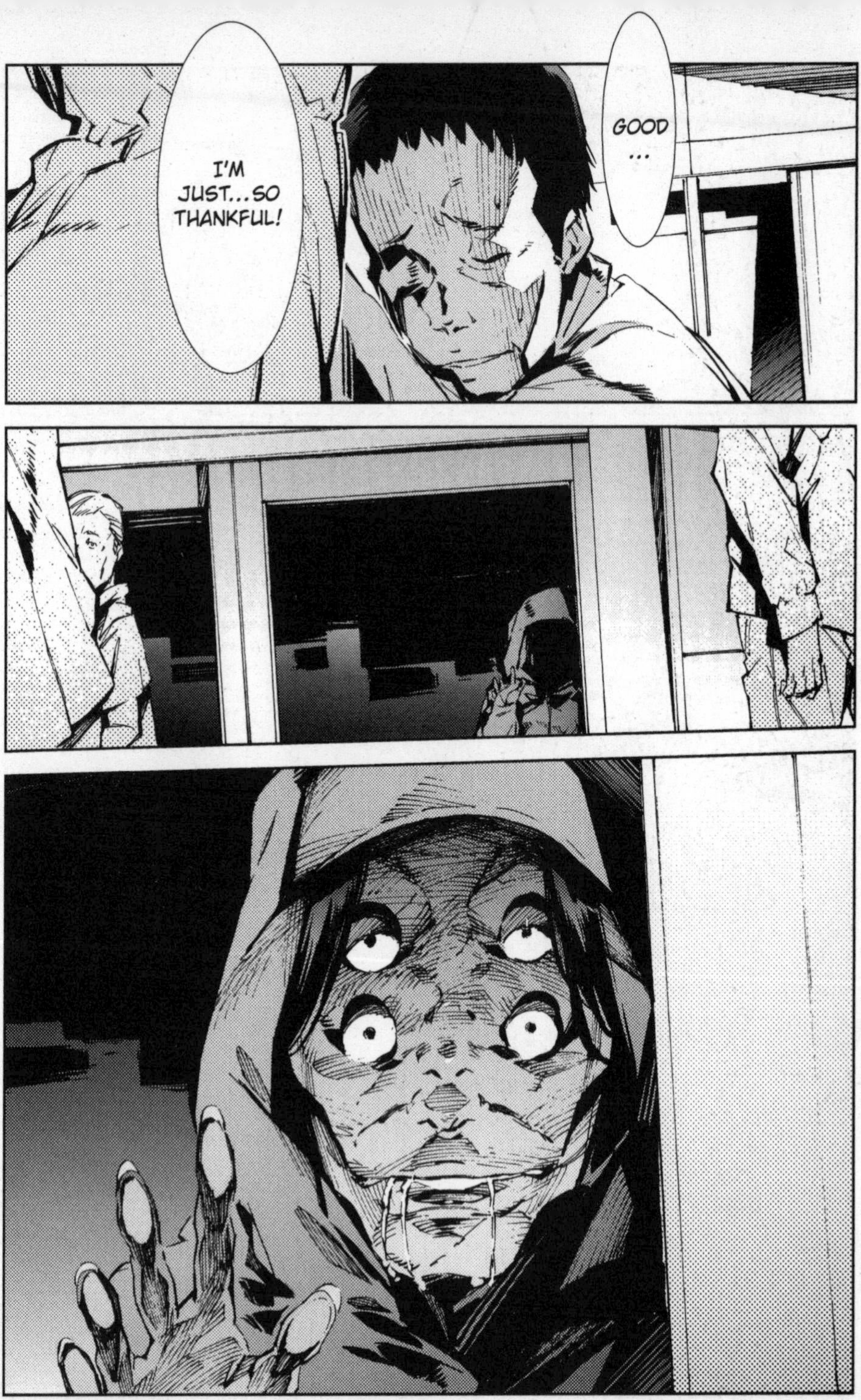
GOOD ...
I'M JUST...SO THANKFUL!

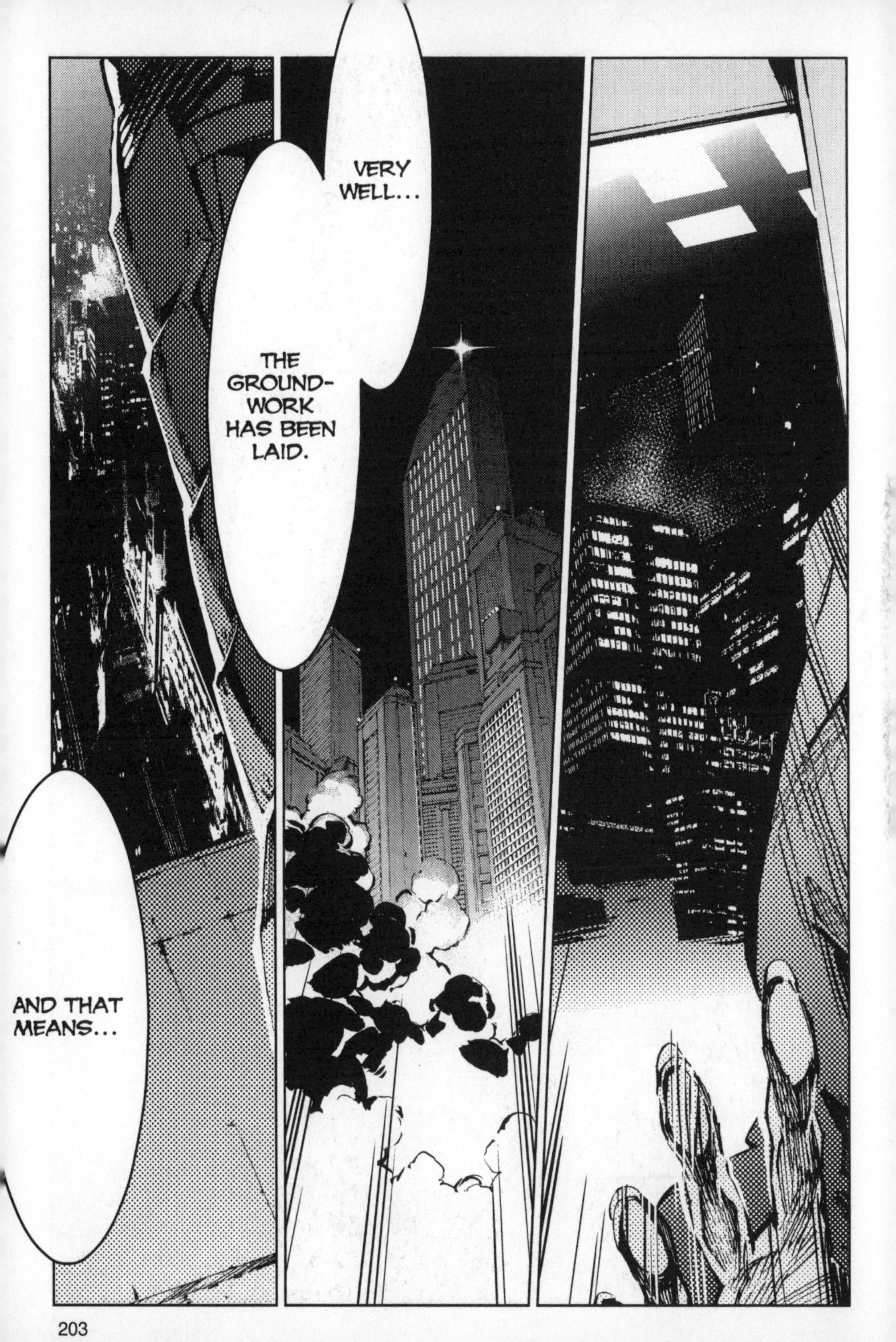
VERY WELL...
THE GROUND-WORK HAS BEEN LAID.
AND THAT MEANS...

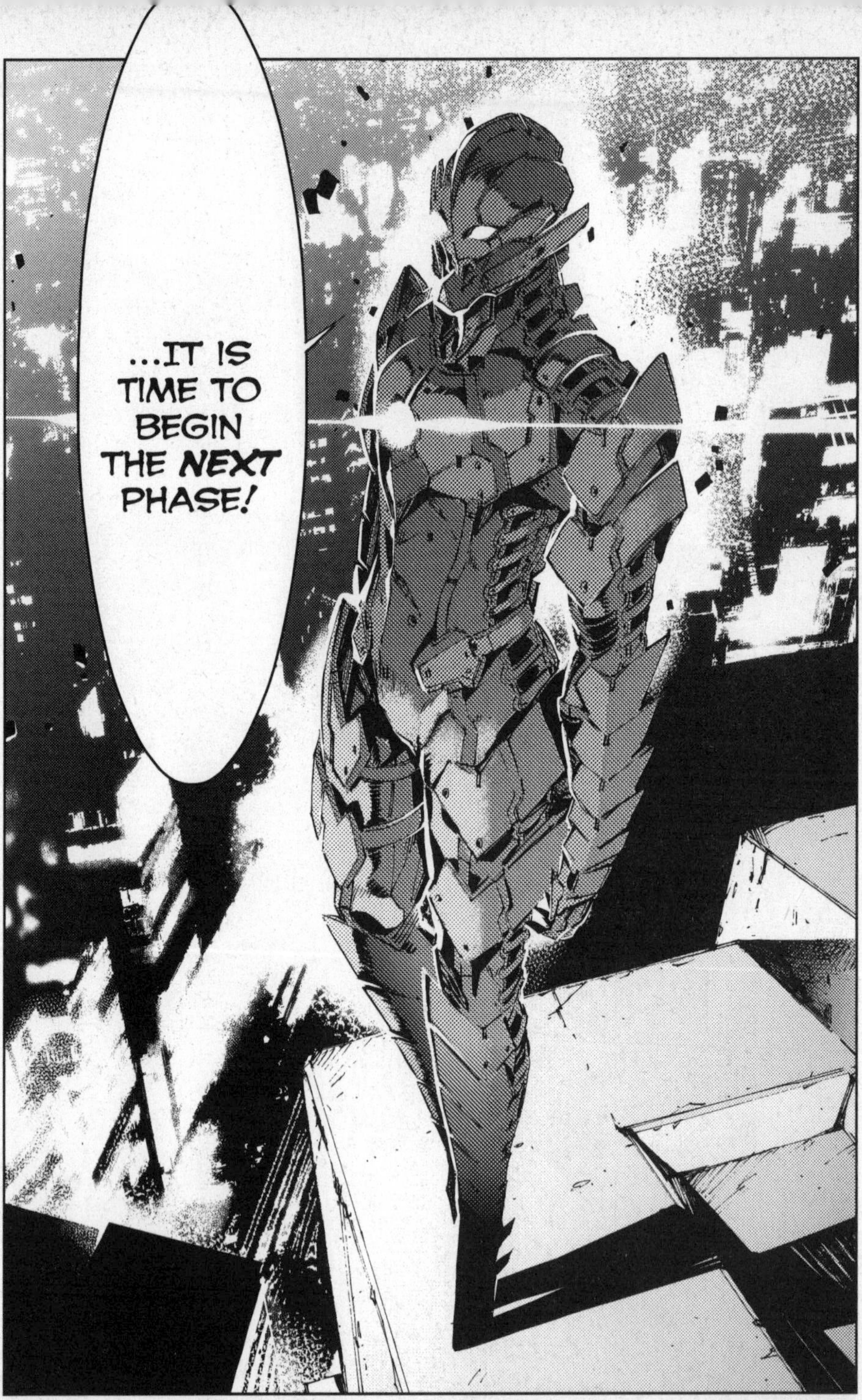
...IT IS TIME TO BEGIN THE NEXT PHASE!

ULTRAMAN 2 - END

THIS IS THE BEGINNING OF A NEW AGE

A hybrid warrior race created through interstellar crossbreeding, the Adacics are highly intelligent and highly aggressive. As a result, the Star Cluster Council does not permit Adacic emigration to Earth. It is all but certain that this individual Adacic came to Earth through unlawful means.

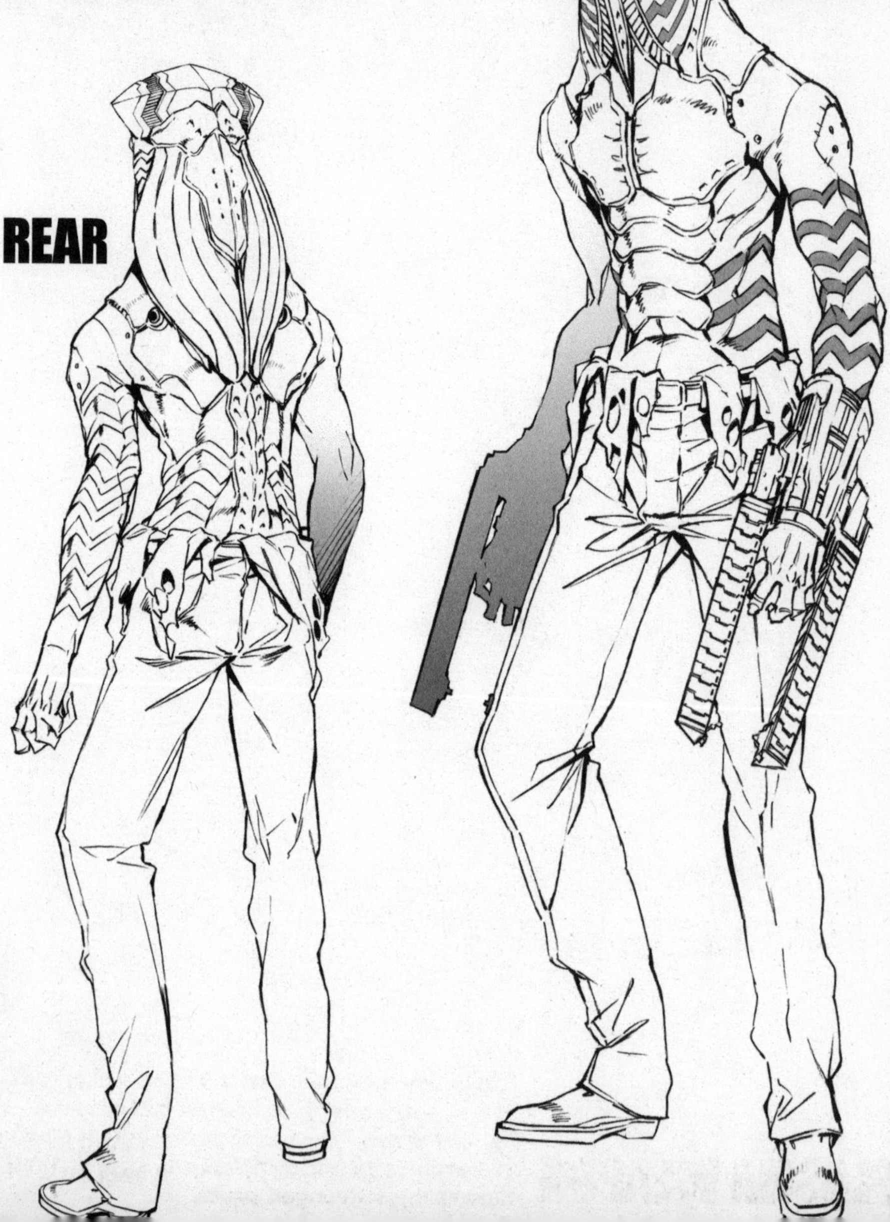
REAR
FRONT

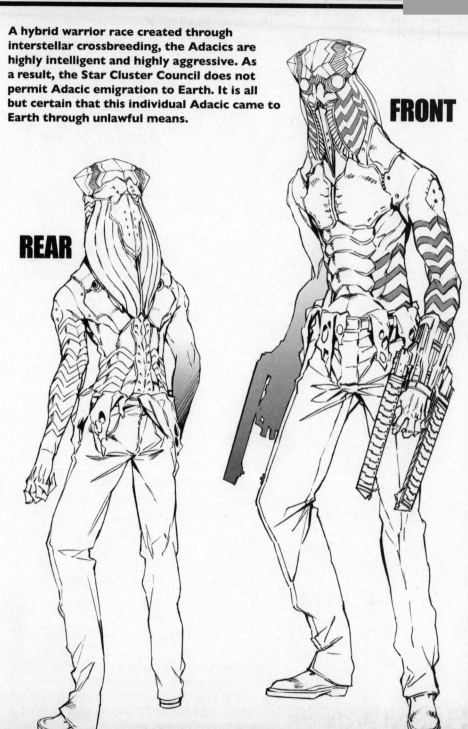

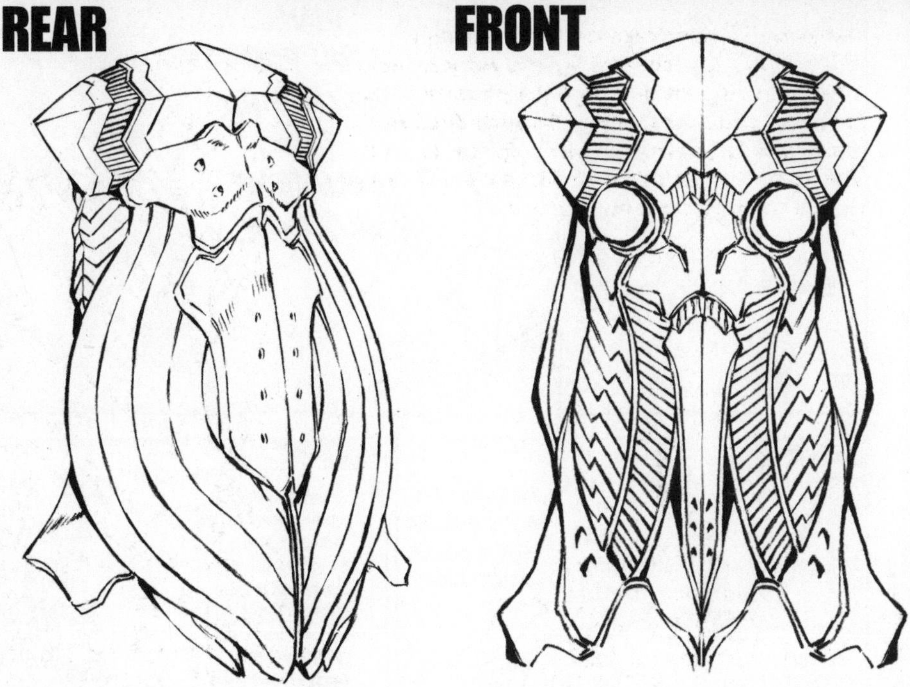
REAR
FRONT

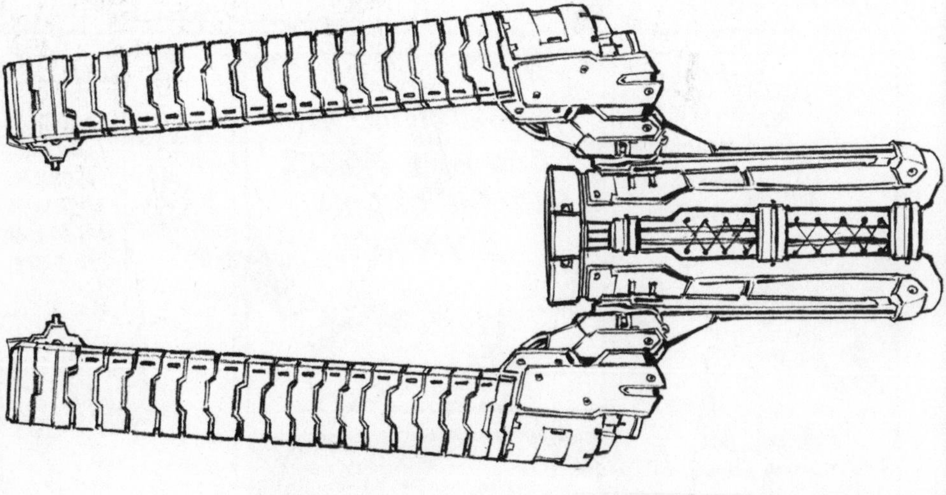

PLASMA WEAPON

The plasma weapon used by the Adacic alien. When retracted, it is housed below the skin of his forearms. This is not something he brought to Earth. It's an illegal weapon that he built here using scavenged parts.

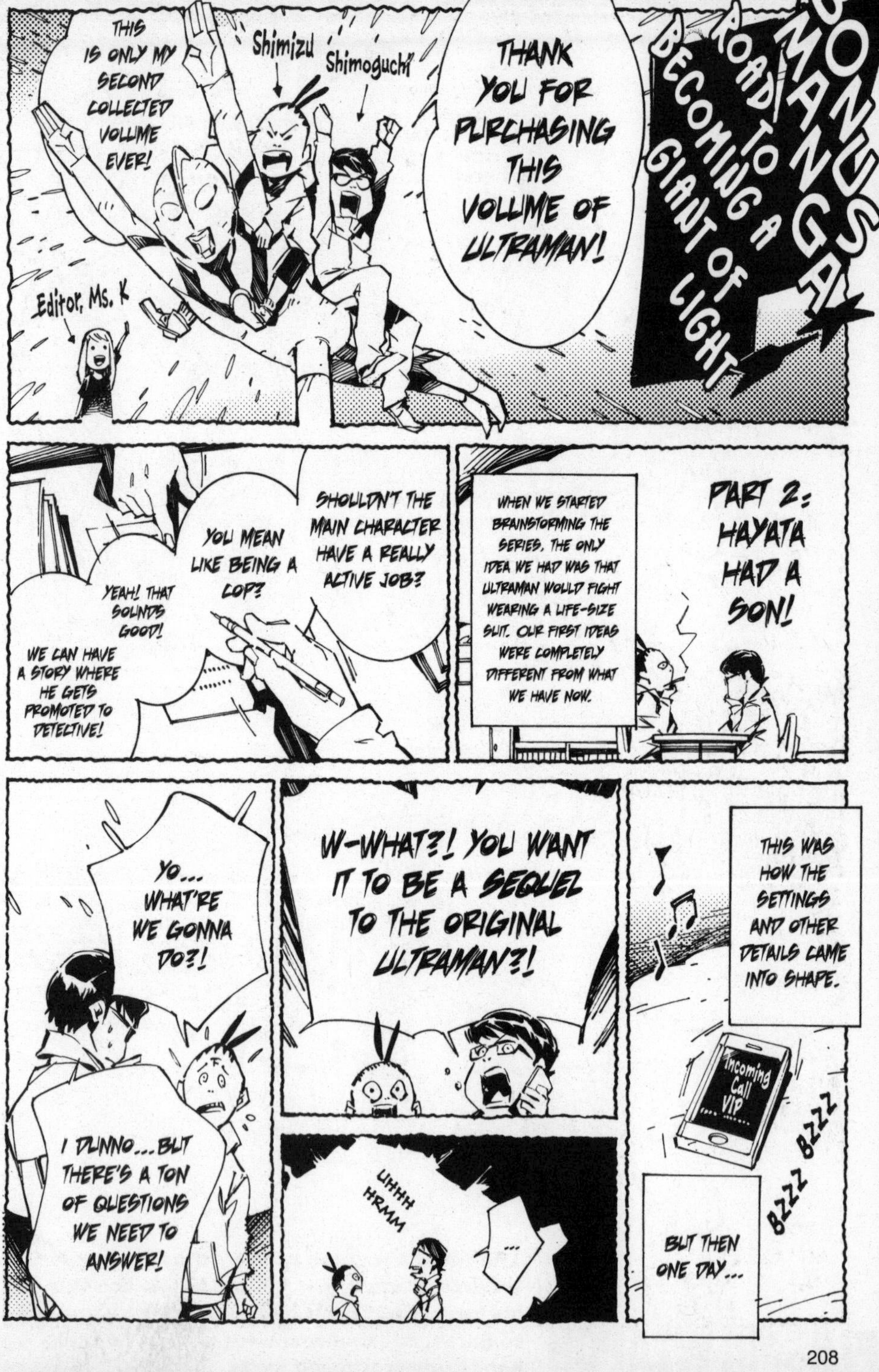
BONUS MANGA★
ROAD TO BECOMING A GIANT OF LIGHT
THANK YOU FOR PURCHASING THIS VOLUME OF ULTRAMAN!
Shimoguchi
Shimizu
THIS IS ONLY MY SECOND COLLECTED VOLUME EVER!
Editor, Ms. K
PART 2: HAYATA HAD A SON!
WHEN WE STARTED BRAINSTORMING THE SERIES, THE ONLY IDEA WE HAD WAS THAT ULTRAMAN WOULD FIGHT WEARING A LIFE-SIZE SUIT. OUR FIRST IDEAS WERE COMPLETELY DIFFERENT FROM WHAT WE HAVE NOW.
SHOULDN'T THE MAIN CHARACTER HAVE A REALLY ACTIVE JOB?
YOU MEAN LIKE BEING A COP?
YEAH! THAT SOUNDS GOOD!
WE CAN HAVE A STORY WHERE HE GETS PROMOTED TO DETECTIVE!
THIS WAS HOW THE SETTINGS AND OTHER DETAILS CAME INTO SHAPE.
Incoming Call VIP
BZZZ BZZZ
BUT THEN ONE DAY...
W-WHAT?! YOU WANT IT TO BE A SEQUEL TO THE ORIGINAL ULTRAMAN?!
UHHH HRMM
...
YO... WHAT'RE WE GONNA DO?!
I DUNNO... BUT THERE'S A TON OF QUESTIONS WE NEED TO ANSWER!

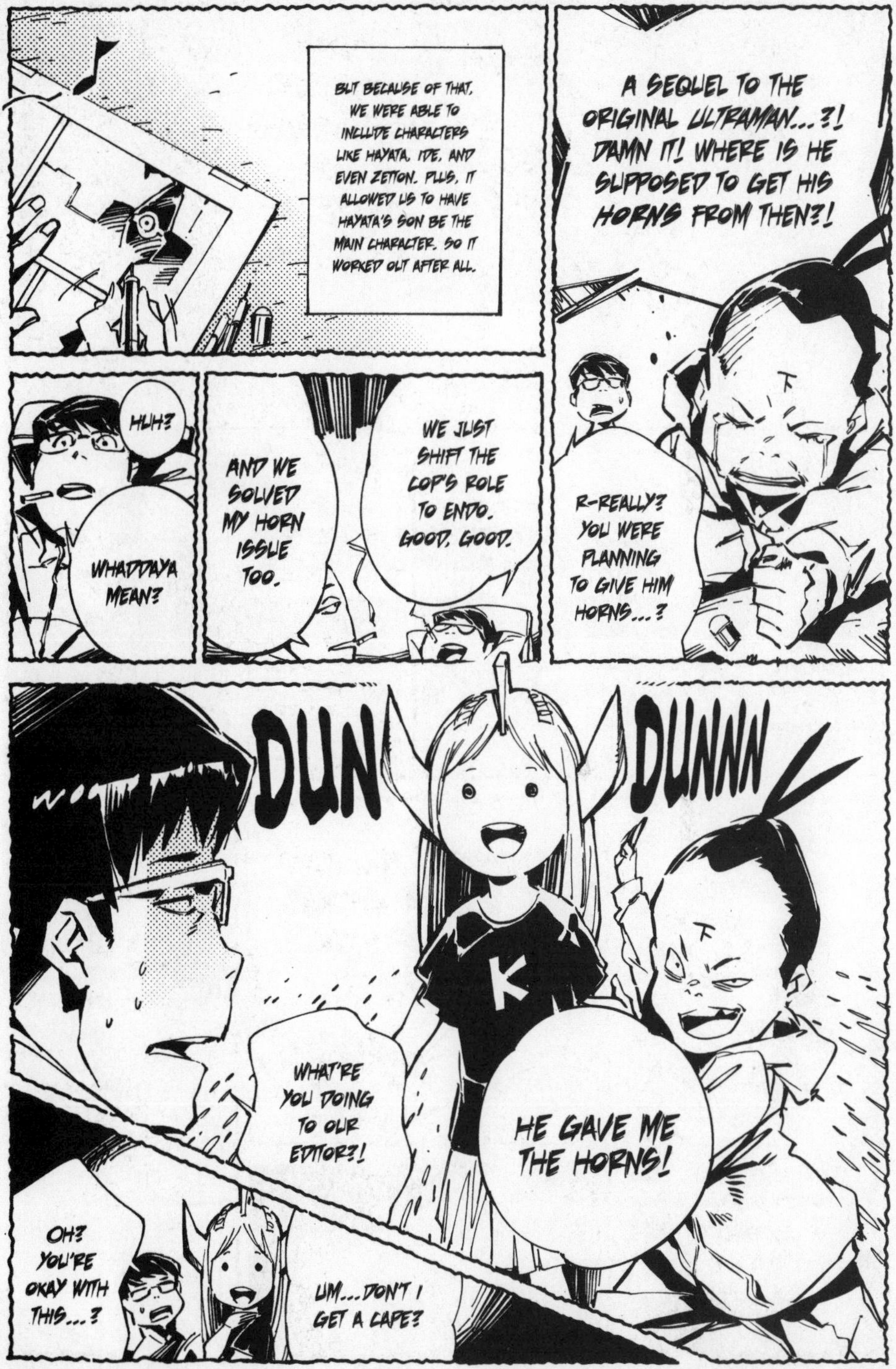
A SEQUEL TO THE ORIGINAL ULTRAMAN...?! DAMN IT! WHERE IS HE SUPPOSED TO GET HIS HORNS FROM THEN?!
BUT BECAUSE OF THAT, WE WERE ABLE TO INCLUDE CHARACTERS LIKE HAYATA, IDE, AND EVEN ZETTON. PLUS, IT ALLOWED US TO HAVE HAYATA'S SON BE THE MAIN CHARACTER. SO IT WORKED OUT AFTER ALL.
R-REALLY? YOU WERE PLANNING TO GIVE HIM HORNS...?
WE JUST SHIFT THE COP'S ROLE TO ENDO. GOOD, GOOD.
AND WE SOLVED MY HORN ISSUE TOO.
HUH?
WHADDAYA MEAN?
DUN
DUNNN
HE GAVE ME THE HORNS!
WHAT'RE YOU DOING TO OUR EDITOR?!
UM...DON'T I GET A CAPE?
OH? YOU'RE OKAY WITH THIS...?

EIICHI SHIMIZU × TOMOHIRO SHIMOGUCHI

This version of *Ultraman* is a sequel to the original *Ultraman*. It takes place in a world where subsequent series don't exist. It's what's called a reboot. But if you ask us if the other series are completely unrelated... That actually may not be the case...

ULTRAMAN

VOLUME 2
VIZ SIGNATURE EDITION

STORY/ART BY **EIICHI SHIMIZU** AND **TOMOHIRO SHIMOGUCHI**

©2013 Eiichi Shimizu and Tomohiro Shimoguchi / TSUBURAYA PROD.
Originally published by HERO'S INC.

TRANSLATION **JOE YAMAZAKI**
ENGLISH ADAPTATION **STAN!**
TOUCH-UP ART & LETTERING **EVAN WALDINGER**
DESIGN **FAWN LAU**
EDITOR **MIKE MONTESA**

Printed in the U.S.A.

Published by VIZ Media, LLC
P.O. Box 77010
San Francisco, CA 94107

10 9 8 7 6 5 4 3 2 1
First printing, November 2015

VIZ SIGNATURE

www.viz.com